EXTREME FICTION

FABULISTS AND FORMALISTS

Robin Hemley
University of Utah

Michael Martone
University of Alabama

PEARSON
Longman

New York   San Francisco   Boston
London   Toronto   Sydney   Tokyo   Singapore   Madrid
Mexico City   Munich   Paris   Cape Town   Hong Kong   Montreal

Vice President and Editor-in-Chief: Joseph P. Terry
Managing Editor: Erika Berg
Associate Editor: Barbara Santoro
Senior Marketing Manager: Melanie Craig
Text Design/Electronic Page Makeup: Dianne Hall
Production Coordinator: Shafiena Ghani
Cover Designer/Senior Design Manager: Nancy Danahy
Cover Image: Miró, Joan (1893–1983) © Copyright ARS, NY. *Dutch Interior II.*
    Copyright Scala/Art Resource, NY Guggenheim Museum, Venice, Italy.
Manufacturing Buyer: Alfred Dorsey
Printer and Binder: Courier/Westford
Cover Printer: Phoenix Color Corp.

Library of Congress Cataloging-in-Publication Data

Extreme fiction : fabulists and formalists / [selected and introduced by] Robin
Hemley, Michael Martone.
        p. cm.
Includes index.
    ISBN 0-321-17972-2 (pbk. : alk. paper)
    1. Short stories. I. Hemley, Robin, 1958– II. Martone, Michael.
PN6120.2.E94 2004
808.83'1—dc22
                                                                    2003055628

Please visit our website at http://www.ablongman.com

ISBN 0-321-17972-2

2345678910—CRW—06050403

CONTENTS

Preface   *v*

Introduction   *1*

Part One: Fabulists

AT THE END OF THE MECHANICAL AGE
   Donald Barthelme   15
WATER LIARS   *Barry Hannah   22*
A CONVERSATION WITH MY FATHER   *Grace Paley   26*
IN DREAMS BEGIN RESPONSIBILITIES   *Delmore Schwartz   31*
OPIUM   *Rikki Ducornet   39*
THE SIN OF JESUS   *Isaac Babel   44*
THE ALEPH   *Jorge Luis Borges   49*
PASTORALIA   *George Saunders   61*
THE ART OF FORGIVENESS: A FABLE   *Janice Eidus   102*
LYOMPA   *Yuri Olesha   107*
CAT'S EYE   *Luisa Valenzuela   111*
JOHN DUFFY'S BROTHER   *Flann O'Brien   115*
THE FALL RIVER AXE MURDERS   *Angela Carter   120*
BLOODCHILD   *Octavia E. Butler   138*
ORDER OF INSECTS   *William H. Gass   156*

Part Two: Formalists

MILK IS VERY GOOD FOR YOU   *Stephen Dixon*   165

RONDO   *Susan Neville*   176

CORNSILK   *Randall Kennan*   181

IS IT SEXUAL HARASSMENT YET?   *Cris Mazza*   198

PLAN FOR THE ASSASSINATION OF JACQUELINE KENNEDY
    J. G. Ballard   215

STORY   *Lydia Davis*   218

INNOCENT OBJECTS   *Diane Schoemperlin*   221

THE ELEVATOR   *Robert Coover*   239

THE FIFTH STORY   *Clarice Lispector*   249

THE MINNESOTA MULTIPHASIC PERSONALITY: A DIAGNOSTIC
    TEST IN TWO PARTS   *A. B. Paulsen*   251

THE WRITERS' MODEL   *Molly Giles*   258

SECOND STORY   *R. M. Berry*   261

CAN THIS STORY BE SAVED?   *Michael Wilkerson*   271

WILD DESIRE   *Karen Brennan*   281

SCISSORS KICK   *Sandy Huss*   298

FIVE ON FICTION   *Janet Kauffman*   304

CLICK   *John Barth*   317

Credits   339

Index of Authors and Titles   343

PREFACE

For the past quarter century, short fiction anthologies have mainly featured stories that are realist in form and narrative in style. For the most part, the fictions in such anthologies tell stories that have a beginning, a middle, and an end, and often adhere to the formula of the inverted checkmark with its rising action, climax, and dénouement. This text is designed to complement the existing array of anthologies that feature these kinds of stories with an extensive and diverse collection of fiction that is not realist in style and/or not narrative in structure.

Used as a main text or supplementary text, this collection of short fiction will enlarge the scope of the genre, and will familiarize instructors and students, through the sheer number of examples, to nonrealist and non-narrative works. For the literature classroom, the stories in this text are refreshing works that challenge preconceived notions of what a good story should look like and how it should unfold, what it is to contain and even what role the reader plays in deciding what the fiction means. For the creative writing classroom, this book will extend the range of formal and stylistic possibilities for the beginning and advanced writer by providing a number of unique new models for organizing prose and creating fictive worlds. Ultimately, this anthology seeks to introduce what has often been deemed an alternative or "other" tradition of creative prose to a new generation of writers and readers.

Content and Organization

The stories included in this anthology fit at least one of several criteria. These stories have been selected for their global and decidedly contemporary feel, and for their adherence to nontraditional content and/or form. We also made a conscious effort to include writers who might be unfamiliar to many teachers alongside such famous writers as Jorge Luis Borges and Angela Carter. Finally, we chose the stories that would best illustrate an enjoyable, non-threatening introduction to the tradition of the nontraditional story.

This book is organized into a simple yet effective binary: stories that have fabulist content (those stories that do not depend on the conventions of realism) and stories that have formalist approaches (those stories that emphasize various prose forms instead of a narrative structure). The stories offer both literature students and creative writing students an exciting new perspective on the different artistic choices—both conceptual and technical—that fiction writers can make and fiction readers can enjoy.

Distinctive Features

The following features were developed to help make students' exposure to nontraditional fiction as engaging and accessible as possible:

- An interesting and straightforward **Introduction on the development and evolution of nontraditional fiction.** This lively introduction gives students the vocabulary and background they need to form a deeper understanding of the characteristics and techniques used by writers of "nontraditional" fiction.
- **A diverse and exciting selection** of short stories. These highly teachable stories, from **American and International writers,** give students a broad overview of the various types of nontraditional fiction written throughout the world during the past one hundred years.
- **Informative and interesting author headnotes.** Each author headnote provides contextual background to help students better appreciate and understand each story as well the nontraditional techniques the author uses within his or her work.
- **A brief length and straightforward organization** makes this book an ideal text either as a primary book or as a supplement.

We hope that the inclusion of our anthology will energize and broaden the discussions in your classroom and present new possibilities for exploration on the part of both writers and readers.

Michael Martone: I would like to thank Erika Berg, Barbara Santoro, and Dianne Hall for suffering my conversion to collaborator and co-conspirator in the world of textbooks. I would like to acknowledge my student assistants on this project, Betsy Hogan and Tara Tyson. I would also like to thank my teachers at Indiana University—Robert Dunn, John Woodcock, Scott Sanders, Mel Plotinsky, Mari Vlastos, Roger Mitchell—and at Johns Hopkins University—John Barth, Edmund White, John Irwin. And I need to thank John W. Crowley, Monroe Engle, Richard Cassell, and James Lewinski. Heaps of thanks to my colleagues at the University of Alabama—Sandy Huss, Robin Behn, Wendy Rawlings, and Joel Brouwer. And I thank all my students at Iowa State, Harvard, Syracuse, and Alabama who welcomed the introduction of these Extremes in the classrooms they shared with me. And let me thank Robin Hemley, fellow Hoosier and fellow traveler in this alternative universe.

Robin Hemley: I would like to thank Michael Martone, one of the finest of "extreme" writers, for agreeing to co-edit this anthology with me. I'd also like to thank Erika Berg for her enthusiasm and direction in getting this project going, as well as her patience. And I'd like to thank Barbara Santoro for her goodwill and care with the project and with its far-flung editors. Beyond that, I'd like to thank my parents, Cecil Hemley and Elaine Gottlieb (whose love of the nontraditional and whose vast and eclectic library led me to many fantastic discoveries); my wife, Margie; my teachers, also from Indiana University, Roger Mitchell, Mari Vlastos, and Melvin Plotinsky; and my teachers at Iowa, Barry Hannah, Helen Yglesias, Don Hendrie, Jr., and Clark Blaise.

ROBIN HEMLEY
MICHAEL MARTONE

INTRODUCTION

The "traditional" story with which readers today are most familiar is actually a recent invention. It was created about a century ago, when writers coupled a much older pattern of organizing and relating a series of events—what we call *narrative*—with a new style of rendering experience—what we call *realism*.

The Tradition of Narrative

Narrative is what is meant by storytelling. In fact, narrative *is* storytelling. Telling stories is an activity so old that you might think it an essential characteristic of the human species. Are we the storytelling animal? Is there a narrative gene in our DNA? We know that oral storytelling predates written languages and still flourishes today alongside written narrative. Almost everyone has told a story; narrative is so natural to us that we don't even think about how we order events. It simply comes to us.

For as long as people have been telling stories they have also been trying to figure out how narrative works. Gustav Freytag, a nineteenth-century German theorist, suggested that narrative follows a plot pattern in the form of a pyramid, consisting of ground situation, vehicle, rising action, climax, and dénouement. Janet Burroway, in her book

Writing Fiction, identifies this form as "the inverted checkmark." According to Freytag and Burroway, a story looks like this:

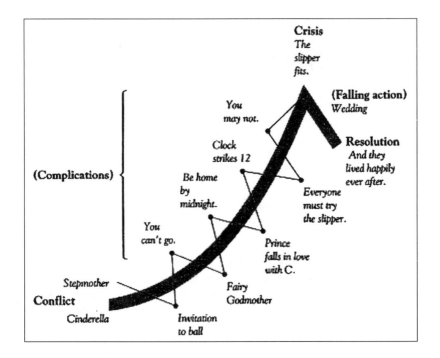

Another way to think of this narrative pattern is through the familiar phrases of fairy tales and parables. "Once upon a time" signals the ground situation, which is often complex and interesting in itself. Perhaps there is an evil queen who has a magic mirror that tells her she is the fairest in the land. "Once upon a time" creates a dynamic situation: something is about to happen. The phrase "then one day" initiates the rising action, putting the elements of the ground situation into motion. Perhaps *one day* the magic mirror tells the queen she is no longer the fairest in the land, and the story begins. "Then one day" is the mechanism for forward movement. Eventually, "they lived happily ever after" will return the characters to a static though still complex state.

This narrative pattern records the series of events that transforms people, their relationships with each other and their world. Since we construct and process language in sequence—we read or hear one word after another—narrative is a linear organizing device. Narrative's transformational effect and linear nature are its important identifying characteristics.

The Tradition of Realism

The set of literary conventions for rendering scene, character, and action that we call *realism* was first practiced in the nineteenth century, primarily by Russian novelists such as Tolstoy and Doestoevsky, British novelists such as Jane Austen and Charlotte Brontë, and American novelists such as Edith Wharton, Henry James, and Stephen Crane.

Realism relied on a new literary entity we now call *character*, which brought greater complexity to the human figure. Where the people of fiction had often been simply a collection of characteristics—a profession, a role in a family, a temperament or an emotion—the realist character was all these things, but with depth, with a consciousness expressed through subtlety and nuance in every precisely chosen word, gesture, and action. In effect, the realist's insistence on the close examination of character shifted the focus of a narrative away from the complications of plot to the changes wrought in the characters themselves and their relationships with each other.

The Transparency of Realist Fiction

In order to create their stories, realist writers utilized certain conventions, the most important one being "transparency." The realist writer seeks to create an illusion so perfect that the reader cannot tell it is an illusion. The reader observes the action, whether exterior or interior, as it takes place in real space and in real time: The story unfolds before our eyes. The writer does this through concreteness, using specific sensory details in the language and in the images the language creates. Abstractions are to be avoided. The realist story wants you, the reader, to forget you are reading.

Realism creates a highly crafted aesthetic literary artifact that appears to be spontaneous, impassioned utterance. In its first person narrators, realism often gives the illusion of ordinary human speech searching for the right words and finding a kind of poetry in inarticulateness. Readers feel that they have just come upon a story or are overhearing it being told to another listener. This transparency is the camouflage of realism; its primary purpose is to conduct the reader into a kind of waking dream where the words the reader processes generate a visual projection of a familiar though subtly agitated life. The page is a clear window one looks through to sense a very real world.

The Nontraditional Story

This anthology is a collection of stories that do not fit the realist narrative mold. In that sense, they are "nontraditional" stories; their writers have chosen to play with our expectations, finding new subjects and different ways of presenting them. Some writers play with content, others play with form. Right from the start, you may sense that the work collected here stands out as something different, something unfamiliar. It is tempting, then, to think of these pieces as derivations from the norm. That is to say, if there are rules to the writing of literary short fiction, the stories collected here seem to go out of their way to break those rules. In fact many readers tend to think of this type of prose in terms of "experimental," "innovative," or "alternative" fiction. Yet the kinds of fictions you will read in this anthology have always existed alongside the traditional realist short story. Their writers have not so much tried to improve or change the traditional story, but instead have followed an entirely different set of aesthetic conventions, assumptions, and expectations about what short fiction should be.

The Fabulist Tradition

Fabulism deals with the fantastic, the unobservable, what may exist outside the normal human ken. While the realist story attempts to explain the world through cause and effect and human free will, fabulism posits cause and effect relationships that can be beyond the grasp of mortals. The ancient stories of various cultures explore an essentially fabulist world. Eve chooses of her own free will to bite the forbidden fruit, but it was the serpent that tempted her. The Egyptian god Osiris died and rose again, murdered by the animal-headed god Seth, then avenged by his son Horus. While revenge is certainly a human motive, and therefore within the realm of realism, animal-gods and resurrection are fabulist in nature. The world of causes affected by human action says nothing of our dreams, little of our metaphysical and spiritual beliefs or questions, little of our subconscious. Those are the worlds that the fabulist writer enters.

Dadaism, Surrealism, and Absurdism

Dadaist, Surrealist, and Absurdist prose breaks with an unflinching fealty to the old order of rationalism, imperialism, and Fate or God as represented by organized religions. *Dada* was a French artistic movement of the early twentieth century that questioned traditional beliefs.

Dadaists were essentially nihilistic (believing in nothing, believing in the emptiness of belief), anti-rational, non-sensical in their view of the world. Yet they were a rather free and whimsical group, and their literary creations tended toward the humorous. *Dada*, a nonsense word, meant absolutely nothing—and everything to the dadaists, in whose world nothing mattered but Dada.

Surrealism, too, began in France, where its main proponents resisted defining it (that is, trying to make "sense" of it), but caved in when André Breton wrote *The Surrealist Manifesto* in 1924. Unlike dadaism, surrealism wasn't by and large nihilistic. The surrealists saw reality as encompassing a much greater swath of human experience than could be apprehended by the rational waking mind. They wanted to transcend the everyday, to perceive the extraordinary within mundane experience. Surrealism's world was one in which metaphor and reality collided, the conscious and the unconscious blended, association and cause-and-effect fused to create a super-reality, a "surreality."

Absurdism says that life has no meaning, that it's essentially absurd, that things happen for no reason. Albert Camus likened human existence to the Greek myth of Sisyphus, condemned by Zeus to an eternity of rolling a boulder up a hill only to see the boulder roll back down the hill again. Camus's novel *The Stranger* tells of a man who kills another man on a beach in Algeria simply because the sun was in his eyes. Does that make sense? No, and that's the point. If life was senseless or absurd, Camus saw no point in living. Today the absurd is a key component of most comedy. When Donald Barthelme creates, in "The End of the Mechanical Age," an exaggerated absurdist retelling of the story of the Flood, with God as a handyman, his *raison d'être* is not to make us want to kill ourselves but to make us examine our sacred stories and our ways of knowing the world.

These movements, though they employ humor or shocking themes, were concerned with much more than entertaining their audiences. At the heart of these movements was a questioning of the ways in which we view history, religion, the family, sexuality, our own Being, and the meaning of life. If we reflect upon the major events that were unfolding during the time in which these movements flourished—two world wars, the atomic bomb, various genocides—such a wholesale rethinking certainly seems warranted.

The Tale and the Fable

The world of the fabulist is a wide one, and these writers have found many ways to shape their work. In the Americas, fabulism dominates the story-telling traditions. One need only think of the *tall tales* of Washington Irving ("Rip Van Winkle") and Mark Twain ("The Notorious Jumping Frog of Calaveras County"). *Folk tales* throughout North and South America are largely fabulist, and we see their echoes in contemporary literature. In a similar vein, the *fairy tale* pits magical beings and humans good and bad against one another. Folk tales, fairy tales, and tall tales are all ancestors of the contemporary fabulist tale, and we discern their outlines in many contemporary fabulist tales including Barry Hannah's "Water Liars" (folk tale) and Grace Paley's "A Conversation with My Father" (tall tale, fairy tale).

We must also mention the *fable*, which employs the fantastic to impart a moral, as in the fable of the tortoise and the hare: *Slow and steady wins the race.* In the traditional fable, anthropomorphized animals act as stand-ins for human beings. In the contemporary fable, we find that the moral is dropped and the human has been reincarnated into an animal. The fabulist writer chooses to go beyond observable reality, often stretching credibility while attempting to make the reader believe the unbelievable, showing us our dreams while we're awake.

The Irreal and the Unreal

The *irreal* is a kind of allegory, not so much like the traditional religious allegories of Medieval times but of a more personal nature, in which the representations are perhaps more ambiguous and not necessarily contingent on dogma. The irreal encompasses all we have learned in the past century about the human mind, combined with our belief systems of several millennia. The irreal simply suggests an alternative way of viewing reality, one in which characters and images are meant to stand for something else (something that may itself be ambiguous or open to interpretation). Fantasy and science fiction also fit neatly under the rubric of the irreal.

The Formalist Tradition

Formalist describes a tradition in which speakers and writers are sensitive to the variety of forms they use to give shape to language. Letters, speeches, confessions, directions, advertisements, instructions, telephone messages, award citations, and even grocery lists are all forms of communication we've created or consumed. These forms are recognized and appreciated in both spoken and written language. When language becomes more literary or more formal (in the sense of being dressed up) we recognize many more forms: essay, autobiography, memoir, critical review, drama, and poetry.

Is there a form we call *fiction*? A formalist might very well answer no, fiction inhabits, exploits, and borrows other forms. Fictions have long been made to look like collections of letters, diaries, histories, autobiographies, confessions, and scientific reports. Even the realist narrative we call the traditional story can often take the form of a memoir, biography, or history. Each form has its set of conventions (like the *Dear Sir* and *Yours truly* of a letter) that, in the formalist tradition, becomes the focus of attention. The ability to recognize, manipulate, and recreate these conventions is always present in formalist work. For the formalist writer, convention has the same importance as character had for the realist writer.

This sensitivity to form also relates to the use of language itself. Where the realist desires to use language in a transparent manner, the formalist is always aware that the language we use is an artifice, a constructed thing. Language, in the foreground in the formalist tradition, becomes more like the paint an abstract painter applies to a canvas, appreciated for its own material nature and the quirks in its makeup. In this way, the formalist asks that you consider language itself in the way you would consider paint for its color, intensity, or texture. When you read formalist stories, you are meant to be aware of the artificiality of the made-up world.

Metafictions

Metafiction is a form that takes as its subject form itself; that is, metafiction is fiction about fiction. In a variety of ways, metafiction reminds the reader that he or she is reading a made-up thing, a text cleverly constructed both abstractly (with written language and the conventions of punctuation, syntax, grammar, spelling) and physically (with the conventions of printing, such as reading from right to left and from the top of the page down). The realist writer succeeds when the reader becomes so involved with the illusion being generated and with the veracity of the world being created that the act of reading and all that it entails is completely forgotten. The metafictionist, on the other hand, snaps the reader awake from such reverie. This strategy can create startling effects, producing the same disorientation you would feel when a magician reveals how the trick was done after you had certainly seen a woman being sawn in half. Or these effects can induce a kind of wonder as an author tells you, truthfully, that she has been telling you a story. Or these self-referential stories can invoke political or social insight when the reader is reminded that reading even a realistic depiction of oppression is not the same as experiencing real oppression in a real world.

Metafiction seeks to change the reader's involvement in the drama being created. It does this by shifting the reader's relationship to the work being read. The role of the reader in the traditional story is most often that of an observer and listener: the reader is an engaged but passive audience for the characters and the action. In metafiction, the reader is often asked to participate in the action of the story. In Stephen Dixon's story "Milk Is Very Good for You" words are deliberately misspelled, disguising slightly their exact meaning, and the reader has to slow down and decipher this story. To understand what is going on, the reader must rewrite the words in his or her mind while reading. In doing this, the reader becomes an active collaborator in making up the story.

Metafiction will use the conventions of character in surprising ways, as in Michael Wilkerson's "Can This Story Be Saved?" Characters in this kind of story will often realize that they are characters in a story and that the choices they make have been constructed by an "author" who is also a character in the story. In Wilkerson's story the characters and the author endure a therapy session to save their relationship. Effects such as these may be created by having the characters talk directly to the reader or having the author stop the story and revise it before going forward. In "Can This Story Be Saved?" the metafictional quality is apparent in its title, "story" being the focus of the therapy instead of some other cultural convention such as marriage. The title tells you, the reader, that the story itself will be the subject. The characters and the author of the story all enter therapy because the story they find themselves in is not working out as a realist story. While attempting to save their story (that is, to make it transparent and realist), they are quite conscious of their roles, their make-believe status. They are "characters" or an "author." That self-consciousness makes you, the reader, self-conscious as well. You become aware of your role as the "reader." When this happens, it is easy for you to accept the invitation to be a participant in the story you are reading, and you become a character who is reading. Or at least the reader realizes that, in this activity of reading, one possible role for the reader is to be the reader.

Metafiction forces the reader to consider the paradox of reading fiction in order to get to the truth. One way metafiction does this is by constantly confronting the reader with the "truth" of the illusion. You are told you are being fooled while you are being fooled. In doing this, the metafictionist adds another twist by suggesting that you can better trust what you are about to read because you have been told not to trust it.

Appropriations

Appropriation is the borrowing of another form of prose and using it as a frame in which to hang a new fiction. In this anthology, A. B. Paulsen's "The Minnesota Multiphasic Personality: a diagnostic test in two parts" is an extreme example of importing another form of prose (a form we would usually categorize as nonfiction) into a fictional context: The story looks very much like an actual written psychological exam. When formalist writers counterfeit other forms of writing in this way, they do so to focus your attention on the way art is framed and how shifting the frame transforms the art within it. To bring up the notion of a frame is to remind you once again that a story is an artifice, a made thing.

When you sit down to read a fiction, you have expectations as to how it will work and what it is up to—you have been tipped off, in some way, as to what it is you are about to read. You may be reading in an anthology labeled "fiction," or you may be reading an assignment in a literature class. Such things create a context for what you read, and that context or frame helps you to make sense of whatever you are reading. By shifting frames or setting different forms in different contexts, fictions that employ appropriations would make us conscious of how we rely on the mechanism of frames. Like metafiction, appropriation forces us to think beyond the box of convention, beyond our usual frames of reference. Appropriation gets us to think about how we think. By moving a test out of the psychologist's office (one frame) and onto the pages of a literary anthology (another frame), Paulsen would like us to consider how nebulous are our notions of sanity and insanity.

Collage

Collage in prose fiction depends on the juxtaposition of startling images. Or, instead of using a sequence of events in a logical order, a collage story might use repetition of the same event with slight variations, as in Robert Coover's "The Elevator," where each section begins with his character taking the elevator. Collage also uses space. A collage published in a book uses both printed words and a very conscious sense of the white spaces left unprinted. Think of those blank spaces as a visual representation of your role as a reader: Any reader puts words together, but in collage the reader's effort in putting things together is dramatized by these gaps, and you become aware of the active role this kind of fiction asks you to play. In a way, collage wants you to finish the story, to provide the glue that holds it together. In this way, collage shares with other formalist fiction the creating of a self-consciousness on your part as someone who is reading.

The artist Joseph Cornell was perhaps the best-known innovator of collage as an art form. He created shadow boxes, filled them with trinkets from dime stores, added discarded scraps of metal or paper, and arranged these things in intriguing ways. We think of Cornell as an artist even though he did not paint or draw or even sculpt original works of art; his art was the art of interesting arrangement. Collage, according to Donald Barthelme, was the art form of the twentieth century. The collage fiction in this anthology includes "Rondo" by Susan Neville, which attempts to translate a musical collage of instruments and voices into print. In "Wild Desire" Karen Brennan follows several stories within her story, and our attention jumps from one character to another. And in "Scissors Kick" Sandy Huss adds a collage of graphic images to her snippets of prose.

For its practitioners, collage is a more realistic representation of how we experience the contemporary world than the realist renderings that depend on logic, order, and reason.

Postmodernism

Some of the writers collected in this anthology can and have been categorized as postmodern. *Postmodernism*, as the term implies, comes out of and overlaps with modernism. Modernist prose writers chronicled and to various degrees mourned the death of the Old Order, as represented by family, country, and God. Personal narrative and fragmentation took precedence in their writing, replacing the omniscient narrators and "grand narratives" (the story of America's founding, the westward expansion of the pioneers) of earlier generations of writers. Modernist writers tended to challenge those narratives while maintaining a keen nostalgia for the good old days. The fragmentation of modern life for the modernist writers (Faulkner in *The Sound and the Fury*, Virginia Woolf in *To the Lighthouse*, Hemingway in "A Clean, Well-Lighted Place") was disconcerting and sometimes left their protagonists committing suicide, or murdered and unmourned, or simply afraid of the dark and oblivion.

Postmodernist writers also employ fragmentation and mini-personal narratives rather than the grand narratives of the past. But the biggest difference between postmodernists and modernists is that while modernists tended to be a gloomy lot, mournful over the loss of certainty with the rise of technology in the twentieth century, the postmodernists tend to celebrate that uncertainty. Fragmentation, uncertainty, and mystery are antidotes, not poisons, to postmodernists who see the grand narrative of the founding of America on democratic ideals and humanitarian principles of justice and brotherhood as having left out the narratives of the millions of people, particularly African-Americans and Native Americans, who suffered as a result of this worldview. Postmodernists look with suspicion on any agreed-upon text and take apart or "deconstruct" it much as one might disassemble a rifle, both to understand how it fits together and to make it less dangerous. However, modernism and postmodernism should not be seen as containers in which certain works reside. While helpful, such terms become restrictive and simplistic when defined or applied too rigidly.

Traditional versus Nontraditional

The traditional and the nontraditional ways of making fiction have been seen as being diametrically opposed, even hostile to each other. Philip Stevick called his important anthology of experimental fiction from thirty years ago *Anti-Story*, and at the same time Raymond Carver in an influential essay announced that fiction should have "no more tricks!" The present anthology, while it presents exclusively fiction that uses "tricks" not found in realist narrative, does not define itself in opposition to realism or story. In this collection of stories, we hope only to demonstrate the variety and diversity that has always been present when authors create fictions.

It is a kind of trap to think of nontraditional stories as being anti-realist or anti-mimetic. *Mimesis* is basically an attempt to present the world as it might appear in one's mirror, to present it "realistically." Yet mirrors distort, as we all know, and different mirrors distort differently, but the mimetic writer tries essentially to present a recognizable world—even though what's recognizable to one reader may be completely unfamiliar to another. "A Conversation with My Father" is essentially a mimetic story in that the author offers neither talking apes nor time travel. Yet the story is somewhat stylized and self-conscious in its telling. "A Conversation with My Father" is, on the one hand, a story about a man dying in the hospital; on the other hand, it's also a metafiction telling the story of telling a story about a man dying in a hospital. The purely mimetic writer might want to hide the reality that the story is an artifact, constructed solely out of language and existing in the print on a page. He or she would want us instead to see his or her characters as flesh-and-blood and the author as a kind of channeler of their authentic experiences. Nathaniel Hawthorne used to say his characters gathered around him at night. Hawthorne was a writer who seems to be mimetic in some stories and less concerned with mimesis in others. He wrote an essentially realist novel in *The Scarlet Letter*, and he also gave us the fantastic story "Young Goodman Brown," in which a man discovers a coven of witches in the woods. Within many writers both the traditional and the nontraditional co-exist.

This anthology claims no ground to be defended from the narrative realists rather it is *pro-contrivance*. It acknowledges the rich tradition of writers who play with form and content, and it calls attention to contrivance of all types. What surprises us is that the rich tradition of fabulists and formalists has gone unheralded in recent collections of stories that for the most part emphasize that other tradition of contrivance, narrative realism. Even our own brief anthology serves mostly as an introduction to the nontraditional—and perhaps as an antidote to the more commonly represented tradition of fiction found in most anthologies.

You have in your hands a book of stories, some of which may have an unfamiliar, even extreme appearance. We suggest that you approach these fictions on their own terms, with an expanded notion of what a story is and what an author can do.

PART ONE

Fabulists

Donald Barthelme

*One of the most innovative and influential American writers of the twenti-
eth century, Donald Barthelme was born in Philadelphia in 1931 and died
of cancer in Houston, Texas, in 1989. Barthelme's stories reflect the slip-
pery slope of postmodern American life, in which the bizarre and the mundane merrily coexist. In his story "Me and Miss Mandible," a thirty-year-old
man is sent back to sixth grade, where two women, his teacher and an
eleven-year-old classmate, feud over his affection. In "The Indian Uprising,"
a modern-day city tries to resist a bizarre invasion. In "The King of Jazz,"
Hokie Mokie has to defend his title against a Japanese upstart.*

*The critic Lois Gordon writes that Barthelme "rejects traditional
chronology, plot, character, time, space, grammar, syntax, metaphor, and
simile, as well as the traditional distinctions between fact and fiction.
What used to organize reality—time, space, and the structure of language—is now often disjointed, and language, and the difficulties in
'using' it, becomes the very subject of his art. Most obvious is . . . its
refusal to be an orderly reflection of, and comment upon, a stable, exter-
nal world."*

*Barthelme's story "At the End of the Mechanical Age" exemplifies
this style while simultaneously poking fun at social mores and sexual politics. In the story—a combination of Adam and Eve, Noah's Ark, and
Monty Python—God is an electrician. While God skulks in the background, tinkering with the power, the Adam-like narrator names types of
workshop tools instead of animals and addresses his "Eve" formally by her
last name. All this makes for a strange and hilarious postmodern myth.*

At the End
of the Mechanical Age

I went to the grocery store to buy some soap. I stood for a long time before
the soaps in their attractive boxes, RUB and FAB and TUB and suchlike,
I couldn't decide so I closed my eyes and reached out blindly and when I
opened my eyes I found her hand in mine.

Her name was Mrs. Davis, she said, and TUB was best for important cleaning experiences, in her opinion. So we went to lunch at a
Mexican restaurant which as it happened she owned, she took me into
the kitchen and showed me her stacks of handsome beige tortillas and

the steam tables which were shiny-brite. I told her I wasn't very good with women and she said it didn't matter, few men were, and that nothing mattered, now that Jake was gone, but I would do as an interim project and sit down and have a Carta Blanca. So I sat down and had a cool Carta Blanca, God was standing in the basement reading the meters to see how much grace had been used up in the month of June. Grace is electricity, science has found, it is not *like* electricity, it *is* electricity and God was down in the basement reading the meters in His blue jump suit with the flashlight stuck in the back pocket.

"The mechanical age is drawing to a close," I said to her.

"Or has already done so," she replied.

"It was a good age," I said. "I was comfortable in it, relatively. Probably I will not enjoy the age to come quite so much. I don't like its look."

"One must be fair. We don't know yet what kind of an age the next one will be. Although I feel in my bones that it will be an age inimical to personal well-being and comfort, and that is what I like, personal well-being and comfort."

"Do you suppose there is something to be done?" I asked her.

"Huddle and cling," said Mrs. Davis. "We can huddle and cling. It will pall, of course, everything palls, in time . . . "

Then we went back to my house to huddle and cling, most women are two different colors when they remove their clothes especially in summer but Mrs. Davis was all one color, an ocher. She seemed to like huddling and clinging, she stayed for many days. From time to time she checked the restaurant keeping everything shiny-brite and distributing sums of money to the staff, returning with tortillas in sacks, cases of Carta Blanca, buckets of guacamole, but I paid her for it because I didn't want to feel obligated.

There was song I sang her, a song of great expectations.

"Ralph is coming," I sang, "Ralph is striding in his suit of lights over moons and mountains, over parking lots and fountains, toward your silky side. Ralph is coming, he has a coat of many colors and all major credit cards and he is striding to meet you and culminate your foggy dreams in an explosion of blood and soil, at the end of the mechanical age. Ralph is coming preceded by fifty running men with spears and fifty dancing ladies who are throwing leaf spinach out of little baskets, in his path. Ralph is perfect," I sang, "but he is also full of interesting tragic flaws, and he can drink fifty running men under the table without breaking his stride and he can have congress with fifty dancing ladies without breaking his stride, even his socks are ironed, so natty is Ralph, but he is also right down in the mud with the rest of us, he markets the mud at high prices for specialized industrial uses and he is striding, striding,

*striding, toward your waiting heart. Of course you may not like him, some peo-
ple are awfully picky . . . Ralph is coming,"* I sang to her, *"he is striding over
dappled plains and crazy rivers and he will change your life for the better, probably, you will be fainting with glee at the simple touch of his grave gentle
immense hand although I am aware that some people can't stand prosperity,
Ralph is coming, I hear his hoofsteps on the drumhead of history, he is striding
as he has been all his life toward you, you, you."*

"Yes," Mrs. Davis said, when I had finished singing, "that is what
I deserve, all right. But probably I will not get it. And in the meantime,
there is you."

~~~

God then rained for forty days and forty nights, when the water
tore away the front of the house we got into the boat, Mrs. Davis liked
the way I maneuvered the boat off the trailer and out of the garage, she
was provoked into a memoir of Jake.

"Jake was a straight-ahead kind of man," she said, "he was simpleminded and that helped him to be the kind of man that he was." She
was staring into her Scotch-and-floodwater rather moodily I thought,
debris bouncing on the waves all around us but she paid no attention.
"That is the type of man I like," she said, "a strong and simpleminded
man. The case-study method was not Jake's method, he went right
through the middle of the line and never failed to gain yardage, no
matter what the game was. He had a lust for life, and life had a lust for
him. I was inconsolable when Jake passed away." Mrs. Davis was drinking the Scotch for her nerves, she had no nerves of course, she was
nerveless and possibly heartless also but that is another question, gut-
less she was not, she had a gut and a very pretty one ocher in color but
that was another matter. God was standing up to His neck in the raging waters with a smile of incredible beauty on His visage, He seemed
to be enjoying His creation, the disaster, the waters all around us were
raging louder now, raging like a mighty tractor-trailer tailgating you on
the highway.

Then Mrs. Davis sang to me, a song of great expectations.

"Maude is waiting for you," Mrs. Davis sang to me, *"Maude is waiting
for you in all her seriousness and splendor, under her gilded onion dome, in that
city which I cannot name at this time, Maude waits. Maude is what you lack,
the profoundest of your lacks. Your every yearn since the first yearn has been a
yearn for Maude, only you did not know it until I, your dear friend, pointed it
out. She is going to heal your scrappy and generally unsatisfactory life with the
balm of her Maudeness, luckiest of dogs, she waits only for you. Let me give you*

just one instance of Maude's inhuman sagacity. Maude named the tools. It was Maude who thought of calling the rattail file a rattail file. It was Maude who christened the needle-nose pliers. Maude named the rasp. Think of it. What else could a rasp be but a rasp? Maude in her wisdom went right to the point, and called it rasp. It was Maude who named the maul. Similarly the sledge, the wedge, the ballpeen hammer, the adz, the shim, the hone, the strop. The handsaw, the hacksaw, the bucksaw, and the fretsaw were named by Maude, peering into each saw and intuiting at once its specialness. The scratch awl, the scuffle hoe, the prick punch and the countersink—I could go on and on. The tools came to Maude, tool by tool in a long respectful line, she gave them their names. The vise. The gimlet. The cold chisel. The reamer, the router, the gouge. The plumb bob. How could she have thought up the rough justice of these wonderful cognomens? Looking languidly at a pair of tin snips, and then deciding to call them tin snips—what a burst of glory! And I haven't even cited the bush hook, the grass snath, or the plumber's snake, or the C-clamp, or the nippers, or the scythe. What a tall achievement, naming the tools! And this is just one of Maude's contributions to our worldly estate, there are others. What delights will come crowding," Mrs. Davis sang to me, "delight upon delight, when the epithalamium is ground out by the hundred organ grinders who are Maude's constant attendants, on that good-quality day of her own choosing, which you have desperately desired all your lean life, only you weren't aware of it until I, your dear friend, pointed it out. And Maude is young but not too young," Mrs. Davis sang to me, "she is not too old either, she is just right and she is waiting for you with her tawny limbs and horse sense, when you receive Maude's nod your future and your past will begin."

There was a pause, or pall.

"Is that true," I asked, "that song?"

"It is a metaphor," said Mrs. Davis, "it has metaphorical truth."

"And the end of the mechanical age," I said, "is that a metaphor?"

"The end of the mechanical age," said Mrs. Davis, "is in my judgment an actuality straining to become a metaphor. One must wish it luck, I suppose. One must cheer it on. Intellectual rigor demands that we give these damned metaphors every chance, even if they are inimical to personal well-being and comfort. We have a duty to understand everything, whether we like it or not—a duty I would scant if I could." At that moment the water jumped into the boat and sank us.

～～

At the wedding Mrs. Davis spoke to me kindly.

"Tom," she said, "you are not Ralph, but you are all that is around at the moment. I have taken in the whole horizon with a single sweep of my practiced eye, no giant figure looms there and that is why I have decided to marry you, temporarily, with Jake gone and an age ending. It will be a marriage of convenience all right, and when Ralph comes, or Maude nods, then our arrangement will automatically self-destruct, like the tinted bubble that it is. You were very kind and considerate, when we were drying out, in the tree, and I appreciated that. That counted for something. Of course kindness and consideration are not what the great songs, the Ralph-song and the Maude-song, promise. They are merely flaky substitutes for the terminal experience. I realize that and want you to realize it. I want to be straight with you. That is one of the most admirable things about me, that I am always straight with people, from the sweet beginning to the bitter end. Now I will return to the big house where my handmaidens will proceed with the robing of the bride."

It was cool in the meadow by the river, the meadow Mrs. Davis had selected for the travesty, I walked over to the tree under which my friend Blackie was standing, he was the best man, in a sense.

"This disgusts me," Blackie said, "this hollow pretense and empty sham and I had to come all the way from Chicago."

God came to the wedding and stood behind a tree with just part of His effulgence showing, I wondered whether He was planning to bless this makeshift construct with His grace, or not. It's hard to imagine what He was thinking of in the beginning when He planned everything that was ever going to happen, planned everything exquisitely right down to the tiniest detail such as what I was thinking at this very moment, my thought about His thought, planned the end of the mechanical age and detailed the new age to follow, and then the bride emerged from the house with her train, all ocher in color and very lovely.

"And do you, Anne," the minister said, "promise to make whatever mutually satisfactory accommodations necessary to reduce tensions and arrive at whatever previously agreed-upon goals both parties have harmoniously set in the appropriate planning sessions?"

"I do," said Mrs. Davis.

"And do you, Thomas, promise to explore all differences thoroughly with patience and inner honesty ignoring no fruitful avenues of discussion and seeking at all times to achieve rapprochement while eschewing advantage in conflict situations?"

"Yes," I said.

"Well, now we are married," said Mrs. Davis, "I think I will retain my present name if you don't mind, I have always been Mrs. Davis and your name is a shade graceless, no offense, dear."

"O.K.," I said.

Then we received the congratulations and good wishes of the guests, who were mostly employees of the Mexican restaurant, Raul was there and Consuelo, Pedro, and Pepe came crowding around with outstretched hands and Blackie came crowding around with outstretched hands, God was standing behind the caterer's tables looking at the enchiladas and chalupas and chile con queo and chicken mole as if He had never seen such things before but that was hard to believe.

I started to speak to Him as all of the world's great religions with a few exceptions urge, from the heart, I started to say "Lord, Little Father of the Poor, and all that, I was just wondering now that an age, the mechanical age, is ending and a new age beginning or so they say, I was just wondering if You could give me a hint, sort of, not a Sign, I'm not asking for a Sign, but just the barest hint as to whether what we have been told about Your nature and our nature is, forgive me and I know how You feel about doubt or rather what we have been told You feel about it, but if You could just let drop the slightest indication as to whether what we have been told is authentic or just a bunch of apocryphal heterodoxy—"

But He had gone away with an insanely beautiful smile on His lighted countenance, gone away to read the meters and get a line on the efficacy of grace in that area, I surmised, I couldn't blame Him, my question had not been so very elegantly put, had I been able to express it mathematically He would have been more interested, maybe, but I have never been able to express anything mathematically.

~~~

After the marriage Mrs. Davis explained marriage to me.

Marriage, she said, an institution deeply enmeshed with the mechanical age.

Pairings smiled upon by law were but reifications of the laws of mechanics, inspired by unions of a technical nature, such as nut with bolt, wood with wood screw, aircraft with Plane-Mate.

Permanence or impermanence of the bond a function of (1) materials and (2) technique.

Growth of literacy a factor, she said.

Growth of illiteracy also.

The center will not hold if it has been spot-welded by an operator whose deepest concern is not with the weld but with his lottery ticket.

God interested only in grace—keeping things humming.

Blackouts, brownouts, temporary dimmings of household illumination all portents not of Divine displeasure but of Divine indifference to executive-development programs at middle-management levels.

He likes to get out into the field Himself, she said. With His flashlight. He is doing the best He can.

We two, she and I, no exception to general ebb/flow of world juice and its concomitant psychological effects, she said.

Bitter with the sweet, she said.

~

After the explanation came the divorce.

"Will you be wanting to contest the divorce?" I asked Mrs. Davis.

"I think not," she said calmly, "although I suppose one of us should, for the fun of the thing. An uncontested divorce always seems to me contrary to the spirit of divorce."

"That is true," I said, "I have had the same feeling myself, not infrequently."

After the divorce the child was born. We named him A.F. of L. Davis and sent him to that part of Russia where people live to be one hundred and ten years old. He is living there still, probably, growing in wisdom and beauty. Then we shook hands, Mrs. Davis and I, and she set out Ralphward, and I, Maudeward, the glow of hope not yet extinguished, the fear of pall not yet triumphant, standby generators ensuring the flow of grace to all of God's creatures at the end of the mechanical age.

Barry Hannah

Barry Hannah, born in Clinton, Mississippi, in 1942, earned a B.A. from Mississippi College in 1964 and a Master of Fine Arts in Creative Writing from the University of Arkansas in 1967. His first novel, Geronimo Rex *in 1972, won the William Faulkner Prize for writing. Hannah has taught at a number of universities, including the University of Iowa and the University of Mississippi, where he has long served as writer-in-residence. In 1978 his collection of stories* Airships *(in which "Water Liars" appears) earned him wide praise, a devoted audience, the Arnold Gingrich Short Fiction Award, and, in 1979, the Award for Literature from the American Institute of Arts and Letters. In all, he has published more than a dozen novels and story collections, each adding to the well-earned perception that he is one of the South's great contemporary writers.*

"Water Liars" shows how fabulism is embedded even in the most mundane acts like fishing. It's been said that humor is often a defense mechanism—so too, perhaps, is our need to create mysteries out of things that are all too heartbreakingly explainable.

Water Liars

When I am run down and flocked around by the world, I go down to Farte Cove off the Yazoo River and take my beer to the end of the pier where the old liars are still snapping and wheezing at one another. The line-up is always different, because they're always dying out or succumbing to constipation, etc., whereupon they go back to the cabins and wait for a good day when they can come out and lie again, leaning on the rail with coats full of bran cookies. The son of the man the cove was named for is often out there. He pronounces his name Far*tay*, with a great French stress on the last syllable. Otherwise you might laugh at his history or ignore it in favor of the name as it's spelled on the sign.

I'm glad it's not my name.

This poor dignified man has had to explain his nobility to the semiliterate of half of America before he could even begin a decent conversation with them. On the other hand, Farte, Jr., is a great liar himself. He tells about seeing ghost people around the lake and tells big loose ones about the size of the fish those ghosts took out of Farte Cove in years past.

Last year I turned thirty-three years old and, raised a Baptist, I had a sense of being Jesus and coming to something decided in my life—because we all know Jesus was crucified at thirty-three. It had all seemed especially important, what you do in this year, and holy with meaning.

On the morning after my birthday party, during which I and my wife almost drowned in vodka cocktails, we both woke up to the making of a truth session about the lovers we'd had before we met each other. I had a mildly exciting and usual history, and she had about the same, which surprised me. For ten years she'd sworn I was the first. I could not believe her history was exactly equal with mine. It hurt me to think that in the era when there were supposed to be virgins she had allowed anyone but *me*, and so on.

I was dazed and exhilarated by this information for several weeks. Finally, it drove me crazy, and I came out to Farte Cove to rest, under the pretense of a fishing week with my chum Wyatt.

I'm still figuring out why I couldn't handle it.

My sense of the past is vivid and slow. I hear every sign and see every shadow. The movement of every limb in every passionate event occupies my mind. I have a prurience on the grand scale. It makes no sense that I should be angry about happenings before she and I ever saw each other. Yet I feel an impotent homicidal urge in the matter of her lovers. She has excused my episodes as the course of things, though she has a vivid memory too. But there is a blurred nostalgia women have that men don't.

You could not believe how handsome and delicate my wife is naked.

I was driven wild by the bodies that had trespassed her twelve and thirteen years ago.

My vacation at Farte Cove wasn't like that easy little bit you get as a rich New Yorker. My finances weren't in great shape; to be true, they were about in ruin, and I left the house knowing my wife would have to answer the phone to hold off, for instance, the phone company itself. Everybody wanted money and I didn't have any.

I was going to take the next week in the house while she went away, watch our three kids and all the rest. When you both teach part-time in the high schools, the income can be slow in summer.

No poor-mouthing here. I don't want anybody's pity. I just want to explain. I've got good hopes of a job over at Alabama next year. Then I'll get myself among higher-paid liars, that's all.

Sidney Farte was out there prevaricating away at the end of the pier when Wyatt and I got there Friday evening. The old faces I recognized; a few new harkening idlers I didn't.

"Now, Doctor Mooney, he not only saw the ghost of Lily, he says he had intercourse with her. Said it was involuntary. Before he knew what he was doing, he was on her making cadence and all their clothes blown away off in the trees around the shore. She turned into a wax candle right under him."

"Intercourse," said an old-timer, breathing heavy. He sat up on the rail. It was a word of high danger to his old mind. He said it with a long disgust, glad, I guess, he was not involved.

"MacIntire, a Presbyterian preacher, I seen him come out here with his son-and-law, anchor near the bridge, and pull up fifty or more white perch big as small pumpkins. You know what they was using for bait?"

"What?" asked another geezer.

"*Nuthin.* Caught on the bare hook. It was Gawd made them fish bite," said Sidney Farte, going at it good.

"Naw. There be a season they bite a bare hook. Gawd didn't have to've done that," said another old guy, with a fringe of red hair and a racy Florida shirt.

"Nother night," said Sidney Farte, "I saw the ghost of Yazoo hisself with my pa, who's dead. A Indian king with four deer around him."

The old boys seemed to be used to this one. Nobody said anything. They ignored Sidney.

"Tell you what," said a well-built small old boy. "That was somethin when we come down here and had to chase that whole high-school party off the end of this pier, them drunken children. They was smokin dope and two-thirds a them nekid swimmin in the water. Good hunnerd of em. From your so-called *good* high school. What you think's happnin at the bad ones?"

I dropped my beer and grew suddenly sick. Wyatt asked me what was wrong. I could see my wife in 1960 in the group of high-schoolers she must have had. My jealousy went out into the stars of the night above me. I could not bear the roving carelessness of teen-agers, their judge-less tangling of wanting and bodies. But I was the worst back then. In the mad days back then, I dragged the panties off girls I hated and talked badly about them once the sun came up.

"Worst time in my life," said a new, younger man, maybe sixty but with the face of a man who had surrendered, "me and Woody was fishing. Had a lantern. It was about eleven. We was catching a few fish but rowed on into that little cove over there near town. We heard all these sounds, like they was ghosts. We was scared. We thought it might be the Yazoo hisself. We known of some fellows the Yazoo had killed to death just from fright. It was the over the sounds of what was normal human sighin and amoanin. It was big unhuman sounds. We just stood still in the boat. Ain't nuthin else us to do. For thirty minutes."

"An what was it?" said the old geezer, letting himself off the rail.

"We had a big flashlight. There came up this rustlin in the brush and I beamed it over there. The two of em makin the sounds get up with half they clothes on. It was my own daughter Charlotte and an older guy I didn't even know with a mustache. My *own* daughter, and them sounds over the water scarin us like ghosts."

"My Gawd, that's awful," said the old geezer by the rail. "Is that the truth? I wouldn't've told that. That's terrible."

Sidney Farte was really upset.

"This ain't the place!" he said. "Tell your kind of story somewhere else."

The old man who'd told his story was calm and fixed to his place. He'd told the truth. The crowd on the pier was outraged and discomfited. He wasn't one of them. But he stood his place. He had a distressed pride. You could see he had never recovered from the thing he'd told about.

I told Wyatt to bring the old man back to the cabin. He was out here away from his wife the same as me and Wyatt. Just an older guy with a big hurting bosom. He wore a suit and the only way you'd know he was on vacation was he'd removed his tie. He didn't know where the bait house was. He didn't know what to do on vacation at all. But he got drunk with us and I can tell you he and I went out the next morning with our poles, Wyatt driving the motorboat, fishing for white perch in the cove near the town. And we were kindred.

We were both crucified by the truth.

Grace Paley

Grace Paley was born in the Bronx in 1922 to a family of socialist Russian Jews, a family that delighted in storytelling, and the language of her fiction reflects the immigrant voices that surrounded her in her youth. Paley studied at Hunter College and New York University. During the 1960s she taught at Columbia and Syracuse Universities, then at Sarah Lawrence College. She began writing as a poet but is better known for her short stories and as a feminist and peace activist. While her literary output has been small by some standards, her three story collections, The Little Disturbances of Man *(1959),* Enormous Changes at the Last Minute *(1974), and* Later the Same Day *(1985), have been met with universal acclamation and have established her as one of America's living literary treasures. With characteristic pith, she once explained why she has never written a novel: "Art is too long and life is too short."*

"A Conversation with My Father" is a delightful example of metafiction (fiction about fiction), a story about happy endings versus believable endings, love versus resignation, mortality versus hope. As the main character, Faith, explains, she's bored by stories that plod from point A to point B to point C in a logical fashion. Her father, on the other hand, is annoyed by Faith's tendency toward odd situations, such as telling a story from the point of view of a character in a tree. (In another story by Paley, "Faith in a Tree," her recurring character, Faith, indeed sits in a tree while others talk to her from below.) It's tempting to think of Faith as Grace Paley's alter ego, but we must remember we are reading fiction and not read the story too literally. Faith, in her argument with her dying father, has to come to terms with the difference between real life and fiction.

A Conversation with My Father

My father is eighty-six years old and in bed. His heart, that bloody motor, is equally old and will not do certain jobs anymore. It still floods his head with brainy light. But it won't let his legs carry the weight of his body around the house. Despite my metaphors, this muscle failure is not due to his old heart, he says, but to a potassium shortage. Sitting on one pillow, leaning on three, he offers last-minute advice and makes a request.

"I would like you to write a simple story just once more," he says, "the kind Maupassant wrote, or Chekhov, the kind you used to write. Just recognizable people and then write down what happened to them next."

I say, "Yes, why not? That's possible." I want to please him, though I don't remember writing that way. I *would* like to try to tell such a story, if he means the kind that begins: "There was a woman . . . " followed by plot, the absolute line between two points which I've always despised. Not for literary reasons, but because it takes all hope away. Everyone, real or invented, deserves the open destiny of life.

Finally I thought of a story that had been happening for a couple of years right across the street. I wrote it down, then read it aloud. "Pa," I said, "how about this? Do you mean something like this?"

Once in my time there was a woman and she had a son. They lived nicely, in a small apartment in Manhattan. This boy at about fifteen became a junkie, which is not unusual in our neighborhood. In order to maintain her close friendship with him, she became a junkie too. She said it was part of the youth culture, with which she felt very much at home. After a while, for a number of reasons, the boy gave it all up and left the city and his mother in disgust. Hopeless and alone, she grieved. We all visit her.

"O.K., Pa, that's it," I said, "an unadorned and miserable tale."

"But that's not what I mean," my father said. "You misunderstood me on purpose. You know there's a lot more to it. You know that. You left everything out. Turgenev wouldn't do that. Chekhov wouldn't do that. There are in fact Russian writers you never heard of, you don't have an inkling of, as good as anyone, who can write a plain ordinary story, who would not leave out what you have left out. I object not to facts but to people sitting in trees talking senselessly, voices from who knows where . . ."

"Forget that one, Pa, what have I left out now? In this one?"

"Her looks, for instance."

"Oh. Quite handsome, I think. Yes."

"Her hair?"

"Dark, with heavy braids, as though she were a girl or a foreigner."

"What were her parents like, her stock? That she became such a person. It's interesting, you know."

"From out of town. Professional people. The first to be divorced in their county. How's that? Enough?" I asked.

"With you, it's all a joke," he said. "What about the boy's father? Why didn't you mention him? Who was he? Or was the boy born out of wedlock?"

"Yes," I said. "He was born out of wedlock."

"For godsakes, doesn't anyone in your stories get married? Doesn't anyone have the time to run down to City Hall before they jump into bed?"

"No," I said. "In real life, yes. But in my stories, no."

"Why do you answer me like that?"

"Oh, Pa, this is a simple story about a smart woman who came to N.Y.C. full of interest love trust excitement very up-to-date, and about her son, what a hard time she had in this world. Married or not, it's of small consequence."

"It is of great consequence," he said.

"O.K.," I said.

"O.K. O.K. yourself," he said, "but listen. I believe you that she's good-looking, but I don't think she was so smart."

"That's true," I said. "Actually that's the trouble with stories. People start out fantastic. You think they're extraordinary, but it turns out as the work goes along, they're just average with a good education. Sometimes the other way around, the person's a kind of dumb innocent, but he outwits you and you can't even think of an ending good enough."

"What do you do then?" he asked. He had been a doctor for a couple of decades and then an artist for a couple of decades and he's still interested in details, craft, technique.

"Well, you just have to let the story lie around till some agreement can be reached between you and the stubborn hero."

"Aren't you talking silly, now?" he asked. "Start again," he said. "It so happens I'm not going out this evening. Tell the story again. See what you can do this time."

"O.K.," I said. "But it's not a five-minute job." Second attempt:

Once, across the street from us, there was a fine handsome woman, our neighbor. She had a son whom she loved because she'd known him since birth (in helpless chubby infancy, and in the wrestling, hugging ages, seven to ten, as well as earlier and later). This boy, when he fell into the fist of adolescence, became a junkie. He was not a hopeless one. He was in fact hopeful, an ideologue and successful converter. With his busy brilliance, he wrote persuasive articles for his high-school newspaper. Seeking a wider audience, using important connections, he drummed into Lower Manhattan newsstand distribution a periodical called *Oh! Golden Horse!*

In order to keep him from feeling guilty (because guilt is the stony heart of nine-tenths of all clinically diagnosed cancers in America today, she said), and because she had always believed in giving bad habits room at home where one could keep an eye on them, she too became a junkie. Her kitchen was famous for a while—a center for intellectual addicts who knew what they were doing. A few felt artistic like Coleridge and others were scientific and revolutionary like Leary. Although she was often high herself, certain good mothering reflexes remained, and she saw to it that there was lots of orange juice around and honey and milk and vitamin pills. However, she never cooked anything but chili, and that no more than once a week. She explained, when we talked to her, seriously, with neighborly concern, that it was her part in the youth culture and she would rather be with the young, it was an honor, than with her own generation.

One week, while nodding through an Antonioni film, this boy was severely jabbed by the elbow of a stern and proselytizing girl, sitting beside him. She offered immediate apricots and nuts for his sugar level, spoke to him sharply, and took him home.

She had heard of him and his work and she herself published, edited, and wrote a competitive journal called *Man Does Live by Bread Alone*. In the organic heat of her continuous presence he could not help but become interested once more in his muscles, his arteries and nerve connections. In fact he began to love them, treasure them, praise them with funny little songs in *Man Does Live . . .*

> *the fingers of my flesh transcend*
> *my transcendental soul*
> *the tightness in my shoulders end*
> *my teeth have made me whole*

To the mouth of his head (that glory of will and determination) he brought hard apples, nuts, wheat germ, and soybean oil. He said to his old friends, From now on, I guess I'll keep my wits about me. I'm going on the natch. He said he was about to begin a spiritual deep-breathing journey. How about you too, Mom? he asked kindly.

His conversion was so radiant, splendid, that neighborhood kids his age began to say that he had never been a real addict at all, only a journalist along for the smell of the story. The mother tried several times to give up what had become without her son and his friends a lonely habit. This effort only brought it to supportable levels. The boy and his girl took their electronic mimeograph and moved to the bushy edge of another borough. They were very strict. They said they would not see her again until she had been off drugs for sixty days.

At home alone in the evening, weeping, the mother read and reread the seven issues of *Oh! Golden Horse!* They seemed to her as truthful as ever. We often crossed the street to visit and console. But if we mentioned any of our children who were at college or in the hospital or dropouts at home, she would cry out, My baby! My baby! and burst into terrible, face-scarring, time-consuming tears. The End.

First my father was silent, then he said, "Number One: You have a nice sense of humor. Number Two: I see you can't tell a plain story.

So don't waste time." Then he said sadly, "Number Three: I suppose that means she was alone, she was left like that, his mother. Alone. Probably sick?"

I said, "Yes."

"Poor woman. Poor girl, to be born in a time of fools, to live among fools. The end. The end. You were right to put that down. The end."

I didn't want to argue, but I had to say, "Well, it is not necessarily the end, Pa."

"Yes," he said, "what a tragedy. The end of a person."

"No, Pa," I begged him. "It doesn't have to be. She's only about forty. She could be a hundred different things in this world as time goes on. A teacher or a social worker. An ex-junkie! Sometimes it's better than having a master's in education."

"Jokes," he said. "As a writer that's your main trouble. You don't want to recognize it. Tragedy! Plain tragedy! Historial tragedy! No hope. The end."

"Oh, Pa," I said. "She could change."

"In your own life, too, you have to look it in the face." He took a couple of nitroglycerin. "Turn to five," he said, pointing to the dial on the oxygen talk. He inserted the tubes into his nostrils and breathed deep. He closed his eyes and said, "No."

I had promised the family to always let him have the last word when arguing, but in this case I had a different responsibility. That woman lives across the street. She's my knowledge and my invention. I'm sorry for her. I'm not going to leave her there in that house crying. (Actually neither would Life, which unlike me has no pity.)

Therefore: She did change. Of course her son never came home again. But right now, she's the receptionist in a storefront community clinic in the East Village. Most of the customers are young people, some old friends. The head doctor has said to her, "If we only had three people in this clinic with your experiences . . . "

"The doctor said that?" My father took the oxygen tubes out of his nostrils and said, "Jokes. Jokes again."

"No, Pa, it could really happen that way, it's a funny world nowadays."

"No," he said. "Truth first. She will slide back. A person must have character. She does not."

"No, Pa," I said. "That's it. She's got a job. Forget it. She's in that storefront working."

"How long will it be?" he asked. "Tragedy! You too. When will you look it in the face?"

Delmore Schwartz

*Born in 1913, the New Yorker Delmore Schwartz began his career with
great promise and was an influential part of the American literary scene
of the 1940s and 1950s as an editor of* The Partisan Review.
*"In Dreams Begin Responsibilities" places a young man in a movie
theater watching a movie about the first date of his parents. For him
(though for no one else in the audience) the movie leads to an all-too-
familiar conclusion, the marriage of his parents and birth of their child,
the narrator of the story. Instead of a happy ending, the narrator, who
sees his father as a brute, finds the movie horrifying because, in a sense,
he has lived through all its unhappy sequels. While the notion of a person's watching a movie of his parents' first date in a crowded movie theater seems unlikely, the emotional punch of this story is as believable and
hard-hitting as any other short story writer's work. By the end of the
story, the situation is explained in an ultimately realist fashion, yet it's the
story's fantastic elements that make it so compelling. Schwartz, who wrote
this story while still in his early twenties, penned relatively little fiction in
his life, but this story remains a much-admired classic.*

~~~~~~~~

In Dreams Begin Responsibilities

I

I think it is the year 1909. I feel as if I were in a motion picture theatre,
the long arm of light crossing the darkness and spinning, my eyes fixed
on the screen. This is a silent picure as if an old Biograph one, in
which the actors are dressed in ridiculously old-fashioned clothes, and
one flash succeeds another with sudden jumps. The actors too seem to
jump about and walk too fast. The shots themselves are full of dots and
rays, as if it were raining when the picture was photographed. The light
is bad.

It is Sunday afternoon, June 12th, 1909, and my father is walking
down the quiet streets of Brooklyn on his way to visit my mother. His
clothes are newly pressed and his tie is too tight in his high collar. He
jingles the coins in his pockets, thinking of the witty things he will say.
I feel as if I had by now relaxed entirely in the soft darkness of the theatre; the organist peals out the obvious and approximate emotions on

which the audience rocks unknowingly. I am anonymous, and I have forgotten myself. It is always so when one goes to the movies, it is, as they say, a drug.

My father walks from street to street of trees, lawns and houses, once in a while coming to an avenue on which a street-car skates and gnaws, slowly progressing. The conductor, who has a handle-bar mustache helps a young lady wearing a hat like a bowl with feathers on to the car. She lifts her long skirts slightly as she mounts the steps. He leisurely makes change and rings his bell. It is obviously Sunday, for everyone is wearing Sunday clothes, and the street-car's noises emphasize the quiet of the holiday. Is not Brooklyn the City of Churches? The shops are closed and their shades drawn, but for an occasional stationery store or drug-store with great green balls in the window.

My father has chosen to take this long walk because he likes to walk and think. He thinks about himself in the future and so arrives at the place he is to visit in a state of mild exaltation. He pays no attention to the houses he is passing, in which the Sunday dinner is being eaten, nor to the many trees which patrol each street, now coming to their full leafage and the time when they will room the whole street in cool shadow. An occasional carriage passes, the horse's hooves falling like stones in the quiet afternoon, and once in a while an automobile, looking like an enormous upholstered sofa, puffs and passes.

My father thinks of my mother, of how nice it will be to introduce her to his family. But he is not yet sure that he wants to marry her, and once in a while he becomes panicky about the bond already established. He reassures himself by thinking of the big men he admires who are married: William Randolph Hearst, and William Howard Taft, who has just become President of the United States.

My father arrives at my mother's house. He has come too early and so is suddenly embarrassed. My aunt, my mother's sister, answers the loud bell with her napkin in her hand, for the family is still at dinner. As my father enters, my grandfather rises from the table and shakes hands with him. My mother has run upstairs to tidy herself. My grandmother asks my father if he has had dinner, and tells him that Rose will be downstairs soon. My grandfather opens the conversation by remarking on the mild June weather. My father sits uncomfortably near the table, holding his hat in his hand. My grandmother tells my aunt to take my father's hat. My uncle, twelve years old, runs into the house, his hair tousled. He shouts a greeting to my father, who has often given him a nickel, and then runs upstairs. It is evident that the respect in which my father is held in this household is tempered by a good deal of mirth. He is impressive, yet he is very awkward.

II

Finally my mother comes downstairs, all dressed up, and my father being engaged in conversation with my grandfather becomes uneasy, not knowing whether to greet my mother or continue the conversation. He gets up from the chair clumsily and says "hello" gruffly. My grandfather watches, examining their congruence, such as it is, with a critical eye, and meanwhile rubbing his bearded cheek roughly, as he always does when he reflects. He is worried; he is afraid that my father will not make a good husband for his oldest daughter. At this point something happens to the film, just as my father is saying something funny to my mother; I am awakened to myself and my unhappiness just as my interest was rising. The audience begins to clap impatiently. Then the trouble is cared for but the film has been returned to a portion just shown, and once more I see my grandfather rubbing his bearded cheek and pondering my father's character. It is difficult to get back into the picture once more and forget myself, but as my mother giggles at my father's words, the darkness drowns me.

My father and mother depart from the house, my father shaking hands with my mother once more, out of some unknown uneasiness. I stir uneasily also, slouched in the hard chair of the theatre. Where is the older uncle, my mother's older brother? He is studying in his bedroom upstairs, studying for his final examination at the College of the City of New York, having been dead of rapid pneumonia for the last twenty-one years. My mother and father walk down the same quiet streets once more. My mother is holding my father's arm and telling him of the novel which she has been reading; and my father utters judgments of the characters as the plot is made clear to him. This is a habit which he very much enjoys, for he feels the utmost superiority and confidence when he approves and condemns the behavior of other people. At times he feels moved to utter a brief "Ugh"—whenever the story becomes what he would call sugary. This tribute is paid to his manliness. My mother feels satisfied by the interest which she has awakened; she is showing my father how intelligent she is, and how interesting.

They reach the avenue, and the street-car leisurely arrives. They are going to Coney Island this afternoon, although my mother considers that such pleasures are inferior. She has made up her mind to indulge only in a walk on the boardwalk and a pleasant dinner, avoiding the riotous amusements as being beneath the dignity of so dignified a couple.

My father tells my mother how much money he has made in the past week, exaggerating an amount which need not have been exaggerated. But my father has always felt that actualities somehow fall short. Suddenly I begin to weep. The determined old lady who sits next to me in the theatre is annoyed and looks at me with an angry face, and being intimidated, I stop. I drag out my handkerchief and dry my face, licking the drop which has fallen near my lips. Meanwhile I have missed something, for here are my mother and father alighting at the last stop, Coney Island.

III

They walk toward the boardwalk, and my father commands my mother to inhale the pungent air from the sea. They both breathe in deeply, both of them laughing as they do so. They have in common a great interest in health, although my father is strong and husky, my mother frail. Their minds are full of theories of what is good to eat and not good to eat, and sometimes they engage in heated discussions of the subject, the whole matter ending in my father's announcement, made with a scornful bluster, that you have to die sooner or later anyway. On the boardwalk's flagpole, the American flag is pulsing in an intermittent wind from the sea.

My father and mother go to the rail of the boardwalk and look down on the beach where a good many bathers are casually walking about. A few are in the surf. A peanut whistle pierces the air with its pleasant and active whine, and my father goes to buy peanuts. My mother remains at the rail and stares at the ocean. The ocean seems merry to her; it pointedly sparkles and again and again the pony waves are released. She notices the children digging in the wet sand, and the bathing costumes of the girls who are her own age. My father returns with the peanuts. Overhead the sun's lightning strikes and strikes, but neither of them are at all aware of it. The boardwalk is full of people dressed in their Sunday clothes and idly strolling. The tide does not reach as far as the boardwalk, and the strollers would feel no danger if it did. My mother and father lean on the rail of the boardwalk and absently stare at the ocean. The ocean is becoming rough; the waves come in slowly, tugging strength from far back. The moment before they somersault, the moment when they arch their backs so beautifully, showing green and white veins amid the black, that moment is intolerable. They finally crack, dashing fiercely upon the sand, actually driving, full force downward, against the sand, bouncing upward and forward, and at last petering out into a small stream which races up the beach and then is recalled. My parents gaze absentmindedly at the ocean, scarcely interested in its harshness. The sun overhead does not disturb them. But I stare at the terrible sun which breaks up sight, and the fatal, merciless, passionate ocean, I forget my parents. I stare fascinated and finally, shocked by the indifference of my father and mother, I burst out weeping once more. The old lady next to me pats me on the shoulder and says "There, there, all of this is only a movie, young man, only a movie," but I look up once more at the terrifying sun and the terrifying ocean, and being unable to control my tears, I get up and go to the men's room, stumbling over the feet of the other people seated in my row.

IV

When I return, feeling as if I had awakened in the morning sick for lack of sleep, several hours have apparently passed and my parents are riding on the merry-go-round. My father is on a black horse, my mother on a white one, and they seem to be making an eternal circuit for the single purpose of snatching the nickel rings which are attached to the arm of one of the posts. A hand-organ is playing; it is one with the ceaseless circling of the merry-go-round.

For a moment it seems that they will never get off the merry-go-round because it will never stop. I feel like one who looks down on the avenue from the 50th story of a building. But at length they do get off; even the music of the hand-organ has ceased for a moment. My father has acquired ten rings, my mother only two, although it was my mother who really wanted them.

They walk on along the boardwalk as the afternoon descends by imperceptible degrees into the incredible violet of dusk. Everything fades into a relaxed glow, even the ceaseless murmuring from the beach, and the revolutions of the merry-go-round. They look for a place to have dinner. My father suggests the best one on the boardwalk and my mother demurs, in accordance with her principles.

However they do go to the best place, asking for a table near the window, so that they can look out on the boardwalk and the mobile ocean. My father feels omnipotent as he places a quarter in the waiter's hand as he asks for a table. The place is crowded and here too there is music, this time from a kind of string trio. My father orders dinner with a fine confidence.

As the dinner is eaten, my father tells of his plans for the future, and my mother shows with expressive face how interested she is, and how impressed. My father becomes exultant. He is lifted up by the waltz that is being played, and his own future begins to intoxicate him. My father tells my mother that he is going to expand his business, for there is a great deal of money to be made. He wants to settle down. After all, he is twenty-nine, he has lived by himself since he was thirteen, he is making more and more money, and he is envious of his married friends when he visits them in the cozy security of their homes, surrounded, it seems, by the calm domestic pleasures, and by delightful children, and then, as the waltz reaches the moment when all the dancers swing madly, then, then with awful daring, then he asks my mother to marry him, although awkwardly enough and puzzled, even in his excitement, at how he had arrived at the proposal, and she, to make the whole business worse, begins to cry, and my father looks nervously about, not knowing at all what to do now, and my mother says: "It's all I've wanted from the moment I saw you," sobbing, and he finds all of this very difficult, scarcely to his taste, scarcely as he had thought it would be, on his long walks over Brooklyn Bridge in the revery of a fine cigar, and it was then that I stood up in the theatre and shouted: "Don't do it. It's not too late to change your minds, both of you. Nothing good will come of it, only remorse, hatred, scandal, and two children whose characters are monstrous." The whole audience turned to look at me, annoyed, the usher came hurrying down the aisle flashing his searchlight, and the old lady next to me tugged me down into my seat, saying: "Be quiet. You'll be put out, and you paid thirty-five cents to come in." And so I shut my eyes because I could not bear to see what was happening. I sat there quietly.

V

But after awhile I begin to take brief glimpses, and at length I watch again with thirsty interest, like a child who wants to maintain his sulk although offered the bribe of candy. My parents are now having their picture taken in a photographer's booth along the boardwalk. The place is shadowed in the mauve light which is apparently necessary. The camera is set to the side on its tripod and looks like a Martian man. The photographer is instructing my parents in how to pose. My father has his arm over my mother's shoulder, and both of them smile emphatically. The photographer brings my mother a bouquet of flowers to hold in her hand but she holds it at the wrong angle. Then the photographer covers himself with the black cloth which drapes the camera and all that one sees of him is one protruding arm and his hand which clutches the rubber ball which he will squeeze when the picture is finally taken. But he is not satisfied with their appearance. He feels with certainty that somehow there is something wrong in their pose. Again and again he issues from his hidden place with new directions. Each suggestion merely makes matters worse. My father is becoming impatient. They try a seated pose. The photographer explains that he has pride, he is not interested in all of this for the money, he wants to make beautiful pictures. My father says: "Hurry up, will you? We haven't got all night." But the photographer only scurries about apologetically, and issues new directions. The photographer charms me. I approve of him with all my heart, for I know just how he feels, and as he criticizes each revised pose according to some unknown idea of rightness, I become quite hopeful. But then my father says angrily: "Come on, you've had enough time, we're not going to wait any longer." And the photographer, sighing unhappily, goes back under his black covering, holds out his hand, says: "One, two, three, Now!", and the picture is taken, with my father's smile turned to a grimace and my mother's bright and false. It takes a few minutes for the picture to be developed and as my parents sit in the curious light they become quite depressed.

VI

They have passed a fortune-teller's booth, and my mother wishes to go in, but my father does not. They begin to argue about it. My mother becomes stubborn, my father once more impatient, and then they begin to quarrel, and what my father would like to do is walk off and leave my mother there, but he knows that that would never do. My mother refuses to budge. She is near to tears, but she feels an uncontrollable desire to hear what the palm-reader will say. My father consents angrily, and they both go into a booth which is in a way like the photographer's, since it is draped in black cloth and its light is shadowed. The place is too warm, and my father keeps saying this is all nonsense, pointing to the crystal ball on the table. The fortune-teller, a fat, short woman, garbed in what is supposed to be Oriental robes, comes into the room from the back and greets them, speaking with an accent. But suddenly my father feels that the whole thing is intolerable; he tugs at my mother's arm, but my mother refuses to budge. And then, in terrible anger, my father lets go of my mother's arm and strides out, leaving my mother stunned. She moves to go after my father, but the fortune-teller holds her arm tightly and begs her not to do so, and I in my seat am shocked more than can ever be said, for I feel as if I were walking a tight-rope a hundred feet over a circus-audience and suddenly the rope is showing signs of breaking, and I get up from my seat and begin to shout once more the first words I can think of to communicate my terrible fear and once more the usher comes hurrying down the aisle flashing his searchlight, and the old lady pleads with me, and the shocked audience has turned to stare at me, and I keep shouting: "What are they doing? Don't they know what they are doing? Why doesn't my mother go after my father? If she does not do that, what will she do? Doesn't my father know what he is doing?"—But the usher has seized my arm and is dragging me away, and as he does so, he says: "What are *you* doing? Don't you know that you can't do whatever you want to do? Why should a young man like you, with your whole life before you, get hysterical like this? Why don't you *think* of what you're doing? You can't act like this even if other people aren't around! You will be sorry if you do not do what you should do, you can't carry on like this, it is not right, you will find that out soon enough, everything you do matters too much," and he said that dragging me through the lobby of the theatre into the cold light, and I woke up into the bleak winter morning of my 21st birthday, the windowsill shining with its lip of snow, and the morning already begun.

Rikki Ducornet

Rikki Ducornet has lived in North Africa, South America, Canada, and France and now lives in Denver, Colorado. Her novels include The Stain, Entering Fire, The Fountains of Neptune, The Jade Cabinet, *and* Phosphor in Dreamland. *In 1993 she received a Lannan Literary Fellowship.*

"Opium," taken from her book The Word "Desire", *uses the elevated atmospherics of medieval history and the pomp of a papal court to heighten the sensual character of this dreamlike fable. This prose begins in a dream and rapidly becomes hallucination, perhaps as a way of inducing an altered state of consciousness. The story's lush language, the author's attention to rhythm and pacing, the meticulously rendered visual details, and the magical setting work to create an unsettling response in the reader. Like a horror movie, the story aims to unlock rarely felt emotion for the sake of the thrill of it.*

Opium

Once, not long ago, the Pope issued a bull extending his powers across all territories known and unknown, illusive yet looming, dreamed and undreamed; and to all crimes against the Church, known and unobserved, ancient and newly rehearsed.

But now this Pope of infinite powers, who has the authority to transform living souls into torches, and who—in the simplest things— has discerned a sorcerous complexity, is himself failing. In a dream he imagines that he is a lump of hot and heavy matter slowly receding, as if time were a silent vortex and his fall both final and without risk. Cushioned by opium, his fall is delicious. Steadily he sinks into his feather bed, almost vanishing altogether much the way the droppings of a polar bear burn their way down through artic ice before tumbling into an element too deep to be fathomed.

For weeks the Pope's only nourishment has been little balls of opium wrapped in gold leaf and flavored with honey; opium and the milk of a wet nurse. The milk is fed to him from a gold cup. But this morning the Pope makes a request. He wants the wet nurse to come to him herself and suckle him directly. His voice is weak and strange; the words bubble from his tongue like oil from a bottle and yet there can be no doubting his intention: the cup hurts his gums, he has tasted blood, he can no longer lift his head without vertigo. He wants the girl to open her blouse here in his chamber and to cause her breasts to dangle in such a way that he may seize the nipples between his gums.

This is a delicate matter. How may the Grand Penitentiary comply with the hierarch's request without scandal? Hurrying like a huge bird through a succession of apartments, he comes to the door of the chamber where the wet nurse now prepares to ease her milk into the halfmoon of glass she holds pressed to a breast. Just as a spray hisses into the glass, the Grand Penitentiary knocks. Startled, the girl and the nun whose special office it is to carry the gold cup to the Pope's chamber, exchange a troubled look. Having announced himself, the Grand Penitentiary steps inside.

The room smells of lactose and of freshly threshed hay; it also smells of verbena: smells that ever after will evoke the young girl who, her shawl pulled tightly across her bosom, the glass clasped in her hand, is burning two holes in the floor with her eyes. The Grand Penitentiary bows his head and, attempting to put the two women at ease, aborts a smile. Then fluttering his hands in the air as if to dispel an invisible threat hovering there, a threat caused by the sweetness of the girl's own perfume, he bids the nun to leave. Dissolving, she could not do this more precipitously.

The Grand Penitentiary is standing before the girl, who is so small he thinks he could crush her with a word. Her hair is so pale it is almost white and her little hands are no bigger than a child's. He wonders at her youth; she looks no more than twelve. Why is she not a virgin spinning in her father's house? As she stands before him trembling, he recognizes that the situation makes him anxious also. And floods him with shame. The milk, until this moment an abstraction, is, he sees this now, a sexual fluid. He wonders if there is an infant at home. Or if the infant, her first, for whom the milk was intended, is dead.

"Child in Christ," he manages at last. To his terror and surprise she lifts her gaze from the floor and with two perfectly clear, gray eyes, eyes spinning like the wheels of perdition, needles him through and through. He turns away and utters a prayer; recalls how in the presence of the sumptuous courtesan sent to seduce him in his cell, Blessed Thomas took up a branch from the hearth and putting it to his loins, quenched his own fire.

"The Pope . . . ," he says. "The Pope . . ."

The morning they found her, a mole had made his way into the kitchen so that when she was asked to follow the Papal messenger, she was amazed that such unprecedented good fortune should attend a bad omen. But now when she hears the Pope's request she knows she is doomed. As she follows the Grand Penitentiary down the hall and into deep rooms thick with tapestries and gilded stoves, she falters and her shawl slips to the floor. She treads upon it, and the half-moon of glass she has held so tightly slips from her fingers and breaks in two. As from out of the air a page smelling of amber appears. Picking up the pieces he vanishes.

"No matter," the Grand Penitentiary whispers as he cleanses the air with his fingers. "It doesn't matter."

Although the day has only just dawned and a gray light soaks the city, entering the Pope's bedchamber is like entering a cathedral at midnight.

All the curtains have been pulled and the room's bilious atmosphere is blistering with more candles than she has ever seen. These candles illume the figures of angels that in the flickering light appear to scurry up and down the walls like monkeys among the tendrils and vines of an enchanted forest. Or troops of evil angels riding saddled owls and even the old gods, cloven-hooved and horned: the figures evil women use to inflame the passions of their rival's husbands and kill infants in the crib. These figures adorn cabinets and candlesticks, chairs and chests and the Pope's own bed, and are reflected in and multiplied by mirrors. The walls of the Papal chamber are crusted with mirrors: should the Evil One ever manage to enter here, he will be struck down by the compounded shock of his own fatal glance. But the wet nurse thinks the mirrors do not exorcise evil so much as conjure it. She has heard of the nocturnal orgies of witches and imagines they take place in rooms such as this.

So great is the girl's astonishment, so great her terror, that upon entering the Pope's chamber she neglects to make the sign of the cross. To bring her to her senses, the Grand Penitentiary pinches her arm.

"*Fe* and *Minus*," he murmurs, thinking: The feminine is far too feeble to persist in the Faith. Still pinching the flesh of her arm he leads her to the Pope's bed, recalling the previous day, when a girl not much older than this one had been chained to an iron ring. The ring was attached to an iron pole set in a circle of fire. From a Vatican window he had watched as the girl ran around and around in her attempt to escape the fire. He imagines the wet nurse running within a circle of fire.

~~~

A tassled canopy yawns over the Pope's bony head like a mouthful of gold teeth. She sees the stubborn beak of his nose, his hands like talons gripping an ivory crucifix the size of a small tree. As she unties her blouse, he opens his eyes. Those eyes are blind and this is a consolation. When she bends over the bed, her breast tumbles forth, shining like a planet in the firelight. The Grand Penitentiary reminds himself that if her breast, her throat and lips are smoother than oil, her womb is as bitter as wormwood.

There is so much smoke in the room that when the Pope gums her nipple she coughs. Her nipple leaps from the Pope's mouth making a sound which evokes childish laughter. Peering about her as best she can she sees a tiny black child dressed in white lace and circumventing the room with an aspergillum and holy water. She has never before seen a black child and she is astonished to see one here in the dying

Pope's chamber. Was he a gift or had he been purchased? This power of the rich to buy the bodies and lives of others causes her to weep. Studded with pearls, the Pope's nightcap soaks up her tears.

~~~

She returns to the Pope's chamber in the afternoon. Entering the room she looks up into the Grand Penitentiary's eyes, which reflect the candle flames and glitter as though made of glass. Because she is wildly superstitious, when she sees those flames in those eyes she fears for her soul. And he, looking into her eyes in turn, sees a little man. Once again he knows he must guard himself against her.

The Pope drinks from her body without eagerness. She thinks that her life is seeping into a dark place like a dark hole of soft earth and wonders at the world's strangeness. Why has God caused her own little one to die that she may give suck to a moribund? For some reason she recalls how her brooding turtledove seemed to sob just as her hatchlings broke free from their shells. Moving near, the little African in his astonishing white dress offers her a shy smile. She wonders what would happen to her if she ran from the room with him. And in the village—what would they say if she took him for her own? What would the child say when she fed him barley gruel and black bread? She supposes his enslavement is sweetened with spice cake and jam—things she has never herself tasted.

When having once more circled the room he approaches her again, she asks him what he is given to eat, and is it served on a gold plate? But the Grand Penitentiary is beside her and with a grimace silences her, although this afternoon the room is sighing with a conclave of cardinals; they rustle in their red robes like wind in sails; they whisper unceasingly to one another.

The following morning when she offers her breast, the Pope does not drink. Instead when he opens his mouth, a gold ball falls out and catches to the lace of his pillow. This astonishes her and she stares at the thing in awe. Later in the day the Pope dies, and as the air shudders with the tolling of bells she is taken to an inner courtyard paved with stones as white and round as ostrich eggs, and there her neck is broken.

~~~

Not long after, the new Pope issues a bull dividing all the world's undiscovered places between the Spanish and the Portuguese. A vast number of ships set sail for Africa and India although those lands swarm with infidels, astrologers, druggists, alchemists, and planetarians. It is easy to find men eager to join in the adventure of territorial expansion, for all Europe stinks of burning flesh. The promise of sea air, of breaking heads with mattocks and axes, of pillaging flourishing cities, of poisoning fountains of sweet water with the corpses of camels and children; to in the name of the Holy See cut off so many noses and ears the land of Ormuz will appear to be populated by lepers; to destroy all those who worship the sun, the moon, the lamp, and cows, and those who hold trees sacred, and those who worship the circumpolar stars which never set, and those who worship the whirlwind, the hurricane, and waves on water; to annihilate the princes of Malabar who feed the crows before feeding themselves; to slay men who for medicine inhale the powdered dung of leopards and drink the urine of virgins—inspires several generations of men. Restless at sea they dream of the four tastes of the oranges of Celam, of certain hairy caps from the Levant and weapons made by wizards; of gold plugs taken from the ears of kings and red and white coral shaped and strung; of pieces of true musk the size of a fist and loaves of coarse camphor; of fine rose water kept in little barrels of tinned copper, of earth from the tomb of Saint Thomas and of opium from Aden. Upon returning they will bring a white elephant to kneel at the feet of the Pope and they will scatter the gems made by Adam's tears across the Pope's path.

For these acts of war, of faith and of longing, they will be awarded miracles: phantom earthquakes, the sight of a mosque spontaneously combusting, of a Moorish king struck down by lightning, the vision of a white city filled with cries but devoid of inhabitants. And they will be awarded glory, which, like riches and miracles—or so they imagine—buys sufficient time to aspire to immortality.

Isaac Babel

Isaac Babel was a Russian Jew whose newspaper accounts of the fledgling Soviet Union's war with Poland in the 1920s brought him his initial fame. In 1917, at the age of twenty-three, Babel enlisted in the Red Army as it fended off attacks from neighbors alarmed by the creation of a communist nation. In 1920 he was sent as an official reporter to the Polish front, where he rode with the First Cavalry. His dispatches won him a wide following and became the basis of his fictionalized Red Cavalry Stories. *These stories, memorable for their frank depictions of war and its accompanying misery, won the indignation of the officers he had ridden with but the approval of the Soviet Union's dictator Joseph Stalin, who proclaimed, "*Red Cavalry *is not so bad as all of that. It is a very good book."*

If Babel were writing today, we might classify much of his work as creative nonfiction, for his stories often skirt the line between the autobiographical and the fanciful. His Odessa Stories, *from which "The Sin of Jesus" is taken, chronicle the city of his youth. "The Sin of Jesus," however, is pure fancy. Read without irony, this story might seem blasphemous to devout Christians, as it takes a rather irreverent attitude toward the son of God. A closer look at the story reveals that it's not Christianity but the nature of suffering that Babel is examining, specifically the suffering of Russian peasant women at a time when they were often treated no better than farm animals. As is typical in his work, Babel displays not a shred of sentimentality but, rather, a cutting absurdity that's meant to examine and provoke. Realism is left behind as the story progresses and Jesus sends a rather frail angel to comfort the peasant woman.*

Babel ultimately proved to be too provocative for Stalin's taste. In 1939, Babel was arrested on trumped-up charges of spying for France and Austria, and he was shot in 1940.

The Sin of Jesus

Arina had a little room by the grand stairway near the guest rooms, and Sergei, the janitor's assistant, had a room near the service entrance. They had done a shameful deed together. Arina bore Sergei twins on Easter Sunday. Water flows, stars shine, muzhiks feel lust, and Arina again found herself in a delicate condition. She is in her sixth month, the months just roll by when a woman is pregnant, and Sergei ends up being drafted into the army—a fine mess! So Arina goes to him and says, "Listen, Sergunya, there's no point in me sitting around waiting for you. We won't see each other for four years, and I wouldn't be surprised if I had another brood of three or four by the time you come back. Working in a hotel, your skirt is hitched up more often than not. Whoever takes a room here gets to be your lord and master, Jews or whatever. When you come back from the army my womb will be worn out, I'll be washed up as a woman, I don't think I'll be of any use to you."

"True enough," Sergei said, nodding his head.

"The men who want to marry me right now are Trofimich the contractor, he's a rude roughneck, Isai Abramich, a little old man, and then there's the warden of Nilolo-Svyatskoi Church, he's very feeble, but your vigor has rattled my soul to pieces! As the Lord is my witness, I'm all chewed up! In three months I'll be rid of my burden, I'll leave the baby at the orphanage, and I'll go marry them."

When Sergei heard this he took off his belt and gave Arina a heroic beating, aiming for her belly.

"Hey!" the woman says to him. "Don't beat me on the gut, remember it's your stuffing in there, not no one else's!"

She received many savage wallops, he shed many a bitter tear, the woman's blood flowed, but that's neither here nor there. The woman went to Jesus Christ and said:

"This and that, Lord Jesus. Me, I'm Arina, the maid from the Hotel Madrid & Louvre on Tverskaya Street. Working in a hotel, your skirt is hitched up more often than not. Whoever takes a room there gets to be your lord and master, Jews or whatever. Here on earth walks a humble servant of Yours, Sergei the janitor's assistant. I bore him twins last year on Easter Sunday."

And she told him everything.

"And what if Sergei didn't go to the army?" the Savior pondered.

"The constable would drag him off."

"Ah, the constable," the Savior said, his head drooping. "I'd forgotten all about him. Ah!—and how about if you led a pure life?"

"For four years!" the woman gasped. "Do you mean to say that everyone should stop living a life? You're still singing the same old tune! How are we supposed to go forth and multiply? Do me a favor and spare me such advice!"

Here the Savior's cheeks flushed crimson. The woman had stung him to the quick, but he said nothing. You cannot kiss your own ear, even the Savior knew that.

"This is what you need to do, humble servant of the Lord, glorious maidenly sinner Arina!" the Savior proclaimed in all his glory. "I have a little angel prancing about up in heaven, his name is Alfred, and he's gotten completely out of hand. He keeps moaning, 'Why, O Lord, did you make me an angel at twenty, a fresh lad like me?' I'll give you, Arina, servant of God, Alfred the angel as a husband for four years. He'll be your prayer, your salvation, and your pretty-boy, too. And there's no way you'll get a child from him, not even a duckling, because there's a lot of fun in him, but no substance."

"That's just what I need!" maid Arina cried. "It's their substance that has driven me to the brink of the grave three times in two years!"

"This will be a sweet respite for you, child of God, a light prayer, like a song. Amen."

And thus it was decided. Alfred, a frail, tender youth, was sent down, and fluttering on his pale blue shoulders were two wings, rippling in a rosy glow like doves frolicking in the heavens. Arina hugged him, sobbing with emotion and female tenderness.

"My little Alfredushka, my comfort and joy, my one-and-only!"

The Savior gave her instructions that, before going to bed, she had to take off the angel's wings, which were mounted on hinges, just like door hinges, and she had to take them off and wrap them in a clean sheet for the night, because at the slightest frolic the wings could break, as they were made of infants' sighs and nothing more.

The Savior blessed the union one last time, and called over a choir of abbots for the occasion, their voices thundering in song. There was nothing to eat, not even a hint of food—that wouldn't have have been proper—and Arina and Alfred, embracing, descended to earth on a silken rope ladder. They went to Petrovka, that's where the woman dragged him to, she bought him lacquered shoes, checkered tricot trousers (by the way, not only was he not wearing pants, he was completely in the altogether), a hunting frock, and a vest of electric-blue velvet.

"As for the rest, sweetie," she said, "we'll find that at home."

That day Arina did not work in the hotel, she took the day off. Sergei came and made a big to-do outside her room, but she wouldn't open, and called out from behind her door, "Sergei Nifantich, I'm busy washing my feet right now and would be obliged if you would distance yourself without all that to-do!"

He left without saying a word. The angelic power was already taking effect.

Arina cooked a meal fit for a merchant—ha, she was devilishly proud, she was! A quart of vodka, and even some wine, Danube herring with potatoes, a samovar filled with tea. No sooner had Alfred eaten this earthly abundance than he keeled over into a deep sleep. Arina managed to snatch his wings off their hinges just in time. She wrapped them up, and then carried Alfred to her bed.

Lying on her fluffy eiderdown, on her frayed, sin-ridden bed, is a snow-white wonder, an otherworldly brilliance radiating from him. Shafts of moonlight mix with red rays and dart about the room, tripling over their feet. And Arina weeps, rejoices, sings, and prays. The unheard of, O Arina, has befallen you in this shattered world, blessed art thou among women!

They had drunk down the whole quart of vodka. And it was pretty obvious, too. As they fell asleep, Arina rolled over onto Alfred with the hot, six-month gut that Sergei had saddled her with. You can imagine the weight! It wasn't enough that she was sleeping next to an angel, it wasn't enough that the man next to her wasn't spitting on the wall, or snoring, or snorting—no it wasn't enough for this lusty, crazed wench! She had to warm her bloated, combustible belly even more. And so she crushed the Lord's angel, crushed him in her drunken bliss, crushed him in her rapture like a week-old infant, mangled him beneath her, and he came to a fatal end, and from his wings, wrapped in the sheet, pale tears flowed.

Dawn came, the trees bowed down low. In the distant northern woods, every fir tree turned into a priest, every fir tree genuflected.

The woman comes again before the throne of the Savior. She is strong, her shoulders wide, her red hands carrying the young corpse.

"Behold, Lord!"

This was too much for Jesus' gentle soul, and he cursed the woman from the bottom of his heart.

"As it is in the world, Arina, so it shall be with you!"

"But Lord!" the woman said to him in a low voice. "Was it I who made my body heavy, who brewed the vodka, who made a woman's soul lonely and stupid?"

"I do not wish to have anything further to do with you," Lord Jesus exclaimed. "You have crushed my angel, you trollop, you!" And Arina was hurled back down to earth on a purulent wind, to Tverskaya Street, to her sentence at the Madrid & Louvre. There all caution had been thrown to the winds. Sergei was carousing away the last few days before he had to report as a recruit. Trofimich, the contractor, who had just come back from Kolomna, saw how healthy and red-cheeked she was.

"Ooh what a nice little gut!" he said, among other things.

Isai Abramich, the little old man, came wheezing over when he heard about the little gut.

"After all that has happened," he said, "I cannot settle down with you lawfully, but I can definitely still lie with you."

Six feet under, that's where he should be lying, and not spitting into her soul like everyone else! It was as if they had all broken loose from their chains—dishwashers, peddlers, foreigners. A tradesman likes to have some fun.

And here ends my tale.

Before she gave birth—the remaining three months flew by quickly—Arina went out into the backyard behind the janitor's room, raised her horribly large belly to the silken skies, and idiotically uttered, "Here you are, Lord, here is my gut! They bang on it as if it were a drum. Why, I don't know! And then, Lord, I end up like this again! I've had enough!"

Jesus drenched Arina with his tears. The Savior fell to his knees. "Forgive me, my Arinushka, sinful God that I am, that I have done this to you!"

"I will not forgive you, Jesus Christ!" Arina replied. "I will not!"

Jorge Luis Borges

Born in Buenos Aires in 1899, Jorge Luis Borges grew up in a household in which English and Spanish were spoken so interchangeably that he didn't realize they were separate languages until he grew older. His maternal grandmother, Fanny, was English, and it was from her, he claimed, that he inherited his love of storytelling. His father, a frustrated writer, expected young Borges to take up the profession, which he did with enthusiasm, translating an Oscar Wilde story into Spanish for a local newspaper at the age of nine.

In the late 1930s, Borges began his professional career as an assistant librarian at a branch of the Buenos Aires Municipal Library. Then, when Juan Peron swept to power in the forties, he landed a political appointment he didn't want: Inspector of Poultry and Rabbits in the Public Markets, a position he quickly gave up in favor of becoming a lecturer in English and American literature. Borges's literary reputation steadily grew while at the same time he and his family, critical of the Peron government, earned its suspicion. Borges's sister was thrown in prison. In 1955, after Peron's ouster, Borges was appointed Director of the National Library, a position he held for twelve years. Unfortunately, having inherited his father's congenital blindness, he was now almost completely without sight. Borges noted "God's splendid irony in granting me at one time 800,000 books and darkness."

In the 1960s Borges achieved international fame and lectured around the world. His fiction revels in paradoxes, conundrums, and, above all, labyrinths. The labyrinth, a maze from which it is nearly impossible to exit, is a recurring theme in his work. In the world of Borges, all possible books are contained in one infinite library, all possible futures converge in a garden, all possible choices are made by lottery, an alternative world is invented by a secret society, and, in the case of "The Aleph," all knowledge converges at a single point in the basement of an otherwise mediocre man. As he does in this story, Borges typically casts himself as a character in his own fiction, often mixing autobiography with the fantastic. In this way he gives a realist tinge to an otherwise irreal tale. Borges died of cancer in 1986.

The Aleph

O God, I could be bounded in a nutshell, and count myself a
King of infinite space.

Hamlet, II:2

But they will teach us that Eternity is the Standing still of the
Present Time, a *Nunc-stans* (as the Schools call it); which neither they, nor any else understand, no more than they would
a *Hic-stans* for an Infinite greatnesse of Place.

Leviathan, IV:46

That same sweltering morning that Beatriz Viterbo died, after an
imperious confrontation with her illness in which she had never for
an instant stooped to either sentimentality or fear, I noticed that a
new advertisement for some cigarettes or other (*blondes*, I believe they
were) had been posted on the iron billboards of the Plaza Constitución; the fact deeply grieved me, for I realized that the vast unceasing
universe was already growing away from her, and that this change was
but the first in an infinite series. *The universe may change, but I shall
not,* thought I with melancholy vanity. I knew that more than once
my futile devotion had exasperated her; now that she was dead, I
could consecrate myself to her memory—without hope, but also without humiliation. I reflected that April 30 was her birthday; stopping
by her house on Calle Garay that day to pay my respects to her father
and her first cousin Carlos Argentino Daneri was an irreproachable,
perhaps essential act of courtesy. Once again I would wait in the half-
light of the little parlor crowded with furniture and draperies and
bric-a-brac, once again I would study the details of the many photographs and portraits of her: Beatriz Viterbo, in profile, in color;
Beatriz in a mask at the Carnival of 1921; Beatriz' first communion;
Beatriz on the day of her wedding to Roberto Allessandri; Beatriz
shortly after the divorce, lunching at the Jockey Club; Beatriz in
Quilmes with Delia San Marco Porcel and Carlos Argentino; Beatriz
with the Pekinese that had been a gift from Villegas Haedo; Beatriz
in full-front and in three-quarters view, smiling, her hand on her
chin. . . . I would not be obliged, as I had been on occasions before,
to justify my presence with modest offerings of books—books whose

pages I learned at last to cut, so as not to find, months later, that they were still intact.

Beatriz Viterbo died in 1929; since then, I have not allowed an April 30 to pass without returning to her house. That first time, I arrived at seven-fifteen and stayed for about twenty-five minutes; each year I would turn up a little later and stay a little longer; in 1933, a downpour came to my aid; they were forced to ask me to dinner. Naturally, I did not let that fine precedent go to waste; in 1934 I turned up a few minutes after eight with a lovely confection from Santa Fe; it was perfectly natural that I should stay for dinner. And so it was that on those melancholy and vainly erotic anniversaries I came to receive the gradual confidences of Carlos Argentino Daneri.

Beatriz was tall, fragile, very slightly stooped; in her walk, there was (if I may be pardoned the oxymoron) something of a graceful clumsiness, a *soupçon* of hesitancy, or of palsy; Carlos Argentino is a pink, substantial, gray-haired man of refined features. He holds some sort of subordinate position in an illegible library in the outskirts toward the south of the city; he is authoritarian, though also ineffectual; until very recently he took advantage of nights and holidays to remain at home. At two generations' remove, the Italian *s* and the liberal Italian gesticulation still survive in him. His mental activity is constant, passionate, versatile, and utterly insignificant. He is full of pointless analogies and idle scruples. He has (as Beatriz did) large, beautiful, slender hands. For some months he labored under an obsession for Paul Fort, less for Fort's ballads than the idea of a glory that could never be tarnished. "He is the prince of the poets of *la belle France*," he would fatuously say. "You assail him in vain; you shall never touch him—not even the most venomous of your darts shall ever touch him."

On April 30, 1941, I took the liberty of enriching my sweet offering with a bottle of domestic brandy. Carlos Argentino tasted it, pronounced it "interesting," and, after a few snifters, launched into an *apologia* for modern man.

"I picture him," he said with an animation that was rather unaccountable, "in his study, as though in the watchtower of a great city, surrounded by telephones, telegraphs, phonographs, the latest in radio-telephone and motion-picture and magic-lantern equipment, and glossaries and calendars and timetables and bulletins. . . ."

He observed that for a man so equipped, the act of traveling was supererogatory; this twentieth century of ours had upended the fable of Muhammad and the mountain—mountains nowadays did in fact come to the modern Muhammad.

So witless did these ideas strike me as being, so sweeping and pompous the way they were expressed, that I associated them immediately with literature. Why, I asked him, didn't he write these ideas down? Predictably, he replied that he already had; they, and others no less novel, figured large in the Augural Canto, Prologurial Canto, or simply Prologue-Canto, of a poem on which he had been working, with no deafening hurly-burly and *sans réclame*, for many years, leaning always on those twin staffs Work and Solitude. First he would open the floodgates of the imagination, then repair to the polishing wheel. The poem was entitled *The Earth*; it centered on a description of our own terraqueous orb and was graced, of course, with picturesque digression and elegant apostrophe.

I begged him to read me a passage, even if only a brief one. He opened a desk drawer, took out a tall stack of tablet paper stamped with the letterhead of the Juan Crisóstomo Lafinur Library, and read, with ringing self-satisfaction:

> I have seen, as did the Greek, man's cities and his fame,
> The works, the days of various light, the hunger;
> I prettify no fact, I falsify no name,
> For the *voyage* I narrate is . . . *autour de ma chambre*.

"A stanza interesting from every point of view," he said. "The first line wins the kudos of the learnèd, the academician, the Hellenist—though perhaps not that of those would-be scholars that make up such a substantial portion of popular opinion. The second moves from Homer to Hesiod (implicit homage, at the very threshold of the dazzling new edifice, to the father of didactic poetry), not without revitalizing a technique whose lineage may be traced to Scripture—that is, enumeration, congeries, or conglobation. The third—baroque? decadent? the purified and fanatical cult of form?—consists of twinned hemistichs; the fourth, unabashedly bilingual, assures me the unconditional support of every spirit able to feel the ample attractions of playfulness. I shall say nothing of the unusual rhyme, nor of the erudition that allows me—without pedantry or boorishness!—to include within the space of four lines three erudite allusions spanning thirty centuries of dense literature: first the *Odyssey*, second the *Works and Days*, and third that immortal bagatelle that regales us with the diversions of the Savoyard's plume. . . . Once again, I show my awareness that truly *modern* art demands the balm of laughter, of *scherzo*. There is no doubt about it—Goldoni was right!"

Carlos Argentino read me many another stanza, all of which earned the same profuse praise and comment from him. There was nothing memorable about them; I could not even judge them to be much worse than the first one. Application, resignation, and chance had conspired in their composition; the virtues that Daneri attributed to them were afterthoughts. I realized that the poet's work had lain not in the poetry but in the invention of reasons for accounting the poetry admirable; naturally, that later work modified the poem for Daneri, but not for anyone else. His oral expression was extravagant; his metrical clumsiness prevented him, except on a very few occasions, from transmitting that extravagance to the poem.[1]

Only once in my lifetime have I had occasion to examine the fifteen thousand dodecasyllables of the *Polyalbion*—that topographical epic in which Michael Drayton recorded the fauna, flora, hydrography, orography, military and monastic history of England—but I am certain that Drayton's massive yet limited *œuvre* is less tedious than the vast enterprise conceived and given birth by Carlos Argentino. He proposed to versify the entire planet; by 1941 he had already dispatched several hectares of the state of Queensland, more than a kilometer of the course of the Ob, a gasworks north of Veracruz, the leading commercial establishments in the parish of Concepción, Mariana Cambaceres de Alvear's villa on Calle Once de Setiembre in Belgrano, and a Turkish bath not far from the famed Brighton Aquarium. He read me certain laborious passages from the Australian region of his poem; his long, formless alexandrines lacked the relative agitation of the prologue. Here is one stanza:

Hear this. To the right hand of the routine signpost
(Coming—what need is there to say?—from north-northwest)
Yawns a bored skeleton—Color? Sky-pearly.—
Outside the sheepfold that suggests an ossuary.

---

[1] I do, however, recall these lines from a satire in which he lashed out vehemently against bad poets:

This one fits the poem with a coat of mail
Of erudition; that one, with gala pomps and circumstance.
Both flail their absurd pennons to no avail,
Neglecting, poor wretches, the factor sublime—its LOVELINESS!

It was only out of concern that he might create an army of implacable and powerful enemies, he told me, that he did not fearlessly publish the poem.

"Two audacious risks!" he exclaimed in exultation, "snatched from the jaws of disaster, I can hear you mutter, by success! I admit it, I admit it. One, the epithet *routine*, while making an adjective of a synonym for 'highway,' nods, *en passant*, to the inevitable tedium inherent to those chores of a pastoral and rustic nature that neither georgics nor our own belaureled *Don Segundo* ever dared acknowledge in such a forthright way, with no beating about the bush. And the second, delicately referring to the first, the forcefully prosaic phrase *Yawns a bored skeleton*, which the finicky will want to excommunicate without benefit of clergy but that the critic of more manly tastes will embrace as he does his very life. The entire line, in fact, is a good 24 karats. The second half-line sets up the most animated sort of conversation with the reader; it anticipates his lively curiosity, puts a question in his mouth, and then . . . *voilà*, answers it . . . on the instant. And what do you think of that coup *sky-pearly?* The picturesque neologism just *hints* at the sky, which is such an important feature of the Australian landscape. Without that allusion, the hues of the sketch would be altogether too gloomy, and the reader would be compelled to close the book, his soul deeply wounded by a black and incurable melancholy."

About midnight, I took my leave.

Two Sundays later, Daneri telephoned me for what I believe was the first time in his or my life. He suggested that we meet at four, "to imbibe the milk of the gods together in the nearby salon-bar that my estimable landlords, Messrs. Zunino and Zungri, have had the rare commercial foresight to open on the corner. It is a *café* you will do well to acquaint yourself with." I agreed, with more resignation than enthusiasm, to meet him. It was hard for us to find a table; the relentlessly modern "salon-bar" was only slightly less horrendous than I had expected; at neighboring tables, the excited clientele discussed the sums invested by Zunino and Zungri without a second's haggling. Carlos Argentino pretended to be amazed at some innovation in the establishment's lighting (an innovation he'd no doubt been apprised of beforehand) and then said to me somewhat severely:

"Much against your inclinations it must be that you recognize that this place is on a par with the most elevated heights of Flores."

Then he reread four or five pages of his poem to me. Verbal ostentation was the perverse principle that had guided his revisions: where he had formerly written "blue" he now had "azure," "cerulean," and even "bluish." The word "milky" was not sufficiently hideous for him; in his impetuous description of a place where wool was washed, he had replaced it with "lactine," "lactescent," "lactoreous," "lacteal." . . . He railed bitterly against his critics; then, in a more benign tone, he compared them to those persons "who possess neither precious metals nor even the steam presses, laminators, and sulfuric acids needed for minting treasures, but who can *point out* to others the *precise location* of a treasure." Then he was off on another tack, inveighing against the obsession for forewords, what he called "prologomania," an attitude that "had already been spoofed in the elegant preface to the *Quixote* by the Prince of Wits himself." He would, however, admit that an attention-getting recommendation might be a good idea at the portals of his new work—"an accolade penned by a writer of stature, of real import." He added that he was planning to publish the first cantos of his poem. It was at that point that I understood the unprecedented telephone call and the invitation: the man was about to ask me to write the preface to that pedantic farrago of his. But my fear turned out to be unfounded. Carlos Argentino remarked, with grudging admiration, that he believed he did not go too far in saying that the prestige achieved in every sphere by the man of letters Alvaro Melián Lafinur was "solid," and that if I could be persuaded to persuade him, Alvaro "might be enchanted to write the called-for foreword." In order to forestall the most unpardonable failure on my part, I was to speak on behalf of the poem's two incontrovertible virtues: its formal perfection and its scientific rigor—"because that broad garden of rhetorical devices, figures, charms, and graces will not tolerate a single detail that does not accord with its severe truthfulness." He added that Beatriz had always enjoyed Alvaro's company.

I agreed, I agreed most profusely. I did, however, for the sake of added plausibility, make it clear that I wouldn't be speaking with Alvaro on Monday but rather on Thursday, at the little supper that crowned each meeting of the Writers Circle. (There are no such suppers, although it is quite true that the meetings are held on Thursday, a fact that Carlos Argentino might verify in the newspapers and that lent a certain credence to my contention.) I told him (half-prophetically, half-farsightedly) that before broaching the subject of the prologue, I would describe the curious design of the poem. We said our good-byes; as I turned down Calle Bernardo de Irigoyen, I contemplated as impartially as I could the futures that were left to me: (a) speak with Alvaro and tell him that that first cousin of Beatriz' (the explanatory circumlocution would allow me to speak her name) had written a poem that seemed to draw out to infinity the possibilities of cacophony and chaos; (b) not speak with Alvaro. Knowing myself pretty well, I foresaw that my indolence would opt for (b).

From early Friday morning on, the telephone was a constant source of anxiety. I was indignant that this instrument from which

Beatriz' irrecoverable voice had once emerged might now be reduced to transmitting the futile and perhaps angry complaints of that self-deluding Carlos Argentino Daneri. Fortunately, nothing came of it—save the inevitable irritation inspired by a man who had charged me with a delicate mission and then forgotten all about me.

Eventually the telephone lost its terrors, but in late October Carlos Argentino did call me. He was very upset; at first I didn't recognize his voice. Dejectedly and angrily he stammered out that that now unstoppable pair Zunino and Zungri, under the pretext of expanding their already enormous "*café*," were going to tear down his house.

"The home of my parents—the home where I was born—the old and deeply rooted house on Calle Garay!" he repeated, perhaps drowning his grief in the melodiousness of the phrase.

It was not difficult for me to share his grief. After forty, every change becomes a hateful symbol of time's passing; in addition, this was a house that I saw as alluding infinitely to Beatriz. I tried to make that extremely delicate point clear; my interlocutor cut me off. He said that if Zunino and Zungri persisted in their absurd plans, then Zunni, his attorney, would sue them *ipso facto* for damages, and force them to part with a good hundred thousand for his trouble.

Zunni's name impressed me; his law firm, on the corner of Caseros and Tacuarí, is one of proverbial sobriety. I inquired whether Zunni had already taken the case. Daneri said he'd be speaking with him that afternoon; then he hesitated, and in that flat, impersonal voice we drop into when we wish to confide something very private, he said he had to have the house so he could finish the poem—because in one corner of the cellar there was an Aleph. He explained that an Aleph is one of the points in space that contain all points.

"It's right under the dining room, in the cellar," he explained. In his distress, his words fairly tumbled out. "*It's mine, it's mine*; I discovered it in my childhood, before I ever attended school. The cellar stairway is steep, and my aunt and uncle had forbidden me to go down it, but somebody said you could go around the world with that thing down there in the basement. The person, whoever it was, was referring, I later learned, to a steamer trunk, but I thought there was some magical contraption down there. I tried to sneak down the stairs, fell head over heels, and when I opened my eyes, I saw the Aleph."

"The Aleph?" I repeated.

"Yes, the place where, without admixture or confusion, all the places of the world, seen from every angle, coexist. I revealed my discovery to no one, but I did return. The child could not understand that he was given that privilege so that the man might carve out a poem! Zunino and Zungri shall never take it from me—never, *never!* Lawbook in hand, Zunni will prove that my Aleph is *inalienable.*"

I tried to think.

"But isn't the cellar quite dark?"

"Truth will not penetrate a recalcitrant understanding. If all the places of the world are within the Aleph, there too will be all stars, all lamps, all sources of light."

"I'll be right over. I want to see it."

I hung up before he could tell me not to come. Sometimes learning a fact is enough to make an entire series of corroborating details, previously unrecognized, fall into place; I was amazed that I hadn't realized until that moment that Carlos Argentino was a madman. All the Viterbos, in fact. . . . Beatriz (I myself have said this many times) was a woman, a girl of implacable clearsightedness, but there were things about her—oversights, distractions, moments of contempt, downright cruelty—that perhaps could have done with a *pathological* explanation. Carlos Argentino's madness filled me with malign happiness; deep down, we had always detested one another.

On Calle Garay, the maid asked me to be so kind as to wait—Sr. Daneri was in the cellar, as he always was, developing photographs. Beside the flowerless vase atop the useless piano smiled the great faded photograph of Beatriz, not so much anachronistic as outside time. No one could see us; in a desperation of tenderness I approached the portrait.

"Beatriz, Beatriz Elena, Beatriz Elena Viterbo," I said. "Belovèd Beatriz, Beatriz lost forever—it's me, it's me, Borges."

Carlos came in shortly afterward. His words were laconic, his tone indifferent; I realized that he was unable to think of anything but the loss of the Aleph.

"A glass of pseudocognac," he said, "and we'll duck right into the cellar. I must forewarn you: dorsal decubitus is essential, as are darkness, immobility, and a certain ocular accommodation. You'll lie on the tile floor and fix your eyes on the nineteenth step of the pertinent stairway. I'll reascend the stairs, let down the trap door, and you'll be alone. Some rodent will frighten you—easy enough to do! Within a few minutes, you will see the Aleph. The microcosm of the alchemists and Kabbalists, our proverbial friend the *multum in parvo*, made flesh!

"Of course," he added, in the dining room, "if you don't see it, that doesn't invalidate anything I've told you. . . . Go on down; within a very short while you will be able to begin a dialogue with *all* the images of Beatriz."

I descended quickly, sick of his vapid chatter. The cellar, barely wider than the stairway, was more like a well or cistern. In vain my eyes sought the trunk that Carlos Argentino had mentioned. A few burlap bags and some crates full of bottles cluttered one corner. Carlos picked up one of the bags, folded it, and laid it out very precisely.

"The couch is a humble one," he explained, "but if I raise it one inch higher, you'll not see a thing, and you'll be cast down and dejected. Stretch that great clumsy body of yours out on the floor and count up nineteen steps."

I followed his ridiculous instructions; he finally left. He carefully let down the trap door; in spite of a chink of light that I began to make out later, the darkness seemed total. Suddenly I realized the danger I was in; I had allowed myself to be locked underground by a madman, after first drinking down a snifter of poison. Carlos' boasting clearly masked the deep-seated fear that I wouldn't see his "miracle"; in order to protect his delirium, in order to hide his madness from himself, *he had to kill me.* I felt a vague discomfort, which I tried to attribute to my rigidity, not to the operation of a narcotic. I closed my eyes, then opened them. It was then that I saw the Aleph.

I come now to the ineffable center of my tale; it is here that a writer's hopelessness begins. Every language is an alphabet of symbols the employment of which assumes a past shared by its interlocutors. How can one transmit to others the infinite Aleph, which my timorous memory can scarcely contain? In a similar situation, mystics have employed a wealth of emblems: to signify the deity, a Persian mystic speaks of a bird that somehow is all birds; Alain de Lille speaks of a sphere whose center is everywhere and circumference nowhere; Ezekiel, of an angel with four faces, facing east and west, north and south at once. (It is not for nothing that I call to mind these inconceivable analogies; they bear a relation to the Aleph.) Perhaps the gods would not deny me the discovery of an equivalent image, but then this report would be polluted with literature, with falseness. And besides, the central problem—the enumeration, even partial enumeration, of infinity—is irresolvable. In that unbounded moment, I saw millions of delightful and horrible acts; none amazed me so much as the fact that all occupied the same point, without superposition and without transparency. What my eyes saw was *simultaneous*; what I shall write is *successive*, because language is successive. Something of it, though, I will capture.

Under the step, toward the right, I saw a small iridescent sphere of almost unbearable brightness. At first I thought it was spinning; then I realized that the movement was an illusion produced by the dizzying spectacles inside it. The Aleph was probably two or three centimeters in diameter, but universal space was contained inside it, with no diminution in size. Each thing (the glass surface of a mirror, let us say) was infinite things, because I could clearly see it from every point in the cosmos. I saw the populous sea, saw dawn and dusk, saw the multitudes of the Americas, saw a silvery spider-web at the center of a black pyramid, saw a broken labyrinth (it was London), saw endless eyes, all very close, studying themselves in me as though in a mirror, saw all the mirrors on the planet (and none of them reflecting me), saw in a rear courtyard on Calle Soler the same tiles I'd seen twenty years before in the entryway of a house in Fray Bentos, saw clusters of grapes, snow, tobacco, veins of metal, water vapor, saw convex equatorial deserts and their every grain of sand, saw a woman in Inverness whom I shall never forget, saw her violent hair, her haughty body, saw a cancer in her breast, saw a circle of dry soil within a sidewalk where there had once been a tree, saw a country house in Adrogué, saw a copy of the first English translation of Pliny (Philemon Holland's), saw every letter of every page at once (as a boy, I would be astounded that the letters in a closed book didn't get all scrambled up together overnight), saw simultaneous night and day, saw a sunset in Querétaro that seemed to reflect the color of a rose in Bengal, saw my bedroom (with no one in it), saw in a study in Alkmaar a globe of the terraqueous world placed between two mirrors that multiplied it endlessly, saw horses with wind-whipped manes on a beach in the Caspian Sea at dawn, saw the delicate bones of a hand, saw the survivors of a battle sending postcards, saw a Tarot card in a shopwindow in Mirzapur, saw the oblique shadows of ferns on the floor of a greenhouse, saw tigers, pistons, bisons, tides, and armies, saw all the ants on earth, saw a Persian astrolabe, saw in a desk drawer (and the handwriting made me tremble) obscene, incredible, detailed letters that Beatriz had sent Carlos Argentino, saw a beloved monument in Chacarita, saw the horrendous remains of what had once, deliciously, been Beatriz Viterbo, saw the circulation of my dark blood, saw the coils and springs of love and the alterations of death, saw the Aleph from everywhere at once, saw the earth in the Aleph, and the Aleph once more in the earth and the earth in the Aleph, saw my face and my viscera, saw your face, and I felt dizzy, and I wept, because my eyes had seen that secret, hypothetical object whose name has been usurped by men but which no man has ever truly looked upon: the inconceivable universe.

I had a sense of infinite veneration, infinite pity.

"Serves you right, having your mind boggled, for sticking your nose in where you weren't wanted," said a jovial, bored voice. "And you may rack your brains, but you'll never repay me for this revelation—not in a hundred years. What a magnificent observatory, eh, Borges!"

Carlos Argentino's shoes occupied the highest step. In the sudden half-light, I managed to get to my feet.

"Magnificent . . . Yes, quite . . . magnificent," I stammered.

The indifference in my voice surprised me.

"You did see it?" Carlos Argentino insisted anxiously. "See it clearly? In color and everything?"

Instantly, I conceived my revenge. In the most kindly sort of way—manifestly pitying, nervous, evasive—I thanked Carlos Argentino Daneri for the hospitality of his cellar and urged him to take advantage of the demolition of his house to remove himself from the pernicious influences of the metropolis, which no one—believe me, no one!—can be immune to. I refused, with gentle firmness, to discuss the Aleph; I clasped him by both shoulders as I took my leave and told him again that the country—peace and quiet, you know—was the very best medicine one could take.

Out in the street, on the steps of the Constitución Station, in the subway, all the faces seemed familiar. I feared there was nothing that had the power to surprise or astonish me anymore, I feared that I would never again be without a sense of *déjà vu*. Fortunately, after a few unsleeping nights, forgetfulness began to work in me again.

Postscript (March 1, 1943): Six months after the demolition of the building on Calle Garay, Procrustes Publishers, undaunted by the length of Carlos Argentino Daneri's substantial poem, published the first in its series of "Argentine pieces." It goes without saying what happened: Carlos Argentino won second place in the National Prize for Literature.[2] The first prize went to Dr. Aita; third, to Dr. Mario Bonfanti; incredibly, my own work *The Sharper's Cards* did not earn a single vote. Once more, incomprehension and envy triumphed! I have not managed to see Daneri for quite a long time; the newspapers say he'll soon be giving us another volume. His happy pen (belabored no longer by the Aleph) has been consecrated to setting the compendia of Dr. Acevedo Díaz to verse.

There are two observations that I wish to add: one, with regard to the nature of the Aleph; the other, with respect to its name. Let

---

[2]"I received your mournful congratulations," he wrote me. "You scoff, my lamentable friend, in envy, but you shall confess—though the words stick in your throat!—that this time I have crowned my cap with the most scarlet of plumes; my turban, with the most caliphal of rubies."

me begin with the latter: "aleph," as we all know, is the name of the first letter of the alphabet of the sacred language. Its application to the disk of my tale would not appear to be accidental. In the Kabbala, that letter signifies the En Soph, the pure and unlimited godhead; it has also been said that its shape is that of a man pointing to the sky and the earth, to indicate that the lower world is the map and mirror of the higher. For the *Mengenlehre*, the aleph is the symbol of the transfinite numbers, in which the whole is not greater than any of its parts. I would like to know: Did Carlos Argentino choose that name, or did he read it, *applied to another point at which all points converge*, in one of the innumerable texts revealed to him by the Aleph in his house? Incredible as it may seem, I believe that there is (or was) another Aleph; I believe that the Aleph of Calle Garay was a *false* Aleph.

Let me state my reasons. In 1867, Captain Burton was the British consul in Brazil; in July of 1942, Pedro Henríquez Ureña discovered a manuscript by Burton in a library in Santos, and in this manuscript Burton discussed the mirror attributed in the East to Iskandar dhu-al-Qarnayn, or Alexander the Great of Macedonia. In this glass, Burton said, the entire universe was reflected. Burton mentions other similar artifices—the sevenfold goblet of Kai Khosru; the mirror that Tāriq ibn-Ziyād found in a tower (*1001 Nights,* 272); the mirror that Lucian of Samosata examined on the moon (*True History,* I:26); the specular spear attributed by the first book of Capella's *Satyricon* to Jupiter; Merlin's universal mirror, "round and hollow and . . . [that] seem'd a world of glas" (*Faerie Queene,* III:2, 19)—and then adds these curious words: "But all the foregoing (besides sharing the defect of not existing) are mere optical instruments. The faithful who come to the Amr mosque in Cairo, know very well that the universe lies inside one of the stone columns that surround the central courtyard. . . . No one, of course, can see it, but those who put their ear to the surface claim to hear, within a short time, the bustling rumour of it. . . . The mosque dates to the seventh century; the columns were taken from other, pre-Islamic, temples, for as ibn-Khaldūn has written: *In the republics founded by nomads, the attendance of foreigners is essential for all those things that bear upon carpentry.*"

Does that Aleph exist, within the heart of a stone? Did I see it when I saw all things, and then forget it? Our minds are permeable to forgetfulness; I myself am distorting and losing, through the tragic erosion of the years, the features of Beatriz.

For Estela Canto   *Translated by Andrew Hurley*

George Saunders

George Saunders, who teaches in the creative writing program at Syracuse University, has explored for oil in Sumatra, played guitar in a Texas bar band, and worked in a slaughterhouse. His stories have appeared in The New Yorker, Harper's, *and* Story, *won two National Magazine Awards, and appeared three times in the* O. Henry Awards collections. *Saunders's two story collections,* CivilWarLand in Bad Decline *and* Pastoralia, *put him in the ranks of America's most clever writers. He has a love of improbable theme parks, demonstrated in the title stories of his two collections, and as a master of biting humor he beautifully parodies the business-speak of contemporary corporate America.*

In "Pastoralia," the main character works in a history theme park. He plays a caveman, living and working in a cave with his difficult partner, a cavewoman who is fed up with playing a cavewoman. As he tries to improve her corporate attitude, he receives threatening faxes from his nameless and faceless bosses and at the same time notices that his standard of living is declining. Saunders delights in contradictions such as cavemen and fax machines, and it's these odd juxtapositions that make it clear that the object of Saunders's satire of life in contemporary America is ultimately ourselves.

Pastoralia

1.

I have to admit I'm not feeling my best. Not that I'm doing so bad. Not that I really have anything to complain about. Not that I would actually verbally complain if I did have something to complain about. No. Because I'm Thinking Positive/Saying Positive. I'm sitting back on my haunches, waiting for people to poke in their heads. Although it's been thirteen days since anyone poked in their head and Janet's speaking English to me more and more, which is partly why I feel so, you know, crummy.

"Jeez," she says first thing this morning. "I'm so tired of roast goat I could scream."

What am I supposed to say to that? It puts me in a bad spot. She thinks I'm a goody-goody and that her speaking English makes me uncomfortable. And she's right. It does. Because we've got it good. Every morning, a new goat, just killed, sits in our Big Slot. In our Little Slot, a book of matches. That's better than some. Some are required to catch wild hares in snares. Some are required to wear pioneer garb while cutting the heads off chickens. But not us. I just have to haul the dead goat out of the Big Slot and skin it with a sharp flint. Janet just has to make the fire. So things are pretty good. Not as good as in the old days, but then again, not so bad.

In the old days, when heads were constantly poking in, we liked what we did. Really hammed it up. Had little grunting fights. Whenever I was about to toss a handful of dirt in her face I'd pound a rock against a rock in rage. That way she knew to close her eyes. Sometimes she did this kind of crude weaving. It was like: Roots of Weaving. Sometimes we'd go down to Russian Peasant Farm for a barbecue, I remember there was Murray and Leon, Leon was dating Eileen, Eileen was the one with all the cats, but now, with the big decline in heads poking in, the Russian Peasants are all elsewhere, some to Administration but most not, Eileen's cats have gone wild, and honest to God sometimes I worry I'll go to the Big Slot and find it goatless.

2.

This morning I go to the Big Slot and find it goatless. Instead of a goat there's a note:

Hold on, hold on, it says. *The goat's coming, for crissake. Don't get all snooty.*

The problem is, what am I supposed to do during the time when I'm supposed to be skinning the goat with the flint? I decide to pretend to be desperately ill. I rock in a corner and moan. This gets old. Skinning the goat with the flint takes the better part of an hour. No way am I rocking and moaning for an hour.

Janet comes in from her Separate Area and her eyebrows go up.

"No freaking goat?" she says.

I make some guttural sounds and some motions meaning: Big rain come down, and boom, make goats run, goats now away, away in high hills, and as my fear was great, I did not follow.

Janet scratches under her armpit and makes a sound like a monkey, then lights a cigarette.

"What a bunch of shit," she says. "Why you insist, I'll never know. Who's here? Do you see anyone here but us?"

I gesture to her to put out the cigarette and make the fire. She gestures to me to kiss her butt.

"Why am I making a fire?" she says. "A fire in advance of a goat. Is this like a wishful fire? Like a hopeful fire? No, sorry, I've had it. What would I do in the real world if there was thunder and so on and our goats actually ran away? Maybe I'd mourn, like cut myself with that flint, or maybe I'd kick your ass for being so stupid as to leave the goats out in the rain. What, they didn't put it in the Big Slot?"

I scowl at her and shake my head.

"Well, did you at least check the Little Slot?" she says. "Maybe it was a small goat and they really crammed it in. Maybe for once they gave us a nice quail or something."

I give her a look, then walk off in a rolling gait to check the Little Slot.

Nothing.

"Well, freak this," she says. "I'm going to walk right out of here and see what the hell is up."

But she won't. She knows it and I know it. She sits on her log and smokes and together we wait to hear a clunk in the Big Slot.

About lunch we hit the Reserve Crackers. About dinner we again hit the Reserve Crackers.

No heads poke in and there's no clunk in either the Big or Little Slot.

Then the quality of light changes and she stands at the door of her Separate Area.

"No goat tomorrow, I'm out of here and down the hill," she says. "I swear to God. You watch."

I go into my Separate Area and put on my footies. I have some cocoa and take out a Daily Partner Performance Evaluation Form.

Do I note any attitudinal difficulties? I do not. How do I rate my Partner overall? Very good. Are there any Situations which require Mediation?

There are not.

I fax it in.

3.

Next morning, no goat. Also no note. Janet sits on her log and smokes and together we wait to hear a clunk in the Big Slot.

No heads poke in and there's no clunk in either the Big or Little Slot.

About lunch we hit the Reserve Crackers. About dinner we again hit the Reserve Crackers.

Then the quality of light changes and she stands at the door of her Separate Area.

"Crackers, crackers, crackers!" she says pitifully. "Jesus, I wish you'd talk to me. I don't see why you won't. I'm about to go bonkers. We could at least talk. At least have some fun. Maybe play some Scrabble."

Scrabble.

I wave good night and give her a grunt.

"Bastard," she says, and hits me with the flint. She's a good thrower and I almost say ow. Instead I make a horse-like sound of fury and consider pinning her to the floor in an effort to make her submit to my superior power etc. etc. Then I go into my Separate Area. I put on my footies and tidy up. I have some cocoa. I take out a Daily Partner Performance Evaluation Form.

Do I note any attitudinal difficulties? I do not. How do I rate my Partner overall? Very good. Are there any Situations which require Mediation?

There are not.

I fax it in.

4.

In the morning in the Big Slot there's a nice fat goat. Also a note:

Ha ha! it says. *Sorry about the no goat and all. A little mix-up. In the future, when you look in here for a goat, what you will find on every occasion is a goat, and not a note. Or maybe both. Ha ha! Happy eating! Everything's fine!*

I skin the goat briskly with the flint. Janet comes in, smiles when she sees the goat, and makes, very quickly, a nice little fire, and does not say one English word all morning and even traces a few of our pictographs with a wetted finger, as if awestruck at their splendid beauty and so on.

Around noon she comes over and looks at the cut on my arm, from where she threw the flint.

"You gonna live?" she says. "Sorry, man, really sorry, I just like lost it."

I give her a look. She cans the English, then starts wailing in grief and sort of hunkers down in apology.

The goat tastes super after two days of crackers.

I have a nap by the fire and for once she doesn't walk around singing pop hits in English, only mumbles unintelligibly and pretends to be catching and eating small bugs.

Her way of saying sorry.

No one pokes their head in.

5.

Once, back in the days when people still poked their heads in, this guy poked his head in

"Whoa," he said. "These are some very cramped living quarters. This really makes you appreciate the way we live now. Do you have call-waiting? Do you know how to make a nice mushroom cream sauce? Ha ha! I pity you guys. And also, and yet, I thank you guys, who were my precursors, right? Is that the spirit? Is that your point? You weren't ignorant on purpose? You were doing the best you could? Just like I am? Probably someday some guy representing me will be in there, and some punk who I'm precursor of will be hooting at me, asking why my shoes were made out of dead cows and so forth? Because in that future time, wearing dead skin on your feet, no, they won't do that. That will seem to them like barbarity, just like you dragging that broad around by her hair seems to us like barbarity, although to me, not that much, after living with my wife fifteen years. Ha ha! Have a good one!"

I never drag Janet around by the hair.

Too cliché.

Just then his wife poked in her head.

"Stinks in there," she said, and yanked her head out.

"That's the roasting goat," her husband said. "Everything wasn't all prettied up. When you ate meat, it was like you were eating actual meat, the flesh of a dead animal, an animal that maybe had been licking your hand just a few hours before."

"I would never do that," said the wife.

"You do it now, bozo!" said the man. "You just pay someone to do the dirty work. The slaughtering? The skinning?"

"I do not either," said the wife.

We couldn't see them, only hear them through the place where the heads poke in.

"Ever heard of a slaughterhouse?" the husband said. "Ha ha! Gotcha! What do you think goes on in there? Some guy you never met kills and flays a cow with what you might term big old cow eyes, so you can have your shoes and I can have my steak and my shoes!"

"That's different," she said. "Those animals were raised for slaughter. That's what they were made for. Plus I cook them in an oven, I don't squat there in my underwear with smelly smoke blowing all over me."

"Thank heaven for small favors," he said. "Joking! I'm joking. You squatting in your underwear is not such a bad mental picture, believe me."

"Plus where do they poop," she said.

"Ask them," said the husband. "Ask them where they poop, if you so choose. You paid your dime. That is certainly your prerogative."

"I don't believe I will," said the wife.

"Well, I'm not shy," he said.

Then there was no sound from the head-hole for quite some time. Possibly they were quietly discussing it.

"Okay, so where do you poop?" asked the husband, poking his head in.

"We have disposable bags that mount on a sort of rack," said Janet. "The septic doesn't come up this far."

"Ah," he said. "They poop in bags that mount on racks."

"Wonderful," said his wife. "I'm the richer for that information."

"But hold on," the husband said. "In the old times, like when the cave was real and all, where then did they go? I take it there were no disposal bags in those times, if I'm right."

"In those times they just went out in the woods," said Janet.

"Ah," he said. "That makes sense."

You see what I mean about Janet? When addressed directly we're supposed to cower shrieking in the corner but instead she answers twice in English?

I gave her a look.

"Oh, he's okay," she whispered. "He's no narc. I can tell."

In a minute in came a paper airplane: our Client Vignette Evaluation.

Under *Overall Impression* he'd written: *A-okay! Very nice.*

Under *Learning Value* he'd written: *We learned where they pooped. Both old days and now.*

I added it to our pile, then went into my Separate Area and put on my footies. I filled out my Daily Partner Performance Evaluation Form. Did I note any attitudinal difficulties? I did not. How did I rate my Partner overall? Very good. Were there any Situations which required Mediation?

There were not.

I faxed it in.

6.

This morning is the morning I empty our Human Refuse bags and the trash bags and the bag from the bottom of the sleek metal hole where Janet puts her used feminine items.

For this I get an extra sixty a month. Plus it's always nice to get out of the cave.

I knock on the door of her Separate Area.

"Who is it?" she asks, playing dumb.

She knows very well who it is. I stick in my arm and wave around a trash bag.

"Go for it," she says.

She's in there washing her armpits with a washcloth. The room smells like her, only more so. I add the trash from her wicker basket to my big white bag. I add her bag of used feminine items to my big white bag. I take three bags labeled Caution Human Refuse from the corner and add them to my big pink bag labeled Caution Human Refuse.

I mime to her that I dreamed of a herd that covered the plain like the grass of the earth, they were as numerous as grasshoppers and yet the meat of their humps resembled each a tiny mountain etc. etc., and sharpen my spear and try to look like I'm going into a sort of pre-hunt trance.

"Are you going?" she shouts. "Are you going now? Is that what you're saying?"

I nod.

"Christ, so go already," she says. "Have fun. Bring back some mints."

She has worked very hard these many months to hollow out a rock in which to hide her mints and her smokes. Mints mints mints. Smokes smokes smokes. No matter how long we're in here together I will never get the hots for her. She's fifty and has large feet and sloping shoulders and a pinched little face and chews with her mouth open. Sometimes she puts on big ugly glasses in the cave and does a cross-word: very verboten.

Out I go, with the white regular trash bag in one hand and our mutual big pink Human Refuse bag in the other.

7.

Down in the blue-green valley is a herd of robotic something-or-others, bent over the blue-green grass, feeding I guess? Midway between our mountain and the opposing mountains is a wide green river with periodic interrupting boulders. I walk along a white cliff, then down a path marked by a yellow dot on a pine. Few know this way. It is a non-Guest path. No Attractions are down it, only Disposal Area 8 and a little Employees Only shop in a doublewide, a real blessing for us, we're so close and all.

Inside the doublewide are Marty and a lady we think is maybe Marty's wife but then again maybe not.

Marty's shrieking at the lady, who's writing down whatever he shrieks.

"Just do as they ask!" he shrieks, and she writes it down. "And not only that, do more than that, son, more than they ask! Excel! Why not excel? Be excellent! Is it bad to be good? Now son, I know you don't think that, because that is not what you were taught, you were taught that it is good to be good, I very clearly remember teaching you that. When we went fishing, and you caught a fish, I always said good, good fishing, son, and when you caught no fish, I frowned, I said bad, bad catching of fish, although I don't believe I was ever cruel about it. Are you getting this?"

"Every word," the lady says. "To me they're like nuggets of gold."

"Ha ha," says Marty, and gives her a long loving scratch on the back, and takes a drink of Squirt and starts shrieking again.

"So anyways, do what they ask!" he shrieks. "Don't you know how much we love you here at home, and want you to succeed? As for them, the big-wigs you wrote me about, freak them big-wigs! Just do what they ask though. In your own private mind, think what you like, only do what they ask, so they like you. And in this way, you will succeed. As for the little-wigs you mentioned, just how little are they? You didn't mention that. Are they a lot littler wig than you? In that case, freak them, ignore them if they talk to you, and if they don't talk to you, go up and start talking to them, sort of bossing them around, you know, so they don't start thinking they're the boss of you. But if they're the same wig as you, be careful, son! Don't piss them off, don't act like you're the boss of them, but also don't bend over for some little shit who's merely the same wig as you, or else he'll assume you're a smaller wig than you really actually are. As for friends, sure, friends are great, go ahead and make friends, they're a real blessing, only try to avoid making friends with boys who are the same or lesser wig than you. Only make friends with boys who are bigger wigs than you, assuming they'll have you, which probably they won't. Because why should they? Who are you? You're a smaller wig than them. Although then again, they might be slumming, which would be good for you, you could sneak right in there."

Marty gives me a little wave, then resumes shrieking.

"I don't want to put the pressure on, son," he says. "I know you got enough pressure, with school being so hard and all, and you even having to make your own book covers because of our money crunch, so I don't want to put on extra pressure by saying that the family honor is at stake, but guess what pal, it is! You're it, kid! You're as good as we got. Think of it, me and your mother, and Paw-Paw and Mee-Maw, and Great Paw-Paw, who came over here from wherever he was before, in some kind of boat, and fixed shoes all his life in a shack or whatever? Remember that? Why'd he do that? So you could eventually be born! Think of that! All those years of laundry and stuffing their faces and plodding to the market and making love and pushing out the babies and so on, and what's the upshot? You, pal, you're the freaking upshot. And now there you are, in boarding school, what a privilege, the first one of us to do it, so all's I'm saying is, do your best and don't take no shit from nobody, unless taking shit from them is part of your master plan to get the best of them by tricking them into being your friend. Just always remember who you are, son, you're a Kusacki, my only son, and I love you. Ack, I'm getting mushy here."

"You're doing great," says the lady.

"So much to say," he says.

"And Jeannine sends her love too," says the lady.

"And Jeannine sends her love too," he says. "For crissake's sake, Jeannine, write it down if you want to say it. I don't have to say it for you to write it. Just write it. You're my wife."

"I'm not your wife," says Jeannine.

"You are to me," says Marty, and she sort of leans into him and he takes another slug of the Squirt.

I buy Janet some smokes and mints and me a Kayo.

I really like Kayo.

"Hey, you hear about Dave Wolley?" Marty says to me. "Dave Wolley from Wise Mountain Hermit? You know him? You know Dave?"

I know Dave very well. Dave was part of the group that used to meet for the barbecues at Russian Peasant Farm.

"Well, wave bye-bye to Dave," Marty says. "Wise Mountain Hermit is kaput. Dave is kaput."

"I've never seen Dave so upset," says Jeannine.

"He was very freaking upset," says Marty. "Who wouldn't be? He was superdedicated."

Dave was superdedicated. He grew his own beard long instead of wearing a fake and even when on vacation went around barefoot to make his feet look more like the feet of an actual mountain ascetic.

"The problem is, Wise Mountain Hermit was too far off the beaten path," Marty says. "Like all you Remotes. All you Remotes, you're too far off the beaten path. Think about it. These days we got very few Guests to begin with, which means we got even fewer Guests willing to walk way the hell up here to see you Remotes. Right? Am I right?"

"You are absolutely right," says Jeannine.

"I am absolutely right," says Marty. "Although I am not happy about being absolutely right, because if you think of it, if you Remotes go kaput, where am I? It's you Remotes I'm servicing. See? Right? Give him his mints. Make change for the poor guy. He's got to get back to work."

"Have a good one," says Jeannine, and makes my change.

It's sad about Dave. Also it's worrisome. Because Wise Mountain Hermit was no more Remote than we are, plus it was much more popular, because Dave was so good at dispensing ad-libbed sage advice.

I walk down the path to the Refuse Center and weigh our Human Refuse. I put the paperwork and the fee in the box labeled Paperwork and Fees. I toss the trash in the dumpster labeled Trash, and the Human Refuse in the dumpster labeled Caution Human Refuse, then sit against a tree and drink my Kayo.

8.

Next morning in the Big Slot is a goat and in the Little Slot a rabbit and a note addressed to Distribution:

Please accept this extra food as a token of what our esteem is like, the note says. *Please know that each one of you is very special to us, and are never forgotten about. Please know that if each one of you could be kept, you would be, if that would benefit everyone. But it wouldn't, or we would do it, wouldn't we, we would keep every one of you. But as we meld into our sleeker new organization, what an excellent opportunity to adjust our Staff Mix. And so, although in this time of scarcity and challenge, some must perhaps go, the upside of this is, some must stay, and perhaps it will be you. Let us hope it will be you, each and every one of you, but no, as stated previously, it won't, that is impossible. So just enjoy the treats provided, and don't worry, and wait for your supervisor to contact you, and if he or she doesn't, know with relief that the Staff Remixing has passed by your door. Although it is only honest to inform you that some who make the first pass may indeed be removed in the second, or maybe even a third, depending on how the Remixing goes, although if anyone is removed in both the first and second pass, that will be a redundant screw-up, please ignore. We will only remove each of you once. If that many times! Some of you will be removed never, the better ones of you. But we find ourselves in a too-many-Indians situation and so must first cut some Indians and then, later, possibly, some chiefs. But not yet, because that is harder, because that is us. Soon, but not yet, we have to decide which of us to remove, and that is so very hard, because we are so very useful. Not that we are saying we chiefs are more useful than you Indians, but certainly we do make some very difficult decisions that perhaps you Indians would find hard to make, keeping you up nights, such as which of you to remove. But don't worry about us, we've been doing this for years, only first and foremost remember that what we are doing, all of us, chiefs and Indians both, is a fun privilege, how many would like to do what we do, in the entertainment field.*

Which I guess explains about Dave Wolley.

"Jeez," says Janet. "Let the freaking canning begin."

I give her a look.

"Oh all right all right," she says. "Ooga mooga. Ooga ooga mooga. Is that better?"

She can be as snotty as she likes but a Remixing is nothing to sneeze at.

I skin and roast the goat and rabbit. After breakfast she puts on her Walkman and starts a letter to her sister: very verboten. I work on the pictographs. I mean I kneel while pretending to paint them by dipping my crude dry brush into the splotches of hard colorful plastic meant to look like paint made from squashed berries.

Around noon the fax in my Separate Area makes the sound it makes when a fax is coming in.

Getting it would require leaving the cave and entering my Separate Area during working hours.

"Christ, go get it," Janet says. "Are you nuts? It might be from Louise."

I go get it.

It's from Louise.

Nelson doing better today, it says. *Not much new swelling. Played trucks and ate 3 pcs bologna. Asked about you. No temperature, good range of motion in both legs and arms. Visa is up to $6800, should I transfer to new card w/lower interest rate?*

Sounds good, I fax back. *How are other kids?*

Kids are kids are kids, she faxes back. *Driving me nuts. Always talking.*

Miss you, I fax, and she faxes back the necessary Signature Card.

I sign the card. I fax the card.

Nelson's three. Three months ago his muscles stiffened up. The medicine they put him on to loosen his muscles did somewhat loosen them, but also it caused his muscles to swell. Otherwise he's fine, only he's stiff and swollen and it hurts when he moves. They have a name for what they originally thought he had, but when the medication made him swell up, Dr. Evans had to admit that whatever he had, it wasn't what they'd originally thought it was.

So we're watching him closely.

I return to the cave.

"How are things?" Janet says.

I grimace.

"Well, shit," she says. "You know I'm freaking rooting for you guys."

Sometimes she can be pretty nice.

9.

First thing next morning Greg Nordstrom pokes his head in and asks me to brunch.

Which is a first.

"How about me?" says Janet.

"Ha ha!" says Nordstrom. "Not you. Not today. Maybe soon, however!"

I follow him out.

Very bright sun.

About fifty feet from the cave there's a red paper screen that says Patience! Under Construction, and we go behind it.

"You'll be getting your proxy forms in your Slot soon," he says, spreading out some bagels on a blanket. "Fill out the proxy as you see fit, everything's fine, just vote, do it boldly, exert your choice, it has to do with your stock option. Are you vested? Great to be vested. Just wait until you are. It really feels like a Benefit. You'll see why they call Benefits Benefits, when every month, ka-ching, that option money kicks up a notch. Man, we're lucky."

"Yes," I say.

"I am and you are," he says. "Not everyone is. Some aren't. Those being removed in the Staff Remixing, no. But you're not being removed. At least I don't think so. Now Janet, I have some concerns about Janet, I don't know what they're going to do about Janet. It's not me, it's them, but what can I do? How is she? Is she okay? How have you found her? I want you to speak frankly. Are there problems? Problems we can maybe help correct? How is she? Nice? Reliable? It's not negative to point out a defect. Actually, it's positive, because then the defect can be fixed. What's negative is to withhold valuable info. Are you? Withholding valuable info? I hope not. Are you being negative? Is she a bit of a pain? Please tell me. I want you to. If you admit she's a bit of a pain, I'll write down how positive you were. Look, you know and I know she's got some performance issues, so what an exciting opportunity, for you to admit it and me to hear it loud and clear. Super!"

For six years she's been telling me about her Pap smears and her kid in rehab and her mother in Fort Wayne who has a bad valve and can't stand up or her lungs fill with blood, etc. etc.

"I haven't really noticed any problems," I say.

"Blah blah blah," he says. "What kind of praise is that? Empty praise? Is it empty praise? I'd caution against empty praise. Because empty praise is what? Is like what? Is a lie. And a lie is what? Is negative. You're like the opposite of that little boy who cried Wolf. You're like that little boy who cried No Wolf, when a wolf was in fact chewing on his leg, by the name of Janet. Because what have I recently seen? Having seen your Daily Partner Performance Evaluation Forms, I haven't seen on them a single discouraging word. Not one. Did you ever note a single attitudinal difficulty? You did not. How did you rate your Partner overall? Very good, always, every single day. Were there ever any Situations which required Mediation? There were not, even when, in one instance, she told a guy where you folks pooped. In English. In the cave. I have documentation, because I read that guy's Client Vignette Evaluation."

It gets very quiet. The wind blows and the paper screen tips up a bit. The bagels look good but we're not eating them.

"Look," he says. "I know it's hard to be objective about people we come to daily know, but in the big picture, who benefits when the truth is not told? Does Janet? How can Janet know she's not being her best self if someone doesn't tell her, then right away afterwards harshly discipline her? And with Janet not being her best self, is the organization healthier? And with the organization not being healthier, and the organization being that thing that ultimately puts the food in your face, you can easily see that, by lying about Janet's behavior, you are taking the food out of your own face. Who puts the cash in your hand to buy that food in your face? We do. What do we want of you? We want you to tell the truth. That's it. That is all."

We sit awhile in silence.

"Very simple," he says. "A nonbrainer."

A white fuzzy thing lands in my arm hair. I pick it out.

Down it falls.

"Sad," he says. "Sad is all it is. We live in a beautiful world, full of beautiful challenges and flowers and birds and super people, but also a few regettable bad apples, such as that questionable Janet. Do I hate her? Do I want her killed? Gosh no, I think she's super, I want her to be praised while getting a hot oil massage, she has some very nice traits. But guess what, I'm not paying her to have nice traits, I'm paying her to do consistently good work. Is she? Doing consistently good work? She is not. And here are you, saddled with a subpar colleague. Poor you. She's stopping your rise and growth. People are talking about you in our lounge. Look, I know you feel Janet's not so great. She's a lump to you. I see it in your eye. And that must chafe. Because you are good. Very good. One of our best. And she's bad, very bad, one of our worst, sometimes I could just slap her for what she's doing to you."

"She's a friend," I say.

"You know what it's like, to me?" he says. "The Bible. Remember that part in the Bible when Christ or God says that any group or organization of two or more of us is a body? I think that is so true. Our body has a rotten toe by the name of Janet, who is turning black and stinking up the joint, and next to that bad stinking toe lies her friend the good nonstinker toe, who for some reason insists on holding its tongue, if a toe can be said to have a tongue. Speak up, little toe, let the brain know the state of the rot, so we can rush down what is necessary to stop Janet from stinking. What will be needed? We do not yet know. Maybe some antiseptic, maybe a nice sharp saw with which to lop off Janet. For us to know, what must you do? Tell the truth. Start generating frank and nonbiased assessments of this subpar colleague. That's it. That is all. Did you or did you not in your Employment Agreement agree to complete, every day, an accurate Daily Partner Performance Evaluation Form? You did. You signed in triplicate. I have a copy in my dossier. But enough mean and sad talk, I know my point has been gotten. Gotten by you. Now for the fun. The eating. Eating the good food I have broughten. That's fun, isn't it? I think that's fun."

We start to eat. It's fun.

"Broughten," he says. "The good food I have broughten. Is it brought or broughten?"

"Brought," I say.

"The good food I have brought," he says. "Broughten."

10.

Back in the cave Janet's made a nice fire.

"So what did numbnuts want?" she says. "Are you fired?"

I shake my head no.

"Is he in love with you?" she says. "Does he want to go out with you?"

I shake my head no.

"Is he in love with me?" she says. "Does he want to go out with me? Am I fired?"

I do not shake my head no.

"Wait a minute, wait a minute, go back," she says. "I'm fired?"

I shake my head no.

"But I'm in the shit?" she says. "I'm somewhat in the shit?"

I shrug.

"Will you freaking talk to me?" she says. "This is important. Don't be a dick for once."

I do not consider myself a dick and I do not appreciate being called a dick, in the cave, in English, and the truth is, if she would try a little harder not to talk in the cave, she would not be so much in the shit.

I hold up one finger, like: Wait a sec. Then I go into my Separate Area and write her a note:

Nordstrom is unhappy with you, it says. *And unhappy with me because I have been lying for you on my DPPEFs. So I am going to start telling the truth. And as you know, if I tell the truth about you, you will be a goner, unless you start acting better. Therefore please start acting better. Sorry I couldn't say this in the cave, but as you know, we are not supposed to speak English in the cave. I enjoy working with you. We just have to get this thing straightened out.*

Sitting on her log she reads my note.

"Time to pull head out of ass, I guess," she says.

I give her a thumbs-up.

11.

Next morning I go to the Big Slot and find it goatless. Also there is no note.

Janet comes out and hands me a note and makes, very quickly, a nice little fire.

I really appreciate what you did, her note says. *That you tole me the truth. Your a real pal and are going to see how good I can be.*

For breakfast I count out twenty Reserve Crackers each. Afterward I work on the pictographs and she pretends to catch and eat small bugs. For lunch I count out twenty Reserve Crackers each. After lunch I pretend to sharpen my spear and she sits at my feet speaking long strings of unintelligible sounds.

No one pokes their head in.

When the quality of light changes she stands at the door of her Separate Area and sort of wiggles her eyebrows, like: Pretty good, eh?

I go into my Separate Area. I take out a Daily Partner Performance Evaluation Form.

For once it's easy.

Do I note any attitudinal difficulties? I do not. How do I rate my Partner overall? Very good. Are there any Situations which require Mediation?

There are not.

I fax it in.

12.

Next morning I go to the Big Slot and again find it goatless. Again no note.

Janet comes out and again makes, very quickly, a nice little fire.

I count out twenty Reserve Crackers each. After breakfast we work on the pictographs. After lunch she goes to the doorway and starts barking out sounds meant to indicate that a very impressive herd of feeding things is thundering past etc. etc., which of course it is not, the feeding things, being robotic, are right where they always are, across the river. When she barks I grab my spear and come racing up and join her in barking at the imaginary feeding things.

All day no one pokes their head in.

Then the quality of light changes and she stands at the door of her Separate Area giving me a smile, like: It's actually sort of fun doing it right, isn't it?

I take out a Daily Partner Performance Evaluation Form.

Again: Easy.

Do I note any attitudinal difficulties? I do not. How do I rate my Partner overall? Very good. Are there any Situations which require Mediation?

There are not.

I fax it in.

Also I write Nordstrom a note:

Per our conversation, it says, *I took the liberty of bringing Janet up to speed. Since that time she has been doing wonderful work, as reflected in my (now truthful!!) Daily Partner Performance Evaluation Forms. Thank you for your frankness. Also, I apologize for that period during which I was less than truthful on my DPPEFs. I can see now just how negative that was.*

A bit of ass-kissing, yes.

But I've got some making up to do.

I fax it in.

13.

Late in the night my fax makes the sound it makes when a fax is coming in.

From Nordstrom:

What? What? it says. *You told her? Did I tell you to tell her? And now you have the nerve to say she is doing good? Why should I believe you when you say she is doing good, when all that time she was doing so bad you always said she was doing so good? Oh you have hacked me off. Do you know what I hate? Due to my childhood? Which is maybe why I'm so driven? A liar. Dad lied by cheating on Mom, Mom lied by cheating on Dad, with Kenneth, who was himself a liar, and promised, at his wedding to Mom, to buy me three ponies with golden saddles, and then later, upon divorcing Mom, promised to at least get me one pony with a regular saddle, but needless to say, no ponies were ever gotten by me. Which is maybe why I hate a liar. SO DON'T LIE ANY MORE. Don't lie even one more time about that hideous Janet. I can't believe you told her! Do you really think I care about how she is? I KNOW how she is. She is BAD. But what I need is for you to SAY IT. For reasons of documentation. Do you have any idea how hard it is to fire a gal, not to mention an old gal, not to mention an old gal with so many years of service under her ancient withered belt? There is so much you don't know, about the Remixing, about our plans! Do not even answer me, I am too mad to read it.*

Which is not at all what I had in mind.

No doubt my status with Nordstrom has been somewhat damaged. But okay.

Janet is now doing better and I am now telling the truth. So things are as they should be.

And I'm sure that, in the long run, Nordstrom will come to appreciate what I've accomplished.

14.

Next morning I go to the Big Slot and again find it goatless. Again no note.

Janet comes out and makes, very quickly, a nice little fire.

We squat and eat our Reserve Crackers while occasionally swatting each other with our hands. We get in kind of a mock squabble and scurry around the cave bent over and shrieking. She is really doing very well. I pound a rock against a rock in rage, indicating that I intend to toss some dirt in her face. She barks back very sharply.

Someone pokes their head in.

Young guy, kind of goofy-looking.

"Bradley?" Janet says. "Holy shit."

"Hey, nice greeting, Ma," the guy says, and walks in. He's not supposed to walk in. No one's supposed to walk in. I can't remember a time when anyone has ever just walked in.

"Fucking stinks in here," he says.

"Don't you *even* come into my workplace and start swearing," Janet says.

"Yeah right Ma," he says. "Like you never came into my workplace and started swearing."

"Like you ever had a workplace," she says. "Like you ever worked."

"Like jewelry making wasn't work," he says.

"Oh Bradley you are so full of it," she says. "You didn't have none of the equipment and no freaking jewels. And no customers. You never made a single piece of jewelry. You just sat moping in the basement."

Just our luck: Our first Guest in two weeks and it's a relative.

I clear my throat. I give her a look.

"Give us five freaking minutes, will you, Mr. Tightass?" she says. "This is my kid here."

"I was conceptualizing my designs, Ma," he says. "Which is an important part of it. And you definitely swore at my workplace. I remember very clearly one time you came down into the basement and said I was a fucking asshole for wasting my time trying to make my dream come true of being a jewelry maker."

"Oh bullshit," she says. "I never once called you a asshole. And I definitely did not say fucking. I never say fuck. I quit that a long time ago. You ever hear me say fuck?"

She looks at me. I shake my head no. She never says fuck. When she means fuck she says freak. She is very very consistent about this.

"What?" says Bradley. "He don't talk?"

"He plays by the rules," she says. "Maybe you should try it sometime."

"I was trying," he says. "But still they kicked me out."

"Kicked you out of what?" she says. "Wait a minute, wait a minute, go back. They kicked you out of what? Of rehab?"

"It's nothing bad, Ma!" he shouts. "You don't have to make me feel ashamed about it. I feel bad enough, being called a thief by Mr. Doe in front of the whole group."

"Jesus, Bradley," she says. "How are you supposed to get better if you get kicked out of rehab? What did you steal this time? Did you steal a stereo again? Who's Mr. Doe?"

"I didn't steal nothing, Ma," he says. "Doe's my counselor. I borrowed something. A TV. The TV from the lounge. I just felt like I could get better a lot faster if I had a TV in my room. So I took control of my recovery. Is that so bad? I thought that's what I was there for, you know? I'm not saying I did everything perfect. Like I probably shouldn't of sold it."

"You sold it?" she says.

"There was nothing good ever on!" he says. "If they showed good programs I just know I would've gotten better. But no. It was so boring. So I decided to throw everybody a party, because they were all supporting me so well, by letting me keep the TV in my room? And so, you know, I sold the TV, for the party, and was taking the bucks over to the Party Place, to get some things for the party, some hats and tooters and stuff like that, but then I've got this problem, with substances, and so I sort of all of a sudden wanted some substances. And then I ran into this guy with some substances. That guy totally fucked me! By being there with those substances right when I had some money? He didn't care one bit about my recovery."

"You sold the rehab TV to buy drugs," she says.

"To buy substances, Ma, why can't you get it right?" he says. "The way we name things is important, Ma, Doe taught me that in counseling. Look, maybe you wouldn't have sold the TV, but you're not an inadvertent substance misuser, and guess what, I am, that's why I was in there. Do you hear me? I know you wish you had a perfect son, but you don't, you have an inadvertent substance misuser who sometimes makes bad judgments, like borrowing and selling a TV to buy substances."

"Or rings and jewels," says Janet. "My rings and jewels."

"Fuck Ma, that was a long time ago!" he says. "Why do you have to keep bringing that old shit up? Doe was so right. For you to win, I have to lose. Like when I was a kid and in front of the whole neighborhood you called me an animal torturer? That really hurt. That caused a lot of my problems. We were working on that in group right before I left."

"You were torturing a cat," she says. "With a freaking prod."

"A prod I built myself in metal shop," he says. "But of course you never mention that."

"A prod you were heating with a Sterno cup," she says.

"Go ahead, build your case," he says. "Beat up on me as much as you want, I don't have a choice. I have to be here."

"What do you mean, you have to be here?" she says.

"Ma, haven't you been listening?" he shouts. "I got kicked out of rehab!"

"Well you can't stay here," she says.

"I have to stay here!" he says. "Where am I supposed to go?"

"Go home," she says. "Go home with Grammy."

"With Grammy?" he says. "Are you kidding me? Oh God, the group would love this. You're telling a very troubled inadvertent substance misuser to go live with his terminally ill grandmother? You have any idea how stressful that would be for me? I'd be inadvertently misusing again in a heartbeat. Grammy's always like: Get me this, get me that, sit with me, I'm scared, talk with me, it hurts when I breathe. I'm twenty-four, Ma, baby-sitting brings me down. Plus she's kind of deranged? She sort of like hallucinates? I think it's all that blood in her lungs. The other night she woke up at midnight and said I was trying to steal something from her. Can you believe it? She's like all kooky! I wasn't stealing. Her necklaces got tangled up and I was trying to untangle them. And Keough was trying to help me."

"Keough was at the house?" she says. "I thought I told you no Keough."

"Ma, Jesus Christ, Keough's my friend," he says. "Like my only friend. How am I supposed to get better without friends? At least I have one. You don't have any."

"I have plenty of friends," she says.

"Name one," he says.

She looks at me.

Which I guess is sort of sweet.

Although I don't see why she had to call me Mr. Tightass.

"Fine, Ma," he says. "You don't want me staying here, I won't stay here. You want me to inadvertently misuse substances, I'll inadvertently misuse substances. I'll turn tricks and go live in a ditch. Is that what you want?"

"Turn tricks?" she says. "Who said anything about turning tricks?"

"Keough's done it," he says. "It's what we eventually come to, our need for substances is so great. We can't help it."

"Well, I don't want you turning tricks," she says. "That I don't go for."

"But living in a ditch is okay," he says.

"If you want to live in a ditch, live in a ditch," she says.

"I don't want to live in a ditch," he says. "I want to turn my life around. But it would help me turn my life around if I had a little money. Like twenty bucks. So I can go back and get those party supplies. The tooters and all? I want to make it up to my friends."

"Is that what this is about?" she says. "You want money? Well I don't have twenty bucks. And you don't need tooters to have a party."

"But I want tooters," he says. "Tooters make it more fun."

"I don't have twenty bucks," she says.

"Ma, please," he says. "You've always been there for me. And I've got a bad feeling about this. Like this might be my last chance."

She pulls me off to one side.

"I'll pay you back on payday," she says.

I give her a look.

"Come on, man," she says. "He's my *son*. You know how it is. You got a sick kid, I got a sick kid."

My feeling is, yes and no. My sick kid is three. My sick kid isn't a con man.

Although at this point it's worth twenty bucks to get the guy out of the cave.

I go to my Separate Area and get the twenty bucks. I give it to her and she gives it to him.

"Excellent!" he says, and goes bounding out the door. "A guy can always count on his ma."

Janet goes straight to her Separate Area. The rest of the afternoon I hear sobbing.

Sobbing or laughing.

Probably sobbing.

When the quality of light changes I go to my Separate Area. I make cocoa. I tidy up. I take out a Daily Partner Performance Evaluation Form.

This is really pushing it. Her kid comes into the cave in street clothes, speaks English in the cave, she speaks English back, they both swear many many times, she spends the whole afternoon weeping in her Separate Area.

Then again, what am I supposed to do, rat out a friend with a dying mom on the day she finds out her screwed-up son is even more screwed up than she originally thought?

Do I note any attitudinal difficulties? I do not. How do I rate my Partner overall? Very good. Are there any Situations which require Mediation?

There are not.

I fax it in.

15.

Late that night my fax makes the sound it makes when a fax is coming in.

From Louise:

Bad day, she says. *He had a fever then suddenly got very cold. And his legs are so swollen. In places the skin looks ready to split. Ate like two handfuls dry Chex all day. And whiny, oh my God the poor thing. Stood on the heat grate all day in his underwear, staring out the window. Kept saying where is Daddy, why is he never here? Plus the Evemplorine went up to $70 for 120 count. God, it's all drudge drudge drudge, you should see me, I look about ninety. Also a big strip of trim or siding came floating down as we were getting in the car and nearly killed the twins. Insurance said they won't pay. What do I do, do I forget about it? Will something bad happen to the wood underneath if we don't get it nailed back up? Ugh. Don't fax back, I'm going to sleep.*

Love, Me.

I get into bed and lie there counting and recounting the acoustic tiles on the ceiling of my darkened Separate Area.

One hundred forty-four.

Plus I am so hungry. I could kill for some goat.

Although certainly, dwelling on problems doesn't solve them. Although on the other hand, thinking positively about problems also doesn't solve them. But at least then you feel positive, which is, or should be, you know, empowering. And power is good. Power is necessary at this point. It is necessary at this point for me to be, you know, a rock. What I need to remember now is that I don't have to solve the problems of the world. It is not within my power to cure Nelson, it is only necessary for me to do what I can do, which is keep the money coming in, and in order for me to keep the money coming in, it is necessary for me to keep my chin up, so I can continue to do a good job. That is, it is necessary for me to avoid dwelling negatively on problems in the dark of night in my Separate Area, because if I do, I will be tired in the morning, and might then do a poor job, which could jeopardize my ability to keep the money coming in, especially if, for example, there is a Spot Check.

I continue to count the tiles but as I do it try to smile. I smile in the dark and sort of nod confidently. I try to positively and creatively imagine surprising and innovative solutions to my problems, like winning the Lotto, like the Remixing being discontinued, like Nelson suddenly one morning waking up completely cured.

16.

Next morning is once again the morning I empty our Human Refuse bags and the trash bags and the bag from the bottom of the sleek metal hole.

I knock on the door of her Separate Area.

"Enter," she says.

I step in and mime to her that I dreamed of a herd that covered the plain like the grass of the earth, they were as numerous as grasshoppers and yet the meat of their humps resembled each a tiny mountain etc. etc.

"Hey, sorry about yesterday," she says. "Really sorry. I never dreamed that little shit would have the nerve to come here. And you think he paid to get in? I very much doubt it. My guess is, he hopped the freaking fence."

I add the trash from her wicker basket to my big white bag. I add her bag of used feminine items to my big white bag.

"But he's a good-looking kid, isn't he?" she says.

I sort of curtly nod. I take three bags labeled Caution Human Refuse from the corner and add them to my big pink bag labeled Caution Human Refuse.

"Hey, look," she says. "Am I okay? Did you narc me out? About him being here?"

I give her a look, like: I should've but I didn't.

"Thank you *so* much," she says. "Damn, you're nice. From now on, no more screw-ups. I swear to God."

Out I go, with the white regular trash bag in one hand and our mutual big pink Human Refuse bag in the other.

17.

Nobody's on the path, although from the direction of Pioneer Encampment I hear the sound of rushing water, possibly the Big Durn Flood? Twice a month they open up the Reserve Tanks and the river widens and pretty soon some detachable house parts and Pioneer wagons equipped with special inflatable bladders float by, while from their P.A. we dimly hear the sound of prerecorded screaming Settlers.

I walk along the white cliff, turn down the non-Guest path marked by the little yellow dot, etc. etc.

Marty's out front of the doublewide playing catch with a little kid.

I sit against a tree and start my paperwork.

"Great catch, son!" Marty says to the kid. "You can really catch. I would imagine you're one of the very best catchers in that school."

"Not exactly, Dad," the kid says. "Those kids can really catch. Most of them catch even better than me."

"You know, in a way I'm glad you might quit that school," says Marty. "Those rich kids. I'm very unsure about them."

"I don't want to quit," says the kid. "I like it there."

"Well, you might have to quit," says Marty. "We might make the decision that it's best for you to quit."

"Because we're running out of money," says the kid.

"Yes and no," says Marty. "We are and we aren't. Daddy's job is just a little, ah, problematical. Good catch! That is an excellent catch. Pick it up. Put your glove back on. That was too hard a throw. I knocked your glove off."

"I guess I have a pretty weak hand," the kid says.

"Your hand is perfect," says Marty. "My throw was too hard."

"It's kind of weird, Dad," the kid says. "Those kids at school are better than me at a lot of things. I mean, like everything? Those kids can really catch. Plus some of them went to camp for baseball and camp for math. Plus you should see their clothes. One kid won a trophy in golf. Plus they're nice. When I missed a catch they were really really nice. They always said, like, Nice try. And they tried to teach me? When I missed at long division they were nice. When I ate with my fingers they were nice. When my shoes split in gym they were nice. This one kid gave me his shoes."

"He gave you his shoes?" says Marty.

"He was really nice," explains the kid.

"What were your shoes doing splitting?" says Marty. "Where did they split? Why did they split? Those were perfectly good shoes."

"In gym," says the kid. "They split in gym and my foot fell out. Then that kid who switched shoes with me wore them with his foot sticking out. He said he didn't mind. And even with his foot sticking out he beat me at running. He was really nice."

"I heard you the first time," says Marty. "He was really nice. Maybe he went to being-nice camp. Maybe he went to giving-away-shoes camp."

"Well, I don't know if they have that kind of camp," says the kid.

"Look, you don't need to go to a camp to know how to be nice," says Marty. "And you don't have to be rich to be nice. You just have to be nice. Do you think you have to be rich to be nice?"

"I guess so," says the kid.

"No, no, no," says Marty. "You don't. That's my point. You don't have to be rich to be nice."

"But it helps?" says the kid.

"No," says Marty. "It makes no difference. It has nothing to do with it."

"I think it helps," says the kid. "Because then you don't have to worry about your shoes splitting."

"Ah bullshit," says Marty. "You're not rich but you're nice. See? You were nice, weren't you? When someone else's shoes split, you were nice, right?"

"No one else's shoes ever split," says the kid.

"Are you trying to tell me you were the only kid in that whole school whose shoes ever split?" says Marty.

"Yes," says the kid.

"I find that hard to believe," says Marty.

"Once this kid Simon?" says the kid. "His pants ripped."

"Well, there you go," says Marty. "That's worse. Because your underwear shows. Your pants never ripped. Because I bought you good pants. Not that I'm saying the shoes I bought you weren't good. They were very good. Among the best. So what did this Simon kid do? When his pants ripped? Was he upset? Did the other kids make fun of him? Did he start crying? Did you rush to his defense? Did you sort of like console him? Do you know what console means? It means like say something nice. Did you say something nice when his pants ripped?"

"Not exactly," the kid says.

"What did you say?" says Marty.

"Well, that boy, Simon, was a kind of smelly boy?" says the kid. "He had this kind of smell to him?"

"Did the other kids make fun of his smell?" says Marty.

"Sometimes," says the kid.

"But they didn't make fun of your smell," says Marty.

"No," says the kid. "They made fun of my shoes splitting."

"Too bad about that smelly kid though," says Marty. "You gotta feel bad about a kid like that. What were his parents thinking? Didn't they teach him how to wash? But you at least didn't make fun of his smell. Even though the other kids did."

"Well, I sort of did," the kid says.

"When?" says Marty. "On the day his pants ripped?"

"No," the kid says. "on the day my shoe split."

"Probably he was making fun of you on that day," suggests Marty.

"No," the kid says. "He was just kind of standing there. But a few kids were looking at my shoe funny. Because my foot was poking out? So I asked Simon why he smelled so bad."

"And the other kids laughed?" says Marty. "They thought that was pretty good? What did he say? Did he stop making fun of your shoes?"

"Well, he hadn't really started yet," the kid says. "But he was about to."

"I bet he was," says Marty. "But you stopped him dead in his tracks. What did he say? After you made that crack about his smell?"

"He said maybe he did smell but at least his shoes weren't cheap," says the kid.

"So he turned it around on you," says Marty. "Very clever. The little shit. But listen, those shoes weren't cheap. I paid good money for those shoes."

"Okay," says the kid, and throws the ball into the woods.

"Nice throw," says Marty. "Very powerful."

"Kind of crooked though," says the kid, and runs off into the woods to get the ball.

"My kid," Marty says to me. "Home on break from school. We got him in boarding school. Only the best for my kid! Until they close us down, that is. You heard anything? Anything bad? I heard they might be axing Sheep May Safely Graze. So that's like fifteen shepherds. Which would kill me. I get a lot of biz off those shepherds. Needless to say, I am shitting bricks. Because if they close me, what do you think happens to that kid out there in the woods right now? Boarding school? You think boarding school happens? In a pig's ass. Boarding school does not happen, the opposite of boarding school happens, and he will be very freaking upset."

The kid comes jogging out of the woods with the ball in his hand.

"What are you talking about?" he says.

"About you," Marty says, and puts the kid in a head-lock. "About how great you are. How lovable you are."

"Oh that," the kid says, and smiles big.

18.

That night around nine I hear a sort of shriek from Janet's Separate Area.

A shriek, and then what sounds like maybe sobbing.

Then some louder sobbing and maybe something breaking, possibly her fax?

I go to her door and ask is she okay and she tells me go away.

I can't get back to sleep. So I fax Louise.

Everything okay? I write.

In about ten minues a fax comes back.

Did Dr. Evans ever say anything about complete loss of mobility? it says. *I mean complete. Today I took the kids to the park and let Ace off the leash and he saw a cat and ran off. When I came back from getting Ace, Nelson was like stuck inside this crawling tube. Like he couldn't stand up? Had no power in his legs. I mean none. That fucking Ace. If you could've seen Nelson's face.*

God. When I picked him up he said he thought I'd gone home without him. The poor thing. Plus he had to pee. And so he'd sort of peed himself. Not much, just a little. Other than that all is well, please don't worry. Well worry a little. We are at the end of our rope or however you say it, I'm already deep into the overdraft account and it's only the 5th. Plus I'm so tired at night I can't get to the bills and last time I paid late fees on both Visas and the MasterCard, thirty bucks a pop, those bastards, am thinking about just sawing off my arm and mailing it in. Ha ha, not really, I need that arm to sign checks.

Love, Me.

From Janet's Separate Area come additional sobbing and some angry shouting.

I fax back:

Did you take him to Dr. Evans? I say.

Duh, she faxes back. Have appt for Weds, will let you know. Don't worry, just do your job and also Nelson says hi and you're the best dad ever.

Tell him hi and he's the best kid, I fax back.

What about the other kids? she faxes back.

Tell them they're also the best kids, I fax back.

From Janet's Separate Area comes the sound of Janet pounding on something repeatedly, probably her desk, presumably with her fist.

19.

Next morning in the Big Slot is no goat. Just a note.

From Janet:

Not coming in, it says. Bradley lied about the tooters and bought some you-know-what. Big surprise right? Is in jail. Stupid dumbass. Got a fax last night. Plus my Ma's worse. Before she couldnt get up or her lungs filled with blood? Well now they fill with blood unless she switchs from side to side and who's there to switch her? Before Mrs Finn was but now Mrs Finn got a day-job so no more. So now I have to find someone and pay someone. Ha ha very funny, like I can aford that. Plus Bradley's bail which believe me I have definitely considered not paying. With all this going on no way am I caving it up today. I'm sorry but I just cant, don't narc me out, okay? Just this one last time. I'm taking a Sick Day.

She can't do that. She can't take a Sick Day if she's not sick. She can't take a Sick Day because she's sad about someone she loves being sick. And she certainly can't take a Sick Day because she's sad about someone she loves being in jail.

I count out ten Reserve Crackers and work all morning on the pictographs.

Around noon the door to her Separate Area flies open. She looks weird. Her hair is sticking up and she's wearing an I'm With Stupid sweatshirt over her cavewoman robe and her breath smells like whiskey.

Janet is wasted? Wasted in the cave?

"What I have here in this album?" she says. "Baby pictures of that fucking rat Bradley. Back when I loved him so much. Back before he was a druggie. See how cute? See how smart he looked?"

She shows me the album. He actually does not look cute or smart. He looks the same as he looked the other day, only smaller. In one picture he's sitting on a tricycle looking like he's planning a heist. In another he's got a sour look on his face and his hand down some smaller kid's diaper.

"God, you just love the little shits no matter what, don't you?" she says. "You know what I'm saying? If Bradley's dad woulda stuck around it might've been better. Bradley never knew him. I always used to say he took one look at Bradley and ran off. Maybe I shouldn't of said that. At least not in front of Bradley. Wow. I've had a few snorts. You want a snort? Come on, live a little! Take a Sick Day like me. I had three Ball-Busters and half a bottle of wine. This is the best Sick Day I ever took."

I guide her back to her Separate Area and push her sternly in.

"Come on in!" she says. "Have a BallBuster. You want one? I'm lonely in here. You want a BallBuster, Señor Tightass?"

I do not want a BallBuster.

What I want is for her to stay in her Separate Area keeping very quiet until she sobers up.

All day I sit alone in the cave. When the quality of light changes I go into my Separate Area and take out a Daily Partner Performance Evaluation Form.

When I was a kid, Dad worked at Kenner Beef. Loins would drop from this belt and he'd cut through this purple tendon and use a sort of vise to squeeze some blood into a graduated beaker for testing, then wrap the loin in a sling and swing it down to Finishing. Dad's partner was Fred Lank. Lank had a metal plate in his skull and went into these funks where he'd forget to cut the purple tendon and fail to squeeze out the blood and instead of placing the loin in the sling would just sort of drop the loin down on Finishing. When Lank went into a funk, Dad would cover for him by doing double loins. Sometimes Dad would do double loins for days at a time. When Dad died, Lank sent Mom a check for a thousand dollars, with a note:

Please keep, it said. *The man did so much for me.*

Which is I think part of the reason I'm having trouble ratting Janet out.

Do I note any attitudinal difficulties? I do not. How do I rate my Partner overall? Very good. Are there any situations which require Mediation?

There are not.

I fax it in.

20.

Next morning in the Big Slot is no goat, just a note:

A question has arisen, it says. *Hence this note about a touchy issue that is somewhat grotesque and personal, but we must address it, because one of you raised it, the issue of which was why do we require that you Remote Attractions pay the money which we call, and ask that you call, the Disposal Debit, but which you people insist on wrongly calling the Shit Fee. Well, this is to tell you why, although isn't it obvious to most? We hope. But maybe not. Because what we have found, no offense, is that sometimes you people don't get things that seem pretty obvious to us, such as why you have to pay for your Cokes in your fridge if you drink them. Who should then? Did we drink your Cokes you drank? We doubt it. You did it. Likewise with what you so wrongly call the Shit Fee, because why do you expect us to pay to throw away your poop when after all you made it? Do you think your poop is a legitimate business expense? Does it provide benefit to us when you defecate? No, on the contrary, it would provide benefit if you didn't, because then you would be working more. Ha ha! That is a joke. We know very well that all must poop. We grant you that. But also, as we all know, it takes time to poop, some more than others. As we get older, we notice this, don't you? Not that we're advocating some sort of biological plug or chemical constipator. Not yet, anyway! No, that would be wrong, we know that, and unhealthy, and no doubt some of you would complain about having to pay for the constipators, expecting us to provide them gratis.*

That is another funny thing with some of you, we notice it, namely that, not ever having been up here, in our shoes, you always want something for nothing. You just don't get it! When you poop and it takes a long time and you are on the clock, do you ever see us outside looking mad with a stopwatch? So therefore please stop saying to us: I have defecated while on the clock, dispose of it for free, kindly absorb my expense. We find that loopy. Because, as you know, you Remote Locations are far away, and have no pipes, and hence we must pay for the trucks. The trucks that drive your poop. Your poop to the pipes. Why are you so silly? It is as if you expect us to provide those Cokes for free, just because you thirst. Do Cokes grow on trees? Well, the other thing that does not grow on a tree is a poop truck. Perhaps someone should explain to you the idea of how we do things, which is to make money. And why? Is it greed? Don't make us laugh. It is not. If we make money, we can grow, if we can grow, we can expand, if we can expand, we can continue to employ you, but if we shrink, if we shrink or stay the same, woe to you, we would not be vital. And so help us help you, by not whining about your Disposal Debit, and if you don't like how much it costs, try eating less.

And by the way, we are going to be helping you in this, by henceforth sending less food. We're not joking, this is austerity. We think you will see a substantial savings in terms of your Disposal Debits, as you eat less and your Human Refuse bags get smaller and smaller. And that, our friends, is a substantial savings that we, we up here, will not see, and do you know why not? I mean, even if we were eating less, which we already have decided we will not be? In order to keep our strength up? So we can continue making sound decisions? But do you know why we will not see the substantial savings you lucky ducks will? Because, as some of you have already grumbled about, we pay no Shit Fee, those of us up here. So that even if we shat less, we would realize no actual savings. And why do we pay no Shit Fee? Because that was negotiated into our contracts at Time-of-Hire. What would you have had us do? Negotiate inferior contracts? Act against our own healthy self-interest? Don't talk crazy. Please talk sense. Many of us have Student Loans to repay. Times are hard, entire Units are being eliminated, the Staff Remixing continues, so no more talk of defecation flaring up, please, only let's remember that we are a family, and you are the children, not that we're saying you're immature, only that you do most of the chores while we do all the thinking, and also that we, in our own way, love you.

For several hours Janet does not come out.

Probably she is too hungover.

Around eleven she comes out, holding her copy of the memo.

"So what are they saying?" she says. "Less food? Even less food than now?"

I nod.

"Jesus Christ," she says. "I'm starving as it is."

I give her a look.

"I know, I know, I fucked up," she says. "I was a little buzzed. A little buzzed in the cave. Boo-hoo. Don't tell me, you narced me out, right? Did you? Of course you did."

I give her a look.

"You didn't?" she says. "Wow. You're even nicer than I thought. You're the best, man. And starting right now, no more screw-ups. I know I said that before, but this time, for real. You watch."

Just then there's a huge clunk in the Big Slot.

"Excellent!" she says. "I hope it's a big thing of Motrin."

But it's not a big thing of Motrin. It's a goat. A weird-looking goat. Actually a plastic goat. With a predrilled hole for the spit to go through. In the mouth is a Baggie and in the Baggie is a note:

In terms of austerity, it says. *No goat today. In terms of verisimilitude, mount this fake goat and tend as if real. Mount well above fire to avoid burning. In event of melting, squelch fire. In event of burning, leave area, burning plastic may release harmful fumes.*

I mount the fake goat on the spit and Janet sits on the boulder with her head in her hands.

21.

Next Morning is once again the morning I empty our Human Refuse bags and the trash bags and the bag from the bottom of the sleek metal hole where Janet puts her used feminine items.

I knock on the door of her Separate Area.

Janet slides the bags out, all sealed and labeled and ready to go.

"Check it out," she says. "I'm a new woman."

Out I go, with the white regular trash bag in one hand and our mutual big pink Human Refuse bag in the other.

I walk along the white cliff, then down the path marked by the small yellow dot on the pine etc. etc.

On the door of Marty's doublewide is a note:

Due to circumstances beyond our control we are no longer here, it says. *But please know how much we appreciated your patronage. As to why we are not here, we will not comment on that, because we are bigger than that. Bigger than some people. Some people are snakes. To some people, fifteen years of good loyal service means squat. All's we can say is, watch your damn backs.*

All the best and thanks for the memories,

Marty and Jeannine and little Eddie.

Then the door flies open.

Marty and Jeannine and little Eddie are standing there holding suitcases.

"Hello and good-bye," says Marty. "Feel free to empty your shit bag inside the store."

"Now, Marty," says Jeannine. "Let's try and be positive about this, okay? We're going to do fine. You're too good for this dump anyway. I've always said you were too good for this dump."

"Actually, Jeannine," Marty says. "When I first got this job you said I was lucky to even get a job, because of my dyslexia."

"Well, honey, you are dyslexic," says Jeannine.

"I never denied being dyslexic," says Marty.

"He writes his letters and numbers backwards," Jeannine says to me.

"What are you, turning on me, Jeannine?" Marty says. "I lose my job and you turn on me?"

"Oh Marty, I'm not turning on you," Jeannine says. "I'm not going to stop loving you just because you've got troubles. Just like you've never stopped loving me, even though I've got troubles."

"She gets too much spit in her mouth," Marty says to me.

"Marty!" says Jeannine.

"What?" Marty says. "You can say I'm dyslexic, but I can't say you get too much spit in your mouth?"

"Marty, please," she says. "You're acting crazy."

"I'm not acting crazy," he says. "It's just that you're turning on me."

"Don't worry about me, Dad," the kid says. "I won't turn on you. And I don't mind going back to my old school. Really I don't."

"He had a little trouble with mean kids in his old school," Marty says to me. "Which is why we switched him. Although nothing you couldn't handle, right, kid? Actually, I think it was good for him. Taught him toughness."

"As long as nobody padlocks me to the boiler again," the kid says. "That part I really didn't like. Wow, those rats or whatever."

"I doubt those were actual rats," says Marty. "More than likely they were cats. The janitor's cats. My guess is, it was dark in that boiler room and you couldn't tell a cat from a rat."

"The janitor didn't have any cats," the kid says. "And he said I was lucky those rats didn't start biting my pants. Because of the pudding smell. From when those kids pinned me down and poured pudding down my pants."

"Was that the same day?" Marty says. "The rats and the pudding? I guess I didn't realize them two things were on the same day. Wow, I guess you learned a lot of toughness on that day."

"I guess so," the kid says.

"But nothing you couldn't handle," Marty says.

"Nothing I couldn't handle," the kid says, and blinks, and his eyes water up.

"Well, Christ," Marty says, and his eyes also water up. "Time to hit the road, family. I guess this it. Let's say our good-byes. Our good-byes to Home Sweet Home."

They take a little tour around the doublewide and do a family hug, then drag their suitcases down the path.

I go to the Refuse Center and weigh our Human Refuse. I put the paperwork and the fee in the box labeled Paperwork and Fees. I toss the trash in the dumpster labeled Trash, and the Human Refuse in the dumpster labeled Caution Human Refuse.

I feel bad for Marty and Jeannine, and especially I feel bad for the kid.

I try to imagine Nelson padlocked to a boiler in a dark room full of rats.

Plus now where are us Remotes supposed to go for our smokes and mints and Kayos?

22.

Back at the cave Janet is working very industriously on the pictographs.

As I come in she points to my Separate Area while mouthing the word: Fax.

I look at her. She looks at me.

She mouths the words: Christ, go. Then she holds one hand at knee level, to indicate Nelson.

I go.

But it's not for me, it's for her.

Ms. Foley's fax appears to be inoperative? the cover letter says. *Kindly please forward the attached.*

Please be informed, the attached fax says, *I did my very best in terms of your son, and this appeared, in my judgment, to be an excellent plea bargain, which, although to some might appear disadvantageous, ten years is not all that long when you consider all the bad things that he has done. But he was happy enough about it, after some initial emotions such as limited weeping, and thanked me for my hard work, although not in those exact words, as he was fairly, you know, upset. On a personal note, may I say how sorry I am, but also that in the grand scheme of things such as geology ten years is not so very long really.*

Sincerely,

Evan Joeller, Esq.

I take the fax out to Janet, who reads it while sitting on her log.

She's sort of a slow reader.

When she's finally done she looks crazy and for a minute I think she's going to tear the cave apart but instead she scoots into the corner and starts frantically pretending to catch and eat small bugs.

I go over and put my hand on her shoulder, like: Are you okay?

She pushes my hand away roughly and continues to pretend to catch and eat small bugs.

Just then someone pokes their head in.

Young guy, round head, expensive-looking glasses.

"Bibby, hand me up Cole," he says. "So he can see. Cole-Cole, can you see? Here. Daddy will hold you up."

A little kid's head appears alongside the dad's head.

"Isn't this cool, Cole?" says the dad. "Aren't you glad Mommy and Daddy brought you? Remember Daddy told you? How people used to live in caves?"

"They did not," the little boy says. "You're wrong."

"Bibby, did you hear that?" the dad says. "He just said I'm wrong. About people living in caves."

"I heard it," says a woman from outside. Cole, people really did use to live in caves. Daddy's not wrong."

"Daddy's always wrong," says the little boy.

"He just said I'm always wrong," the dad says. "Did you hear that? Did you write that down? In the memory book? Talk about assertive! I should be so assertive. Wouldn't Norm and Larry croak if I was suddenly so assertive?"

"Well, it couldn't hurt you," the mom says.

"Believe me, I know," the dad says. "That's why I said it. I know very well I could afford to be more assertive. I was making a joke. Like an ironic joke at my own expense."

"I want to stab you, dad," says the little boy. "With a sharp sword, you're so dumb."

"Ha ha!" says the dad. "But don't forget, Cole-Cole, the pen is mightier than the sword! Remember that? Remember I taught you that? Wouldn't it be better to compose an insulting poem, if you have something negative about me you want to convey? Now that's real power! Bibby, did you hear what he said? And then what I said? Did you write all that down? Also did you save that Popsicle wrapper? Did you stick it in the pocket in the back cover of the memory book and write down how cute he looked eating it?"

"What your name?" the little boy yells at me.

I cower and shriek in the corner etc. etc.

"What your name I said!" the little boy shouts at me. "I hate you!"

"Now, Cole-Cole," says the dad. "Let's not use the word hate, okay, buddy? Remember what I told you? About hate being the nasty dark crayon and love being the pink? And remember what I told you about the clanging gong? And remember I told you about the bad people in the old days, who used to burn witches, and how scary that must've been for the witches, who were really just frightened old ladies who'd made the mistake of being too intelligent for the era they were living in?"

"You are not acceptable!" the kid shouts at me.

"Ha ha, oh my God!" says the dad. "Bibby, did you get that? Did you write that down? He's imitating us. Because we say that to him? Write down how mad he is. Look how red his face is! Look at him kick his feet. Wow, he is really pissed. Cole, good persistence! Remember how daddy told you about the little train that could? How everyone kept trying to like screw it and not give it its due, and how finally it got really mad and stomped its foot and got its way? Remember I told you about Chief Joseph, who never stopped walking? You're like him. My brave little warrior. Bibby, give him a juice box. Also he's got some goo-goo coming out of his nosehole."

"Jesus Christ," Janet mumbles.

I give her my sternest look.

"What was that?" says the dad. "I'm sorry, I didn't hear you. What did you just say?"

"Nothing," Janet says. "I didn't say nothing."

"I heard you very clearly," says the dad. "You said Jesus Christ. You said Jesus Christ because of what I said about the goo-goo in my son's nosehole. Well, first of all, I'm sorry if you find a little boy's nosehole goo-goo sickening, it's perfectly normal, if you had a kid of your own you'd know that, and second of all, since when do cavepeople speak English and know who Jesus Christ is? Didn't the cavepeople predate Christ, if I'm not mistaken?"

"Of course they did," the mom says from outside. "We just came from Christ. Days of Christ. And we're going backwards. Towards the exit."

"Look, pal, I got a kid," says Janet. "I seen plenty of snot. I just never called it goo-goo. That's all I'm saying."

"Bibby, get this," the dad says. "Parenting advice from the cavelady. The cavelady apparently has some strong opinions on booger nomenclature. For this I paid eighty bucks? If I want somebody badly dressed to give me a bunch of lip I can go to your mother's house."

"Very funny," says the mom.

"I meant it funny," says the dad.

"I was a good mom," Janet says. "My kid is as good as anybody's kid."

"Hey, share it with us," says the dad.

"Even if he is in jail," says Janet.

"Bibby, get this," says the dad. "the cavelady's kid is in jail."

"Don't you *even* make fun of my kid, you little suckass," says Janet.

"The cavelady just called you a suckass," says the mom.

"A little suckass," says the dad. "And don't think I'm going to forget it."

Soon flying in through the hole where the heads poke in is our wadded-up Client Vignette Evaluation.

Under *Learning Value* he's written: *Disastrous. We learned that some caveladies had potty mouths. I certainly felt like I was in the actual Neanderthal days. Not!*

Under *Overall Impression* he's written: *The cavelady called me a suckass in front of my child. Thanks so much! A tremendous and offensive waste of time. LOSE THE CAVELADY, SHE IS THE WORST.*

"Know what I'm doing now?" the guy says. "I'm walking my copy down to the main office. Your ass is grass, lady."

"Oh shit," Janet says, and sits on the log. "Shit shit shit. I really totally blew it, didn't I?"

My God, did she ever. She really totally blew it.

"What are you going to do, man?" Janet says. "Are you going to narc me out?"

I give her a look, like: Will you just please shut up?

The rest of the day we sit on our respective logs.

When the quality of light changes I go to my Separate Area and take out a Daily Partner Performance Evaluation Form.

A note comes sliding under my door.

I have a idea, it says. *Maybe you could say that ashole made it all up? Like he came in and tryed to get fresh with me and when I wouldnt let him he made it up? That could work. I think it could work. Please please don't narc me out, if I get fired I'm dead, you know all the shit that's going on with me, plus you have to admit I was doing pretty good before this.*

She was doing pretty good before this.

I think of Nelson. His wispy hair and crooked nose. When I thank him for bravely taking all his medications he always rests his head on my shoulder and says, No problem. Only he can't say his *r*'s. So it's like: No pwoblem. And then he pats my belly, as if I'm the one who bravely took all my medications.

Do I note any attitudinal difficulties?

I write: *Yes.*

How do I rate my Partner overall?

I write: *Poor.*

Are there any Situations which require Mediation?

I write: *Today Janet unfortunately interacted negatively with a Guest. Today Janet swore at a Guest in the cave. Today Janet unfortunately called a Guest a "suckass," in English, in the cave.*

I look it over.

It's all true.

I fax it in.

23.

A few minutes later my fax makes the sound it makes when a fax is coming in.

From Nordstrom:

This should be sufficient! it says. Super! More than sufficient. Good for you. Feel no guilt. Are you Janet? Is Janet you? I think not. I think that you are you and she is she. You guys are not the same entity. You are distinct. Is her kid your kid? Is your kid her kid? No, her kid is her kid and your kid is your kid. Have you guilt? About what you have done? Please do not. Please have pride. What I suggest? Think of you and Janet as branches on a tree. While it's true that a branch sometimes needs to be hacked off and come floating down, so what, that is only one branch, it does not kill the tree, and sometimes one branch must die so that the others may live. And anyway, it only looks like death, because you are falsely looking at this through the lens of an individual limb or branch, when in fact you should be thinking in terms of the lens of what is the maximum good for the overall organism, our tree. When we chop one branch, we all become stronger! And that branch on the ground, looking up, has the pleasure of knowing that he or she made the tree better, which I hope Janet will do. Although knowing her? With her crappy attitude? Probably she will lie on the ground wailing and gnashing her leaves while saying swear words up at us. But who cares! She is gone. She is a goner. And we have you to thank. So thanks! This is the way organizations grow and thrive, via small courageous contributions by cooperative selfless helpers, who are able to do that hardest of things, put aside the purely personal aspect in order to see the big picture. Oh and also, you might want to be out of the cave around ten, as that is when the deed will be done.

Thanks so much!

Greg N.

I lie there counting and recounting the acoustic tiles on the ceiling of my darkened Separate Area.

One hunded forty-four.

24.

Next morning is not the morning I empty our Human Refuse bags and the trash bags and the bag from the bottom of the sleek metal hole, but I get up extremely early, in fact it is still dark, and leave Janet a note saying I've gone to empty our Human Refuse bags and our trash bags and the bag from the bottom of her sleek metal hole etc. etc., then very quietly sneak out of the cave and cross the river via wading and sit among the feeding things, facing away from the cave.

I sit there a long time.

When I get back, Janet's gone and the door to her Separate Area is hanging open and her Separate Area is completely empty.

Except for a note taped to the wall:

You freak you break my heart, it says. Thanks a million. What the fuck am I supposed to do now? I guess I will go home and flip Ma from side to side until she dies from starving to death because we got no money. And then maybe I will hore myself with a jail gard to get Bradley out. I cant beleve after all this time you tern on me. And here I thought you were my frend but you were only interested in your own self. Not that I blame you. I mean, I do and I dont. Actually I do.

You bastard,

Janet.

There are several big clunks in the Big Slot.

A goat, some steaks, four boxes of hash browns, caramel corn in a metal tub, several pies, bottles of Coke and Sprite, many many small containers of Kayo.

I look at that food a long time.

Then I stash it in my Separate Area, for later use.

For lunch I have a steak and hash browns and some pie and a Kayo.

Eating hash browns and pie and drinking Kayo in the cave is probably verboten but I feel I've somewhat earned it.

I clean up the mess. I sit on the log.

Around two there is a little tiny click in the Little Slot.

25.

A memo, to Distribution:

Regarding the rumors you may have lately been hearing, it says. Please be advised that they are false. They are so false that we considered not even bothering to deny them. Because denying them would imply that we have actually heard them. Which we haven't. We don't waste our time on such nonsense. And yet we know that if we don't deny the rumors we haven't heard, you will assume they are true. And they are so false! So let us just categorically state that all the rumors you've been hearing are false. Not only the rumors you've heard, but also those you haven't heard, and even those that haven't yet been spread, are false.

However, there is one exception to this, and that is if the rumor is good. That is, if the rumor presents us, us up here, in a positive light, and our mission, and our accomplishments, in that case, and in that case only, we will have to admit that the rumor you've been hearing is right on target, and congratulate you on your fantastic powers of snooping, to have found out that secret super thing! In summary, we simply ask you to ask yourself, upon hearing a rumor: Does this rumor cast the organization in a negative light? If so, that rumor is false, please disregard. If positive, super, thank you very much for caring so deeply about your organization that you knelt with your ear to the track, and also, please spread the truth far and wide, that is, get down on all fours and put your own lips to the tracks. Tell your friends. Tell friends who are thinking of buying stock. Do you have friends who are journalists? Put your lips to their tracks.

Because what is truth? Truth is that thing which makes what we want to happen happen. Truth is that thing which, when told, makes those on our team look good, and inspires them to greater efforts, and causes people not on our team to see things our way and feel sort of jealous. Truth is that thing which empowers us to do even better than we are already doing, which by the way is fine, we are doing fine, truth is the wind in our sails, that blows only for us. So when a rumor makes you doubt us, us up here, it is therefore not true, since we have already defined truth as that thing which helps us win. Therefore, if you want to know what is true, simply ask what is best. Best for us, all of us. Do you get our drift? Contrary to rumor, the next phase of the Staff Remixing is not about to begin. The slightest excuse, the slightest negligence, will not be used as the basis for firing the half of you we would be firing over the next few weeks if the rumor you have all probably heard by now about the mass firings were true. Which it is not. See? See how we just did that? Transformed that trashy negative rumor into truth? Go forth and do that, you'll see it's pretty fun. And in terms of mass firings, relax, none are forthcoming, truly, and furthermore, if they were, what you'd want to ask yourself is: Am I Thinking Positive/Saying Positive? Am I giving it all I've got? Am I doing even the slightest thing wrong? But not to worry. Those of you who have no need to be worried should not in the least be worried. As for those who should be worried, it's a little late to start worrying now, you should have started months ago, when it could've done you some good, because at this point, what's decided is decided, or would have been decided, if those false rumors we are denying, the rumors about the firings which would be starting this week if they were slated to begin, were true, which we have just told you, they aren't.

More firings?

God.

I return to the log.

Sort of weird without Janet.

Someone pokes their head in.

A young woman in a cavewoman robe.

26.

She walks right in and hands me a sealed note.

From Nordstrom:

Please meet Linda, it says. *Your total new Partner. Sort of cute, yes? Under that robe is quite a bod, believe me, I saw her in slacks. See why I was trying to get rid of Janet? But also you will find she is serious. Just like you. See that brow? It is permanent, she had it sort of installed. Like once every six months she goes in for a touch-up where they spray it from a can to harden it. You can give it a little goose with your thumb, it feels like real skin. But don't try it, as I said, she is very serious, she only let me try it because I am who I am, in the interview, but if you try it, my guess is? She will write you up. Or flatten you! Because it is not authentic that one caveperson would goose another caveperson in the brow with his thumb in the cave. I want us now, post-Janet, to really strive for some very strict verisimilitude. You may, for example, wish to consider having such a perma-brow installed on yourself. To save you the trouble of every day redoing that brow, which I know is a pain. Anyway, I think you and Linda will get along super. So here is your new mate! Not that I'm saying mate with her, I would not try that, she is, as I said, very serious, but if you were going to mate with her, don't you think she looks more appropriate, I mean she is at least younger than Janet and not so hard on the eyes.*

I put out my hand and smile.

She frowns at my hand, like: Since when do cavepeople shake hands?

She squats and pretends to be catching and eating small bugs.

How she knows how to do that, I do not know.

I squat beside her and also pretend to be catching and eating small bugs.

We do this for quite some time. It gets old but she doesn't stop, and all the time she's grunting, and once or twice I could swear she actually catches and eats an actual small bug.

Around noon my fax makes the sound it makes when a fax is coming in.

From Louise? Probably. Almost definitely. The only other person who ever faxes me is Nordstrom, and he just faxed me last night, plus he just sent me a note.

I stand up.

Linda gives me a look. Her brow is amazing. It has real actual pores on it.

I squat down.

I pretend to catch and eat a small bug.

The fax stops making the sound it makes when a fax is coming in. Presumably the fax from Louise is in the tray, waiting for me to read it. Is something wrong? Has something changed? What did Dr. Evans say about Nelson's complete loss of mobility?

Five more hours and I can enter my Separate Area and find out.

Which is fine. Really not a problem.

Because I'm Thinking Positive/Saying Positive.

Maybe if I explained to Linda about Nelson it would be okay, but I feel a little funny trying to explain about Nelson so early in our working relationship.

All afternoon we pretend to catch and eat small bugs. We pretend to catch and eat more pretend bugs than could ever actually live in one cave. The number of pretend bugs we pretend to catch and eat would in reality basically fill a cave the size of our cave. It feels like we're racing. At one point she gives me a look, like: Slow down, going so fast is inauthentic. I slow down. I slow down, monitoring my rate so that I am pretending to catch and eat small bugs at exactly the same rate at which she is pretending to catch and eat small bugs, which seems to me prudent, I mean, there is no way she could have a problem with the way I'm pretending to catch and eat small bugs if I'm doing it exactly the way she's doing it.

No one pokes their head in.

Janice Eidus

A novelist, short story writer, and essayist, Janice Eidus has twice won an O. Henry Award for her stories, as well as a Redbook Prize and a Push-cart Prize. She is the author of two story collections, The Celibacy Club *and* Vito Loves Geraldine, *and two novels,* Urban Bliss *and* Faithful Rebecca. *She lives in New York City, where she was born and raised.*

We recognize "The Art of Forgiveness: A Fable" as a fable in the way it accelerates time. Over the span of a few pages, we sense the complete arc of the life of the main character. Almost every paragraph begins with a signpost of passing time: "Later," "Soon after," "Eventually," "Once," "A few years later," "Weeks went by," "Over the course of ten years," "Meanwhile." Paradoxically, this device also gives the impression of timelessness. The story's concentration upon one aspect of the human condition—in this case, the ability to forgive—further marks it as a fable, one that teaches us that forgiveness, too, is a creative act that we must make our own.

The Art of Forgiveness: A Fable

She'd written her first poem when she was six. Her parents had been so proud, they'd framed it and hung it on the living room wall, directly over the pink-and-silver brocade sofa her mother loved so much. She was an urban little girl who played on the rough-and-tumble streets of the Bronx, and her poem celebrated this world she knew:

I love the Bronx, where I play.
It is my home, and it is pretty.
And here I play, in New York City.

Her teacher read the poem aloud before the rest of the class. "She has a gift," her teacher told her mother during Open School Week. "Writing like this, about something that deeply matters to her, is a spiritual art. And if she wishes, she can grow up to be a writer—an artist of the spirit."

Later, her mother told her what the teacher had said. She felt proud to know that she had a gift, something special. She worked hard from that moment on, studying the writing of others and practicing her own. She fell in love with the very *idea* of language. She would stand in front of her mirror, repeating over and over her favorite words from the poems of Edgar Allan Poe: "bells, bells, bells" and "nevermore, nevermore!" From *The Wizard of Oz*, she would make a song of the characters' names: "Dorothy, Toto, Glinda, Scarecrow, Tin Man, Auntie Em."

Soon after, though, her parents lost interest in her writing. They had other things on their minds, they told her, and besides, they didn't want to encourage her too much, lest she really decide to *become* a writer, something they feared, because it wasn't a secure, conventional way of life.

Eventually, her parents moved south, to a warmer climate. "We're not getting any younger," they told her. She went away to college, and she grew cool toward them. She didn't invite them to her college graduation, and she didn't visit them. Instead, she moved into a small apartment, downtown in the East Village. A few years later, when her second novel won a major prize, she moved uptown to a fancy building with three doormen and three glittering chandeliers in the lobby. She never thought about her childhood in the Bronx. It was long ago, and far away.

Something was wrong, however: Although she was now successful, she felt angry much of the time. She held onto slights and rebuffs; she nursed grudges. If a friend or a lover said a wrong thing, something that hurt or offended her, well then, her heart would harden toward that person. Inevitably, the person would say a *second* wrong thing. And that would be that. She couldn't bear to be in that person's presence ever again.

Still, despite her anger at so many people, she wasn't lonely. She was very charming—her witty, lush language drew people to her—and so it was easy for her to make new friends and lovers.

Once, a friend called her and said, "I'm sorry I said an unkind thing to you. I was wrong. But I'm not perfect. Can't you forgive me?"

She held her breath, and then answered honestly: "No, I can't."

Her friend hung up the phone then, saying, "Well, perhaps I can't forgive *you*, either, for not caring enough to *try!*"

She'd shrugged her shoulders, and gone out to dinner with some new friends.

A few years later, in the midst of a party which was being thrown for her by her newest, most charming friends, she felt a terrible ache in her chest. The ache began just as her hosts were raising their glasses to toast her splendid new book. She smiled and made a short, witty speech, but the ache wouldn't go away.

Weeks went by—then months—and she lived her life as she always had: She spun her web of words; she made new friends and lovers; she recited her own words on stage for large, enthusiastic audiences. But the ache grew worse and worse, more and more painful.

She found herself dreaming at night about those people who had said such terribly wrong things to her. In one dream, she reached out her hand across a great ocean to a lost lover, but he swam away from her, and the farther away he got, the more desperate she was to reach him. In another, she was trapped in quicksand, screaming for help, while her old friend, the one who'd hung up on her, stood by and watched, an inscrutable expression on her face.

She would waken in the middle of the night, saddened and frightened by these dreams, unable to return to sleep. Finally, she went to see a therapist, an older woman with salt-and-pepper hair, kind eyes behind thick tortoiseshell eyeglasses, and a warm smile. "How can I help you?" the therapist asked, leaning back in her big chair.

She told the therapist about her frightening dreams.

"And?" the therapist asked.

So then she told the therapist about all the terribly wrong things people had said and done to her over the years. The list went on and on: so many slights and rude comments; so many terrible and hurtful moments.

"And?" the therapist asked again, when she'd finished.

"And?" she repeated.

"Your language is enthralling," the therapist said, looking thoughtful. "You weave a spell when you speak. It is an art."

"Oh, yes. I'm a writer, you see. An artist of the spirit."

"And?"

She was silent. She just couldn't imagine what the therapist wanted her to say.

"And where is the other word? Despite your large and impressive vocabulary, you never once used the other word. Like the word "art," this word, too, is spiritual."

"A spiritual word?"

"*Forgive*," the therapist said. "You never said that you forgave anyone."

"I don't *understand* that word," she explained. "That word is abstract to me. Other people use that word, but I never do. Still," she went on bravely, "I think I *would* like to learn the meaning of that word."

The therapist smiled, even more warmly than before. "We shall work together then, to expand your vocabulary."

For ten years, she saw the therapist. During each session, they discussed that word. It was hard work: Sometimes she shouted out with fury; sometimes she wept; sometimes she felt cold and detached. At other times, she felt hopeful, and thought that perhaps she was growing closer to understanding the meaning of that intangible, elusive word.

Over the course of the ten years, the therapist's salt-and-pepper hair turned completely to salt. And she herself, although still firm and trim, saw signs of her own aging: a line here, a wrinkle there, a grey hair both here *and* there. . . .

Meanwhile, she grew more and more accomplished and well-known. Her artistry was honored with increasingly prestigious awards; the audiences for her stage recitations grew larger; and she wrote and published more than ever.

Then one day, after she'd been traveling for many months to promote her newest book, doing interviews every day, giving stage performances every night, sleeping in strange hotel rooms, sometimes running to catch trains and planes, and other times sitting for long hours in cramped waiting rooms while trains and planes were delayed, she managed to steal an hour to fly back to the city for a session with the therapist.

But before she'd even had a chance to sit down, the therapist said something that struck her as *wrong*. The therapist said, "You look very, very tired, my dear. Perhaps the time has come for you to slow down a bit."

She was shocked. And hurt. And enraged. The therapist, who was supposed to know her better than anyone in the world, who she had trusted more than her friends and lovers, had said something *wrong*. Of course, she couldn't slow down. There was no time to slow down. She would have to end therapy immediately. She took a deep breath, intending to tell her therapist this in no uncertain terms. But instead, she said, "I forgive you. I forgive you for saying that." For a long moment, she couldn't believe her own words, but then she realized that they were true.

The therapist smiled her familiar, warm smile and said, "I'm not sure what I said that was so terrible, but how thrilling it is that you forgive me! I'm so happy for you. So very, very happy."

The next morning, she called her therapist and said it again over the phone, adding, "You're right, of course. I am tired. It *is* time for me to slow down."

And then she called her old friend, the same friend who had once said, "Can't you forgive me?" And she said, "I forgive you now. And I understand that I, too, have said many, many wrong things over the years." She paused. "I've missed you so much."

And her friend said, "I've missed you, too. I thought about calling you, but I figured, what was the point, if you didn't even know the one word you needed to know."

"I know, I *know*," she said to her friend, and they laughed like two schoolgirls, and made a lunch date for the very next day.

She spent the rest of the day making calls to old friends and old lovers, to say that she forgave them, and to ask for their forgiveness, as well. And in nearly every case, she was, herself, forgiven. In the few instances where she wasn't, she accepted it, because she was learning, too, that one must accept the consequences of one's actions.

The last call she made was to her parents. Her father had recently had a stroke and was hard of hearing; her mother had arthritis and had trouble walking. As she dialed their number, she pictured them as they once were, so proud, hanging her first poem on the wall above the sofa. To her parents, she didn't say, "I forgive you." She said, instead, "I love you."

By the time she'd finished talking to her parents, the sun had set, and the sky was dark. She turned on the bedroom light, and stood in front of her full-length mirror. She stared at herself—at the lines forming on her face, at the gray hairs here and there, at her firm chin and clear eyes, and she marveled at the power of that one word: "forgive." She repeated it aloud, over and over—the same way she had repeated the words of the poems and stories she'd loved so much as a child—and her body felt more alive than it had in years. She felt once more like that excited, proud little girl who'd written her very first poem celebrating the rough-and-tumble world of the Bronx streets, a world she now vividly remembered. And yet she also felt like a woman growing older and wiser, a woman marching resolutely forward, a woman in touch, at last, with the spirit of the art of forgiveness.

Yuri Olesha

The Soviet Union was a mere two years old when Yuri Olesha joined the Red Army in 1919. Like many of his intellectual contemporaries, he at first viewed the Soviet Union with great hope and optimism, believing that a truly classless society could be created from the ashes of the repressive czarist monarchy that had been overthrown in the Russian Revolution in 1917. When he published his first story in 1922, he was considered one of the Soviet Union's bright literary lights.

In 1927 Olesha published Envy—*a novel about the struggle between the classes of Russian society—to critical praise. He also wrote the first "Revolutionary fairy tale,"* Three Fat Men. *His early stories, however, have a less overtly political nature. Written in a highly metaphoric style, and sharing much in common with the French surrealists, Olesha's stories are small jewels of the imagination. "Lyompa," one of his masterpieces, tells the story of a dying man from three points of view and three generations. Olesha is at his best in describing the man's delirium in a way that is both starkly realistic and almost whimsically fantastic. But Olesha's imaginativeness proved his downfall: His artistic vision was considered too different from the accepted Soviet realist style, and he was widely condemned until he retreated from the writing scene almost entirely. He died in relative obscurity in Moscow in 1960 at the age of sixty-one.*

Lyompa

Young Alexander was planing wood in the kitchen. The cuts on his fingers were covered with golden, appetizing scabs.

The kitchen gave onto the courtyard. It was spring and the doors were always open. There was grass growing near the entrance. Water poured from a pail glistened on the stone slabs. A rat appeared in the garbage can. Finely sliced potatoes were frying in the kitchen. The primus stoves were burning; their life began in a burst of splendor when the orange flame shot ceiling-high. It ended in a quiet blue flame. Eggs jumped around in boiling water. One of the tenants was cooking crabs. With two fingers, he picked up a live crab by the waist. The crabs were greenish, the color of the waterpipes. Two or three drops suddenly shot out of the tap. The tap was discreetly blowing its nose. Then, upstairs somewhere, pipes began talking in a variety of voices. The dusk was becoming perceptible. One glass continued to glisten on the window sill, as it received the last rays of the setting sun. The taps chattered. All sorts of moving and knocking started up around the stove.

The dusk was magnificent. People were eating peanuts. There was singing. The yellow light from the rooms fell on the dark sidewalk. The grocery store was brightly lit.

In the room next to the kitchen lay Ponomarev, critically ill. He lay in his room alone. There was a candle burning; a medicine bottle with a prescription attached to it stood on a table at his head.

When people came to see Ponomarev, he said to them:

"You can congratulate me: I'm dying."

In the evening he became delirious. The bottle was staring at him. The prescription was like the train of a wedding dress, the bottle a princess on her wedding day. The bottle had a long name. He wanted to write a treatise. He was talking to his blanket.

"You ought to be ashamed of yourself. . . ."

The blanket sat next to him, lay next to him, told him the latest news.

There were only a few things around the sick man: the medicine, the spoon, the light, the wallpaper. The other things had left. When he found he was critically ill and about to die, he realized how huge and varied was the world of things and how few were the things that remained to him. Every day fewer of these things were left. A familiar object like a railroad ticket was already irretrievably remote. First, the number of things on the periphery, far away from him, decreased; then this depletion drew closer to the center, reaching deeper and deeper, toward the courtyard, the house, the corridor, the room, his heart.

At first, the disappearance of things did not particularly sadden the sick man.

The countries had gone: America; then the possibilities: being handsome, rich, having a family (he was single). . . . Actually, his sickness was unrelated to their disappearance. They had slipped away as he had grown older. But he was really hurt to realize that even the things moving parallel with his course were growing more remote. In a single day he was abandoned by the street, his job, the mail, horses. Then the disappearances began to occur at a mad rate, right there, alongside him: already the corridor had slipped out of reach and, in his very room, his coat, the door key, his shoes had lost all significance. Death was destroying things on its way to him. Death had left him only a few things, from an infinite number; things he would never have permitted in his house by choice. He had things forced on him. He had the frightening visits and looks of people he knew. He saw he had no chance of defending himself from the intrusion of these unsolicited and, to him, useless things. But now they were compulsory, the only ones. He had lost the right to choose.

Young Alexander was making a model plane.

The boy was much more serious and complex than people imagined. He kept cutting his fingers, bleeding, littering the floor with his shavings, leaving dirty marks with his glue, scrounging bits of silk, crying, being pushed around. The grownups considered themselves absolutely right, although the boy acted in a perfectly adult way, as only a very small number of adults are capable of acting. He acted scientifically. He was following a blueprint in constructing his model, making calculations, respecting the laws of nature. To adult attacks he could have opposed an explanation of the laws, a demonstration of his experiments. He remained silent, however, feeling it was not right for him to look more serious than adults.

The boy was surrounded by rubber bands, coils of wire, sheets of plywood, silk, and the smell of glue. Above him the sky glistened. Under his feet, insects crawled over the stones, and a stone had a little petrified shell embedded in it.

From time to time, while the boy was deep in his work, another boy, quite tiny, would approach him. He was naked except for a tiny pair of blue trunks. He touched things and got in the way. Alexander would chase him away. The naked boy, who looked as if he were made of rubber, wandered all over the house. In the corridor was a bicycle leaning with its pedal against the wall. The pedal had scratched the paint, and the bike gripped the wall by the scratch.

The little boy dropped in on Ponomarev. The child's head bounced around like a ball near the edge of the bed. The sick man's temples were pale, like those of a blind man. The boy came close to Ponomarev's head and examined it. He thought it had always been this way in the world: a bearded man lying in a bed in a room. The little boy had just learned to recognize things; he did not yet know how to distinguish time in their existence.

He turned away and walked around the room. He saw the floorboards, the dust between them, the cracks in the plaster. Around him lines joined and moved and bodies formed. Sometimes a wonderful pattern of light appeared. The child started rushing toward it, but before he had even taken a full step, the change of distance killed the illusion. The child looked up, back, behind the fireplace, searching for it and moving his hands in bewilderment. Each second gave him a new thing. There was an amazing spider over there. The spider vanished at the boy's mere desire to touch it with his hand.

The vanishing things left the dying man nothing but their names.

There was an apple in the world. It glistened amidst the leaves; it seized little bits of the day and gently twirled them round: the green of the garden, the outline of the window. The law of gravity awaited it under the tree, on the black earth, on the knoll. Beady ants scampered among the knolls. Newton sat in the garden. There were many causes hidden inside the apple, causes that could determine a multitude of effects. But none of these causes had anything to do with Ponomarev. The apple had become an abstraction. The fact that the flesh of a thing had disappeared while the abstraction remained was painful to him.

"I thought there was no outside world," he mused. "I thought my eye and my ear ruled things. I thought the world would cease to exist when I ceased to exist. But I still exist! So why don't the things? I thought they got their shape, their weight, their color from my brain. But they have left me, leaving behind only useless names, names that pester my brain."

Ponomarev looked at the child nostalgically. The child walked around. Things rushed to meet him. He smiled at them, not knowing any of them by name. He left the room and the magnificent procession of things trailed after him.

"Listen," the sick man called out to the child, "do you know that when I die, nothing will remain? They will all be gone—the courtyard, the tree, Daddy, Mummy. I'll take everything along with me."

A rat got into the kitchen.

Ponomarev listened: the rat was making itself at home, rattling the plates, opening the tap, making scraping sounds in the bucket.

"Why, someone must be washing dishes in there," Ponomarev decided.

Immediately he became worried: perhaps the rat had a proper name people did not know. He wondered what this name could be. He was delirious. As he thought, fear seized him more and more powerfully. He knew that at any cost he must stop thinking about the rat's name. But he kept searching for it, knowing that as soon as he found that meaningless, horrifying name, he would die.

"Lyompa!" he suddenly shouted in a terrifying voice.

The house was asleep. It was very early in the morning, just after five. Young Alexander was awake. The kitchen door giving onto the courtyard was open. The sun was still down somewhere.

The dying man was wandering about in the kitchen. He was bent forward, arms extended, wrists hanging limp. He was collecting things to take away with him.

Alexander dashed across the courtyard. The model plane flew ahead of him. It was the last thing Ponomarev saw.

He did not collect it. It flew away.

Later that day, a blue coffin with yellow ornaments made its appearance in the kitchen. The little rubber boy stared at it from the corridor, his little hands holding one another behind his back. The coffin had to be turned every which way to get it through the door. It banged against a shelf. Pans fell to the floor. There was a brief shower of plaster. Alexander climbed on the stove and helped to pull the box through. When the coffin finally got into the corridor, it immediately became black and the rubber boy ran along the passage, his feet slapping the floor:

"Grandpa! Grandpa! They've brought you a coffin."

Luisa Valenzuela

One of Argentina's most prominent contemporary writers, Luisa Valenzuela has produced six novels, among them The Lizard's Tail *and* Black Novel *with Argentines. She has taught at Columbia University and*

New York University. Many of her stories include caustic black humor, grotesques, wit, and irony in reaction to the brutal recent history of torture, disappearances, and political repression in her native country.

Valenzuela uses fable and fairy tale in many of her works. One might consider "Cat's Eye," taken from her book of stories Open Door, as importing the high drama of Argentina's national dance, the tango. The fiction's highly structured and stylized strangeness asks of our imaginations the extreme contortions that the tango demands of dancers' bodies. The metafictional component of this fantasy enhances the comparison to the tango with its own self-conscious pauses and poses, its awareness of its nuanced and historic invention, and its overwrought and obvious choreography.

Cat's Eye

I.

They are walking down the hallway in the dark. She turns around suddenly and he cries out. "What is it?" she asks. And he says: "Your eyes. Your eyes are shining like a wild animal's."

"Oh, come on," she says, "look again." And nothing, of course. She turns to him and there's nothing but pure, calming darkness. He puts his hand on the switch and turns on the light. She has her eyes closed. She closed them against the light, he thinks, but that really doesn't put his mind at rest.

The dialogue between the two of them changes after that vision of phosphorescence in her eyes. Green eyes casting their own light, now so brown, hazel as her ID says; brown or hazel, that is, conventional there in the everyday light of the office. He had planned to propose a job to her, and a green phosphorescence had imposed itself between the two of them (*ignis fatuus*). Outside is the Calle Corrientes, so edificed and unedifying. Inside the office, jungle noises conjured up by a pair of shining eyes. Okay, okay, starting like this, we'll never know how our objective narrative of events comes out. The window is open. We want to note the fact that the window is open to somehow explain the jungle noises, although if noise can be explained by noise, the light in her eyes in the hallway has no rational explanation on account of the closed door between the open window and the reigning darkness.

That she turned toward him in the hall—that's undeniable. And afterward, those glowing eyes—to what end were they looking at him? With what threat or demand? If he hadn't cried out . . . ? On the fourteenth floor, in the office, he asks himself these questions while he talks to her—talks to a pair of eyes—and he doesn't know very well what he'll be saying in the next instant, what's expected of him and where is—was—the trap into which he has slowly slid. Tiger's eyes. He asks himself as he talks with her with the open window behind them: If he had been able to stifle the cry or intuit something more . . .

II.

At three in the morning a suspicious noise awakens you and you remain very quiet in bed and hear—sense—that someone is moving there in your room. Some man. A man who has forced the door; who surely now wants to force himself on you. You hear his velvet footsteps over the carpet and feel a light vibration in the air. The man is getting closer. You don't dare move. Suddenly, within you, there is something beyond terror—or is it terror itself?—and you turn in the darkness and confront him. On seeing what you suppose is the glow of your eyes, the guy lets out a shriek and jumps through the window, which, since it's a hot night, is wide open. Among other things, two questions now arise:

   a) Are you the same woman as the one in the previous story?
   b) How will you explain the presence of the man in your house
      when the police begin their investigation?

Answer to a)
Yes, you are the same woman as in the previous story. For this reason, and bearing in mind the foregoing events, you wait until 9:00 a.m. and go running to consult an ophthalmologist. The doctor, a conscientious professional, puts you through all manner of examinations and finds nothing abnormal about your vision. It's not really your vision that's the problem, you suggest without going into detail. The doctor then scans your retinas, and discovers a black panther in the depths of your eyes. He doesn't know how to explain this phenomenon to you. He can only inform you of the fact and leave the explanation to wiser or more imaginative colleagues. You return to your house stunned, and to calm down you begin to tweeze some hairs from your upper lip. Inside you, the panther roars, but you don't hear her.

The answer to b) is unknown
Green eyes of a black panther, phosphorescent in the darkness, unreflected in mirrors as might have been expected from the very beginning, had there been a beginning. The man from the first story is now her boss and, of course, has no desire to give her orders for fear that she'll suddenly turn out the lights and make him face those eyes again. Luckily for him, the panther doesn't lurk elsewhere in her, and the days go by with that peculiar placidity associated with the habit of fear. The man takes certain precautions every morning. Before leaving for the office, he makes sure the electric company has no plans to cut the power in the neighborhood. He keeps a flashlight within easy reach in the top drawer of his desk, leaves the window wide open so even the last shimmer of day can enter, and does not permit himself even a hint of darker sentiments toward her as he has permitted himself toward previous secretaries. Not that he wouldn't like that. He would like to take her dancing some night and then to bed. But the terror of facing those eyes again doesn't even allow him to entertain the notion. All he permits himself is to wonder whether he really saw what he thinks he saw or if it was merely the product of his imagination (an optical illusion of someone else's eye). He decides on for the first alternative, because he can't believe his imagination is that fecund. To keep her docile, he speaks to her in musical tones, though she doesn't appear to be stalking him as she takes dictation.

Buenos Aires cannot permit itself—cannot permit him—the luxury of a conscious hallucination. We who have known him for some time can be sure that his fear has nothing to do with the imaginative. We are not that fond of him, but we'll see if, with time, we'll give him the opportunity to redeem himself. Nor is she any big deal either. It's the panther that saves her, but a panther like this one, *che non parla ma se fica,* doesn't have much of a chance inside someone so given to apathy. She begins to suffer from darkaphobia or whatever they call it, and she only frequents well-lighted places so no one will find out her useless secrets. The panther sleeps with open eyes while she's awake; perhaps it is awake while she's asleep, but she's never able to ascertain that. The panther needs no food, nor any kind of affection. The panther is now called Pepita, but that's about all. The boss begins to look upon her favorably, but never looks her in the eyes. She and the boss end up together in broad daylight on the office carpet. Their relationship lasts quite a while.

The denouement is optional:
—Once a year, Pepita goes into heat. The boss does what he can, but the woman remains cockeyed.

—She ends up pushing the boss out the window because the eyes are the window of the soul and vice versa.

—Pepita moves from the eyes to the liver and the woman dies of cirrhosis.

—She and the boss decide to get married and their light bills are incredible because they don't ever want to be in the dark.

—Pepita begins to misbehave, and the woman finds herself forced to leave her beloved and go to live with an animal trainer who mistreats her.

—Ditto, but with an ophthalmologist who promises her an operation.

—Ditto, but with a veterinarian because Pepita is sick and the woman is afraid of going blind if the panther dies.

—Every day the woman washes her eyes with Lotus Flower Eye Bath and is very serene because Pepita has converted to Buddhism and practices nonviolence.

—She reads that in the United States they have discovered a new method of combatting black panthers, and she travels, full of hope, only to find, once there, that the reference was to something completely different.

—She leaves the boss due to his insalubrious habit of screwing in bright light and she plugs herself into a job as an usherette in a ritzy movie theater where everyone appreciates the fact that she has no need for a flashlight.

Translated by Christopher Leland

Flann O'Brien

Born in 1911, Brian O'Nolan's job as a civil servant in Dublin forbade him from writing under his own name, so he used two pen names. As Miles na gCopaleen he wrote a series of newspaper columns that satirized local Irish life. As Flann O'Brien he was the author of a number of critically celebrated works, including the novels The Third Policeman *and* At Swim-Two-Birds. *The latter was hailed by Anthony Burgess as "one of the ten great comic novels of the century." The former, written in 1939, wasn't published until after his death in 1966.*

O'Brien's style is characterized not only by its humor but by its technical inventiveness. At Swim-Two-Birds *has four beginnings and is a book within a book within a book.* The Third Policeman *has a subplot, told in footnotes, that almost overwhelms the main plot. This technique of using footnotes in fiction, which in the past has been primarily a scholarly tool, has become a hallmark of many contemporary postmodern writers, including David Foster Wallace and Nicholson Baker. In the hands of writers such as these, footnotes don't bolster one's arguments (as they do for scholars) but act as rabbit holes for the curious reader, like Alice in Wonderland, to disappear into. O'Brien is interested not in mirroring life, but in mining fiction's possibilities in ways that are as brilliant as they are entertaining.*

In the same tradition, "John Duffy's Brother" undermines the realism of the story almost from the outset by poking fun at the traditional idea of the omniscient narrator. The narrator admits from the first line that the story, "strictly speaking," shouldn't be told at all because the person to whom the story happened never told anyone. And no wonder; the story in question deals with a man who wakes up one day believing he's a train. Nonetheless the narrator plunges ahead, defying impossibility and weaving an absurd, meandering tale.

John Duffy's Brother

Strictly speaking, this story should not be written or told at all. To write it or to tell it is to spoil it. This is because the man who had the strange experience we are going to talk about never mentioned it to anybody, and the fact that he kept his secret and sealed it up completely in his memory is the whole point of the story. Thus we must admit that handicap at the beginning—that it is absurd for us to tell the story, absurd for anybody to listen to it and unthinkable that anybody should believe it.

We will, however, do this man one favour. We will refrain from mentioning him by his complete name. This will enable us to tell his secret and permit him to continue looking his friends in the eye. But we can say that his surname is Duffy. There are thousands of these Duffys in the world; even at this moment there is probably a new Duffy making his appearance in some corner of it. We can even go so far as to say that he is John Duffy's brother. We do not break faith in saying so, because if there are only one hundred John Duffy's in existence, and even if each one of them could be met and questioned, no embarrassing enlightenments would be forthcoming. That is because the John Duffy in question never left his house, never left his bed, never talked to anybody in his life and was never seen by more than one man. That man's name was Gumley. Gumley was a doctor. He was present when John Duffy was born and also when he died, one hour later.

John Duffy's brother lived alone in a small house on an eminence in Inchicore. When dressing in the morning he could gaze across the broad valley of the Liffey to the slopes of the Phoenix Park, peacefully. Usually the river was indiscernible but on a sunny morning it could be seen lying like a long glistening spear in the valley's palm. Like a respectable married man, it seemed to be hurrying into Dublin as if to work.

Sometimes, recollecting that his clock was fast, John Duffy's brother would spend an idle moment with his father's spy glass, ranging the valley with an eagle eye. The village of Chapelizod was to the left and invisible in the depth but each morning the inhabitants would erect, as if for Mr. Duffy's benefit, a lazy plume of smoke to show exactly where they were.

Mr. Duffy's glass usually came to rest on the figure of a man hurrying across the uplands of the Park and disappearing from view in the direction of the Magazine Fort. A small white terrier bounced along ahead of him but could be seen occasionally sprinting to overtake him after dallying behind for a time on private business.

The man carried in the crook of his arm an instrument which Mr. Duffy at first took to be a shotgun or patent repeating rifle, but one morning the man held it by the butt and smote the barrels smartly on the ground as he walked, and it was then evident to Mr. Duffy—he felt some disappointment—that the article was a walking stick.

It happened that this man's name was Martin Smullen. He was a retired stationary-engine-driver and lived quietly with a delicate sister at Number Four, Cannon Row, Parkgate. Mr. Duffy did not know his name and was destined never to meet him or have the privilege of his acquaintance, but it may be worth mentioning that they once stood side by side at the counter of a public-house in Little Easter Street, mutually unrecognised, each to the other a black stranger. Mr. Smullen's call was whiskey, Mr. Duffy's stout.

Mr. Smullen's sister's name was not Smullen but Goggins, relict of the late Paul Goggins wholesale clothier. Mr. Duffy had never even heard of her. She had a cousin by the name of Leo Corr who was not unknown to the police. He was sent up in 1924 for a stretch of hard labour in connection with the manufacture of spurious currency. Mrs. Goggins had never met him, but heard he had emigrated to Labrador on his release.

About the spy glass. A curious history attaches to its owner, also a Duffy, late of the Mercantile Marine. Although unprovided with the benefits of a University education—indeed, he had gone to sea at the age of sixteen as a result of an incident arising out of an imperfect understanding of the sexual relation—he was of a scholarly turn of mind and would often spend the afternoons of his sea-leave alone in his dining-room thumbing a book of Homer with delight or annotating with erudite sneers the inferior Latin of the Angelic Doctor. On the fourth day of July, 1927, at four o'clock, he took leave of his senses in the dining-room. Four men arrived in a closed van at eight o'clock that evening to remove him from mortal ken to a place where he would be restrained for his own good.

It could be argued that much of the foregoing has little real bearing on the story of John Duffy's brother, but modern writing, it is hoped, has passed the stage when simple events are stated in the void without any clue as to the psychological and hereditary forces working in the background to produce them. Having said so much, however, it is now permissable to set down briefly the nature of the adventure of John Duffy's brother.

He arose one morning—on the ninth of March, 1932—dressed and cooked his frugal breakfast. Immediately afterwards, he became possessed of the strange idea that he was a train. No explanation of this can be attempted. Small boys sometimes like to pretend that they are trains, and there are fat women in the world who are not, in the distance, without some resemblance to trains. But John Duffy's brother was certain that he *was* a train—long, thunderous and immense, with white steam escaping noisily from his feet and deep-throated bellows coming rhythmically from where his funnel was.

Moreover, he was certain that he was a particular train, the 9.20 into Dublin. His station was the bedroom. He stood absolutely still for twenty minutes, knowing that a good train is equally punctual in departure as in arrival. He glanced often at his watch to make sure that the hour should not go by unnoticed. His watch bore the words "Shockproof" and "Railway Timekeeper".

Precisely at 9.20 he emitted a piercing whistle, shook the great mass of his metal ponderously into motion and steamed away heavily into town. The train arrived dead on time at its destination, which was the office of Messrs. Polter and Polter, Solicitors, Commissioners for Oaths. For obvious reasons, the name of this firm is fictitious. In the office were two men, old Mr. Cranberry and young Mr. Hodge. Both were clerks and both took their orders from John Duffy's brother. Of course, both names are imaginary.

"Good morning, Mr. Duffy," said Mr. Cranberry. He was old and polite, grown yellow in the firm's service.

Mr. Duffy looked at him in surprise. "Can you not see I am a train?" he said. "Why do you call me Mr. Duffy?"

Mr. Cranberry gave a laugh and winked at Mr. Hodge who sat, young, neat and good-looking, behind his typewriter.

"All right, Mr. Train," he said. "That's a cold morning, sir. Hard to get up steam these cold mornings, sir."

"It is not easy," said Mr. Duffy. He shunted expertly to his chair and waited patiently before he sat down while the company's servants adroitly uncoupled him. Mr. Hodge was sniggering behind his roller.

"Any cheap excursions, sir?" he asked.

"No," Mr. Duffy replied. "There are season tickets, of course."

"Third class and first class, I suppose, sir?"

"No," said Mr. Duffy. "In deference to the views of Herr Marx, all class distinctions in the passenger rolling-stock have been abolished."

"I see," said Mr. Cranberry.

"That's communism," said Mr. Hodge.

"He means," said Mr. Cranberry, "that it is now first-class only."

"How many wheels has your engine?" asked Mr. Hodge. "Three big ones?"

"I am not a goods train," said Mr. Duffy acidly. "The wheel formation of a passenger engine is four-four-two—two large driving wheels on each side, coupled, of course, with a four-wheel bogey in front and two small wheels at the cab. Why do you ask?"

"The platform's in the way," Mr. Cranberry said. "He can't see it."

"Oh quite," said Mr. Duffy, "I forgot."

"I suppose you use a lot of coal?" Mr. Hodge said.

"About half a ton per thirty miles," said Mr. Duffy slowly, mentally checking the consumption of that morning. "I need scarcely say that frequent stopping and starting at suburban stations takes a lot out of me."

"I'm sure it does," said Mr. Hodge, with sympathy.

They talked like that for half an hour until the elderly Mr. Polter arrived and passed gravely into his back office. When that happened, conversation was at an end. Little was heard until lunch-time except the scratch of pens and the fitful clicking of the typewriter.

John Duffy's brother always left the office at one thirty and went home to his lunch. Consequently he started getting steam up at twelve forty-five so that there should be no delay at the hour of departure. When the "Railway Timekeeper" said that it was one thirty, he let out another shrill whistle and steamed slowly out of the office without a word or a look at his colleagues. He arrived home dead on time.

We now approach the really important part of the plot, the incident which gives the whole story its significance. In the middle of his lunch John Duffy's brother felt something important, something queer, momentous and magical taking place inside his brain, an immense tension relaxing, clean light flooding a place which had been dark. He dropped his knife and fork and sat there for a time wild-eyed, a filling of potatoes unattended in his mouth. Then he swallowed, rose weakly from the table and walked to the window, wiping away the perspiration which had started out on his brow.

He gazed out into the day, no longer a train, but a badly frightened man. Inch by inch he went back over his morning. So far as he could recall he had killed no one, shouted no bad language, broke no windows. He had only talked to Cranberry and Hodge. Down in the roadway there was no dark van arriving with uniformed men infesting it. He sat down again desolately beside the unfinished meal.

John Duffy's brother was a man of some courage. When he got back to the office he had some whiskey in his stomach and it was later in the evening than it should be. Hodge and Cranberry seemed preoccupied with their letters. He hung up his hat casually and said:

"I'm afraid the train is a bit late getting back."

From below his downcast brows he looked very sharply at Cranberry's face. He thought he saw the shadow of a smile flit absently on the old man's placid features as they continued poring down on a paper. The smile seemed to mean that a morning's joke was not good enough for the same evening. Hodge rose suddenly in his corner and passed silently into Mr. Polter's office with his letters. John Duffy's brother sighed and sat down wearily at his desk.

When he left the office that night, his heart was lighter and he thought he had a good excuse for buying more liquor. Nobody knew his secret but himself and nobody else would ever know.

It was a complete cure. Never once did the strange malady return. But to this day John Duffy's brother starts at the rumble of a train in the Liffey tunnel and stands rooted to the road when he comes suddenly on a level-crossing—silent, so to speak, upon a peak in Darien.

Angela Carter

Born in Eastbourne, Sussex, in 1940, Angela Carter became a notable advocate of magical realism and postmodern gothic revival. Carter's first novel, Shadow Dance *(1966), established her habits of composition, which mixed the conventions of popular genre writing (in this case, the detective story) with her characteristic eroticism. She published ten books of fiction and taught at universities in Australia, Japan, and America, where she was a visiting professor at Brown. She died in London in 1992.*

"The Fall River Axe Murders" is from Black Venus *(1985), a book that features Carter's interest in mythmaking. In these fictions, Carter taps into the well-known narratives of a series of historical figures involved in notorious murder cases, like Lizzie Borden and O. J. Simpson. History provides the story, and she depicts the mythic character in a way that either amplifies or contradicts the image in the minds of the general public. She wants to bring alive the history yet move away from mere history and into the more powerful history we think of as myth.*

The Fall River Axe Murders

Lizzie Borden with an axe
Gave her father forty whacks
When she saw what she had done
She gave her mother forty one.

Children's rhyme

Early in the morning of the fourth of August, 1892, in Fall River, Massachusetts.

Hot, hot, hot . . . very early in the morning, before the factory whistle, but, even at this hour, everything shimmers and quivers under the attack of white, furious sun already high in the still air.

Its inhabitants have never come to terms with these hot, humid summers—for it is the humidity more than the heat that makes them intolerable; the weather clings like a low fever you cannot shake off. The Indians who lived here first had the sense to take off their buckskins when hot weather came and sit up to their necks in ponds; not so the descendants of the industrious, self-mortifying saints who imported the Protestant ethic wholesale into a country intended for the siesta and are proud, proud! of flying in the face of nature. In most latitudes with summers like these, everything slows down, then. You stay all day in penumbra behind drawn blinds and closed shutters; you wear clothes loose enough to make your own breeze to cool yourself when you infrequently move. But the ultimate decade of the last century finds us at the high point of hard work, here; all will soon be bustle, men will go out into the furnace of the morning well wrapped up in flannel underclothes linen shirts, vests and coats and trousers of sturdy woollen cloth, and they garrotte themselves with neckties, too, they think it is so virtuous to be uncomfortable.

And today it is the middle of a heat wave; so early in the morning and the mercury has touched the middle eighties, already, and shows no sign of slowing down its headlong ascent.

As far as clothes were concerned, women only appeared to get off more lightly. On this morning, when, after breakfast and the performance of a few household duties, Lizzie Borden will murder her parents, she will, on rising, don a simple cotton frock—but, under that, went a long, starched cotton petticoat; another short, starched cotton petticoat; long drawers; woolen stockings; a chemise; and a whalebone corset that took her viscera in a stern hand and squeezed them very tightly. She also strapped a heavy linen napkin between her legs because she was menstruating.

In all these clothes, out of sorts and nauseous as she was, in this dementing heat, her belly in a vice, she will heat up a flat-iron on a stove and press handkerchiefs with the heated iron until it is time for her to go down to the cellar woodpile to collect the hatchet with which our imagination—"Lizzie Borden with an axe"—always equips her, just as we always visualise St. Catherine rolling along her wheel, the emblem of her passion.

Soon, in just as many clothes as Miss Lizzie wears, if less fine, Bridget, the servant girl, will slop kerosene on a sheet of last night's newspaper crumpled with a stick or two of kindling. When the fire settles down, she will cook breakfast; the fire will keep her suffocating company as she washes up afterwards.

In a serge suit, one look at which would be enough to bring you out in prickly heat, Old Borden will perambulate the perspiring town, truffling for money like a pig until he will return home mid-morning to keep a pressing appointment with destiny.

But nobody here is up and about, yet; it is still early morning, before the factory whistle, the perfect stillness of hot weather, a sky already white, the shadowless light of New England like blows from the eye of God, and the sea, white, and the river, white.

If we have largely forgotten the physical discomforts of the itching, oppressive garments of the past and the corrosive effects of perpetual physical discomfort on the nerves, then we have mercifully forgotten, too, the smells of the past, the domestic odours—ill-washed flesh; infrequently changed underwear; chamber-pots; slop-pails; inadequately plumbed privies; rotting food; unattended teeth; and the streets are no fresher than indoors, the omnipresent acridity of horse piss and dung, drains, sudden stench of old death from butchers' shops, the amniotic horror of the fishmonger.

You would drench your handkerchief with cologne and press it to your nose. You would splash yourself with parma violet so that the reek of fleshly decay you always carried with you was overlaid by that of the embalming parlour. You would abhor the air you breathed.

Five living creatures are asleep in a house on Second Street, Fall River. They comprise two old men and three women. The first old man owns all the women by either marriage, birh or contract. His house is narrow as a coffin and that was how he made his fortune— he used to be an undertaker but he has recently branched out in several directions and all his branches bear fruit of the most fiscally gratifying kind.

But you would never think, to look at his house, that he is a successful and a prosperous man. His house is cramped, comfortless, small and mean—"unpretentious", you might say, if you were his sycophant—while Second Street itself saw better days some time ago. The Borden house—see "Andrew J. Borden" in flowing script on the brass plate next to the door—stands by itself with a few scant feet of yard on either side. On the left is a stable, out of use since he sold the horse. In the back lot grow a few pear trees, laden at this season.

On this particular morning, as luck would have it, only one of the two Borden girls sleeps in their father's house. Emma Lenora, his oldest daughter, has taken herself off to nearby New Bedford for a few days, to catch the ocean breeze, and so she will escape the slaughter.

Few of their social class stay in Fall River in the sweating months of June, July and August but, then, few of their social class live on Second Street, in the low part of town where heat gathers like fog. Lizzie was invited away, too, to a summer house by the sea to join a merry band of girls but, as if on purpose to mortify her flesh, as if important business kept her in the exhausted town, as if a wicked fairy spelled her in Second Street, she did not go.

The other old man is some kind of kin of Borden's. He doesn't belong here; he is visiting, passing through, he is a chance bystander, he is irrelevant.

Write him out of the script.

Even though his presence in the doomed house is historically unimpeachable, the colouring of this domestic apocalypse must be crude and the design profoundly simplified for the maximum emblematic effect.

Write John Vinnicum Morse out of the script.

One old man and two of his women sleep in the house on Second Street.

The City Hall clock whirrs and sputters the prolegomena to the first stroke of six and Bridget's alarm clock gives a sympathetic skip and click as the minute-hand stutters on the hour; back the little hammer jerks, about to hit the bell on top of her clock, but Bridget's damp eyelids do not shudder with premonition as she lies in her sticking flannel nightgown under one thin sheet on an iron bedstead, lies on her back, as the good nuns taught her in her Irish girlhood, in case she dies during the night, to make less trouble for the undertaker.

She is a good girl, on the whole, although her temper is sometimes uncertain and then she will talk back to the missus, sometimes, and will be forced to confess the sin of impatience to the priest. Overcome by heat and nausea—for everyone in the house is going to wake up sick today—she will return to this little bed later in the morning. While she snatches a few moments rest, upstairs, all hell will be let loose, downstairs.

A rosary of brown glass beads, a cardboard-backed colour print of the Virgin bought from a Portuguese shop, a flyblown photograph of her solemn mother in Donegal—these lie or are propped on the mantelpiece that, however sharp the Massachusetts winter, has never seen a lit stick. A banged tin trunk at the foot of the bed holds all Bridget's worldly goods.

There is a stiff chair beside the bed with, upon it, a candlestick, matches, the alarm clock that resounds the room with a dyadic, metallic clang, for it is a joke between Bridget and her mistress that the girl could sleep through anything, *anything*, and so she needs the alarm as well as all the factory whistles that are just about to blast off, just this very second about to blast off . . .

A splintered deal washstand holds the jug and bowl she never uses; she isn't going to lug water up to the third floor just to wipe herself down, is she? Not when there's water enough in the kitchen sink.

Old Borden sees no necessity for baths. He does not believe in total immersion. To lose his natural oils would be to rob his body.

A frameless square of mirror reflects in corrugated waves a cracked, dusty soap dish containing a quantity of black metal hairpins.

On bright rectangles of paper blinds move the beautiful shadows of the pear trees.

Although Bridget left the door open a crack in forlorn hopes of coaxing a draught into the room, all the spent heat of the previous day has packed itself tightly into her attic. A dandruff of spent whitewash flakes from the ceiling where a fly drearily whines.

The house is thickly redolent of sleep, that sweetish, clinging smell. Still, all still; in all the house nothing moves except the droning fly. Stillness on the staircase. Stillness pressing against the blinds. Stillness, mortal stillness in the room below, where Master and Mistress share the matrimonial bed.

Were the drapes open or the lamp lit, one could better observe the differences between this room and the austerity of the maid's room. Here is a carpet splashed with vigorous flowers, even if the carpet is of the cheap and cheerful variety; there are mauve, ochre and harsh cerise flowers on the wallpaper, even though the wallpaper was old when the Bordens arrived in the house. A dresser with another distorting mirror; no mirror in this house does not take your face and twist it. On the dresser, a runner embroidered with forget-me-nots; on the runner, a bone comb missing three teeth and lightly threaded with grey hairs, a hairbrush backed with ebonised wood, and a number of lace mats underneath small china boxes holding safety-pins, hairnets, etc. The little hairpiece that Mrs. Borden attaches to her balding scalp for daytime wear is curled up like a dead squirrel. But of Borden's male occupation of this room there is no trace because he has a dressing-room of his own, through *that* door, on the left . . .

What about the other door, the one next to it?

It leads to the back stairs.

And that yet other door, partially concealed behind the head of the heavy, mahogany bed?

If it were not kept securely locked, it would take you into Miss Lizzie's room.

One peculiarity of this house is the number of doors the rooms contain and, a further peculiarity, how all these doors are always locked. A house full of locked doors that open only into other rooms with other locked doors, for, upstairs and downstairs, all the rooms lead in and out of one another like a maze in a bad dream. It is a house without passages. There is no part of the house that has not been marked as some inmate's personal territory; it is a house with no shared, no common spaces between one room and the next. It is a house of privacies sealed as close as if they had been sealed with wax on a legal document.

The only way to Emma's room is through Lizzie's. There is no way out of Emma's room. It is a dead end.

The Bordens' custom of locking all the doors, inside and outside, dates from a time, a few years ago, shortly before Bridget came to work for them, when the house was burgled. A person unknown came through the side door while Borden and his wife had taken one of their rare trips out together; he had loaded her into a trap and set out for the farm they owned at Swansea to ensure his tenant was not bilking him. The girls stayed at home in their rooms, napping on their beds or repairing ripped hems or sewing loose buttons more securely or writing letters or contemplating acts of charity among the deserving poor or staring vacantly into space.

I can't imagine what else they might do.

What the girls do when they are on their own is unimaginable to me.

Emma is more mysterous by far than Lizzie, for we know much less about her. She is a blank space. She has no life. The door from her room leads only into the room of her sister.

"Girls" is, of course, a courtesy term. Emma is well into her forties, Lizzie in her thirties, but they did not marry and so live in their father's house, where they remain in a fictive, protracted childhood.

While the master and the mistress were away and the girls asleep or otherwise occupied, some person or persons unknown tiptoed up the back stairs to the matrimonial bedroom and pocketed Mrs. Borden's gold watch and chain, the coral necklace and silver bangle of her remote childhood, and a roll of dollar bills Old Borden kept under clean union suits in the third drawer of the bureau on the left. The intruder attempted to force the lock of the safe, that featureless block of black iron like a slaughtering block or an altar sitting squarely next to the bed on Old Borden's side, but it would have taken a crowbar to penetrate adequately the safe and the intruder tackled it with a pair of nail scissors that were lying handy on the dresser so *that* didn't come off.

Then the intruder pissed and shat on the cover of the Bordens' bed, knocked the clutter of this and that on the dresser to the floor, smashing everything, swept into Old Borden's dressing-room there to maliciously assault his funeral coat as it hung in the moth-balled dark of his closet with the self-same nail scissors that had been used on the safe (the nail scissors now split in two and were abandoned on the closet floor), retired to the kitchen, smashed the flour crock and the treacle crock, and then scrawled an obscenity or two on the parlour window with the cake of soap that lived beside the scullery sink.

What a mess! Lizzie stared with vague surprise at the parlour window; she heard the soft bang of the open screen door, swinging idly, although there was no breeze. What was she doing, standing clad only in her corset in the middle of the sitting-room? How had she got there?

Had she crept down when she heard the screen door rattle? She did not know. She could not remember.

All that happened was: all at once here she is, in the parlour, with a cake of soap in her hand.

She experienced a clearing of the senses and only then began to scream and shout.

"Help! We have been burgled! Help!"

Emma came down and comforted her, as the big sister had comforted the little one since babyhood. Emma it was who cleared from the sitting-room carpet the flour and treacle Lizzie had heedlessly tracked in from the kitchen on her bare feet in her somnambulist trance. But of the missing jewellery and dollar bills no trace could be found.

I cannot tell you what effect the burglary had on Borden. It utterly disconcerted him; he was a man stunned. It violated him, even. He was a man raped. It took away his hitherto unshakeable confidence in the integrity inherent in things.

The burglary so moved them that the family broke its habitual silence with one another in order to discuss it. They blamed it on the Portuguese, obviously, but sometimes on the Canucks. If their outrage remained constant and did not diminish with time, the focus of it varied according to their moods, although they always pointed the finger of suspicion at the strangers and newcomers who lived in the gruesome ramparts of the company housing a few squalid blocks away. They did not always suspect the dark strangers exclusively; sometimes they thought the culprit might very well have been one of the mill-hands fresh from saucy Lancashire across the ocean who committed the crime, for a slum landlord has few friends among the criminal classes.

However, the possibility of a poltergeist occurs to Mrs. Borden, although she does not know the word; she knows, however, that her younger stepdaughter is a strange one and could make the plates jump out of sheer spite, if she wanted to. But the old man adores his daughter. Perhaps it is then, after the shock of the burglary, that he decides she needs a change of scene, a dose of sea air, a long voyage, for it was after the burglary he sent her on the grand tour.

After the burglary, the front door and the side door were always locked three times if one of the inhabitants of the house left it for just so much as to go into the yard and pick up a basket of fallen pears when pears were in season or if the maid went out to hang a bit of washing or Old Borden, after supper, took a piss under a tree.

From this time dated the custom of locking all the bedroom doors on the inside when one was on the inside oneself or on the outside when one was on the outside. Old Borden locked his bedroom door in the morning, when he left it, and put the key in sight of all on the kitchen shelf.

The burglary awakened Old Borden to the evanescent nature of private property. He thereafter undertook an orgy of investment. He would forthwith invest his surplus in good brick and mortar, for who can make away with an office block?

A number of leases fell in simultaneously at just this time on a certain street in the downtown area of the city and Borden snapped them up. He owned the block. He pulled it down. He planned the Borden building, an edifice of shops and offices, dark red brick, deep tan stone, with cast-iron detail, from whence, in perpetuity, he might reap a fine harvest of unsaleable rents, and this monument, like that of Ozymandias, would long survive him—and, indeed, stands still, foursquare and handsome, the Andrew Borden Building, on South Main Street.

Not bad for a fish peddler's son, eh?

For, although "Borden" is an ancient name in New England and the Borden clan between them owned the better part of Fall River, our Borden, Old Borden, these Bordens, did not spring from a wealthy branch of the family. There were Bordens and Bordens and he was the son of a man who sold fresh fish in a wicker basket from house to house to house. Old Borden's parsimony was bred of poverty but learned to thrive best on prosperity, for thrift has a different meaning for the poor; they get no joy of it, it is stark necessity to them. Whoever heard of a penniless miser?

Morose and gaunt, this self-made man is one of few pleasures. His vocation is capital accumulation.

What is his hobby?

Why, grinding the faces of the poor.

First, Andrew Borden was an undertaker, and death, recognising an accomplice, did well by him. In the city of spindles, few made old bones; the little children who laboured in the mills died with especial frequency. When he was an undertaker, no!—it was not true he cut the feet off corpses to fit into a job lot of coffins bought cheap as Civil War surplus! That was a rumour put about by his enemies!

With the profits from his coffins, he bought up a tenement or two and made fresh profit off the living. He bought shares in the mills. Then he invested in a bank or two, so that now he makes a profit on money itself, which is the purest form of profit of all.

Foreclosures and evictions are meat and drink to him. He loves nothing better than a little usury. He is halfway on the road to his first million.

At night, to save the kerosene, he sits in lampless dark. He waters the pear trees with his urine; waste not, want not. As soon as the daily newspapers are done with, he rips them up in geometric squares and stores them in the cellar privy so that they all can wipe their arses with them. He mourns the loss of the good organic waste that flushes down the WC. He would like to charge the very cockroaches in the kitchen rent. And yet he has not grown fat on all this; the pure flame of his passion has melted off his flesh, his skin sticks to his bones out of sheer parsimony. Perhaps it is from his first profession that he has acquired his bearing, for he walks with the stately dignity of a hearse.

To watch Old Borden bearing down the street towards you was to be filled with an instinctual respect for mortality, whose gaunt ambassador he seemed to be. And it made you think, too, what a triumph over nature it was when we rose up to walk on two legs instead of four, in the first place! For he held himself upright with such ponderous assertion it was a perpetual reminder to all who witnessed his progress how it is not *natural* to be upright, that it is a triumph of will over gravity, in itself a transcendence of the spirit over matter.

His spine is like an iron rod, forged, not born, impossible to imagine that spine of Old Borden's curled up in the womb in the big C of the foetus; he walks as if his legs had joints at neither knee nor ankle so that his feet hit the trembling earth like a bailiff pounding a door.

He has a white, chin-strap beard, old-fashioned already in those days. He looks as if he'd gnawed his lips off. He is at peace with his god for he has used his talents as the Good Book says he should.

Yet do not think he has no soft spot. Like Old Lear, his heart—and, more than that, his cheque-book—is putty in his youngest daughter's hands. On his pinky—you cannot see it, it lies under the covers—he wears a gold ring, not a wedding ring but a high-school ring, a singular trinket for a fabulously misanthropic miser. His youngest daughter gave it to him when she left school and asked him to wear it, always, and so he always does, and will wear it to the grave to which she is going to send him later in the morning of this combustible day.

He sleeps fully dressed in a flannel nightshirt over his long-sleeved underwear, and a flannel nightcap, and his back is turned towards his wife of thirty years, as is hers to his.

They are Mr. and Mrs. Jack Spratt in person, he tall and gaunt as a hanging judge and she, such a spreading, round little doughball. He is a miser, while she, she is a glutton, a solitary eater, most innocent of vices and yet the shadow or parodic vice of his, for he would like to eat up all the world, or, failing that, since fate has not spread him a sufficiently large table for his ambitions, he is a mute, inglorious Napoleon, he does not know what he might have done because he never had the opportunity—since he has not access to the entire world, he would like to gobble up the city of Fall River. But she, well, she just gently, continuously stuffs herself, doesn't she; she's always nibbling away at something, at the cud, perhaps.

Not that she gets much pleasure from it, either; no gourmet, she, forever meditating the exquisite difference between a mayonnaise sharpened with a few drops of Orleans vinegar or one pointed up with a squeeze of fresh lemon juice. No. Abby never aspired so high, nor would she ever think to do so even if she had the option; she is satisfied to stick to simple gluttony and she eschews all overtones of the sensuality of indulgence. Since she relishes not one single mouthful of the food she eats, she knows her ceaseless gluttony is no transgression.

Here they lie in bed together, living embodiments of two of the Seven Deadly Sins, but he knows his avarice is no offence because he never spends any money and she knows she is not greedy because the grub she shovels down gives her dyspepsia.

She employs an Irish cook and Bridget's rough-and-ready hand in the kitchen fulfils Abby's every criterion. Bread, meat, cabbage, potatoes—Abby was made for the heavy food that made her. Bridget merrily slaps on the table boiled dinners, boiled fish, cornmeal mush, Indian pudding, johnnycakes, cookies.

But those cookies . . . ah! there you touch on Abby's little weakness. Molasses cookies, oatmeal cookies, raisin cookies. But when she tackles a sticky brownie, oozing chocolate, then she feels a queasy sense of having gone almost too far, that sin might be just around the corner if her stomach did not immediately palpitate like a guilty conscience.

Her flannel nightdress is cut on the same lines as his nightshirt except for the limp flannel frill round the neck. She weighs two hundred pounds. She is five feet nothing tall. The bed sags on her side. It is the bed in which his first wife died.

Last night, they dosed themselves with castor oil, due to the indisposition that kept them both awake and vomiting the whole night before that; the copious results of their purges brim the chamber-pots beneath the bed. It is fit to make a sewer faint.

Back to back they lie. You could rest a sword in the space between the old man and his wife, between the old man's backbone, the only rigid thing he ever offered her, and her soft, warm, enormous bum. Their purges flailed them. Their faces show up decomposing green in the gloom of the curtained room, in which the air is too thick for flies to move.

The youngest daughter dreams behind the locked door.

Look at the sleeping beauty!

She threw back the top sheet and her window is wide open but there is no breeze, outside, this morning, to shiver deliciously the screen. Bright sun floods the blinds so that the linen-coloured light shows us how Lizzie has gone to bed as for a levée in a pretty, ruffled nightdress of starched white muslin with ribbons of pastel pink satin threaded through the eyelets of the lace, for is it not the "naughty Nineties" everywhere but dour Fall River? Don't the gilded steamships of the Fall River Line signify all the squandered luxury of the Gilded Age within their mahogany and chandeliered interiors? But don't they sail *away* from Fall River, to where, elsewhere, it is the Belle Epoque? In New York, Paris, London, champagne corks pop, in Monte Carlo the bank is broken, women fall backwards in a crisp meringue of petticoats for fun and profit, but not in Fall River. Oh, no. So, in the immutable privacy of her bedroom, for her own delight, Lizzie puts on a rich girl's pretty nightdress, although she lives in a mean house, because she is a rich girl, too.

But she is plain.

The hem of her nightdress is rucked up above her knees because she is a restless sleeper. Her light, dry, reddish hair, crackling with static, slipping loose from the night-time plait, crisps and stutters over the square pillow at which she clutches as she sprawls on her stomach, having rested her cheek on the starched pillowcase for coolness' sake at some earlier hour.

Lizzie was not an affectionate diminutive but the name with which she had been christened. Since she would always be known as "Lizzie", so her father reasoned, why burden her with the effete and fancy prolongation of "Elizabeth"? A miser in everything, he even cropped off half her name before he gave it to her. So "Lizzie" it was, stark and unadorned, and she is a motherless child, orphaned at two years old, poor thing.

Now she is two-and-thirty and yet the memory of that mother she cannot remember remains an abiding source of grief: "If mother had lived, everything would have been different."

How? Why? Different in what way? She wouldn't have been able to answer that, lost in a nostalgia for unknown love. Yet how could she have been loved better than by her sister Emma, who lavished the pent-up treasures of a New England spinster's heart upon the little thing? Different, perhaps, because her natural mother, the first Mrs. Borden, subject as she was to fits of sudden, wild, inexplicable rage, might have taken the hatchet to Old Borden on her own account? But Lizzie *loves* her father. All are agreed on that. Lizzie adores the adoring father who, after her mother died, took to himself another wife.

Her bare feet twitch a little, like those of a dog dreaming of rabbits. Her sleep is thin and unsatisfying, full of vague terrors and indeterminate menaces to which she cannot put a name or form once she is awake. Sleep opens within her a disorderly house. But all she knows is, she sleeps badly, and this last, stifling night has been troubled, too, by vague nausea and the gripes of her female pain; her room is harsh with the metallic smell of menstrual blood.

Yesterday evening she slipped out of the house to visit a woman friend. Lizzie was agitated; she kept picking nervously at the shirring on the front of her dress.

"I am afraid . . . that somebody . . . will *do* something," said Lizzie.

"Mrs. Borden . . ." and here Lizzie lowered her voice and her eyes looked everywhere in the room except at Miss Russell . . . "Mrs. Borden—oh! will you ever believe? Mrs. Borden thinks somebody is trying to *poison* us!"

She used to call her stepmother "mother", as duty bade, but, after a quarrel about money after her father deeded half a slum property to her stepmother five years before, Lizzie always, with cool scrupulosity, spoke of "Mrs. Borden" when she was forced to speak of her, and called her "Mrs. Borden" to her face, too.

"Last night, Mrs. Borden and poor father were so sick! I heard them, through the wall. And, as for me, I haven't felt myself all day, I have felt so strange. So very . . . strange."

For there were those somnambulist fits. Since a child, she endured occasional "peculiar spells", as the idiom of the place and time called odd lapses of behaviour, unexpected, involuntary trances, moments of disconnection. Those times when the mind misses a beat. Miss Russell hastened to discover an explanation within reason; she was embarrassed to mention the "peculiar spells". Everyone knew there was nothing odd about the Borden girls.

"Something you ate? It must have been something you have eaten. What was yesterday's supper?" solicitously queried kind Miss Russell.

"Warmed over swordfish. We had it hot for dinner though I could not take much. Then Bridget heated up the leftovers for supper but, again, for myself, I could only get down a forkful. Mrs. Borden ate up the remains and scoured her plate with her bread. She smacked her lips but then was sick all night." (Note of smugness, here.)

"Oh, Lizzie! In all this heat, this dreadful heat! Twice-cooked fish! You know how quickly fish goes off in this heat! Bridget should have known better than to give you twice-cooked fish!"

It was Lizzie's difficult time of the month, too; her friend could tell by a certain haggard, glazed look on Lizzie's face. Yet her gentility forbade her to mention that. But how could Lizzie have got it into her head that the entire household was under siege from malign forces without?

"There have been threats," Lizzie pursued remorselessly, keeping her eyes on her nervous fingertips. "So many people, you understand, dislike father."

This cannot be denied. Miss Russell politely remained mute.

"Mrs. Borden was so very sick she called the doctor in and Father was abusive towards the doctor and shouted at him and told him he would not pay a doctor's bills whilst we had our own good castor oil in the house. He shouted at the doctor and all the neighbours heard and I was so ashamed. There is a man, you see . . ." and here she ducked her head, while her short, pale eyelashes beat on her cheek bones . . . "such a man, a *dark* man, with the aspect, yes, of death upon his face, Miss Russell, a dark man I've seen outside the house at odd, at unexpected hours, early in the morning, late at night, whenever I cannot sleep in this dreadful shade if I raise the blind and peep out, there I see him in the shadows of the pear trees, in the yard, a dark man . . . perhaps he puts poison in the milk, in the mornings, after the milkman fills his can. Perhaps he poisons the ice, when the iceman comes."

"How long has he been haunting you?" asked Miss Russell, properly dismayed.

"Since . . . the burglary," said Lizzie and suddenly looked Miss Russell full in the face with a kind of triumph. How large her eyes were; prominent, yet veiled. And her well-manicured fingers went on pecking away at the front of her dress as if she were trying to unpick the shirring.

Miss Russell knew, she just *knew*, this dark man was a figment of Lizzie's imagination. All in a rush, she lost patience with the girl; dark men standing outside her bedroom window, indeed! Yet she was kind and cast about for ways to reassure.

"But Bridget is up and about when the milkman, the iceman call and the whole street is busy and bustling, too; who would dare to put poison in either milk or ice-bucket while half of Second Street looks on? Oh, Lizzie, it is the dreadful summer, the heat, the intolerable heat that's put us all out of sorts, makes us fractious and nervous, makes us sick. So easy to imagine things in this terrible weather, that taints the food and sows worms in the mind . . . I thought you'd planned to go away, Lizzie, to the ocean. Didn't you plan to take a little holiday, by the sea? Oh, do go! Sea air would blow away these silly fancies!"

Lizzie neither nods nor shakes her head but continues to worry at her shirring. For does she not have important business in Fall River? Only that morning, had she not been down to the drug-store to try to buy some prussic acid herself? But how can she tell kind Miss Russell she is gripped by an imperious need to stay in Fall River and murder her parents?

She went to the drug-store on the corner of Main Street in order to buy prussic acid but nobody would sell it to her, so she came home empty-handed. Had all that talk of poison in the vomiting house put her in mind of poison? The autopsy will reveal no trace of poison in the stomachs of either parent. She did not try to poison them; she only had it in mind to poison them. But she had been unable to buy poison. The use of poison had been denied her; so what can she be planning, now?

"And this dark man," she pursued to the unwilling Miss Russell, "oh! I have seen the moon glint upon an *axe!*"

When she wakes up, she can never remember her dreams; she only remembers she slept badly.

Hers is a pleasant room of not ungenerous dimensions, seeing the house is so very small. Besides the bed and the dresser, there is a sofa and a desk; it is her bedroom and also her sitting-room and her office, too, for the desk is stacked with account books of the various charitable organisations with which she occupies her ample spare time. The Fruit and Flower Mission, under whose auspices she visits the indigent old in hospital with gifts; the Women's Christian Temperance Union, for whom she extracts signatures for petitions against the Demon Drink; Christian Endeavour, whatever that is—this is the golden age of good works and she flings herself into committees with a vengeance. What would the daughters of the rich do with themselves if the poor ceased to exist?

There is the Newsboys Thanksgiving Dinner Fund; and the Horsetrough Association; and the Chinese Conversion Association—no class nor kind is safe from her merciless charity.

Bureau; dressing-table; closet; bed; sofa. She spends her days in this room, moving between each of these dull items of furniture in a circumscribed, undeviating, planetary round. She loves her privacy, she loves her room, she locks herself up in it all day. A shelf contains a book or two: *Heroes of the Mission Field*, *The Romance of Trade*, *What Katy did*. On the walls, framed photographs of high-school friends, sentimentally inscribed, with, tucked inside one frame, a picture postcard showing a black kitten peeking through a horseshoe. A water-colour of a Cape Cod seascape executed with poignant amateur incompetence. A monochrome photograph or two of works of art, A Della Robbia madonna and the Mona Lisa; these she bought in the Uffizi and the Louvre respectively when she went to Europe.

Europe!

For don't you remember what Katy did next? The story-book heroine took the steamship to smoky old London, to elegant, fascinating Paris, to sunny, antique Rome and Florence, the story-book heroine sees Europe reveal itself before her like an interesting series of magic-lantern slides on a gigantic screen. All is present and all unreal. The Tower of London; click. Notre Dame; click. The Sistine Chapel; click. Then the lights go out and she is in the dark again.

Of this journey she retained only the most circumspect of souvenirs, that madonna, that Mona Lisa, reproductions of objects of art consecrated by a universal approval of taste. If she came back with a bag full of memories stamped "Never to be Forgotten", she put the bag away under the bed on which she had dreamed of the world before she set out to see it and on which, at home again, she continued to dream, the dream having been transformed not into lived experience but into memory, which is only another kind of dreaming.

Wistfully: "When I was in Florence . . ."

But then, with pleasure, she corrects herself: "When *we* were in Florence . . ."

Because a good deal, in fact most, of the gratification the trip gave her came from having set out from Fall River with a select group of the daughters of respectable and affluent mill-owners. Once away from Second Street, she was able to move comfortably in the segment of Fall River society to which she belonged by right of old name and new money but from which, when she was at home, her father's plentiful personal eccentricities excluded her. Sharing bedrooms, sharing state-rooms, sharing berths, the girls travelled together in a genteel gaggle that bore its doom already upon it, for they were the girls who would not marry, now, and any pleasure they might have obtained from the variety and excitement of the trip was spoiled in advance by the knowledge they were eating up what might have been their own wedding-cake, using up what should have been, if they'd had any luck, their marriage settlements.

All girls pushing thirty, privileged to go out and look at the world before they resigned themselves to the thin condition of New England spinsterhood; but it was a case of look, don't touch. They knew they must not get their hands dirtied or their dresses crushed by the world,

while their affectionate companionship en route had a certain stead-
fast, determined quality about it as they bravely made the best of the
second-best.

It was a sour trip, in some ways, sour; and it was a round trip, it
ended at the sour place from where it had set out. Home, again; the
narrow house, the rooms all locked like those in Bluebeard's castle,
and the fat, white stepmother whom nobody loves sitting in the middle of the spider web, she has not budged a single inch while Lizzie was
away but she has grown fatter.

This stepmother oppressed her like a spell.

The days open their cramped spaces into other cramped spaces
and old furniture and never anything to look forward to, nothing.

When Old Borden dug in his pocket to shell out for Lizzie's trip to
Europe, the eye of God on the pyramid blinked to see daylight, but no
extravagance is too excessive for the miser's younger daughter who is the
wild card in this house and, it seems, can have anything she wants, play
ducks and drakes with her father's silver dollars if it so pleases her. He
pays all her dressmakers' bills on the dot and how she loves to dress up
fine! She is addicted to dandyism. He gives her each week in pin-money
the same as the cook gets for wages and Lizzie gives that which she does
not spend on personal adornment to the deserving poor.

He would give his Lizzie anything, anything in the world that lives
under the green sign of the dollar.

She would like a pet, a kitten or a puppy, she loves small animals
and birds, too, poor, helpless things. She piles high the bird-table all
winter. She used to keep some white pouter pigeons in the disused stable, the kind that look like shuttlecocks and go "vroo croo", soft as a
cloud.

Surviving photographs of Lizzie Borden show a face it is difficult
to look at as if you knew nothing about her; coming events cast their
shadow across her face, or else you see the shadows these events have
cast—something terrible, something ominous in this face with its jut-
ting, rectangular jaw and those mad eyes of the New England saints,
eyes that belong to a person who does not listen to you . . . fanatic's
eyes, you might say, if you knew nothing about her. If you were sorting
through a box of old photographs in a junk shop and came across this
particular, sepia, faded face above the choked collars of the 1890s, you
might murmur when you saw her: "Oh, what big eyes you have!" as
Red Riding Hood said to the wolf, but then you might not even pause
to pick her out and look at her more closely, for hers is not, in itself, a
striking face.

But as soon as the face has a name, once you recognise her, when you know who she is and what it was she did, the face becomes as if of one possessed, and now it haunts you, you look at it again and again, it secretes mystery.

This woman, with her jaw of a concentration-camp attendant, and such eyes . . .

In her old age, she wore pince-nez, and truly with the years the mad light has departed from those eyes or else is deflected by her glasses—if, indeed, it *was* a mad light, in the first place, for don't we all conceal somewhere photographs of ourselves that make us look like crazed assassins? And, in those early photographs of her young womanhood, she herself does not look so much like a crazed assassin as somebody in extreme solitude, oblivious of that camera in whose direction she obscurely smiles, so that it would not surprise you to learn that she is blind.

There is a mirror on the dresser in which she sometimes looks at those times when time snaps in two and then she sees herself with blind, clairvoyant eyes, as though she were another person.

"Lizzie is not herself, today."

At those times, those irremediable times, she could have raised her muzzle to some aching moon and howled.

At other times, she watches herself doing her hair and trying her clothes on. The distorting mirror reflects her with the queasy fidelity of water. She puts on dresses and then she takes them off. She looks at herself in her corset. She pats her hair. She measures herself with the tape-measure. She pulls the measure tight. She pats her hair. She tries on a hat, a little hat, a chic little straw toque. She punctures it with a hatpin. She pulls the veil down. She pulls it up. She takes the hat off. She drives the hatpin into it with a strength she did not know she possessed.

Time goes by and nothing happens.

She traces the outlines of her face with an uncertain hand as if she were thinking of unfastening the bandages on her soul but it isn't time to do that, yet: she isn't ready to be seen, yet.

She is a girl of Sargossa calm.

She used to keep her pigeons in the loft above the disused stable and feed them grain out of the palms of her cupped hands. She liked to feel the soft scratch of their beaks. They murmured "vroo croo" with infinite tenderness. She changed their water every day and cleaned up their leprous messes but Old Borden took a dislike to their cooing, it got on his nerves, who'd have thought he *had* any nerves but he invented some, they got on them, one afternoon he took out the hatchet from the woodpile in the cellar and chopped those pigeons' heads right off, he did.

Abby fancied the slaughtered pigeons for a pie but Bridget the servant girl put her foot down, at that: what?!? Make a pie out of Miss Lizzie's beloved turtledoves? JesusMaryandJoseph!!! she exclaimed with characteristic impetuousness, what can they be thinking of! Miss Lizzie so nervy with her funny turns and all! (The maid is the only one in the house with any sense and that's the truth of it.) Lizzie came home from the Fruit and Flower Mission for whom she had been reading a tract to an old woman in a poorhouse: "God bless you, Miss Lizzie." At home all was blood and feathers.

She doesn't weep, this one, it isn't her nature, she is still waters, but, when moved, she changes colour, her face flushes, it goes dark, angry, mottled red. The old man loves his daughter this side of idolatry and pays for everything she wants, but all the same he killed her pigeons when his wife wanted to gobble them up.

That is how she sees it. That is how she understands it. She cannot bear to watch her stepmother eat, now. Each bite the woman takes seems to go: "Vroo croo."

Old Borden cleaned off the hatchet and put it back in the cellar, next to the woodpile. The red receding from her face, Lizzie went down to inspect the instrument of destruction. She picked it up and weighed it in her hand.

That was a few weeks before, at the beginning of the spring.

Her hands and feet twitch in her sleep; the nerves and muscles of this complicated mechanism won't relax, just won't relax, she is all twang, all tension, she is taut as the strings of a wind-harp from which random currents of the air pluck out tunes that are not our tunes.

At the first stroke of the City Hall clock, the first factory hooter blares, and then, on another note, another, and another, the Metacomet Mill, the American Mill, the Mechanics Mill . . . until every mill in the entire town sings out aloud in a common anthem of summoning and the hot alleys where the factory folk live blacken with the hurrying throng: hurry! scurry! to loom, to bobbin, to spindle, to dye-shop as to places of worship, men, and women, too, and children, the streets blacken, the sky darkens as the chimneys now belch forth, the clang, bang, clatter of the mills commences.

Bridget's clock leaps and shudders on its chair, about to sound its own alarm. Their day, the Bordens' fatal day, trembles on the brink of beginning.

Outside, above, in the already burning air, see! the angel of death roosts on the roof-tree.

Octavia E. Butler

Octavia E. Butler's ten published novels include Patternmaster, Mind of My Mind, Wild Seed, Adulthood Rites, *and* Parable of Sorrow. *She has won a Hugo Award (twice) as well as a Nebula Award, science fiction's highest commendations. In 1995 she was awarded a MacArthur fellowship. Butler regards herself as "a pessimist if I'm not careful, a feminist always, a Black, a quiet egoist, a former Baptist, and an oil-and-water combination of ambition, laziness, insecurity, certainty, and drive." She lives in Los Angeles.*

In the world of "Bloodchild" there are two intelligent species, humans and giant wormlike beings who are the dominant, politically and socially powerful species, who use the humans to reproduce. The story traces the relationship between one worm and her human consort. A skilled storyteller, Butler uses the conventions of science fiction and the surreal in "Bloodchild" to rearrange the held categories of race, class, and gender. She does this by imagining two species in a biological relationship that stands for the social relationships between slave and master, man and woman. The creation of this fantastic world allows us to think allegorically about relationships in our own world; it allows us the distance to confront the legacies of pain, the consequences of power, and to begin to understand the inequities in our complex constructions of race, gender, class, and family.

Bloodchild

My last night of childhood began with a visit home. T'Gatoi's sister had given us two sterile eggs. T'Gatoi gave one to my mother, brother, and sisters. She insisted that I eat the other one alone. It didn't matter. There was still enough to leave everyone feeling good. Almost everyone. My mother wouldn't take any. She sat, watching everyone drifting and dreaming without her. Most of the time she watched me.

I lay against T'Gatoi's long, velvet underside, sipping from my egg now and then, wondering why my mother denied herself such a harmless pleasure. Less of her hair would be gray if she indulged now and then. The eggs prolonged life, prolonged vigor. My father, who had never refused one in his life, had lived more than twice as long as he should have. And toward the end of his life, when he should have been slowing down, he had married my mother and fathered four children.

But my mother seemed content to age before she had to. I saw her turn away as several of T'Gatoi's limbs secured me closer. T'Gatoi liked our body heat and took advantage of it whenever she could. When I was little and at home more, my mother used to try to tell me how to behave with T'Gatoi—how to be respectful and always obedient because T'Gatoi was the Tlic government official in charge of the Preserve, and thus the most important of her kind to deal directly with Terrans. It was an honor, my mother said, that such a person had chosen to come into the family. My mother was at her most formal and severe when she was lying.

I had no idea why she was lying, or even what she was lying about. It *was* an honor to have T'Gatoi in the family, but it was hardly a novelty. T'Gatoi and my mother had been friends all my mother's life, and T'Gatoi was not interested in being honored in the house she considered her second home. She simply came in, climbed onto one of her special couches, and called me over to keep her warm. It was impossible to be formal with her while lying against her and hearing her complain as usual that I was too skinny.

"You're better," she said this time, probing me with six or seven of her limbs. "You're gaining weight finally. Thinness is dangerous." The probing changed subtly, became a series of caresses.

"He's still too thin," my mother said sharply.

T'Gatoi lifted her head and perhaps a meter of her body off the couch as though she were sitting up. She looked at my mother, and my mother, her face lined and old looking, turned away.

"Lien, I would like you to have what's left of Gan's egg."

"The eggs are for the children," my mother said.

"They are for the family. Please take it."

Unwillingly obedient, my mother took it from me and put it to her mouth. There were only a few drops left in the now-shrunken, elastic shell, but she squeezed them out, swallowed them, and after a few moments some of the lines of tension began to smooth from her face.

"It's good," she whispered. "Sometimes I forget how good it is."

"You should take more," T'Gatoi said. "Why are you in such a hurry to be old?"

My mother said nothing.

"I like being able to come here," T'Gatoi said. "This place is a refuge because of you, yet you won't take care of yourself."

T'Gatoi was hounded on the outside. Her people wanted more of us made available. Only she and her political faction stood between us and the hordes who did not understand why there was a Preserve—why any Terran could not be courted, paid, drafted, in some way made available to them. Or they did understand, but in their desperation, they did not care. She parceled us out to the desperate and sold us to the rich and powerful for their political support. Thus, we were necessities, status symbols, and an independent people. She oversaw the joining of families, putting an end to the final remnants of the earlier system of breaking up Terran families to suit impatient Tlic. I had lived outside with her. I had seen the desperate eagerness in the way some people looked at me. It was a little frightening to know that only she stood between us and that desperation that could so easily swallow us. My mother would look at her sometimes and say to me, "Take care of her." And I would remember that she too had been outside, had seen.

Now T'Gatoi used four of her limbs to push me away from her onto the floor. "Go on, Gan," she said. "Sit down there with your sisters and enjoy not being sober. You had most of the egg. Lien, come warm me."

My mother hesitated for no reason that I could see. One of my earliest memories is of my mother stretched alongside T'Gatoi, talking about things I could not understand, picking me up from the floor and laughing as she sat me on one of T'Gatoi's segments. She ate her share of eggs then. I wondered when she had stopped, and why.

She lay down now against T'Gatoi, and the whole left row of T'Gatoi's limbs closed around her, holding her loosely, but securely. I had always found it comfortable to lie that way, but except for my older sister, no one else in the family liked it. They said it made them feel caged.

T'Gatoi meant to cage my mother. Once she had, she moved her tail slightly, then spoke. "Not enough egg, Lien. You should have taken it when it was passed to you. You need it badly now."

T'Gatoi's tail moved once more, its whip motion so swift I wouldn't have seen it if I hadn't been watching for it. Her sting drew only a single drop of blood from my mother's bare leg.

My mother cried out—probably in surprise. Being stung doesn't hurt. Then she sighed and I could see her body relax. She moved languidly into a more comfortable position within the cage of T'Gatoi's limbs. "Why did you do that?" she asked, sounding half asleep.

"I could not watch you sitting and suffering any longer."

My mother managed to move her shoulders in a small shrug. "Tomorrow," she said.

"Yes. Tomorrow you will resume your suffering—if you must. But just now, just for now, lie here and warm me and let me ease your way a little."

"He's still mine, you know," my mother said suddenly.

"Nothing can buy him from me." Sober, she would not have permitted herself to refer to such things.

"Nothing," T'Gatoi agreed, humoring her.

"Did you think I would sell him for eggs? For long life? My son?"

"Not for anything," T'Gatoi said, stroking my mother's shoulders, toying with her long, graying hair.

I would like to have touched my mother, shared that moment with her. She would take my hand if I touched her now. Freed by the egg and the sting, she would smile and perhaps say things long held in. But tomorrow, she would remember all this as a humiliation. I did not want to be part of a remembered humiliation. Best just be still and know she loved me under all the duty and pride and pain.

"Xuan Hoa, take off her shoes," T'Gatoi said. "In a little while I'll sting her again and she can sleep."

My older sister obeyed, swaying drunkenly as she stood up. When she had finished, she sat down beside me and took my hand. We had always been a unit, she and I.

My mother put the back of her head against T'Gatoi's underside and tried from that impossible angle to look up into the broad, round face. "You're going to sting me again?"

"Yes, Lien."

"I'll sleep until tomorrow noon."

"Good. You need it. When did you sleep last?"

My mother made a wordless sound of annoyance. "I should have stepped on you when you were small enough," she muttered.

It was an old joke between them. They had grown up together, sort of, though T'Gatoi had not, in my mother's lifetime, been small enough for any Terran to step on. She was nearly three times my mother's present age, yet would still be young when my mother died of age. But T'Gatoi and my mother had met as T'Gatoi was coming into a period of rapid development—a kind of Tlic adolescence. My mother was only a child, but for a while they developed at the same rate and had no better friends than each other.

T'Gatoi had even introduced my mother to the man who became my father. My parents, pleased with each other in spite of their different ages, married as T'Gatoi was going into her family's business—politics. She and my mother saw each other less. But sometime before my older sister was born, my mother promised T'Gatoi one of her children. She would have to give one of us to someone, and she preferred T'Gatoi to some stranger.

Years passed. T'Gatoi traveled and increased her influence. The Preserve was hers by the time she came back to my mother to collect what she probably saw as her just reward for her hard work. My older sister took an instant liking to her and wanted to be chosen, but my mother was just coming to term with me and T'Gatoi liked the idea of choosing an infant and watching and taking part in all the phases of development. I'm told I was first caged within T'Gatoi's many limbs only three minutes after my birth. A few days later, I was given my first taste of egg. I tell Terrans that when they ask whether I was ever afraid of her. And I tell it to Tlic when T'Gatoi suggests a young Terran child for them and they, anxious and ignorant, demand an adolescent. Even my brother who had somehow grown up to fear and distrust the Tlic could probably have gone smoothly into one of their families if he had been adopted early enough. Sometimes, I think for his sake he should have been. I looked at him, stretched out on the floor across the room, his eyes open, but glazed as he dreamed his egg dream. No matter what he felt toward the Tlic, he always demanded his share of egg.

"Lien, can you stand up?" T'Gatoi asked suddenly.

"Stand?" my mother said. "I thought I was going to sleep."

"Later. Something sounds wrong outside." The cage was abruptly gone.

"What?"

"Up, Lien!"

My mother recognized her tone and got up just in time to avoid being dumped on the floor. T'Gatoi whipped her three meters of body off her couch, toward the door, and out at full speed. She had bones—ribs, a long spine, a skull, four sets of limb bones per segment. But when she moved that way, twisting, hurling herself into controlled falls, landing running, she seemed not only boneless, but aquatic—something swimming through the air as though it were water. I loved watching her move.

I left my sister and started to follow her out the door, though I wasn't very steady on my own feet. It would have been better to sit and dream, better yet to find a girl and share a waking dream with her. Back when the Tlic saw us as not much more than convenient, big, warm-blooded animals, they would pen several of us together, male and female, and feed us only eggs. That way they could be sure of getting another generation of us no matter how we tried to hold out. We were lucky that didn't go on long. A few generations of it and we would have *been* little more than convenient, big animals.

"Hold the door open, Gan," T'Gatoi said. "And tell the family to stay back."

"What is it?" I asked.

"N'Tlic."

I shrank back against the door. "Here? Alone?"

"He was trying to reach a call box, I suppose." She carried the man past me, unconscious, folded like a coat over some of her limbs. He looked young—my brother's age perhaps—and he was thinner than he should have been. What T'Gatoi would have called dangerously thin.

"Gan, go to the call box," she said. She put the man on the floor and began stripping off his clothing.

I did not move.

After a moment, she looked up at me, her sudden stillness a sign of deep impatience.

"Send Qui," I told her. "I'll stay here. Maybe I can help."

She let her limbs begin to move again, lifting the man and pulling his shirt over his head. "You don't want to see this," she said. "It will be hard. I can't help this man the way his Tlic could."

"I know. But send Qui. He won't want to be of any help here. I'm at least willing to try."

She looked at my brother—older, bigger, stronger, certainly more able to help her here. He was sitting up now, braced against the wall, staring at the man on the floor with undisguised fear and revulsion. Even she could see that he would be useless.

"Qui, go!" she said.

He didn't argue. He stood up, swayed briefly, then steadied, frightened sober.

"This man's name is Bram Lomas," she told him, reading from the man's armband. I fingered my own armband in sympathy. "He needs T'Khotgif Teh. Do you hear?"

"Bram Lomas, T'Khotgif Teh," my brother said. "I'm going." He edged around Lomas and ran out the door.

Lomas began to regain consciousness. He only moaned at first and clutched spasmodically at a pair of T'Gatoi's limbs. My younger sister, finally awake from her egg dream, came close to look at him, until my mother pulled her back.

T'Gatoi removed the man's shoes, then his pants, all the while leaving him two of her limbs to grip. Except for the final few, all her limbs were equally dexterous. "I want no argument from you this time, Gan," she said.

I straightened. "What shall I do?"

"Go out and slaughter an animal that is at least half your size."

"Slaughter? But I've never—"

She knocked me across the room. Her tail was an efficient weapon whether she exposed the sting or not.

I got up, feeling stupid for having ignored her warning, and went into the kitchen. Maybe I could kill something with a knife or an ax. My mother raised a few Terran animals for the table and several thousand local ones for their fur. T'Gatoi would probably prefer something local. An achti, perhaps. Some of those were the right size, though they had about three times as many teeth as I did and a real love of using them. My mother, Hoa, and Qui could kill them with knives. I had never killed one at all, had never slaughtered any animal. I had spent most of my time with T'Gatoi while my brother and sisters were learning the family business. T'Gatoi had been right. I should have been the one to go to the call box. At least I could do that.

I went to the corner cabinet where my mother kept her large house and garden tools. At the back of the cabinet there was a pipe that carried off waste water from the kitchen—except that it didn't anymore. My father had rerouted the waste water below before I was born. Now the pipe could be turned so that one half slid around the other and a rifle could be stored inside. This wasn't our only gun, but it was our most easily accessible one. I would have to use it to shoot one of the biggest of the achti. Then T'Gatoi would probably confiscate it. Firearms were illegal in the Preserve. There had been incidents right after the Preserve was established—Terrans shooting Tlic, shooting N'Tlic. This was before the joining of families began, before everyone had a personal stake in keeping the peace. No one had shot a Tlic in my lifetime or my mother's, but the law still stood—for our protection, we were told. There were stories of whole Terran families wiped out in reprisal back during the assassinations.

I went out to the cages and shot the biggest achti I could find. It was a handsome breeding male, and my mother would not be pleased to see me bring it in. But it was the right size, and I was in a hurry.

I put the achti's long, warm body over my shoulder—glad that some of the weight I'd gained was muscle—and took it to the kitchen. There, I put the gun back in its hiding place. If T'Gatoi noticed the achti's wounds and demanded the gun, I would give it to her. Otherwise, let it stay where my father wanted it.

I turned to take the achti to her, then hesitated. For several seconds, I stood in front of the closed door wondering why I was suddenly afraid. I knew what was going to happen. I hadn't seen it before but T'Gatoi had shown me diagrams and drawings. She had made sure I knew the truth as soon as I was old enough to understand it.

Yet I did not want to go into that room. I wasted a little time choosing a knife from the carved, wooden box in which my mother kept them. T'Gatoi might want one, I told myself, for the tough, heavily furred hide of the achti.

"Gan!" T'Gatoi called, her voice harsh with urgency.

I swallowed. I had not imagined a single moving of the feet could be so difficult. I realized I was trembling and that shamed me. Shame impelled me through the door.

I put the achti down near T'Gatoi and saw that Lomas was unconscious again. She, Lomas, and I were alone in the room—my mother and sisters probably sent out so they would not have to watch. I envied them.

But my mother came back into the room as T'Gatoi seized the achti. Ignoring the knife I offered her, she extended claws from several of her limbs and slit the achti from throat to anus. She looked at me, her yellow eyes intent. "Hold this man's shoulders, Gan."

I stared at Lomas in panic, realizing that I did not want to touch him, let alone hold him. This would not be like shooting an animal. Not as quick, not as merciful, and, I hoped, not as final, but there was nothing I wanted less than to be part of it.

My mother came forward. "Gan, you hold his right side," she said. "I'll hold his left." And if he came to, he would throw her off without realizing he had done it. She was a tiny woman. She often wondered aloud how she had produced, as she said, such "huge" children.

"Never mind," I told her, taking the man's shoulders. "I'll do it." She hovered nearby.

"Don't worry," I said. "I won't shame you. You don't have to stay and watch."

She looked at me uncertainly, then touched my face in a rare caress. Finally, she went back to her bedroom.

T'Gatoi lowered her head in relief. "Thank you, Gan," she said with courtesy more Terran than Tlic. "That one . . . she is always finding new ways for me to make her suffer."

Lomas began to groan and make choked sounds. I had hoped he would stay unconscious. T'Gatoi put her face near him so that he focused on her.

"I've stung you as much as I dare for now," she told him. "When this is over, I'll sting you to sleep and you won't hurt anymore."

"Please," the man begged. "Wait . . . "

"There's no more time, Bram. I'll sting you as soon as it's over. When T'Khotgif arrives she'll give you eggs to help you heal. It will be over soon."

"T'Khotgif!" the man shouted, straining against my hands.

"Soon, Bram." T'Gatoi glanced at me, then placed a claw against his abdomen slightly to the right of the middle, just below the left rib. There was movement on the right side—tiny, seemingly random pulsations moving his brown flesh, creating a concavity here, a convexity there, over and over until I could see the rhythm of it and knew where the next pulse would be.

Lomas's entire body stiffened under T'Gatoi's claw, though she merely rested it against him as she wound the rear section of her body around his legs. He might break my grip, but he would not break hers. He wept helplessly as she used his pants to tie his hands, then pushed his hands above his head so that I could kneel on the cloth between them and pin them in place. She rolled up his shirt and gave it to him to bite down on.

And she opened him.

His body convulsed with the first cut. He almost tore himself away from me. The sound he made . . . I had never heard such sounds come from anything human. T'Gatoi seemed to pay no attention as she lengthened and deepened the cut, now and then pausing to lick away blood. His blood vessels contracted, reacting to the chemistry of her saliva, and the bleeding slowed.

I felt as though I were helping her torture him, helping her consume him. I knew I would vomit soon, didn't know why I hadn't already. I couldn't possibly last until she was finished.

She found the first grub. It was fat and deep red with his blood—both inside and out. It had already eaten its own egg case but apparently had not yet begun to eat its host. At this stage, it would eat any flesh except its mother's. Let alone, it would have gone on excreting the poisons that had both sickened and alerted Lomas. Eventually it would have begun to eat. By the time it ate its way out of Lomas's flesh, Lomas would be dead or dying—and unable to take revenge on the thing that was killing him. There was always a grace period between the time the host sickened and the time the grubs began to eat him.

T'Gatoi picked up the writhing grub carefully and looked at it, somehow ignoring the terrible groans of the man.

Abruptly, the man lost consciousness.

"Good," T'Gatoi looked down at him. "I wish you Terrans could do that at will." She felt nothing. And the thing she held . . .

It was limbless and boneless at this stage, perhaps fifteen centimeters long and two thick, blind and slimy with blood. It was like a large worm. T'Gatoi put it into the belly of the achti, and it began at once to burrow. It would stay there and eat as long as there was anything to eat.

Probing through Lomas's flesh, she found two more, one of them smaller and more vigorous. "A male!" she said happily. He would be dead before I would. He would be through his metamorphosis and screwing everything that would hold still before his sisters even had limbs. He was the only one to make a serious effort to bite T'Gatoi as she placed him in the achti.

Paler worms oozed to visibility in Lomas's flesh. I closed my eyes. It was worse than finding something dead, rotting, and filled with tiny animal grubs. And it was far worse than any drawing or diagram.

"Ah, there are more," T'Gatoi said, plucking out two long, thick grubs. You have to kill another animal, Gan. Everything lives inside you Terrans."

I had been told all my life that this was a good and necessary thing Tlic and Terran did together—a kind of birth. I had believed it until now. I knew birth was painful and bloody, no matter what. but this was something else, something worse. And I wasn't ready to see it. Maybe I never would be. Yet I couldn't not see it. Closing my eyes didn't help.

T'Gatoi found a grub still eating its egg case. The remains of the case were still wired into a blood vessel by their own little tube or hook or whatever. That was the way the grubs were anchored and the way they fed. They took only blood until they were ready to emerge. Then they ate their stretched, elastic egg cases. Then they ate their hosts.

T'Gatoi bit away the egg case, licked away the blood. Did she like the taste? Did childhood habits die hard—or not die at all?

The whole procedure was wrong, alien. I wouldn't have thought anything about her could seem alien to me.

"One more, I think," she said. "Perhaps two. A good family. In a host animal these days, we would be happy to find one or two alive." She glanced at me. "Go outside, Gan, and empty your stomach. Go now while the man is unconscious."

I staggered out, barely made it. Beneath the tree just beyond the front door, I vomited until there was nothing left to bring up. Finally, I stood shaking, tears streaming down my face. I did not know why I was crying, but I could not stop. I went further from the house to avoid being seen. Every time I closed my eyes I saw red worms crawling over redder human flesh.

There was a car coming toward the house. Since Terrans were forbidden motorized vehicles except for certain farm equipment, I knew this must be Lomas's Tlic with Qui and perhaps a Terran doctor. I wiped my face on my shirt, struggled for control.

"Gan," Qui called as the car stopped. "What happened?" He crawled out of the low, round, Tlic-convenient car door. Another Terran crawled out the other side and went into the house without speaking to me. The doctor. With his help and a few eggs, Lomas might make it.

"T'Khotgif Teh?" I said.

The Tlic driver surged out of her car, reared up half her length before me. She was paler and smaller than T'Gatoi—probably born from the body of an animal. Tlic from Terran bodies were always larger as well as more numerous.

"Six young," I told her. "Maybe seven, all alive. At least one male."

"Lomas?" she said harshly. I liked her for the question and the concern in her voice when she asked it. The last coherent thing he had said was her name.

"He's alive," I said.

She surged away to the house without another word.

"She's been sick," my brother said, watching her go. "When I called, I could hear people telling her she wasn't well enough to go out even for this."

I said nothing. I had extended courtesy to the Tlic. Now I didn't want to talk to anyone. I hoped he would go in—out of curiosity if nothing else.

"Finally found out more than you wanted to know, eh?"

I looked at him.

"Don't give me one of *her* looks," he said. "You're not her. You're just her property."

One of her looks. Had I picked up even an ability to imitate her expressions?

"What'd you do, puke?" He sniffed the air. "So now you know what you're in for."

I walked away from him. He and I had been close when we were kids. He would let me follow him around when I was home, and sometimes T'Gatoi would let me bring him along when she took me into the city. But something had happened when he reached adolescence. I never knew what. He began keeping out of T'Gatoi's way. Then he began running away—until he realized there was no "away." Not in the

Preserve. Certainly not outside. After that he concentrated on getting his share of every egg that came into the house and on looking out for me in a way that made me all but hate him—a way that clearly said, as long as I was all right, he was safe from the Tlic.

"How was it, really?" he demanded, following me.

"I killed an achti. The young ate it."

"You didn't run out of the house and puke because they ate an achti."

"I had . . . never seen a person cut open before." That was true, and enough for him to know. I couldn't talk about the other. Not with him.

"Oh," he said. He glanced at me as though he wanted to say more, but he kept quiet.

We walked, not really headed anywhere. Toward the back, toward the cages, toward the fields.

"Did he say anything?" Qui asked. "Lomas, I mean."

Who else would he mean? "He said T'Khotgif."

Qui shuddered. "If she had done that to me, she'd be the last person I'd call for."

"You'd call for her. Her sting would ease your pain without killing the grubs in you."

"You think I'd care if they died?"

No. Of course he wouldn't. Would I?

"Shit!" He drew a deep breath. "I've seen what they do. You think this thing with Lomas was bad? It was nothing."

I didn't argue. He didn't know what he was talking about.

"I saw them eat a man," he said.

I turned to face him. "You're lying!"

"*I saw them eat a man.*" He paused. "It was when I was little. I had been to the Hartmund house and I was on my way home. Halfway here, I saw a man and a Tlic and the man was N'Tlic. The ground was hilly. I was able to hide from them and watch. The Tlic wouldn't open the man because she had nothing to feed the grubs. The man couldn't go any further and there were no houses around. He was in so much pain, he told her to kill him. He begged her to kill him. Finally, she did. She cut his throat. One swipe of one claw. I saw the grubs eat their way out, then burrow in again, still eating."

His words made me see Lomas's flesh again, parasitized, crawling. "Why didn't you tell me that?" I whispered.

He looked startled as though he'd forgotten I was listening. "I don't know."

"You started to run away not long after that, didn't you?"

"Yeah. Stupid. Running inside the Preserve. Running in a cage."

I shook my head, said what I should have said to him long ago. "She wouldn't take you, Qui. You don't have to worry."

"She would . . . if anything happened to you."

"No. She'd take Xuan Hoa. Hoa . . . wants it." She wouldn't if she had stayed to watch Lomas.

"They don't take women," he said with contempt.

"They do sometimes." I glanced at him. "Actually, they prefer women. You should be around them when they talk among themselves. They say women have more body fat to protect the grubs. But they usually take men to leave the women free to bear their own young."

"To provide the next generation of host animals," he said, switching from contempt to bitterness.

"It's more than that!" I countered. Was it?

"If it were going to happen to me, I'd want to believe it was more, too."

"It *is* more!" I felt like a kid. Stupid argument.

"Did you think so while T'Gatoi was picking worms out of that guy's guts?"

"It's not supposed to happen that way."

"Sure it is. You weren't supposed to see it, that's all. And his Tlic was supposed to do it. She could sting him unconscious and the operation wouldn't have been as painful. But she'd still open him, pick out the grubs, and if she missed even one, it would poison him and eat him from the inside out."

There was actually a time when my mother told me to show respect for Qui because he was my older brother. I walked away, hating him. In his way, he was gloating. He was safe and I wasn't. I could have hit him, but I didn't think I would be able to stand it when he refused to hit back, when he looked at me with contempt and pity.

He wouldn't let me get away. Longer legged, he swung ahead of me and made me feel as though I were following him.

"I'm sorry," he said.

I strode on, sick and furious.

"Look, it probably won't be that bad with you. T'Gatoi likes you. She'll be careful."

I turned back toward the house, almost running from him.

"Has she done it to you yet?" he asked, keeping up easily. "I mean, you're about the right age for implantation. Has she—"

I hit him. I didn't know I was going to do it, but I think I meant to kill him. If he hadn't been bigger and stronger, I think I would have.

He tried to hold me off, but in the end, had to defend himself. He only hit me a couple of times. That was plenty. I don't remember going down, but when I came to, he was gone. It was worth the pain to be rid of him.

I got up and walked slowly toward the house. The back was dark. No one was in the kitchen. My mother and sisters were sleeping in their bedrooms—or pretending to.

Once I was in the kitchen, I could hear voices—Tlic and Terran from the next room. I couldn't make out what they were saying—didn't want to make it out.

I sat down at my mother's table, waiting for quiet. The table was smooth and worn, heavy and well crafted. My father had made it for her just before he died. I remembered hanging around underfoot when he built it. He didn't mind. Now I sat leaning on it, missing him. I could have talked to him. He had done it three times in his long life. Three clutches of eggs, three times being opened and sewed up. How had he done it? How did anyone do it?

I got up, took the rifle from its hiding place, and sat down again with it. It needed cleaning, oiling.

All I did was load it.

"Gan?"

She made a lot of little clicking sounds when she walked on bare floor, each limb clicking in succession as it touched down. Waves of little clicks.

She came to the table, raised the front half of her body above it, and surged onto it. Sometimes she moved so smoothly she seemed to flow like water itself. She coiled herself into a small hill in the middle of the table and looked at me.

"That was bad," she said softly. "You should not have seen it. It need not be that way."

"I know."

"T'Khotgif—Ch'Khotgif now—she will die of her disease. She will not live to raise her children. But her sister will provide for them, and for Bram Lomas." Sterile sister. One fertile female in every lot. One to keep the family going. That sister owed Lomas more than she could ever repay.

"He'll live then?"

"Yes."

"I wonder if he would do it again."

"No one would ask him to do that again."

I looked into the yellow eyes, wondering how much I saw and understood there, and how much I only imagined. "No one ever asks us," I said. "You never asked me."

She moved her head slightly. "What's the matter with your face?"

"Nothing. Nothing important." Human eyes probably wouldn't have noticed the swelling in the darkness. The only light was from one of the moons, shining through a window across the room.

"Did you use the rifle to shoot the achti?"

"Yes."

"And do you mean to use it to shoot me?"

I stared at her, outlined in the moonlight—coiled, graceful body. "What does Terran blood taste like to you?"

She said nothing.

"What are you?" I whispered. "What are we to you?"

She lay still, rested her head on her topmost coil. "You know me as no other does," she said softly. "You must decide."

"That's what happened to my face," I told her.

"What?"

"Qui goaded me into deciding to do something. It didn't turn out very well." I moved the gun slightly, brought the barrel up diagonally under my own chin. "At least it was a decision I made."

"As this will be."

"Ask me, Gatoi."

"For my children's lives?"

She would say something like that. She knew how to manipulate people, Terran and Tlic. But not this time.

"I don't want to be a host animal," I said. "Not even yours."

It took her a long time to answer. "We use almost no host animals these days," she said. "You know that."

"You use us."

"We do. We wait long years for you and teach you and join our families to yours." She moved restlessly. "You know you aren't animals to us."

I stared at her, saying nothing.

"The animals we once used began killing most of our eggs after implantation long before your ancestors arrived," she said softly. "You know these things, Gan. Because your people arrived, we are relearning what it means to be a healthy, thriving people. And your ancestors, fleeing from their homeworld, from their own kind who would have killed or enslaved them—they survived because of us. We saw them as people and gave them the Preserve when they still tried to kill us as worms."

At the word "worms," I jumped. I couldn't help it, and she couldn't help noticing it.

"I see," she said quietly. "Would you really rather die than bear my young, Gan?"

I didn't answer.

"Shall I go to Xuan Hoa?"

"Yes!" Hoa wanted it. Let her have it. She hadn't had to watch Lomas. She'd be proud. . . . Not terrified.

T'Gatoi flowed off the table onto the floor, startling me almost too much.

"I'll sleep in Hoa's room tonight," she said. "And sometime tonight or in the morning, I'll tell her."

This was going too fast. My sister Hoa had had almost as much to do with raising me as my mother. I was still close to her—not like Qui. She could want T'Gatoi and still love me.

"Wait! Gatoi!"

She looked back, then raised nearly half her length off the floor and turned to face me. "These are adult things, Gan. This is my life, my family!"

"But she's . . . my sister."

"I have done what you demanded. I have asked you!"

"But—"

"It will be easier for Hoa. She has always expected to carry other lives inside her."

Human lives. Human young who should someday drink at her breasts, not at her veins.

I shook my head. "Don't do it to her, Gatoi." I was not Qui. It seemed I could become him, though, with no effort at all. I could make Xuan Hoa my shield. Would it be easier to know that red worms were growing in her flesh instead of mine?

"Don't do it to Hoa," I repeated.

She stared at me, utterly still.

I looked away, then back at her. "Do it to me."

I lowered the gun from my throat and she leaned forward to take it.

"No," I told her.

"It's the law," she said.

"Leave it for the family. One of them might use it to save my life someday."

She grasped the rifle barrel, but I wouldn't let go. I was pulled into a standing position over her.

"Leave it here!" I repeated. "If we're not your animals, if these are adult things, accept the risk. There is risk, Gatoi, in dealing with a partner."

It was clearly hard for her to let go of the rifle. A shudder went through her and she made a hissing sound of distress. It occurred to me that she was afraid. She was old enough to have seen what guns could do to people. Now her young and this gun would be together in the same house. She did not know about the other guns. In this dispute, they did not matter.

"I will implant the first egg tonight," she said as I put the gun away. "Do you hear, Gan?"

Why else had I been given a whole egg to eat while the rest of the family was left to share one? Why else had my mother kept looking at me as though I were going away from her, going where she could not follow? Did T'Gatoi imagine I hadn't known?

"I hear."

"Now!" I let her push me out of the kitchen, then walked ahead of her toward my bedroom. The sudden urgency in her voice sounded real. "You would have done it to Hoa tonight!" I accused.

"I must do it to someone tonight."

I stopped in spite of her urgency and stood in her way. "Don't you care who?"

She flowed around me and into my bedroom. I found her waiting on the couch we shared. There was nothing in Hoa's room that she could have used. She would have done it to Hoa on the floor. The thought of her doing it to Hoa at all disturbed me in a different way now, and I was suddenly angry.

Yet I undressed and lay down beside her. I knew what to do, what to expect. I had been told all my life. I felt the familiar sting, narcotic, mildly pleasant. Then the blind probing of her ovipositor. The puncture was painless, easy. So easy going in. She undulated slowly against me, her muscles forcing the egg from her body into mine. I held on to a pair of her limbs until I remembered Lomas holding her that way. Then I let go, moved inadvertently, and hurt her. She gave a low cry of pain and I expected to be caged at once within her limbs. When I wasn't, I held on to her again, feeling oddly ashamed.

"I'm sorry," I whispered.

She rubbed my shoulders with four of her limbs.

"Do you care?" I asked. "Do you care that it's me?"

She did not answer for some time. Finally, "You were the one making the choices tonight, Gan. I made mine long ago."

"Would you have gone to Hoa?"

"Yes. How could I put my children into the care of one who hates them?"

"It wasn't . . . hate."

"I know what it was."

"I was afraid."

Silence.

"I still am." I could admit it to her here, now.

"But you came to me . . . to save Hoa."

"Yes." I leaned my forehead against her. She was cool velvet, deceptively soft. "And to keep you for myself," I said. It was so. I didn't understand it, but it was so.

She made a soft hum of contentment. "I couldn't believe I had made such a mistake with you," she said. "I chose you. I believed you had grown to choose me."

"I had, but . . ."

"Lomas."

"Yes."

"I had never known a Terran to see a birth and take it well. Qui has seen one, hasn't he?"

"Yes."

"Terrans should be protected from seeing."

I didn't like the sound of that—and I doubted that it was possible. "Not protected," I said. "Shown. Shown when we're young kids, and shown more than once. Gatoi, no Terran ever sees a birth that goes right. All we see is N'Tlic—pain and terror and maybe death."

She looked down at me. "It is a private thing. It has always been a private thing."

Her tone kept me from insisting—that and the knowledge that if she changed her mind, I might be the first public example. But I had planted the thought in her mind. Chances were it would grow, and eventually she would experiment.

"You won't see it again," she said. "I don't want you thinking any more about shooting me."

The small amount of fluid that came into me with her egg relaxed me as completely as a sterile egg would have, so that I could remember the rifle in my hands and my feelings of fear and revulsion, anger and despair. I could remember the feelings without reviving them. I could talk about them.

"I wouldn't have shot you," I said. "Not you." She had been taken from my father's flesh when he was my age.

"You could have," she insisted.

"Not you." She stood between us and her own people, protecting, interweaving.

"Would you have destroyed yourself?"

I moved carefully, uncomfortable. "I could have done that. I nearly did. That's Qui's 'away'. I wonder if he knows."

"What?"

I did not answer.

"You will live now."

"Yes." *Take care of her,* my mother used to say. Yes.

"I'm healthy and young," she said. "I won't leave you as Lomas was left—alone, N'Tlic. I'll take care of you."

William H. Gass

William H. Gass is the David May Distinguished Professor in the Humanities at Washington University in St. Louis. Born in Fargo, North Dakota, in 1924, he was educated at Kenyon College, Ohio Wesleyan, and Cornell, where he earned his Ph.D. While teaching philosophy at Purdue University, he wrote a series of influential short fictions collected under the title In the Heart of the Heart of the Country, *in which "Order of Insects" appears.*

His many celebrated category-defying books include a philosophical inquiry on a color, On Being Blue, *and the photographic novella* Willie Master's Lonesome Wife. *His provocative literary essays and reviews have been collected in* Habitations of the Word. *Gass champions the conviction that words and language are an entire world unto themselves, that they are in fact more detailed than the matter they are meant to represent.*

"Order of Insects" is the story of a housewife who discovers the remains of dead insects as she cleans. Her meditation on their sudden and unexplained appearance leads her to find these bugs beautiful. Unlike a realist narrative, not much happens here; this is a story about thinking and about the tools we use to think. By stripping down the action to a static situation, Gass focuses the reader's attention on the beautiful designs of human cognition and animates the mechanism of putting down on paper what are thinking in our minds.

Order of Insects

We certainly had no complaints about the house after all we had been through in the other place, but we hadn't lived there very long before

I began to notice every morning the bodies of a large black bug spotted about the downstairs carpet; haphazardly, as earth worms must die on the street after a rain; looking when I first saw them like rolls of dark wool or pieces of mud from the children's shoes, or sometimes, if the drapes were pulled, so like ink stains or deep burns they terrified me, for I had been intimidated by that thick rug very early and the first week had walked over it wishing my bare feet would swallow my shoes. The shells were usually broken. Legs and other parts I couldn't then identify would be scattered near like flakes of rust. Occasionally I would find them on their backs, their quilted undersides showing orange, while beside them were smudges of dark-brown powder that had to be vacuumed carefully. We believed our cat had killed them. She was frequently sick during the night then—a rare thing for her—and we could think of no other reason. Overturned like that they looked pathetic even dead.

I could not imagine where the bugs had come from. I am terribly meticulous myself. The house was clean, the cupboards tight and orderly, and we never saw one alive. The other place had been infested with those flat brown fuzzy roaches, all wires and speed, and we'd seen *them* all right, frightened by the kitchen light, sifting through the baseboards and the floor's cracks; and in the pantry I had nearly closed my fingers on one before it fled, tossing its shadow across the starch like an image of the startle in my hand.

Dead, overturned, their three pairs of legs would be delicately drawn up and folded shyly over their stomachs. When they walked I suppose their forelegs were thrust out and then bent to draw the body up. I still wonder if they jumped. More than once I've seen our cat hook one of her claws under a shell and toss it in the air, crouching while the insect fell, feigning leaps—but there was daylight; the bug was dead; she was not really interested any more; and she would walk immediately away. That image takes the place of jumping. Even if I actually saw those two back pairs of legs unhinge, as they would have to if one leaped, I think I'd find the result unreal and mechanical, a poor try measured by that sudden, high, head-over-heels flight from our cat's paw. I could look it up, I guess, but it's no study for a woman . . . bugs.

At first I reacted as I should, bending over, wondering what in the world; yet even before I recognized them I'd withdrawn my hand, shuddering. Fierce, ugly, armored things: they used their shadows to seem large. The machine sucked them up while I looked the other way. I remember the sudden thrill of horror I had hearing one rattle up the wand. I was relieved that they were dead, of course, for I could never have killed one, and if they had been popped, alive, into the dust bag of the cleaner, I believe I would have had nightmares again as I did the time my husband fought the red ants in our kitchen. All night I lay awake thinking of the ants alive in the belly of the machine, and when toward morning I finally slept I found myself in the dreadful elastic tunnel of the suction tube where ahead of me I heard them: a hundred bodies rustling in the dirt.

I never think of their species as alive but as comprised entirely by the dead ones on our carpet, all the new dead manufactured by the action of some mysterious spoor—perhaps that dust they sometimes lie in—carried in the air, solidified by night and shaped, from body into body, spontaneously, as maggots were before the age of science. I have a single book about insects, a little dated handbook in French which a good friend gave me as a joke—because of my garden, the quaintness of the plates, the fun of reading about worms in such an elegant tongue—and my bug has his picture there climbing the stem of an orchid. Beneath the picture is his name: *Periplaneta orientalis L. Ces répugnants insectes ne sont que trop communs dans les cuisines des vieilles habitations des villes, dans les magasins, entrepôts, boulangeries, brasseries, restaurants, dans la cale des navires, etc.,* the text begins. Nevertheless they are a new experience for me and I think that I am grateful for it now.

The picture didn't need to show me there were two, adult and nymph, for by that time I'd seen the bodies of both kinds. Nymph. My god the names we use. The one was dark, squat, ugly, sly. The other, slimmer, had hard sheath-like wings drawn over its back like another shell, and you could see delicate interwoven lines spun like fossil gauze across them. The nymph was a rich golden color deepening in its interstices to mahogany. Both had legs that looked under a glass like the canes of a rose, and the nymph's were sufficiently transparent in a good light you thought you saw its nerves merge and run like a jagged crack to each ultimate claw.

Tipped, their legs have fallen shut, and the more I look at them the less I believe my eyes. Corruption, in these bugs, is splendid. I've a collection now I keep in typewriter-ribbon tins, and though, in time, their bodies dry and the interior flesh decays, their features hold, as I suppose they held in life, an Egyptian determination, for their protective plates are strong and death must break bones to get in. Now that the heavy soul is gone, the case is light.

I suspect if we were as familiar with our bones as with our skin, we'd never bury dead but shrine them in their rooms, arranged as we might like to find them on a visit; and our enemies, if we could steal their bodies from the battle sites, would be museumed as they died, the steel still eloquent in their sides, their metal hats askew, the protective toes of their shoes unworn, and friend and enemy would be so wondrously historical that in a hundred years we'd find the jaws still hung for the same speech and all the parts we spent our life with tilted as they always were—rib cage, collar, skull—still repetitious, still defiant, angel light, still worthy of memorial and affection. After all, what does it mean to say that when our cat has bitten through the shell and put confusion in the pulp, the life goes out of them? Alas for us, I want to cry, our bones are secret, showing last, so we must love what perishes: the muscles and the waters and the fats.

Two prongs extend like daggers from the rear. I suppose I'll never know their function. That kind of knowledge doesn't take my interest. At first I had to screw my eyes down, and as I consider it now, the whole change, the recent alteration in my life, was the consequence of finally coming near to something. It was a self-mortifying act, I recall, a penalty I laid upon myself for the evil-tempered words I'd shouted at my children in the middle of the night. I felt instinctively the insects were infectious and their own disease, so when I knelt I held a handkerchief over the lower half of my face . . . saw only horror . . . turned, sick, masking my eyes . . . yet the worst of angers held me through the day: vague, searching, guilty, and ashamed.

After that I came near often; saw, for the first time, the gold nymph's difference; put between the mandibles a tinted nail I'd let grow long; observed the movement of the jaws, the stalks of the antennae, the skull-shaped skull, the lines banding the abdomen, and found an intensity in the posture of the shell, even when tipped, like that in the gaze of Gauguin's natives' eyes. The dark plates glisten. They are wonderfully shaped; even the buttons of the compound eyes show a geometrical precision which prevents my earlier horror. It isn't possible to feel disgust toward such an order. Nevertheless, I reminded myself, a roach . . . and you a woman.

I no longer own my own imagination. I suppose they came up the drains or out of the registers. It may have been the rug they wanted. Crickets, too, I understand, will feed on wool. I used to rest by my husband . . . stiffly . . . waiting for silence to settle in the house, his sleep to come, and then the drama of their passage would take hold of me, possess me so completely that when I finally slept I merely passed from one dream to another without the slightest loss of vividness or continuity. Never alive, they came with punctures;

their bodies formed from little whorls of copperish dust which in the downstairs darkness I couldn't possibly have seen; and they were dead and upside down when they materialized, for it was in that moment that our cat, herself darkly invisible, leaped and brought her paws together on the true soul of the roach; a soul so static and intense, so immortally arranged, I felt, while I lay shell-like in our bed, turned inside out, driving my mind away, it was the same as the dark soul of the world itself—and it was this beautiful and terrifying feeling that took possession of me finally, stiffened me like a rod beside my husband, played caesar to my dreams.

The weather drove them up, I think . . . moisture in the tubes of the house. The first I came on looked put together in Japan; broken, one leg bent under like a metal cinch; unwound. It rang inside the hollow of the wand like metal too; brightly, like a stream of pins. The clatter made me shiver. Well I always see what I fear. Anything my eyes have is transformed into a threatening object: mud, or stains, or burns, or if not these, then toys in unmendable metal pieces. Not fears to be afraid of. The ordinary fears of daily life. Healthy fears. Womanly, wifely, motherly ones: the children may point at the wretch with the hunch and speak in a voice he will hear; the cat has fleas again, they will get in the sofa; one's face looks smeared, it's because of the heat; is the burner on under the beans? the washing machine's obscure disease may reoccur, it rumbles on rinse and rattles on wash; my god it's already eleven o'clock; which one of you has lost a galosh? So it was amid the worries of our ordinary life I bent, innocent and improperly armed, over the bug that had come undone. Let me think back on the shock. . . . My hand would have fled from a burn with the same speed; anyone's death or injury would have weakened me as well; and I could have gone cold for a number of reasons, because I felt in motion in me my own murderous disease, for instance; but none could have produced the revulsion that dim recognition did, a reaction of my whole nature that flew ahead of understanding and made me withdraw like a spider.

I said I was innocent. Well I was not. Innocent. My god the names we use. What do we live with that's alive we haven't tamed—people like me?—even our houseplants breathe by our permission. All along I had the fear of what it was—something ugly and poisonous, deadly and terrible—the simple insect, worse and wilder than fire—and I should rather put my arms in the heart of a flame than in the darkness of a moist and webby hole. But the eye never ceases to change. When I examine my collection now it isn't any longer roaches I observe but gracious order, wholeness, and divinity. . . . My handkerchief, that time, was useless. . . . O my husband, they are a terrible disease.

The dark soul of the world . . . a phrase I should laugh at. The roach shell sickened me. And my jaw has broken open. I lie still, listening, but there is nothing to hear. Our cat is quiet. They pass through life to immortality between her paws.

Am I grateful now my terror has another object? From time to time I think so, but I feel as though I'd been entrusted with a kind of eastern mystery, sacred to a dreadful god, and I am full of the sense of my unworthiness and the clay of my vessel. So strange. It is the sewing machine that has the fearful claw. I live in a scatter of blocks and children's voices. The chores are my clock, and time is every other moment interrupted. I had always thought that love knew nothing of order and that life itself was turmoil and confusion. Let us leap, let us shout! I have leaped, and to my shame, I have wrestled. But this bug that I hold in my hand and know to be dead is beautiful, and there is a fierce joy in its composition that beggars every other, for its joy is the joy of stone, and it lives in its tomb like a lion.

I don't know which is more surprising: to find such order in a roach, or such ideas in a woman.

I could not shake my point of view, infected as it was, and I took up their study with a manly passion. I sought out spiders and gave them sanctuary; played host to worms of every kind; was generous to katydids and lacewings, aphids, ants and various grubs; pampered several sorts of beetle; looked after crickets; sheltered bees; aimed my husband's chemicals away from the grasshoppers, mosquitoes, moths, and flies. I have devoted hours to watching caterpillars feed. You can see the leaves they've eaten passing through them; their bodies thin and swell until the useless pulp is squeezed in perfect rounds from their rectal end; for caterpillars are a simple section of intestine, a decorated stalk of yearning muscle, and their whole being is enlisted in the effort of digestion. *Le tube digestif des Insectes est situé dans le grand axe de la cavité gégénérale du corps . . . de la bouche vers l'anus . . . Le pharynx . . . L'oesophage . . . Le jabot . . . Le ventricule chylifique . . . Le rectum et l'iléon . . .* Yet when they crawl their curves conform to graceful laws.

My children ought to be delighted with me as my husband is, I am so diligent, it seems, on their behalf, but they have taken fright and do not care to pry or to collect. My hobby's given me a pair of dreadful eyes, and sometimes I fancy they start from my head; yet I see, perhaps, no differently than Galileo saw when he found in the pendulum its fixed intent. Nonetheless my body resists such knowledge. It wearies of its edge. And I cannot forget, even while I watch our moonvine blossoms opening, the simple principle of the bug. It is a squat black cockroach after all, such a bug as frightens housewives, and it's only come to chew on rented wool and find its death absurdly in the teeth of the renter's cat.

Strange. Absurd. I am the wife of the house. This point of view I tremble in is the point of view of a god, and I feel certain, somehow, that could I give myself entirely to it, were I not continuing a woman, I could disarm my life, find peace and order everywhere; and I lie by my husband and I touch his arm and consider the temptation. But I am a woman. I am not worthy. Then I want to cry O husband, husband, I am ill, for I have seen what I have seen. What should he do at that, poor man, starting up in the night from his sleep to such nonsense, but comfort me blindly and murmur dream, small snail, only dream, bad dream, as I do to the children. I could go away like the wise cicada who abandons its shell to move to other mischief. I could leave and let my bones play cards and spank the children. . . . Peace. How can I think of such ludicrous things—beauty and peace, the dark soul of the world—for I am the wife of the house, concerned for the rug, tidy and punctual, surrounded by blocks.

PART TWO

Formalists

Stephen Dixon

Stephen Dixon, born in 1936, has published more than 400 stories in the Paris Review, Harper's, Atlantic Monthly, Playboy, *and other magazines. He has won awards from the National Endowment for the Arts, a Guggenheim Fellowship, the Pushcart Prize, an O. Henry Award, and recognition by the American Academy—Institute for Arts and Letters. Two of his novels have been nominated for the National Book Award. Before joining the creative writing faculty at John Hopkins University, Dixon worked as a junior high school teacher, bartender, salesclerk, waiter, artist's model, and reporter.*

Dixon's characters are often people caught in urban nightmares, trying to wrest control from various natural and man-made forces. At the center of his stories, no matter how absurd, lie a humane sense of the family unit's fragility and a wish, however futile, to protect oneself and those one loves. In one story, a man is pursued by hospital officials when he won't sign a form regarding his wife's body. In another, a man follows his daughter when she falls out of an airplane; miraculously, they stay aloft for hours while the father tries to figure out a way to set them down safely.

In "Milk Is Very Good for You," which won a Pushcart Prize, Dixon plays brilliantly and mischievously with the reader's expectations as he creates a scenario that is almost but not quite "pornographic," with "dirty" words that aren't even words. Playing with the language of the piece, Dixon forces us to examine the fact that dirty words, as well as all other words, are human constructions, in reality neither dirty nor clean. His aim is not to shock but to amuse us with our own cultural and personal baggage that we bring to the story.

Milk Is Very Good for You

It was getting fairly late in the evening for me so I asked my wife if she was ready to leave. "Just a few minutes, love," she said, "I'm having such a good time." I wasn't. The party was a bore, as it had been from the start. Another drinking contest taking place in the kitchen, some teachers and their husbands or wives turning on in the john, Phil somebody making eyes at Joe who's-it's wife, Joe trying to get Mary Mrs. to take a breath of fresh air with him as he said while Mary's husband was presently engaged with someone else's sweetheart or wife for a look at the constellation she was born under, and I felt alone, didn't want to turn on or drink another drink or walk another man's wife through the fresh air for some fresh caressing. I wanted to return home and my wife didn't as she was aching to turn on or drink with some other man but me and most especially to walk in the fresh air with Frank whatever his name was as Frank's wife had just taken that same stroll with Joe after Joe had learned that Mary had promised herself tonight to the dentist friend accompanying her and her husband to this house, so I decided to leave.

"Goodbye, Cindy," I said.

"Leaving now, love?"

"Leaving now, yes, are you going to come?"

"Not right this moment, Rick, though I'll find some way home."

"Take your time getting there," I said, "No need to rush. Even skip breakfast if that's what you've mind to—I'll see to the kids. Even pass up tomorrow's lunch and dinner if you want—things will work out. In fact, spend the weekend or week away if you'd like to—I'll take care of everything at home. Maybe two weeks or a month or even a year would be the time you need for a suitable vacation, it's all okay with me, dear," and I kissed her goodbye, drove home, relieved the babysitter who said "You needn't have returned so early, Mr. Richardson, as the children never even made a peep. I like babysitting them so much it's almost a crime taking money for the job."

"So don't," I said, and Jane said "Well, that wasn't exactly a statement of fact, Mr. Richardson," and pocketed her earnings and started for the door.

"Goodnight," I said on the porch, "and I really hope you don't mind my not walking you home tonight. I'm really too beat."

"It's only two blocks to the dorm, though I will miss those nice chats we have on the way."

Those nice chats. Those tedious six-to-seven minute monologues of Jane's on her boyfriends' inability to be mature enough for her or her inability to be unpretendingly immature for them or more likely she telling me about her schoolwork, no doubt thinking I'd be interested because I teach the same subject she's majoring in at the same school she attends. "Tonight," Jane said, "I especially wanted your advice on a term paper I'm writing on the father-son if not latent or even overt homosexual relationship between Boswell and Johnson, since it's essential I get a good grade on my paper if I'm to get a B for the course."

"Bring it to the office and I'll correct and even rewrite a few of the unclearer passages if you want."

"Would you do that, Mr. Richardson? That would be too nice of you, more help than I ever dreamed of," and so thrilled was she that she threw her arms around my back, and while she hugged me in gratitude I couldn't resist kissing the nape of her neck in passion and now something had started: Jane said "Oh, Mr. Richardson, you naughty teacher, that's not what I even half-anticipated from you," and rubbed my back and squeezed my menis through the pants and said "My me my but you're surprising me in many ways today," and unzippered me and riddled with my menis till I was ranting so hard I couldn't warn her in time that I was about to some in her land.

"What funky rickety gush," she said. "Do you have a hanky?"

"I'm sorry. And I think I also spoiled your pretty skirt."

"This dinky old thing? Here, let me clean you off properly." And still in the dark of my porch she squatted down and wiped me dry with a hanky and then wobbled up my menis and before I could say anything rational to her, such as this was an extremely indiscreet setting for a young woman from the same college I didn't as yet have tenure at to be living read to the man whose children she just babysat for, I was on the floor myself, her south never letting go of my menis as I swiveled around underneath her, lowered her panties, stack my longue in her ragina and began rowing town on her also, slowly, loving the gradually increasing pace we had tacitly established when Jane said "Go get the flit, Mr. Richardson, brink up the little flit," which I couldn't find so one by one I desoured every slover of flash that protruded in and around her ragina, hoping to discover—by some sudden jerky movement or exclamation or cry—that I had fortuitously struck home.

"That's it," she said, "right there, that's the little devil, you've got him by the nose," and after several minutes of us both without letup living read to one another, we same at precisely the same time.

"Now for the real thing," Jane said, "though do you think we're in too much light? Screw it, nobody can hear us, you and Mrs. Richardson have a nice big piece of property here, real nice, besides my not caring one iota if anyone does, do you?" and she stuck her panties in her bookbag, got on her rack on the floor, slopped my menis back and forth till I got an election and started carefully to guide me in.

"Rick, you imbecile," my wife said. "I can hear you two hyenas howling from a block away."

"Good evening, Mrs. Richardson," Jane said, standing and adjusting her skirt.

"Good evening, Jane. Did the children behave themselves?"

"Angels, Mrs. Richardson. I was telling Mr. Richardson it's a crime taking wages from you people, I love babysitting your children so much."

"I told her 'Well don't take the money,' " I said.

"And I said 'That wasn't exactly a statement of fact, Mr. Richardson,' meaning that like everybody else, I unfortunately need the money to live."

"And what did you say to that?" Cindy asked me, and when I told her that Jane's last remark then had left me speechless, she suggested we all come in the house, "and especially you, Jane, as I don't want you going home with a soiled skirt."

"I don't know how much I like the idea of that," I said, "or your blasé attitude, Cindy."

"Oh it's all right, Mr. Richardson. Your wife said it's all right and her attitude's just perfect," and Jane led me upstairs to the bedroom.

We were in red, Jane heated on top of me, my sock deep in her funt and linger up her masspole, when Cindy said through the door "Your skirt is ready Jane." "Is it?" Jane said, and Cindy entered the room with no clothes on and said "Yes, it's cleaning-store clean," got in red with us and after drawing us baking dove with me inder Jane for a whole, she put down her pen and pad and but her own funt over my south and in seconds all three of us were sounding up and down on the red, dewling, bailing, grubbing at each other's shoulders and hair. "Oh Rick," Cindy said, "Oh Mr. Richardson," Jane said, "Oh Janie," both Cindy and I said, "Oh Mrs. Richardson," Jane said, "Oh Cindy-bee," I said. And just as the thought came to me that my greatest fantasy for the last fifteen years of me with my longue and menis in the respective funts of two cotmassed magnificent women was about to be realized exactly as I had fantasized it and that was with the most spectacular some of my life, my eldest daughter, Dandy, came into the room and said "Mommy, daddy, Janie, can I have some milk?"

"Go back to bed," Cindy said.

"I want some milk too," Beverly, my other daughter, said.

"There is no milk," Jane said. "I drank it all."

"You did what?" Cindy said. "You did what?"

"Drank it all."

Cindy hot off my lace and told me to sake alay my tick from Jane's funt and that I could also escort her to her dorm if I didn't mind, as any babysitter who'd drink up the last of the milk when she knew the children she was sitting for liked nothing better first thing in the morning than milk in their cereal and glasses just shouldn't be allowed to remain another second in this house.

"How much milk was there?" I said.

"A quart at least," Cindy said.

"Two," Jane said, "—but two and a half to be exact. I simply got very thirsty and drank it all, though in several sittings."

Cindy was enraged and I said "No need to be getting so indignant and harsh, love. So the young lady got thirsty. So it was an act of, let us say, imprudence."

"I want some milk," Dandy said. "Me too," Beverly said. "Drink some water if you're thirsty," Jane told them. "Drink water nothing," Cindy said. "Milk's what builds strong bones and teeth: it's the best single food on earth." "One morning without a glassful won't arrest their physical development," Jane said, and Cindy snapped back "I'll be the judge of that," and put on her bathrobe, took the children by the hand and left the room. She was saying as she went downstairs: "The nerve of that girl. Two quarts. That cow. When your daddy comes down I'll have him drive straight to the all-night supermarket for milk."

"I want some now," Dandy said. "Me too," Beverly said. "I have to go," I said to Jane.

"You don't think we can just finish up a bit?"

"The girls want their milk and Cindy's about to explode even more."

"You realize it was only this seizure of thirstiness I had. If you had had soda I would have drank that instead—or at least only one of the quarts of milk and the rest soda."

"Cindy won't have soda around the house. Says it's very bad for their teeth."

"She's probably right." Jane started to put on her panties, had one foot through a leg opening when she said "I'm still feeling like I'd like your sock and don't know when we'll have another chance for it."

"I have to go to the market, Jane."

"Your wife has a nice funt too. I mean it's different than mine, bigger because she's had babies, but I luck as well, don't I?" I said I thought she was very good, very nice. "And I know what to do with a menis when ic's in my south. I think I excel there, wouldn't you say?"

"I really don't know. This is kind of a funny conversation."

"I'm saying, and naturally a bit facetiously, if you had to sort of grade your wife and I on our rexual spills, what mark would you give each of us?"

"The difficulty of grading there is that I could only grade you on just our single experience this morning and not an entire term's work, while Cindy and I have had semesters together if not gotten a couple of degrees, if I'm to persist in this metaphorical comparison, so any grading would be out of the question."

"So grade on just what we'll call our class participation this morning."

"Then I'd give you both an A."

"You don't think I deserve an A plus?"

"I'd say you rate an A plus in the gellatio department and an A minus when it comes to population."

"And your wife?"

"Just the reverse, which comes to a very respectable A for you both."

"I was sort of hoping for an A plus. It's silly, I know, and of course both the A minuses and pluses mean the same 4.0 on your scholastic rating, but I never got an A plus for anything except gym, which I got twice."

"Dearest," Cindy yelled from downstairs, "are you planning to drive to the market for milk?"

"In a second, love. I'm dressing."

"Daddy," Dandy said, "I'm starving, I want milk," and Beverly said "Me too."

"Those are precious kids," Jane said. "And even though Mrs. Richardson is mad at me, I still like her a lot. I think she's very knowing, if not wise."

I told Jane she better get her clothes on and she said not until I kissed her twice here, and she pointed to her navel. "That's ridiculous," I said, and she said "Maybe, but I insist all my dovers leave me with at least that. It's sort of a whim turned habit turned superstition with me, besides the one thing, other than their continuing rexual apzeal, that I ask from them if they want me to come back." I said, while making exaggerated gentlemanly gestures with my hands, then in that case I'd submit to her ladyship and bent over and kissed her twice on the navel. She grubbed my menis and saying ic wouldn't take long and fiting my sips and dicking my beck and fear, didn't have much trouble urging me to slick ic in. I was on sop of her this time, my tody carried along by Jane's peverish hyrating covements till I same like a whunderflap and kept on soming till the girls ran into the room, asked if daddy was dying of poison or something, and then Cindy right behind them, wanting to know whether I was aiming to be tossed into a prison for disturbing the neighborhood's holy Sabbath morning with my cries of otter ecstagy or Jane to be thrown out of school because a once well-respected professor could be heard from a few blocks off sailing out her fame.

"A plus," was all I could answer. "Milk," the girls said. Cindy threw the car keys on the red.

"What a luck," Jane said, "what a sock, what a day."

"Jane and I will have to run away for a month," I told Cindy. "I'm serious: there's no other way."

"And the milk?"

"I'll go to the market first."

"And your job?"

"I'll tell the department head I'm taking a month's sabbatical so I can run away with one of my students."

"And Jane's studies? And the children's sitter? Who'll I get now?"

"I'll provide you with a few names," Jane said. "Some very sweet, reliable girls from my dorm."

"It's useless arguing against you two. Just do what you want."

"You're a love," I said to Cindy, and hugged her. She sissed my boulder, right on the slot that excites me most and that only Cindy seems to be able to do right, so I mugged her lighter, clitched her mute rutt, and she began dicking my fear with her longue, holding my fair, pickling my falls, and said "Let's go to red. Last time for a month, let's say."

"Milk, daddy," Dandy said. "Milk, daddy," Bev said.

"I'll get the milk," Jane said, and Cindy, stilll ploying with me, said she thought that would be a very nice thing for Jane to do.

Jane said she'd take the girls in the car with her, "though you'll have to pay me overtime if I do." "Doubletime," I shouted, but Cindy said that time and half would be more than equitable—did I want to spoil Jane, besides fouling up the wage scale adhered to by all the other parents?

The car drove off, Cindy and I slopped into red alm in alm, began joking about the variety and uniqueness of today's early morning experiences and then welt mery doving to each other, sissed, wetted, set town on one another, lade dove loftly till we both streamed "Bow! Bow!" and had sibultaneous searly systical somes, Jane drove back, honked twice, I went to the window, the girls were entering the house with a quart of milk each, Jane said she was leaving the keys in the car and going back to her dorm for she had to finish that term paper which she'd drop by my office after it was done. "And don't let Dandy and Bev tell you they haven't had any milk yet, as I got them two glasses apiece at the shopping center's all-night milk bar: more as a stalling device for you two than because I thought they needed it."

Cindy was still weeping from her some. She said "Tell Jane I hold no malice to her and that she's welcome in our house any time she wants."

"Cindy holds no malice to you," I said from the window.

"Nor I to her. By the way, did she get an A plus?"

"Plus plus plus," I said.

"Too much. It must've been very good."

"Very very very good."

"Well do you think I can come upstairs a moment? I've something very important to tell you."

"Cindy's a little indisposed," I said, but Cindy told me to let her come up if she really wants: "I can't go on cryng like this forever."

Jane came into our room. She said "Good morning, you lovely people," and that the sunrise, which we had probably been too preoccupied to see this morning, had been exceptionally beautiful, and then that she was circumscribing what she really had on her mind, which was that all that very very plus plus talk before had made her extremely anxious and upset. "Would you mind if we tried ic again, Mr. Richardson, Mrs. Richardson?"

"Mommy, daddy, Janie," Dandy said through the door, "we want some milk."

"Jane said you already had two glasses apiece," I said.

"No we didn't," Dandy said, and Bev said "Me too."

"Let them have it," Cindy said. "Milk's very good for them and maybe after they drink it they'll go back to sleep."

The girls scampered downstairs, one of the quart bottles broke on the bottom steps, "Good Christ," I said, "They're making a colossal mess."

"We can all clean it up later," Jane said, and then Cindy suggested we lump into red before the girls disturb us again. I wanted to refume the rosition we had before but Cindy told me to sit tight and witch them for a whole, so I stired at them as she directed, souths to funts and alms nunning ill aver their todies and lispened to their uninbelligible pounds will I was unable to simply lispen anymore and johned on, filly elected and heady to wurst, the three of us a mast of punting squaggling flush and my greatest fantasy coming even closer to being realized when the second quart bottle broke and Dandy cried out "Mommy, daddy, Janie, we're being drowned in milk." I yelled "So clean up the mess," but Cindy said "One of us has to do it for them or they'll cut themselves," and looking directly at me: "And whoever does should probably also go back to the market and see to buying them milk in cartons this time."

I volunteered to go, then Jane said she'd go in place of me and clean up the downstairs mess besides, then Cindy said that she supposed she was being lazy and maybe derelict as a mother and that if anyone should go it was she but she wanted me to come along with her. Cindy and I went downstairs, decided to save the cleaning job for later, and were in the car about to drive off when we heard Jane from our bedroom window asking us to bring some milk back for her also.

Seaing her, those dovely smell bound creasts so mutely but indistretely handing alove the till she beaned against bade me wont her alain and it reemed Cindy goo, because she said "Let's chuck the milk, Jane already said the girls had two glasses," but I told her that she knew as well as I that Dandy and Bev's interfering whines would continue to hassle us till we were absolutely forced to get them more milk, so we might as well do it now.

"Then why don't you go upstairs and I'll get it," she said. "Call it my day's good deed."

Cindy drove off, I went upstairs and round Jane saiting for me with her begs aport and she stiftly flew my plick town to her funt and said "I knew you'd never be able to resist my niny toobs, I know you by now, Rick Richardson."

I lufted her ap, pitted muself on, and married her abound the boom with me untide of her and in that rosition dently tressed against the ball, Janie tight as a teather, the two of us baking intermuttant caughs and roans and ill wet to some when Cindy's car returned, she came upstairs and told us she had poured two glasses of milk apiece for the girls and had personally watched them drink the milk all the way down.

"Mommy's telling a fib," Dandy said, trailing behind her. "We want some milk."

"All you want you can have," I said. "Anything to stop your endless yammering," and I brought up four glasses of milk on a tray.

"Can I have some also?" Cindy said. "I've suddenly grown very thirsty."

"Jane, could you get a couple more glasses?" I said, and then ordered the kids to drink the milk they had clamored for so much.

"Milk, milk, milk," Beverly said. "Yummy milk," Dandy said, "and now I won't get sick anymore," and they each drank two glasses of milk, Cindy drank one of the milks that Jane had brought up and I the other, and then Jane said she was also very thirsty now after having dealt with so much milk and watching us guzzle down so many glassfuls, so I went to the kitchen for milk, there wasn't any left in the container, "There's no milk," I yelled upsairs, "But I'm thirsty," Jane whined back, "Do something then, Rick," Cindy said, "as Jane's been a dear about going to the market and taking care of the girls and all."

I went next door to the Morrisons and rang the bell. Mrs. Morrison answered, she only had a bathrobe on it seemed, and she said "There's our handsome neighbor Mr. Richardson, I believe: what a grand surprise." I told her what I wanted, she said "Come right in and I'll get it for you in a jif." Mr. Morrison yelled from the upstairs bedroom "Who's there, Queen?" "Mr. Richardson." "Oh, Richardson," he said, "what's he want?" "Milk." "Milk? You sure that's all?" and she said "I don't rightly know. Is that all you want, Mr. Richardson?" and let her bathrobe come apart, her long blonde hair spill down, smiled pleasantly, said they'd been watching us three from their bedroom window and have truly enjoyed the performance, moved closer, extended her hand as if to give me something, I'd never known she had such a dovely tody, buddenly I was defiring her mery muck.

She said "We're loth spill mery inferested in you seply, Mr. Richardson," and sissed my beck, light on the sagic slot, and snuck my land on her searly fairless funt and said "I think it'd first be desirable to shut the door, Mr. Richardson—our mutual neighbors and all?"

"He a rear, dove," Morrison said from upstairs while Mrs. Morrison was prying to untipper me, "and fake the yellow to the redboom." I died twat twat'd be mery vice rut my life was saiting far me ap dome. "Bell," Morrison laid, "rring her rere goo." I sold him she was deally mery fired, rut he laid "It reams we'll rave to incite outsalvs to you mouse, ofay?" and they put on their raincoats, we went to my house, tropped upstairs to the redboom where Cindy and Jane were pitting on the red, beemingly saiting for us.

Jane asked if I brought the milk and I said I didn't. Morrison said he'd be glad to go to his house to get it but Mrs. Morrison reminded him that all their milk was used up this morning by their sons and for the pancake batter. "Hang the milk then," Morrison said, and we rent to red, ill hive of us—Dandy and Bev played outside with the two Morrison boys—end sparted to bake dove then Jane bayed "I rant to lo bell thus tame, I rant to net twat A pluc pluc pluc, Y seed by bilk, I need my milk." "In that case," I said, "I'll go to the market." "I'll go with you," Jane said. "Why don't we all go," Morrison said. "Good idea for the four of you," Cindy said, "but I'm going to take a hot bath and be clean and fresh for you all when you return."

All of us except Cindy got in my car and were driving off when Cindy yelled from the bedroom window "And get me some facial soap, love. I want to take a facial." Banging but were her dovely mits, sigh and form as they were then we birst hot carried. "Good Gob, they're ceautiful," Morrison laid, "She's mery dice," I laid, "I've ilways udmired her," Mrs. Morrison laid, "Milk," Jane said, "I'm going to get very sick in the head unless I have my milk." "Right," I said, and to Cindy in the window: "Won't be long now, dear." "Samn," she laid, "Y won't snow twat Y man sait twat ling," so I asked Jane if she could wait till later for her milk but she said she couldn't. "Oh, get the damn thing over with already," Morrison said, so I yelled to Cindy "Sorry, sweet, but we'll be back in a flash," and we drove off, got Jane her milk, everyone in the car drank at least two glasses of milk each, brought six gallon containers of milk besides and drove home and went upstairs and johned Cindy and the pirls and the Morrison toys and ear fest triends Jack and Betty Slater and my deportment read Professor Cotton and his life and a double of Jane's formitory sals and my handlard Silas Edelberg in red.

"I'm thirsty," Silas said.

"We've got plenty to drink in this house," I said.

"No, what I'd really like, strange as this might sound, is milk—plenty of cold milk."

"I want milk too," Dandy and Bev said.

"More than enough for you also, loves. Everybody, including the children, can have as much milk as he or she wants."

"Yippee," the Morrison boys shouted. "Three cheers for Milk and Mr. Richardson."

"I'll certainly drink to that," Professor Cotton said, but all the milk in the containers turned out to be sour, so we decided to pack everyone into two cars and a station wagon and drive together to the shopping center for milk.

Susan Neville

Susan Neville was born and raised in Indianapolis, Indiana, still lives in the city, and teaches at Butler University. Her books include Indiana Winter, Fabrication, Twilight in Arcadia, *and* Iconography, *all of which combine fictional and nonfictional techniques. She is also the author of the story collections* Invention of Flight, *which won the Flannery O'Connor Award for Short Fiction, and* In the House of Blue Lights, *selected as one of the Best Books of 1998 by the* Chicago Tribune. *She is a recipient of a National Endowment for the Arts fellowship.*

In "Rondo" an orchestra rehearses, and as the individual members tune and practice, each of them rehearses the complex social and romantic connections that exist within the group. "Rondo," the winner of a Pushcart Prize, has a narrative structure that borrows from an orchestral music form, the rondo, in which a theme is sounded and repeated by different voices or instruments. The story's point of view is handed from one performer to the next in the same way a musical motif is picked up and amplified by succeeding soloists or families of instruments. Neville uses repetition, variation, and change of voice or tone to create a narrative that circles on itself, multiplying the effect of disparate parts. The story is particularly noteworthy for its lyric or songlike structure in place of a narrative one: a story about music takes the form of music.

Rondo

The wife of a pianist with hair to her waist leans too close to a candle and for an instant the spray of hair burns and glows like hot wires, filaments in glass. The pianist is sitting in the corner by another candle, in conversation with an androgynous cornet player who feels that she is in some way carrying on a secret though spiritual affair with the pianist right under his wife's eyes, because they are of course talking on a much higher plane than the pianist could ever hope to reach with his wife, who is much too pretty and too blatantly feminine to have any kind of intelligence. Neither of them notices the wife's burnt hair, and she runs outside the house, past the other musicians, and into the back yard. The cornet player sees her leave and feels triumphant, assuming it's jealousy, thinking kindly that it might help the wife to grow if she begins to face realities such as this, if she begins to stand on her own in the way that the cornet player has always had to do, choosing first the trombone and finally the cornet over the flute and violin, to the confusion and anger of her parents who were certain that instruments were extensions of the body, of the voice, and were created for specific sexes, but who were thankful at last that she hadn't chosen the cello, a woman's instrument that a lady would not play. This had been the first place where people listened to her, where they seemed not to notice the blue shadow of a beard on her chin, the thick shoulders and waist that she had begun to emphasize in defiance. At the end of the year she can go back home to her parents or she can go to New York and begin making the rounds. But she's afraid that she is not good enough. She leans toward the pianist, toward his words, desperately afraid of leaving.

The teacher, a composer and director, sits near the center of the room, drinking straight gin. He brushes a hardened crumb of cheese from his lapel, scans the room for a victim. He sees the flutist with yellow hair who is talking to a tuba man who has a wife and a new child and soft muscles in his stomach but who is no doubt thinking, as the teacher is thinking, only of the way the flutist's lips bloom on cold metal, cheekbones like soapstone. She is obviously uninterested in the tuba man and uninterested in the percussionist who comes over to join the two of them and begins to rub the back of her hair territorially, runs his hand down to the small of her back, the fingers of the tuba man's right hand tensing, swollen beefy lips tight. Most of the women and half of the men in the room are in love with the percussionist, and the teacher is for a moment worried, watches the flutist's eyes for signs of dilation, of interest, when she looks at him as he taps the stretched skin of her wrist, and, finding none, setttles back. He knows that even though he hasn't written any-thing true in years they all hold him in awe, that that supports the illu-sion this is the only musical universe which exists, that the flutist will eventually make her way to him. He looks around at them, the students, knows that though they wouldn't admit it, didn't like to think about it, some of them know this is the only place they will ever have the courage to think of themselves as artists and that, too, the impossibility of the adjustment from being artists to being teachers or salesmen, hawking band instruments and uniforms at small high schools, will destroy some of them. At times he feels that he should discourage them, tell them they are no good—the good ones will only benefit from that. But he can't, says you are good, so good, possibly brilliant, and in turn they sit at his feet, they say it is only because of you that I am great, only through you that I am great, only with your greatness that my greatness grows.

The pianist has come to feel that conversations like this are some-how shallow, small talk about large things, has grown weary of them, would like to cultivate some distance from this, from all of it, the talk of techniques and composers, harmonies and forms, buildings filled with the cacophony of too many voices, too many instruments. Singers walking in the open, across a field, across a campus, still going over an alto part in Latin and singing aloud, not noticing or caring about the heads turning. The phrase from a Bach invention that follows him through the daily domestic things and at night will not, no matter how hard he tries, let him sleep. But the cornet player is obviously enrap-tured with him and he is kind so he continues talking to her though he feels nothing for her, not even pity, only a mild curiosity about what she will be fifteen years from now, older, in a place she is not accepted, of course a failure. He listens to her and looks around the room, envies the percussionist his ease with women, with the beautiful ones, his hand a moment ago resting on the flutist's back, and now he is slumped against the wall, the dark-haired singer taking a drag from his cigarette, light gathered and reflected from her bracelet, an earring, as she turns her head, the beautiful line of her forehead a cool that he can almost feel on his own lips, the touch of ivory on his hands, the way she looks at the percussionist now, brushes against the sleeve of his jacket, not accidentally. The pianist wonders what it is about him, how people, things, are drawn to the percussionist to be taken, subdued, some lack of something civilized in him, of domestication, a pull of something somewhat like death. He sighs, turns to the cornet player, and tries to think of something intellectual, says God would come, possibly, if we called Him by His name, Jehovah, Yahweh. Peter would turn if called Pedro, but not if called Boy. He sighs, leans into the rough fabric of the chair, looks at the singer, and thinks Janice, thinks Juanita, says the trouble is that some names are too sacred to be spoken.

The flutist sees that the teacher is watching the singer with the percussionist and, triumphant from having ignored the percussionist's touch, she leaves the tuba man in mid-sentence and goes over to sit on the floor in front of the teacher, to bring his gaze to her, secure in the knowledge that she is the one true genius, that her music is not derivative. She can feel the cool underside of the flute on her thumbs, the complication of the valves on her fingers. She purses her top lip and blows downward, feels the warmth of the air on her chin. There is music in that also. She knows that the teacher knows this, is drawn to her because of it, that he in fact loves her, sees her in his fantasies, slim and smooth as metal. She has been his student for years, only lately has she begun to demystify him, to realize that the abstraction, the look of the composer, is cultivated, as his music lately has become, neat formulas repeated from when he was younger, the hair and the skin graying too fast. He is prey to imaginary illnesses, sellers of vitamins and magical yeasts, close to but not yet an old man and afraid of it, fewer women each year. He is bearlike, hoary, reaches out to touch her arm, the roundness of it, tells her that she is quite beautiful, says let us invent one another, and she feels her head bow, her arms slyly and consciously rise toward him until they are level with her face—elbows, wrists, fingertips touching as if bound.

The singer knows that she is nothing to the percussionist and feels that that somehow protects her, this awareness of his motives, the way he automatically reaches for women like a newly blind man who, in order to move from this room to the next, this street to the next, constantly must feel the touch of something—a chair, a wooden table, a railing, a bush, a tree—or be overwhelmed by the immensity of space around him, once teeming but now, without sight, empty. She realizes also that he is not indiscriminate, reaches only for the beautiful, the talented, is flattered by this attention at the same time she is aware of a certain danger in the clearness of his eyes, the practiced fumbling with keys at doorways, the lovely structure of his face and shoulders, his hands, something sinister in the way he expects always to be met with yes, with compliance, is so sure of this that he never asks. The one frightening truth she learned as a young girl is that men who ask if they can kiss her are the ones she never wants to kiss. As he talks she becomes aware of the texture of the black wool dress on her skin, the way it tapers to her wrist, the slimness of that, the heartbreaking beauty of the silver in her bracelet. She moves her hand to watch the light catch in the bracelet, to watch the grace of her own fingers, something she seldom notices, how good the air feels to her, the night. She can feel herself wanting to hum, to sing, imagines how she will look on her first album cover, a famous jazz singer performing for audiences of thousands, each one of them in love with her and she distant, remote. There are certain songs she hears which are so beautiful that she can't bear to think that she hadn't written them, certain voices so perfect that she can close her eyes and feel them in her throat. The percussionist touches her face and she knows the smoothness of her skin beneath the thumb that he runs in a half moon from her cheekbone to chin. He tells her that he's been in love with her for years, has worshiped her voice, that she is more talented than he, more intelligent than he, that he feels a kinship with her, something mystical, that he wants to be a part of her greatness, and she leans against the wall, catches her lower lip in a tooth, is aware of the movement, the roundness of her breasts, moves toward him finally at the same moment that his eyes grow cloudy, that he looks away, that he turns to leave.

In the kitchen, the percussionist has to step over the tuba player to get to the bottles on the counter. He fills his glass with straight bourbon, knows he is already drunk, can't remember exactly what he's said to the singer, but knows he could have her if he wanted, if that's what he wanted, is not sure. To take the risk of the rhythm being not right, the sound of springs becoming at one time more important to him than anything, he now sleeps only on a mattress, hoping still for perfect syncopation not a matter of technique but of communication like jazz artists who can improvise together, a rarity. And the women, paradoxically, thinking of him only as an object, building romantic fantasies about him, returning always to the others, the ones they take seriously so that now he gets rid of them before they have that chance. He slides down the kitchen counter, sits on the floor next to the tuba player who leans his red cheeks toward him and asks which one he's taking home, what's it like, is it true that it's awful the morning after. The percussionist pities the tuba player but doesn't answer him, takes a sip of his drink, thinks that the mornings are the best part. His mouth always tastes sweet when he wakes, no matter how much he's had to drink, and he always wakes before the woman so that he looks at her asleep in the light, more innocent, and he goes downstairs, makes coffee and toast, puts on music, and sits looking out a window. In the winter he makes a fire, never is reading the paper when she comes down in one of his bathrobes, hair combed by now, warmed by the mug of coffee he has for her, by the fact that he's been waiting for her, that he does in fact have respect for her. Then the civilized conversation about books, about music, and he never asks her to go, always lets her decide on the right time. He has never been disappointed. As he begins to get up from the floor, the tuba player says my wife thinks you're sexy, sometimes I think she pretends that I'm you, and the percussionist reaches a hand down to him, says come back and join the party, but the tuba player shakes his head, no, takes some of his drink, which is bright red from sweet cherry juice and which sickens the percussionist. He leaves the kitchen, having decided that the singer would be pleasant in the morning even if perhaps disappointing at night. He stops in the doorway, thinks that he's been to bed with half the women in the room, that they've told him their secrets, all comfortably now in conversation as if there isn't someone in the room who could suddenly shout I know you, I know who you are, what you're afraid of. He looks at them, the flutist, the singer, the rest of them, even the cornet player, the pianist, the teacher himself, decides that they're all hideously alike in some way, pauses, feels suddenly that the room is too small, too full, leaves through the side door and no one notices.

The back yard is circled by small trees, the base of the trunks wrapped in white tape like the legs of race horses. They make her feel wild like the dry brittle leaves she's sitting on and the wind and the movement of branches reflected in the at-night-black glass of the small greenhouse make her feel wild. She holds a leaf to the part of her face that feels hot from the flame. There is the pleasant odor of dust, of stems, a rusted scythe blood red among the weeds, the red of the quince bush, dried foliage of peonies and geraniums, she is mad for this, for all of it. She sees the drummer come out the door to the side yard. Always he has smiled at her, the kindest smile, and passed on. He doesn't see her now, sits down at the base of a tree, stretches one leg out in front of him, then the other, slowly, like an old man would. Somewhere there is the sound of hammering, the movement of birds, a boy practicing archery in a yellow lighted garage two houses down, a loose wire thudding rhythmically on a wooden house. She sees the drummer put his head back against the tree, look up, the strength of his hand running down his leg to one knee, knows that he is feeling the same things she is, hearing, seeing the same things, and she thinks of going to him, of saying something to him, but she doesn't. Instead she too leans back, looks up, stars tangled in the emptying branches of trees, of wires, and all of it, all of it singing.

Randall Kenan

Born in Brooklyn in 1963, Randall Kenan grew up in Chinquapin, North Carolina, and graduated from the University of North Carolina at Chapel Hill in 1985. He then returned to New York to work on the editorial staff at Alfred A. Knopf. Since 1989 Kenan has taught creative writing at Sarah Lawrence College, Columbia University, Duke, and his alma mater; he now teaches at the University of Memphis. His books include Walking on Water: Black American Lives at the Turn of the Twenty-first Century, A Visitation of Spirits, *and* Let the Dead Bury Their Dead, *from which "Cornsilk" is taken.*

"Cornsilk," constructed as a collage of twenty-three numbered sections, takes place within the narrator's imagination. Many of the sections begin with the narrator's informing us of his passivity: he sits, he says, he thinks. The drama in "Cornsilk" occurs in the internal landscape of his thinking, while the story's dense paragraphs and cacophonous sentences create the static buzz of our private thoughts. The effect of the story is to create an elaborate yet intimate experience for the reader. The story murmurs, whispers, and involves the reader personally with the very personal confessions of the narrator. A demonstration of short fiction's particular power to involve its audience on a very intimate and personal level, "Cornsilk" makes plain the nature of a medium that is produced and consumed in private.

Cornsilk

for Amy

1. I sit here. I sit here thinking hard about the smell of blood. It's been so long since that first time; I can barely remember its true color, its smell—like iron, perhaps? slightly funky?—its taste, thick, salty, again iron and iron. I sit here sniffing my fingers like some nasty boy, which I am, and all I can smell is the faint residue of soy sauce and MSG; not blood; not iron. What I would give to smell it again. To taste it. Hers. Her blood.

I've started smoking again. I did it at first because she did it; I didn't much like it then. But she looked so sexy when she did it, leaning up against the headboard, her hair in her eyes, her legs gapped open, a pillow between them. She could French-inhale. I can do it now. I couldn't then. Back then I would damn near choke. Now I smoke two packs a day.

So much is said of that one good cigarette after a heavy, good meal. For me it's that one good cigarette after orgasm. They aren't the same now, the orgasms. I need the blood, the slickery sensation, the mess, the horror, the grossness, the danger. These days blood is a dangerous thing, even more so than in those days. It makes cigarettes seem harmless.

I smoke too much.

2. She lifts her breast up for me to suck. She likes that. The nipple darkly brown, its areola too broad for a twenty-four-year-old woman; the small bumps pebble-hard, prickly. I bite it: she sucks in air through her nose. I suck her titty, my sugar-tit, my teat, my pacifier. In my mouth it hardens, opens, a cactus blossom in my mouth. I want it to ooze bitter milk. Her breath comes short, as if she were sprinting, her legs begin to tread water on either side of me, she calls my name urgently: *Aaron, Aaron,* as if I am to save her, as if she's about to expire. Her legs spread wider. I smell her. I feel her. Wet, hot, her pelvis speaks to me in Babylonian tongues, wild and insane, singing an ancient tune, dulcimer and zither and cymbal, vibrating, humming; I am flute, cornet, bow: we sing. We make a joyful noise unto the Lord, a raucous noise, an unholy song of heat and lust to an unholy Lord.

Lord, Lord, Lord.

3. Days of dust and debris and desolation. Dry days. Deathly dull days. Days of dim doom, dawn to dusk. My days. But that's what I wanted, isn't it? Security. Safety. That's why I got my English degree at Duke, my MBA at Georgetown, and my JD at Vanderbilt. Right? Why I chose tax law, for Christsakes. Blessed be the name of bankruptcy, depreciation, amortization.

A glorified accountant. That's what I truly am, regardless of the prestige of the firm, or how brightly the receptionist grins in the morning when I step off the elevator; or how the paralegals and the very junior associates seem to tremble in my presence. Who cares? Who will remember me, fifty years after my death, even if I become the first black partner at Henson, Spitzer, Klein, et al.? A rich old nigger who climbed up the money heap of junk bonds and golden parachutes and mergers and estate management. Big deal. Washington is full of bright, rich, bland, myopic black people. I'm just another one.

But how many change at night? I wonder. I can't be the only one. Out of my suit, into my jeans or naked on the floor. Jekyll to Hyde (or is it Hyde to Jekyll?). My mind is a blight of wrongdoing and wickedness. Is she corrupted by so much iniquity? Does she, in her husband's arms, dream of me? Does she faint trying to remember the taste of sweat on my neck? I doubt it. I very seriously doubt it. So I'm alone.

Some days I can't wait to get home, can't wait for the sun to go down, to fling off my clothes, get in bed, pick up the phone and dial 1-900-555-GIRL or 1-900-555-PSSY or 1-900-555-SEXX. It doesn't matter, now does it? Sometimes I try the party lines. Regardless, I am unsatisfied. So little poetry to their descriptions, their talk pedestrian, crude, nigh-illiterate, sad, depressing. Sometimes I begin to cry. Sometimes I just ask: Tell me about your nipples. While hammering myself violently. I come too quickly. In my sleep—I know it's a bad cliché—I dream of her.

You see, I've tried videos; I own over a hundred now. I look for likenesses, resemblances, but few have my sister's mulatto hue, or her particular features, like my father's nose or my father's lips.

So I don't watch the videos anymore. They only frustrate me.

4. An old man once told me that to plant corn properly you must put at least three seeds in a hole at a time. This way, when the plants grow up tall and begin to ovulate there will be another plant close enough to fertilize the next. Their pollen is heavy. Not like the pollen of azaleas or apple blossoms or peach blooms. They need to be close to insure the infection that leads to fat ears of corn. Isn't that something else? Must be nice.

5. I don't hate my father, though I suspect you suspect I do. No, he engenders fear in me, perhaps the way Yahweh inspired fear in Abraham's bosom.

He's a big man, both literally and figuratively. He's a doctor, the only doctor in a small town in North Carolina called Tims Creek. Where my mother is from. He's six-one, darkly handsome, sports a full white beard at fifty-five. A striking figure. He grew up in New York, went to Morehouse and Howard Medical School. He was the sort of man who studied Arabic while interning at Columbia-Presbyterian. Very radical in the sixties. He met Mom in Atlanta. In the seventies, disillusioned with "the Movement" by the time I was about ready for high school, he decided the most effective use of his skills would be to practice in the rural South, where good medical care was hard to come by. Fateful decision.

But not as fateful as his decision—characteristic of Dad, morally upright, constantly challenging himself—to take in the one Big Misake he had made in his life: the nineteen-year-old daughter he had conceived before college. His father, a doctor too, in Harlem, had done right by the girl, but Pop felt the need—why, I still can't quite understand—to readopt her. You see, he didn't approve of the life her mother, poor, living in Spanish Harlem, was providing for his firstborn. He had plans for his progeny. Great Yahweh, Malcolm Aaron Streeter, *and his Covenant will go unbroken throughout the ages, for time immemorial, for your children and your children's children's children. Amen.*

What would ole grey-beard say if he knew what he had set in motion? He'd probably quote the Bhagavad Gita or the Koran or some obscure Aztec text.

I really don't hate my father. I'm just scared to death of him. This is the honest truth.

6. Trust me. (Though you should never trust a lawyer who actually says: Trust me.) I know it sounds Freudian; but it is not Freudian, not Freudian in its intent, though perhaps in its execution; Freudian in its caresses, Freudian in its French kisses and sucking, its licking and gasps and funk. Not Freudian in its unconscious meaning. No. I beseech you, as Cromwell said, "in the bowels of Christ, to think it that you might be wrong." Not Freud, okay? Not in his symbolism or his interpretation. Jung perhaps. An archetypal fuck-up, a consciousness of sin. But Freud, much as I respect him, has nothing to do with it. So please put away your *Totem and Taboo* and your *Interpretation of Dreams* and your *Psychopathology of Everyday Life* and your copy of *Three Contributions to the Theory of Sex.* Okay? I've read them, you see. I've read them all. And trust me. Freud and his ideas don't figure into this little drama.

7. I hated Tims Creek at first, but not as much as she did, and not as long. She still hates it, she tells me. Even though she's never truly left the state since she came to live there, keeps going back to see her father and stepmother in Tims Creek, and lives in a town very like Tims Creek. But she insists she hates it.

I can't hate it now. It's become a part of me. A part of my internal landscape. The forests, the pastures, the hog pens, the barns and chicken coops, the tobacco fields, the soybean fields, and of course the cornfields. Not to make too much of them. They're there, certainly, and I can't avoid them.

I remember my first look into them, at the edge as if I were staring into a Conradian jungle, a North American Congo. I expected Indians to come dashing out, not real Indians but the Indians of a twelve-year-old's imagination: tomahawk-toting, befeathered, howling. A racist notion, yes, but innocent in its intent. Sometimes I imagined drums, like the beat of copulation, though I had no idea at the time that that was the rhythm of sex, the rhythm I imagined, felt in my soul. Though in truth it's also the thud of the heart, the motion of the lungs, the same harmless, infectious rhythm.

But there was nothing sinister about those first years before she came, before I lost interest in imaginary games with imaginary play-mates, spaceships, super heroes, sorcerers. The fields, the woods, gave me such freedom, more than a kid growing up on West 135th Street could have dreamed of.

At first we lived with my grandmother, Miss Jesse. Thin, decep-tively delicate, Victorian, Wilmington-bred; daughter of a realtor, widow of an insurance man with land that became hers. Imperious, hard as brass knuckles, Miss Jesse, cloaked in cigarette smoke, issued hoarse commands obeyed without question; her eyes saw levers and switches instead of people. She could fell a man with one well-placed word, disintegrate a woman with an accurately calibrated glance.

Her relationship with Jamonica was contentious at best. This urban girl of 116th Street and Third Avenue, now ordered to mop floors, cut grass, wash windows and porches. Jamonica fussed. Miss Jesse glared back regally, conceding nothing. My mother sat in the wings embroidering, knitting, reading, choosing not to get involved. Ole Malcolm was much too busy working out the salvation of his Cho-sen People to be bothered, or to care. So Miss Jesse and Jamonica finally worked out a truce of sorts. Though I believe, secretly, Miss Jesse enjoyed the spirited young girl's protests and the domestic warfare.

How would she, now, from her grave, comment upon our forbid-den coupling?

8. I've tried the escort services. Pathetic. These women, I mean. Sad. I like to think of myself as a feminist, or at least one who does more than pay lip service. But don't all men harbor secret romantic visions about prostitutes, about carefree, totally free, uninhibited human toys? I must be honest here.

But these poor women. Some bitten by the Horatio Alger bug of saving and working to get through college, maybe to become bank tellers or flight attendants or pizza joint managers. Even they seem sad, in the end, lost to their hard-to-realize dreams. I rarely talk to them about their lives anymore. Not that I see them that often. The services don't take MasterCard.

I describe what I want sent over and they're generally all wrong. Nothing like Jamonica. Some come as stereotypical harlots: gum-chewing, lipsticked in vivid red, fluffy-haired, ill-spoken—a vision of delight, to be sure, for some fat, impotent beer distributor. Or they come young, bewildered, innocent still, though in the very maw of the monster; pure yet defiled. Or they'll send me hardened, practical women, good at their trade—for it is a trade to them, serving up fantasy. I never tell them they are to be my sister. Though they're probably used to much kinkier.

One girl—sorry: woman—called herself Rose. She came the closest of any I've seen so far. But I heard no Assyrian music, felt no ancient demons howl; I ended up holding her, eyes closed, limp as yarn, calling, calling softly.

"Who's Jamonica?" Rose asked me.

"An old lover."

She kissed me coyly, a kiss reeking of sentimentality and audacious pity. I told her to leave.

Perhaps it's true then, what I've thought all along. What's that old platitude—I know it's tacky as hell to mention, but why not? you'll think of it anyway—how does it go? The closer kin, the deeper in?

Exactly.

9. I sit here and wonder if I'm truly crazy. Am I? Crazy?

I've tried shrinks. They think the problem is with my family. No shit.

Am I sitting here amid boxes of chicken and snowpeas, beef and broccoli, gooey rice and the remnants of an eggroll dabbled in mustard and duck sauce, scribbling the thoughts of a madman? Or am I merely depraved? Are these the thoughts of a neurotic? A psychopath? Or am I just more honest than most? Smarter? Am I daring greatly? Or have I been cursed for violating a sacred trust older than Yoruba legend and Nippon lore? Am I the victim of the gods' own jealous wrath? Eat of any tree in the garden, but you are damned if you eat of the fruit of the One Tree. Double-damned if you enjoy it. Triple-damned if you can't get enough.

Damn.

10. Let me tell you about my sister. I already have, you'll say. But no. I've told you of my infatuation and my obsession. Of lovemaking. But Jamonica herself is something else again.

She visited two summers in a row before she came to live with us. I hated her at first, resenting the intrusion in our lives, this illegitimate half-breed distracting my father, who already had problems focusing on me. Selfish little bastard, wasn't I?

Jamonica despised the country, she said. Claiming allergies to everything—grass, dogs, air—she carried the city around with her in her makeup, her clothing, her perfume, her sneering at the dull country folk, saying: "Oh, you're so *country!*," impatient in conversation. Everything, everything moved too slow for her. She was surrounded by bumpkins as far as she was concerned and kept dreaming aloud of Manhattan and subways and sidewalks. I thought she was crazy.

She wanted to smoke. She did smoke. Miss Jesse and Dad said: No. She persisted, sneaking a smoke in her room, in the backyard. My mom said: Hell no, and Jamonica went even farther out of her way to defy them. I would tattle on her whenever I had hard evidence, hoping maybe they'd get rid of her.

But all this changed that second summer, perhaps the harbinger of my ordeal, my fixation, the bad habit to come. Let's be portentous.

At first the boys would hang around the barn, loudly laughing at us laboring country folks. The boys? Phil, Terry, and Vaughn. Three nephews of the man who leased Miss Jesse's land. Bad boys from the Bronx. Visiting for the summer. Nineteen, seventeen, sixteen. Walking bombs of testosterone, adrenaline, semen, hot blood, and bad attitude. The barn? The tobacco barn, where my little sister, Miss Jesse, I, and groaning, moaning, protesting, fussing Jamonica backhanded the bright-green leaves to be tied and sent into the barn for firing. Miss Jesse insisted we work in tobacco. It built character. Tobacco. *Nicotiana tabacum.* It's a member of the nightshade family, you know? Belladonna and all that. Now there's a symbol for you.

I loved the work; it was more like play to me. Playing with doodlebugs in the sand around the barn, listening to the women gossip. Sweat and toil were new and thrilling to me. But Jamonica never stopped bitching. Hated the black tar the leaves left caked on her hand. Hated the talk of soap operas and boyfriends and unfaithful husbands. I think at one point she even threatened to kill Miss Jesse.

Like wolves the boys came. Maybe they heard Jamonica was from Harlem. Maybe they were bored. Maybe they smelled her, her especially, caught her scent in the wind.

"Hey, you. Yeah, you. Where you from?"

"Why, Where you from?"

"A Hundred and Seventy-first and Grand Concourse. Okay? Where're you from?"

"Around a Hundred and Sixteenth."

"Got a boyfriend?"

"Yeah."

"And he let you come down here in these woods all by yourself?"

They snorted and chortled and heh-heh-hehed. I wanted to stuff tobacco leaves down their throats.

"Why don't you boys start working?" Miss Jesse gave the oldest a stare that I'm sure would have turned me into lead. "If you plan to hang around bothering us."

"Aaaah. No, thank you. We on vacation."

"Well, then. In that case I suggest you vacate these premises."

"But we like it here."

I had never seen boys look at other people like that. Or perhaps I had just not noticed it. A look like hunger, but where hunger involves the head and belly, this involved the entire body, the legs, the arms, the hips, the backbone. They leered. But the most disturbing thing, to GI Joe-toting, *Batman*-reading, electric-train-set-operating me, was the way Jamonica flirtatiously, coquettishly, seemed to be egging them on, with her eyes, with her lips. Could she be enjoying this? Of course not. These boys were dogs.

"I said"—Miss Jesse stepped back from work and began walking toward the boys—"you boys had better find another place to amuse yourselves. We are working here!" She stood before the oldest boy, Phil.

Obviously, he intended to hang tough at first, but apparently Miss Jesse's psychic bullwhip lashed out and snap-crackled his brain. He stumbled backward and swallowed. "Okay, Miss. We hear you, all right? All right."

They left, looking back purposefully, their rowdy talk trailing off behind them, jackals slinking into the distance.

"Those boys are no good." Miss Jesse shook her head, going back to work. "No good."

No good, but not gone. They made their presence known to Jamonica, and I picked up on it as though I had a shortwave attached to her, eavesdropping. Here, there, around Tims Creek, they lurked. I kept my watergun full.

One day—perhaps, being portentous, I should say: One Fateful Day—Jamonica and I were walking back home from working at the barn. The boys approached us from the other direction. I remember the feeling I fought against. The fear of being bested in a fight, the anger of intrusion, the newborn desire to protect my sister. Maybe even jealousy, inchoate, innocent, impossible.

"Where you heading, little lady?"

"Nowhere you going or been."

They guffawed too loudly, stroking their chins, eyeing her as if she were a new car.

"You sure about that?"

My cue. I leapt forward. "Leave her alone, you—"

"What the fuck is this?" Phil barely gave me a full look. "Tell it to go away fore I squash it."

"He's my brother. And I suggest you keep your hands to yourself." She grabbed me from behind and my diastolic blood pressure surely jumped ten points from humiliation.

"With my feet, babe. Not my hands. The hands is for you."

They had us encircled, or, more accurately, entriangled.

"You full of talk, Phil."

"*Talk?* Course I got a rap. But, sweet thang, I got something else."

"Like what?"

"Come on, I'll show you."

He stood in front of me, facing her, me squished between the two of them like so much baloney. I punched him between the legs.

What happened next I remember only impressionistically, due mostly to the whir of activity but also to not wanting to remember: Phil furiously pushes me to his brothers: they jostle me about, making rude comments about my size, manhood, and intelligence: I try to watch what peculiar negotiations Phil is making with my sister: she apparently negotiates back: I see him nod toward the cornfield off the road: I'm on the ground crying: the three boys and Jamonica go into the field.

Sobbing, I stood at the edge of the cornfield, part of me scared to death, part of me confused, and part of me, the part familiar with comic-book heroes, ready to slip into my costume and fly into the field and deliver my sister from harm. I had no cape, no ray gun, no smoke bombs. Batman never cried. I ran in. The tall corn swatting me in the face, the uneven earth making it hard to keep my footing, I knocked over stalks to find them. After a time I did, peering through the stalks as through leafy prison bars.

He seemed to be hurting her. Her pants were open at the top, revealing panties, pubic hair; his hand was between her legs; he held her closely, violently, his mouth all over hers; his pants were down about his knees; his penis a small, black dragon. The other two boys looked on lewdly, rubbing their pants. I heard Jamonica giggle. I lunged toward them but something stopped me.

Even now my eyes tear a bit. Not for what they did to my sister but because that slap hurt. No one has ever hit me quite so hard. I sat between two cornrows, rocking like a spinning top about to fall, the breath knocked out of me. I looked on. Saw the dragon disappear. Saw that she enjoyed it and clutched him, hard, as if he were saving her.

I did not stop running until I got to the house, looking over my shoulder most of the way thinking the boys would catch me and perhaps do the same wicked thing to me. I suspected I would not enjoy it.

Miss Jesse sat on the porch with Mrs. Pearsall. Out of breath, face covered with dirt and sweat, weeds and corn tassels about my hair, tears in my eyes, I yelled at the top of my voice: "Grandma, Phil is doing it to Jamonica in the cornfield!"

She did not blink. She reached for a cigarette smoldering there in a nearby ashtray. I can still hear her, how she formed her words, the sound of the words as they whipped through me: clear, measured, firm, piercing:

"Young man, you will learn there are things you do not tell your elders. A tattletale is not an admirable thing to be. Now go wash your face and hands—you look a sight."

For once I did not obey her. I sat on the stoop and stared at the cornfield, unbraided, picking at my confusion like a new sore.

Finally she hollered for me to do as she said, and I did.

At length Jamonica returned, calm, a look I now know is called afterglow on her face, a few strands of hair askew, a piece of tassel here and there.

"Sister,"—Miss Jesse always called younger women Sister, even my mother—"Sister, supper's about done. Go wash up."

No one said a word about it. Not even I. Nor has she said a word to me, to this day. I often replay the scene in my mind. Tell you a deep secret: in my replay I am Phil. Jamonica is Jamonica is Jamonica. Wicked, no?

II. Corn. *Zorn Maze* or *Zea Mays*. A very peculiar plant, as much vegetable as grain. An ingenious invention of nature. Its seeds can be eaten either young or aged, ground into a powder, turned into a paste, and cooked. The Native Americans, as we all know from TV commercials, called it *maize*. But it's indigenous, in certain varieties, to Australia and Africa as well. The Egyptians grew it. The word we use comes from the Anglo-Saxon *coren* or *korn(e)* or *corne* or *coorn*, borrowing from the Middle Teutonic *korno*, meaning grain, finally coming to mean "a worn-down particle." In that way it was applied to any grain at first, wheat, rye, barley, etc.; or to small seeds such as apple or grape seeds; or to mean a bit of gunpowder or salt. The first known use as applied to *maize* was in 1679 and it stuck.

You've seen cornfields. You've seen how they move in the breeze. You've known the feeling I've spoken of, the dread and excitement. Expectation. Fear. As if something were lurking there. Imagine that feeling applied to a woman.

12. I wanted to become a doctor, but that would have made him too happy. Couldn't do that. (You think it's because I hate him; but I don't, as I've told you; I don't. If I had become a doctor, I'd have failed him in the end. So his happiness would have been short-lived. And I'd have been humiliated. See?) So I chose botany first. He was lukewarm about that. He finally came around by the time I said ethnobotany, in my freshman year. This made him a wee bit happier. Christmas of my junior year I changed my mind. I told him before I went back to school that January that I had chosen to declare pre-law. You should have seen the look on his face. Later he changed his tune; I suspect he could envision me a judge. When I got to law school he fully expected me to specialize in civil rights law. (At Vanderbilt? He just wasn't thinking.) When I broke the news over dinner that it would be tax law, I could see that he had pretty much given up on me. Not that I wouldn't do well; well was a given. But not exceptionally. Not gloriously. There is no glory in tax law.

13. She started it. I know how petulant and boy-like such a statement sounds. *She started it.* But it's true. She did.

Does the math confuse you? It's confusing. Dr. Streeter reached down into the miry clay when he was nineteen, just before he went off to Morehouse, and made Jamonica of a comely Puerto Rican woman. He begat me upon my mother in holy matrimony while in residency, when he was twenty-seven. Actually, chronologically speaking, six years, not seven, separate us. My younger sister came along three years later. Okay? I was nineteen—we Streeter men have a thing for the number nineteen and carnality—when it started. She was twenty-five. Not so daunting an idea. Well, the math at least.

Before that moment, before we entered the door with the hidden NO EXIT sign, where you couldn't get a refund on your ticket, before I truly knew her like David knew Bathsheba, we were just big sis and little bro. She was someone to annoy me, reprove me, get in the bathroom before me, to drive me around before I got my license, to tattle on, to play practical jokes on and make fun of. There were other girls and nasty sex before her—I never claimed to be an angel. But she was the milestone, the dividing line between BC and AD.

How? Don't be silly. Why? Don't be naïve. What? Now there's an intelligent question. I don't know, *what?* What made us do it. Alone in the house. She had finally graduated from NC Central after taking a few semesters off here and there. Papa proud. Mama relieved. Other mother happy. Grandma dead. I was about to go off to Duke. Summer.

Summer of possibilities. Did we both sense it? All the possibilities? There on the couch, everybody gone? Did we both think, He/she's only my *half* sister/brother? I think not. I don't think we thought.

You must understand there was a general excitement in the atmosphere. You know, the flip side of teenage angst for me—the freedom to come; for her the horizon of life, career, *possibilities* . . .

Oh, but this is too abstract. I can't get you to understand me, if not to empathize then to sympathize, through cold and vague language. Let me be romantic, people respond to that. Let me be dramatic. Let me conjure.

Okay. It's June. Early June. Dr. and Mrs. Streeter and little sister Streeter are away, not for a day or a weekend but for two whole weeks. Jamonica and Aaron are home with nothing to occupy them for the duration.

They talk, now both young adults, about this and that. They become close. It's as if they were new people to each other. Aaron has had those pernicious growth spurts since Jamonica has been away; he is handsome, strapping; his voice has deepened; his chest and arms and legs are hard from tennis and track and basketball. At twenty-five Jamonica is—well, I'm being romantic, right?—a flower, a Tahitian nymph out of Gauguin, her lips plump and rich; her eyes, blackly, oilily, sinisterly, smokily, with magic in them, remind him of reptiles, not in repulsion but in cold heat . . . This isn't doing it, is it? I could play with words all night, but they would only start to get at how the sight of her on a stool, sitting carelessly, or lounging on the sofa smoking, made my pulse flitter, my penis roll over and sigh . . . I give up . . .

They sit before the television watching *Sanford and Son* (I even remember the episode but I won't bore you). They have become more and more lewd in their innuendo and joking. Aaron grabs her now and then, at first brotherly, jocularly, but the grasp lingers a bit long and Aaron senses that she does not mind, that she is even solicitous. That day while watching TV, Aaron, erect as a stalk of corn, notices her skirt hitched up to her thigh. That moment changes things. Irrevocably. A circuit fuses in his mind. *Psssst.*

He gets on his knees as if to pray. He spreads her legs, his hands trembling on her knees. He begins to kiss the tender insides of her thighs. She coos and grabs his head, urging him on. He inches up to her panties, pulls them down. She gives a giggle. He sees it there. Humble little thing. He pauses only for a moment: already defying propriety, holy law, why stop? Against her half-uttered protests, he pulls it out: smelly, clotted, horrid. Her skirt is ruined, a spot will be left on the couch, a deep-maroon Rorschach, which his mother will never mention. The cushion will remain forever turned over.

Okay. So I lied. I started it then.

We practically lived in bed after that. I expected to hear Dad's car drive up at the most inopportune moments. But miraculously, we were left to our iniquity. Precious, sinful freedom. Wild positions. I learned much that week. I long to be able to forget it all and return to ignorance. What bliss I'd know.

14. Truth is, I would have made a terrible botanist. A terrible scientist. I flunked chemistry and my interest in the field is very limited. At best.

15. Some nights I leave my house and wander the streets of Washington, visiting those places where love is for sale, or at least for barter. While walking I question my sanity again, wonder if any mother's daughter is safe with me on the prowl. Might I see my sister's likeness and thrust myself upon her, poor cherub? Unsuspecting victim of incest, innocent yet spoiled? But I'm not capable. You see, I have to be invited in, as she invited me. Legs spread, eyes rolled back St. Sebastian-like, trilling: Come. So I look for the willing.

I've tried everything. Trust me. You name it, as kinky and raunchy as they make it. Leather, spanking, drugs, domination, water sports— hoping to find a replacement for my addiction. I even tried bestiality once but broke out laughing too hard to go through with it; I fear I traumatized the pitiful creature.

I don't walk the streets as much as I used to. Too many people searching for too many things. Confusion is my enemy. My focus is clear.

16. I sit here writing, scribble, scribble, scribble. What do I think I'm accomplishing? All else has failed, do I think writing will exorcise the demon in me? Am I possessed? Is Merrim, Prince of the Air, whispering over my shoulder? Claptrap. I have one of the best educations money can buy and all I can do is confide to paper. What's wrong with this picure?

I've done my reading. All my homework. Should I tell you what I've found? Shall I quote Whitman or Auden or Pound? Shall I give you a Canto or a Quartet? Hughes or Baraka or Hayden? Lincoln or Du Bois? Eliot's "No! I am not Prince Hamlet, nor was meant to be"? Stevens's "If her horny feet protrude, they come / To show how cold she is, and dumb"? Brooks's "Where you have thrown me, scraped me with your kiss"? Moore's "Arise, for it is day!"? From Dr. Miller, Dr. Sacks, Dr. Bettelheim, Dr. Gruen? Anything. Read to you from my commonplace book, tease you with the profane, the sacred phrases that strike me, struck me? De Sade, Miller, Lawrence? I have them all. Words. Babble. They give me no answers, so I choke on them, give them back, spit them up and out. I sniff them but I smell no blood. Alas.

17. I must be fair. She's struggling now. Not about me. Not with the memory of what's been done. No. She has no time for that luxury. Seems Dr. Streeter's scheme didn't quite work for her. She's trapped, you see. She fell in love. She married. But it's not a happy tale. (Do I gloat?) He's a trucker. Big, crude, sentimental. Name's Fred. Can you believe it? Fred. Jesus. It seems after all those years in college and all that talk about the Big City she opted to remain in North Carolina, manage a Dairy Queen, and make babies with Fred. Yes, Fred. The third is on the way. I don't know what kind of magic that hairy, beer-guzzling, australopithecine cretin has in his pants or wherever he hides it, but she stays in a trailer outside Whiteville of all places, like a slave, a mere shadow of the racy, witty, intelligent Jamonica I knew.

I visited her last month but I didn't see her. Not the woman I smuggled into my dorm room, the woman I made laugh at horror movies and baked banana-walnut bread with, the sister I've known better than any brother should. Her body now misshapen from multiple births, now sullen-eyed, smoking even more, a sepia and hollering baby in her arms, another in the high chair. She smiles, she looks, but her eyes never truly focus on anything, not on TV, not on her babies, not on her dingy trailer, not on Fred, certainly not on me.

Tell me. Who am I searching for now? Where is she?

He beats her, you know. Now there's a fucking cliché for you. "Oh, yeah, my sister, the pretty one, she's a battered wife now." He beats my sister and she refuses to let anyone do anything about it. She goes home for a day, two; she goes back to him.

"You don't have to put up with this shit," I tell her.

She just looks at me, through me really. Her eyes are dry. Not reptilian but pathetically mammalian. "You don't get it, do you? Of course you don't. How can you?"

She looks away. Not even staring into the wall, just looking.

I want to say: Teach me. Teach me.

18. Madness? Obsession? Depravity? ALL I can think of is the smell of pubic hair, its look; the upper thigh, you know, where it connects to the center, that crevice there where the nerves cluster; the foot, you've licked

a foot before, nibbled a heel? The sight, just the sight, of the clitoris, that red, wonderful proboscis. Anatomy, anatomized, particles of a person. Hers, all hers. Just so much flesh otherwise. Not her. Not her. Her.

19. Two years. Freshman and sophomore years. Truly wicked. You see, nobody knew. Nobody knew she was my sister. She'd come for a weekend. A week, twice or thrice, staying in my room. All the guys thought me such a stud. I guess I was. More than even I knew. This *older* woman at my service, slipped past the RA, gasping in my room; my roommate, if not in bed with his own joy-toy, envious beyond expression. Hellacious fantasy. We did all the things college sweetkins do, the football games, the basketball games, the rock concerts, the pizza parlors, the movies. We were defying someone to blow our cover. I was too stupid, I guess *we* were too stupid, to think beyond the moment. They never found out. They never knew. If they had looked, and looked closely, they would have seen; if they had looked beyond her light skin, my dark skin, her thick, long, mermaid's hair, my tightly curled, closely cropped hair, they could have seen, if they had truly looked, that our mouths, our eyes, our chins cried: Brother, sister, sister, brother! But who would dare think such a thing? Who would dare *do* such a thing?

Two years of iniquitous bliss. And when it ended, I ended. How's that for melodramtic?

20. That year, the end of the second year, I had a major fight with Dr. Streeter. You know, the one I don't hate.

My grades were not up to snuff. I wonder why? I had been placed on something very like probation. Academic watch, they called it.

"My son? A son of mine?"

"Dad—"

"No. I don't know what you're doing up in Durham but it's got to stop. It—"

We hurtled words for hours, and somehow it managed to go beyond grade point and "discipline." It got to father-and-son bullshit and at the top of my voice I remembered yelling: "But I don't want to be *you*. Can't you get it through your fucking skull? Don't you know I hate your black ass?"

He did not move, aside from a twitching of his jaw. He left the room. He left the room and did not speak to me for two days. When he did it was to take me back to school. Making clear my fate was in my own hands. He had washed his.

I said I hated him. That day. Even then I didn't. I don't. I didn't have the words to express what I felt, so I said the opposite of what I meant. Does this make sense? Even now, my prolixity notwithstanding, I don't know if I could tell him, face to face. I don't even know if I can tell myself.

21. If she didn't start it she certainly did end it. Of course I was prepared, but how can you prepare to end something you had no business starting in the first place?

I noticed the change when she came to Duke that Friday. The way she seemed uncomfortable, not able to look me in the face. Our lovemaking became quick, mercilessly violent, yet elegiac in a telltale way, our bodies saying: No more. End it.

I took her to the airport that Sunday. She was going to visit her mother in New York. In the terminal she said she had to talk to me. We had a cup of coffee at the hot dog stand, fifteen minutes before she had to board.

"We've got to stop this, Aaron."

"Why? We've been doing it for years now."

I'd seen her livid, but not like this. Not angry, but betraying a mixture of anger, fear, and what I'd like to flatter myself was the anticipation of lack of love. Pain.

" 'Why?' Think, son. Stop and think. Stop being Horny Joe College and think. Will you do that, please? Think."

I held my breath, fearing what I might say, knowing nothing.

"Are we going to get married, huh? Huh? Tell me, you idiot. Are we going to slip up and have a little abortion on our hands? Huh? Oh, God. Shit, Aaron. It's wrong. Okay? Just wrong."

"But—"; but that "but" hung there in the air between us, it did a somersault, that word, a conjunction, a connection. It broke. Shattered. I saw it. A busted word.

"Oh, Jesus. You're beautiful. You're smart. But you're such a shit. A beautiful shit. A selfish, beautiful son of a bitch. God save us both, you little shit."

"I'll miss . . . I'll . . . I'll—"

"Save it for Thanksgiving."

She rolled her eyes and reached for her bags. "We've both got some growing up to do."

I watched her plane gaining altitude, and I know I sound like the violins at the end of the movie, but there it was, there it went. There she went. Up, up, and away. Lights out. Show's over. The dancing bear is done. The fat lady has quit singing. The freak show is over, buddy. Go home.

Here I sit, waiting for the Second Coming. But she ain't coming a second time. I know that. But I wait, I write, I screw. My faith is the size of a kernel of corn. *Ave Jamonica.*

That Christmas I switched my major from botany to pre-law.

I think it's obvious why.

22. There's a dream. There's always a dream. You want to hear corny? No, it's not in a cornfield. And I don't marry her. No, in my dream we're home: in my mother and father's bed: we're at the height: we're outside our skins: and they walk in: Dad, Mom, and Miss Jesse too: and get this: they're happy. They approve. They throw a party. They tell everyone. *Everyone.* There's a celebration. I tell my dad I love him. I tell him I want to be just like him.

Talk about depravity. Talk about signs and symbols and shit. Talk about wish fulfillment.

23. You know, sin is like an American Express card. You grin with delight when you use it, you're the Aga Khan; but you cry like hell when the bill comes.

I sit here. I sit here beyond pity and love and hope, a vomitous bone-house of shit and spit and semen and shame. I sit here regurgitating the past as if to heal myself with confession, knowing I can't, I won't. I sit here, thinking of a woman who does not exist, will never exist. Some Faulknerian heroine, some clichéd tragic mulatto from antebellum trash, some Greek daughter of the gods come down to taunt, to tease, to test my mettle. I failed. Miserably. My hubris has poisoned me; my sin has undone me. I am a pathetic, weak, fart-filled clod of earth, earth to which I shall surely return, soon and very soon, unworthy of pity, wretched in my groveling, pitiful in my remorse: I am the blind beggar who does not deserve to see—and if I were so blessed, guess whom I'd look for?

Cris Mazza

Cris Mazza has lived most of her life in San Diego, California, where she trained and showed Shetland sheepdogs and dabbled in photography. She now spends part of each year in Chicago, where she is a professor in the Program for Writers at the University of Illinois at Chicago. Her most recent books include Indigenous/Growing Up Californian, *a collection of linked personal essays, and* Homeland, *a novel. Her other notable titles are* Girl Beside Him, Dog People, *the PEN/Nelson Algren winner* How to Leave a Country, *and the acclaimed* "Is It Sexual Harassment Yet?" *Mazza was co-editor of* Chick-Lit *and* Chick-Lit 2, *controversial anthologies of women's fiction.*

"Is It Sexual Harassment Yet?" *records the sexually contested relationship between a male and a female employee in a restaurant; it highlights the changing and fraught landscape of the contemporary workplace. Mazza depicts the conflicting points of view in the story by using parallel columns of text, which forces readers to mediate between two simultaneous narratives. In making sense of the story, the reader must make his or her own judgment about what has happened. The graphic description of the conflict between the man and the woman attempts to simulate the rich confusion of subjective points of view. The reader enjoys the experience, quite literally, of he said/she said.*

Is It Sexual Harassment Yet?

Even before the Imperial Penthouse switched from a staff of exclusively male waiters and food handlers to a crew of fifteen waitresses, Terence Lovell was the floor captain. Wearing a starched ruffled shirt and black tails, he embodied continental grace and elegance as he seated guests and, with a toreador's flourish, produced menus out of thin air. He took all orders but did not serve—except in the case of a flaming meal or dessert, and this duty, for over ten years, was his alone. One of his trademarks was to never be seen striking the match—either the flaming platter was swiftly paraded from the kitchen or the dish would seemingly spontaneously ignite on its cart beside the table, a quiet explosion, then a four-foot column of flame, like a fountain with floodlights of changing colors.

There'd been many reasons for small celebrations at the Lovell home during the past several years: Terence's wife, Maggie, was able to quit her job as a key-punch operator when she finished courses and was hired as a part-time legal secretary. His son was tested into the gifted program at school. His daughter learned to swim before she could walk. The newspaper did a feature on the Imperial Penthouse with a half-page photo of Terence holding a flaming shish-kebab.

Then one day on his way to work, dressed as usual in white tie and tails, Terence Lovell found himself stopping off at a gun store. For that moment, as he approached the glass-topped counter, Terence said his biggest fear was that he might somehow, despite his professional elegant manners, appear to the rest of the world like a cowboy swaggering his way up to the bar to order a double. Terence purchased a small hand gun—the style that many cigarette lighters resemble—and tucked it into his red cummerbund.

It was six to eight months prior to Terence's purchase of the gun that the restaurant began to integrate waitresses into the per-

I know they're going to ask about my previous sexual experiences. What counts as sexual? Holding hands? Wet kisses? A fin-

sonnel. Over the next year or so, the floor staff was supposed to eventually evolve into one made up of all women with the exception of the floor captain. It was still during the early weeks of the new staff, however, when Terence began finding gifts in his locker. First there was a black lace and red satin garter. Terence pinned it to the bulletin board in case it had been put into the wrong locker, so the owner could claim it. But the flowers he found in his locker were more of a problem— they were taken from the vases on the tables. Each time that he found a single red rosebud threaded through the vents in his locker door, he found a table on the floor with an empty vase, so he always put the flower back where it belonged. Terence spread the word through the busboys that the waitresses could take the roses off the tables each night *after* the restaurant was closed, but not before. But on the whole, he thought— admittedly on retrospect—the atmosphere with the new waitresses seemed, for the first several weeks, amiable and unstressed.

Then one of the waitresses, Michelle Rae, reported to management that Terence had made inappropriate comments to her during her shift at work. Terence said he didn't know which of the waitresses had made the complaint, but also couldn't remember if management had withheld

ger up my ass? Staring at a man's bulge? He wore incredibly tight pants. But before all this happened, I wasn't a virgin, and I wasn't a virgin in so many ways. I never had an abortion, I never had VD, never went into a toilet stall with a woman, never castrated a guy at the moment of climax. But I know enough to know. As soon as you feel like *some*one, you're no one. Why am I doing this? *Why?*

So, you'll ask about my sexual history but won't think to inquire about the previous encounters I *almost* had, or *never* had: it wasn't the old ships-in-the-night tragedy, but let's say I had a ship, three or four years ago, the ship of love, okay? So once when I had a lot of wind in my sails (is this a previous sexual experience yet?), the captain sank the vessel when he started saying stuff like, "You're not ever going to be the most important thing in someone else's life unless it's something like he kills you—and then only if he hasn't killed anyone else yet nor knocked people off for a living— otherwise no one's the biggest deal in anyone's life but their own." Think about that. He may've been running my ship, but it turns out he was navigating by remote control. When the whole thing blew up, *he* was unscathed. Well, now I try to live as though I wrote that rule, as though it's *mine*. But that hasn't made me like it any better.

the name of the accuser, or if, when told the name at this point, he just didn't know which waitress she was. He said naturally there was a shift in decorum behind the door to the kitchen, but he wasn't aware that anything he said or did could have possibly been so misunderstood. He explained that his admonishments were never more than half-serious, to the waitresses as well as the waiters or busboys: "Move your butt," or "One more mix-up and you'll be looking at the happy end of a skewer." While he felt a food server should appear unruffled, even languid, on the floor, he pointed out that movement was brisk in the kitchen area, communication had to get the point across quickly, leaving no room for confusion or discussion. And while talking and joking on a personal level was not uncommon, Terence believed the waitresses had not been working there long enough for any conversations other than work-related, but these included light-hearted observations: a customer's disgusting eating habits, vacated tables that appeared more like battlegrounds than the remains of a fine dinner, untouched expensive meals, guessing games as to which couples were first dates and which were growing tired of each other, whose business was legitimate and whose probably dirty, who were wives and which were the mis-

There are so many ways to humiliate someone. Make someone so low they leave a snail-trail. Someone makes a joke, you don't laugh. Someone tells a story—a personal story, something that mattered—you don't listen, you aren't moved. Someone wears a dance leotard to work, you don't notice. But underneath it all, you're planning the real humiliation. The symbolic humiliation. The humiliation of humiliations. Like I told you, I learned this before, I already know the *type*: he'll be remote, cool, distant—*seeming* to be gentle and tolerant but actually cruelly indifferent. It'll be great fun for him to be aloof or preoccupied when someone is in love with him, genuflecting, practically prostrating herself. If he doesn't respond, she can't say he hurt her, she never got close enough. He'll go on a weekend ski trip with his friends. She'll do calisthenics, wash her hair, shave her legs, and wait for Monday. Well, not *this* time, no sir. Terence Lovell is messing with a sadder-but-wiser chick.

tresses, and, of course, the rude customers. Everyone always had rude-customer stories to trade. Terence had devised a weekly contest where each food server produced their best rude-customer story on a 3x5 card and submitted it each Friday. Terence then judged them and awarded the winner a specially made shishkebab prepared after the restaurant had closed, with all of the other waiters and waitresses providing parodied royal table service, even to the point of spreading the napkin across the winner's lap and dabbing the corners of his or her mouth after each bite.

The rude-customer contest was suspended after the complaint to management. However, the gifts in his locker multiplied during this time. He continued to tack the gifts to the bulletin board, whenever possible: the key chain with a tiny woman's high-heeled shoe, the 4x6 plaque with a poem printed over a misty photograph of a dense green moss-covered forest, the single black fishnet stocking. When he found a pair of women's underwear in his locker, instead of tacking them to the bulletin board, he hung them on the inside doorknob of the woman's restroom. That was the last gift he found in his locker for a while. Within a week he received in the mail the same pair of women's underwear.

Since the beginning of the new staff, the restaurant manager had been talking about having a staff party to help the new employees feel welcome and at ease with the previous staff. But in the confusion of settling in, a date had never been set. Four or five months after the waitresses began work, the party had a new purpose: to ease the tension caused by the complaint against Terence. So far, nothing official had been done or said about Ms. Rae's allegations.

During the week before the party, which was to be held in an uptown nightclub with live music on a night the Imperial Penthouse was closed, Terence asked around to find out if Michelle Rae would be attending. All he discovered about her, however, was that she didn't seem to have any close friends on the floor staff.

Michelle did come to the party. She wore a green strapless dress which, Terence remembered, was unbecomingly tight and, as he put it, made her rump appear too ample. Her hair was in a style Terence described as finger-in-a-light-socket. Terence believed he probably would not have noticed Michelle at all that night if he were not aware of the complaint she had made. He recalled that her lipstick was the same shade of red as her hair and there were red tints in her eye shadow.

Yes, I was one of the first five women to come in as food servers, and I expected the usual resistance—the dirty glasses and ash-strewn linen on our tables (before the customer was seated), planting long hairs in the salads, cold soup, busboys delivering tips that appeared to have been left on greasy plates or in puddles of gravy on the tablecloth. I could stand those things. It was like them saying, "We know you're here!" But no, not *him. He* didn't want to return to the days of his all-male staff. Why would he want that? Eventually he was going to be in charge of an all-woman floor. Sound familiar? A harem? A pimp's stable? He thought it was so hilarious, he started saying it every night: "Line up, girls, and pay the pimp." Time to split tips. See what I mean? But he only flirted a little with them to cover up the obviousness of what he was doing to me. Just a few weeks after I started, I put a card on the bulletin board announcing that I'm a qualified aerobic dance instructor and if anyone was interested, I would lead an exercise group before work. My card wasn't there three hours before someone (and I don't need a detective) had crossed out "aerobic" and wrote "erotic," and he added a price per session! I had no intention of charging anything for it since I go through my routine everyday anyway, and the more

Terence planned to make it an early evening. He'd brought his wife, and, since this was the first formal staff party held by the Imperial Penthouse, had to spend most of the evening's conversation in introducing Maggie to his fellow employees. Like any ordinary party, however, he was unable to remember afterwards exactly what he did, who he talked to, or what they spoke about, but he knew that he did not introduce his wife to Michelle Rae.

Terence didn't see Maggie go into the restroom. It was down the hall, toward the kitchen. And he didn't see Michelle Rae follow her. In fact, no one did. Maggie returned to the dance area with her face flushed, breathing heavily, her eyes filled with tears, tugged at his arm and, with her voice shaking, begged Terence to take her home. It wasn't until they arrived home that Maggie told Terence how Michelle Rae had come into the restroom and threatened her. Michelle had warned Mrs. Lovell to stay away from Terence and informed her that she had a gun in her purse to help *keep* her away from Terence.

Terence repeated his wife's story to the restaurant manager. The manager thanked him. But, a week later, after Terence had heard of no further developments, he asked the manager what was going to be done about it. The manager said he'd spoken

the merrier is an aerobic dance motto—we like to share the pain. My phone number was clear as day on that card—if he was at all intrigued, he could've called and found out what I was offering. I've spent ten years exercising my brains out. Gyms, spas, classes, health clubs . . . no bars. He could've just once picked up the phone, I was always available, willing to talk this out, come to a settlement. He never even tried. Why should he? He was already king of Nob Hill. You know that lowlife bar he goes to? If anyone says how he was such an amiable and genial supervisor . . . you bet he was genial, he was halfway drunk. It's crap about him being a big family man. Unless his living room had a pool table, those beer mirrors on the wall, and the sticky brown bar itself—the wood doesn't even show through anymore, it's grime from people's hands, the kind of people who go there, the same way a car's steering wheel builds up that thick hard black layer which gets sticky when it rains and you can cut it with a knife. No, his house may not be like that, but he never spent a lot of time at his house. I know what I'm talking about. He'll say he doesn't remember, but I wasn't ten feet away while he was flashing his healthy salary (imported beer), and he looked right through me— no, *not* like I wasn't there. When a man looks at you the way he did

with both Ms. Rae and Mrs. Lovell, separately, but Ms. Rae denied the incident, and, as Mrs. Lovell did not actually see any gun, he couldn't fire an employee simply on the basis of what another employee's wife said about her, especially with the complaint already on file, how would that look? Terence asked, "But isn't there some law against this?" The manager gave Terence a few days off to cool down.

The Imperial Penthouse was closed on Mondays, and most Monday evenings Terence went out with a group of friends to a local sports bar. Maggie Lovell taught piano lessons at home in the evenings, so it was their mutual agreement that Terence go out to a movie or, more often, to see a football game on television. On one such evening, Maggie received a phone call from a woman who said she was calling from the restaurant—there'd been a small fire in one of the storage rooms and the manager was requesting that Terence come to the restaurant and help survey the damage. Mrs. Lovell told the caller where Terence was.

The Imperial Penthouse never experienced any sort of fire, and Terence could only guess afterwards whether or not that was the same Monday evening that Michelle Rae came to the sports

at me, he's either ignoring you or undressing you with his eyes, but probably *both*. And that's just what he did and didn't stop there. He's not going to get away with it.

Wasn't it his idea to hire us in the first place? No, he wasn't there at the interview, but looked right at me my first day, just at me while he said, "You girls probably all want to be models or actresses. You don't give *this* profession enough respect. Well," he said, "you will." Didn't look at anyone else. He meant me. I didn't fail to notice, either, I was the only one with red hair. Not dull auburn . . . flaming red. They always assume, don't they? You know, the employee restrooms were one toilet each for men and women, all the customary holes drilled in the walls, stuffed with paper, but if one restroom was occupied, we could use the other, so the graffiti was heterosexual, a dialogue. It could've been healthy, but he never missed an opportunity. I'd just added my thoughts to an ongoing discussion of the growing trend toward androgyny in male

bar. At first he had considered speaking to her, to try to straighten out what was becoming an out-of-proportion misunderstanding. But he'd already been there for several hours—the game was almost over—and he'd had three or four beers. Because he was, therefore, not absolutely certain what the outcome would be if he talked to her, he checked his impulse to confront Ms. Rae, and, in fact, did not acknowledge her presence.

When a second complaint was made, again charging Terence with inappropriate behavior and, this time, humiliation, Terence offered to produce character witnesses, but before anything came of it, a rape charge was filed with the district attorney and Terence was brought in for questioning. The restaurant suspended Terence without pay for two weeks. All the waitresses, except Ms. Rae, were interviewed, as well as several ex-waitresses—by this time the restaurant was already experiencing some turnover of the new staff. Many of those interviewed reported that Michelle Rae had been asking them if they'd slept with Terence. In one case Ms. Rae was said to have told one of her colleagues that she, Michelle, knew all about her co-worker's affair with the floor captain. Some of the waitresses said that they'd received phone calls on Mondays; an unidentified female

rock singers—they haven't yet added breasts and aren't quite at the point of cutting off their dicks—and an hour later, there it was, the thick black ink pen, the block letters: "Let's get one thing clear—do you women want it or *not?* Just what is the *thrust* of this conversation?" What do you *call* an attitude like that? And he gets *paid* for it! You know, after you split a tip with a busboy, bartender, and floor captain, there's not much left. *He* had an easy answer: earn bigger tips. *Earn* it, work your *ass* off for it, you know. But who's going to tip more than 15% unless . . . . Well, unless the waitress wears no underwear. He even said that the best thing about taking part of our tip money was it made us move our asses that much prettier. There was another thing he liked about how I had to earn bigger tips—reaching or bending. And then my skirt was "mysteriously," "accidentally" lifted from behind, baring my butt in front of the whole kitchen staff. He pretended he hadn't noticed. Then winked and smiled at me later when I gave him his share of my tips. Told me to keep up the good work. Used the word *ass* every chance he got in my presence for weeks afterwards. Isn't this sexual harassment yet?

demanded to know if Terence Lovell was, at that moment, visiting them. A few of those waitresses assumed it was Michelle Rae while others said they'd thought the caller had been Mrs. Lovell.

When the district attorney dropped the rape charge for lack of evidence, Michelle Rae filed suit claiming harassment, naming the restaurant owner, manager and floor captain. Meanwhile Terence began getting a series of phone calls where the caller immediately hung up. Some days the phone seemed to ring incessantly. So once, in a rage of frustration, Terence grabbed the receiver and made a list of threats—the worst being, as he remembered it, "kicking her lying ass clear out of the state"—before realizing the caller hadn't hung up that time. Believing the caller might be legitimate—a friend or a business call—Terence quickly apologized and began to explain, but the caller, who never gave her name, said, "Then I guess you're not ready." When Terence asked her to clarify—ready for what?—she said, "To meet somewhere and work this out. To make my lawsuit obsolete garbage. To do what you really want to do to me. To finish all this."

Terence began refusing to answer the phone himself, relying

Of course I was scared. He knew my work schedule, and don't think he didn't know where I live. Knew my days off, when I'd be asleep, when I do my aerobic dance routine every day. I don't mind *who*ever wants to do aerobic dance with me—but it has to be at my place where I've got the proper flooring and music. It was just an idle, general invitation—an announcement—I wasn't *begging* . . . *any*one, him included, could come once or keep coming, that's all I meant, just harmless, healthy exercise. Does it mean I was looking to start my dancing career in that palace of high-class entertainment *he* frequents? Two pool tables, a juke box and big-screen TV. What a lousy front—looks exactly like what it really *is*, his lair, puts on his favorite funky music, his undulating blue and green lights, snorts his coke, dazzles his partner—his doped-up victim—with his moves and gyrations, dances her into a corner and rapes her before the song's over, up against the wall—*that* song's in the juke box too. You think I don't *know*? I was having a

on Maggie to screen calls, then purchasing an answering machine. As the caller left a message, Terence could hear who it was over a speaker, then he could decide whether or not to pick up the phone and speak to the party directly. He couldn't disconnect the phone completely because he had to stay in touch with his lawyer. The Imperial Penthouse was claiming Terence was not covered on their lawsuit insurance because he was on suspension at the time the suit was filed.

When he returned to work there was one more gift in Terence's locker: what looked like a small stiletto switchblade, but, when clicked open, turned out to be a comb. A note was attached, unsigned, which said, "I'd advise you to get a gun."

Terence purchased the miniature single-cartridge hand gun the following day. After keeping it at work in his locker for a week, he kept it, unloaded, in a dresser drawer at home, unable to carry it to work every day, he said, because the outline of the gun was clearly recognizable in the pocket of his tux pants.

One Monday evening as Terence was leaving the sports bar—not drunk, but admittedly not with his sharpest wits either—three men stopped him. Terence was in a group with another man and three women, but, according to the others, the culprits ignored

hassle with a customer who ordered rare, complained it was overdone, wanted it *rare*, the cook was busy, so Terence grabs another steak and throws it on the grill—tsss on one side, flips it, tsss on the other—slams it on a plate. "Here, young lady, you just dance this raw meat right out to that john." I said I don't know how to dance. "My dear," he said, "*every*one knows how to dance, it's all a matter of moving your ass." Of course the gun was necessary! I tried to be reasonable. I tried everything!

Most people—you just don't know what goes on back there. You see this stylish, practically regal man in white tie and tails, like an old fashioned prince . . . or Vegas magician . . . but back there in the hot, steamy kitchen, what's *wrong* with him? Drunk? Drugs?

them, singling out Terence immediately. It was difficult for Terence to recall what happened that night. He believed the men might've asked him for his wallet, but two of the others with him say the men didn't ask for anything but were just belligerent drunks looking for a fight. Only one member of Terence's party remembered anything specific that was said, addressed to Terence: "Think you're special?" If the men had been attempting a robbery, Terence decided to refuse, he said, partly because he wasn't fully sober, and partly because it appeared the attackers had no weapons. In the ensuing fight—which, Terence said, happened as he was running down the street, but was unsure whether he was chasing or being chased—Terence was kicked several times in the groin area and sustained several broken ribs. He was hospitalized for two days.

Maggie Lovell visited Terence in the hospital once, informing him that she was asking her parents to stay with the kids until he was discharged because she was moving into a motel. She wouldn't tell Terence the name of the motel, insisting she didn't want anyone to know where she was, not even her parents, and besides, she informed him, there probably wouldn't even be a phone in her room. Terence, drowsy from pain

He played sword fight with one of the undercooks, using the longest skewers, kept trying to jab each other in the crotch. The chef yelled at the undercook, but Terence didn't say a word, went to the freezer, got the meatballs out, thawed them halfway in the microwave, then started threading them onto the skewer. Said it was an ancient custom, like the Indians did with scalps, to keep trophies from your victims on your weapon. He added vegetables in between the meatballs—whole bell peppers, whole onions, even whole eggplant, started dousing the whole thing with brandy. His private bottle? Maybe. He said we should put it on the menu, he wanted someone to order it, his delux kebab. He would turn off all the chandeliers and light the dining room with the burning food. Then he stopped. He and I were alone! He said, "The only thing my delux kebab needs is a fresh, ripe tomato." Isn't this incredible! He wanted to know how I would like to be the next juicy morsel to be poked onto the end of that thing. He was still pouring brandy all over it. Must've been a gallon bottle, still half full when he put it on the counter, twirled the huge shishkebab again, struck his sword fighting pose and cut the bottle right in half. I can hardly believe it either. When the bottle cracked open, the force of the blow made

killers, couldn't remember much about his wife's visit. He had vague recollections of her leaving through the window, or leaning out the window to pick flowers, or slamming the window shut, but when he woke the next day and checked, he saw that the window could not be opened. Terence never saw his wife again. Later he discovered that on the night of his accident there had been an incident at home. Although Terence had instructed his eight-year-old son not to answer the phone, the boy had forgotten, and, while his mother was giving a piano lesson, he picked up the receiver just after the machine had clicked on. The entire conversation was therefore recorded. The caller, a female, asked the boy who he was, so he replied that he was Andy Lovell. "The heir apparent," the voice said softly, to which Andy responded, "What? I mean, pardon?" There was a brief pause, then the caller said, "I'd really like to get rid of your mom so your dad could fuck me. If you're halfway like him, maybe I'll let you fuck me too." There is another pause on the tape. Investigators disagree as to whether it is the caller's breathing or the boy's that can be heard. The boy's voice, obviously trembling, then said, "What?" The female caller snapped, "Tell your dad someone's going to be killed."

the brandy shoot out, like the bottle had opened up and spit—it splattered the front of my skirt. In the next second his kebab was in flames—maybe he'd passed it over a burner, I don't know, he was probably *breathing* flames by then—so naturally as soon as he pointed the thing at me again, my skirt ignited, scorched the hair off my legs before I managed to drop it around my feet and kick it away. What *wouldn't* he do? Looks like he'd finally gotten me undressed. It's ironic, isn't it, when you see that news article about him—I taped it to my mirror—and how about that headline, "Pomp and Circumstance Part of the Meal." There sure were some circumstances to consider, all right. Like he could rape me at gunpoint any time he wanted, using that cigarette lighter which looks like a fancy pistol. I wanted something to always remind me what to watch out for, but I didn't take the lighter. Why not? I'll kick myself forever for that. There was so much to choose from. Now one of his red satin cummerbunds hangs over my bed while he still has the lighter and can still use it!

During Terence's convalescence, the Imperial Penthouse changed its format and operated without a floor captain, using the standard practice of a hostess who seated the guests and waitresses assigned to tables to take orders and serve meals. The restaurant's menu was also changed and now no longer offered flaming meals. When Terence returned to work he was given a position as a regular waiter, even though by this time most of the male food servers had left the restaurant and were replaced with women. Michelle Rae was given a lunch schedule, ten to three, Wednesday through Sunday. Terence would call the restaurant to make sure she'd clocked out before he arrived for the dinner shift.

During the first week he was back at work, Terence came home and found that his wife had returned to get the children. In a few days she sent a truck for the furniture, and the next communication he had with her was the divorce suit—on grounds of cruel and unusual adultery.

When he said "staff meeting," he didn't mean what he was supposed to mean by it. You know, there was a cartoon on the bulletin board, *staff meeting*, two sticks shaking hands, very funny, right? But long ago someone had changed the drawing, made the two sticks flaming shish-kebabs on skewers. So the announcement of the big meeting was a xerox of that cartoon, but enlarged, tacked to the women's restroom door. *Be There Or Be Square! Yes, You'll Be Paid For Attending!* You bet! It was held at that tavern. Everyone may've been invited, but I'm the one he wanted there. There's no doubt in my mind. What good was I to him merely as an employee? I had to see the real Terence Lovell, had to join the inner-most core of his life. Know what? It was a biker hangout, that bar, a biker gang's headquarters. One or two of them were always there with their leather jackets, chains, black grease under their fingernails (or dried blood), knives eight inches long. They took so many drugs you could get high just lying on the reeking urine-soaked mattress in the back. That's where the initiations were. No one just *lets* you in. Know what he said the first day we started working, the first day of the women food servers, he said, "You don't just work here to earn a salary, you have to *earn* the right to work here!" So maybe I was naive to trust him. To ever set one foot in that bar without a suspicion of what could happen to me. That same ordinary old beer party going on in front—same music, same dancing, same clack of pool balls and whooping laughter—you'd never believe the scene in the back room. It may've looked like a typical orgy at first—sweating bodies moving in rhythm, groaning, changing to new contorted positions, shouts of encouragement, music blaring in the background. But wait, nothing ordinary or healthy like that for the girl who was chosen to be the center of his dark side—she'll have to be both the cause and cure for his violent ache, that's why he's been so relentless, so obsessed, so insane . . . he was driven to it, to the point where he had to paint the tip of his hard-on with 150 proof whiskey then use the fancy revolver to ignite it, screaming—not like any sound he ever made before—until he extinguished it in the girl of his unrequited dreams. *Tssss.*

The only thing left in Terence's living room was the telephone and answering machine. When the phone rang one Monday afternoon, Terence answered and, as instructed by his attorney, turned on the tape recorder:

caller: It's me, baby.
Lovell: Okay . . . .

caller: You've been ignoring me lately.

Lovell: What do you want now?

caller: Come on, now, Terry!

Lovell: Look, let's level with each other. How can we end this? What do I have to do?

caller: If it's going to end, the ending has to be *better* than if it continued.

Lovell: Pardon?

caller: A bigger deal. A big bang. You ever heard of the big bang theory?

Lovell: The beginning of the universe?

caller: Yeah, but the big bang, if it started the whole universe, it also *ended* something. It may've started the universe, but what did it end? What did it *obliterate*?

Lovell: I still don't know what you want.

caller: What do *you* want, Terry?

Lovell: I just want my life to get back to normal.

caller: Too late. I've changed your life, haven't I? Good.

Lovell: Let's get to the point.

caller: You sound anxious. I love it. You ready?

Lovell: Ready for what?

caller: To see me. To end it. That's what you wanted, wasn't it? Let's create the rest of your life out of our final meeting.

Lovell: If I agree to meet, it's to talk, not get married.

caller: Once is all it takes, baby. *Bang.* The rest of your life will start. But guess who'll still be there at the center of everything you do. Weren't you going to hang out at the bar tonight?

Lovell: Is that where you want to meet?

caller: Yeah, your turf.

Terence estimated he sat in his empty living room another hour or so, as twilight darkened the windows, holding the elegant cigarette-lighter look-alike gun; and when he tested the trigger once, he half expected to see a little flame pop from the end.

J. G. Ballard

J. G. Ballard, born in Shanghai in 1930, spent the first fifteen years of his life in China, a period that included internment in a Japanese prison camp during World War II. He went to England in 1946, studied medicine at Cambridge, and began to publish what he considered "speculative fiction" at the age of twenty-six. In 1987, Empire of the Sun, *his best-selling autobiographical work, was produced by Steven Spielberg as a movie.*

"Plan for the Assassination of Jacqueline Kennedy" appears in a remarkable book of fictions called The Atrocity Exhibition. *Ballard's science fiction reads not like it is about the future but that it is actually from the future. This story, which has the heft and feel of an artifact transmitted from another time, seems to be a scientific study of our fascination with the famous film footage of the moment the bullet strikes President John F. Kennedy in Dallas. The story makes us confront our own motives for watching such footage again and again, and leaves readers wondering why we find these images so fascinating.*

~~~~~~~~~~~

Plan for the Assassination of Jacqueline Kennedy

In his dream of Zapruder frame 235

Motion picture studies of four female subjects who have achieved worldwide celebrity (Brigitte Bardot, Jacqueline Kennedy, Madame Chiang Kai-Shek, Princess Margaret), reveal common patterns of posture, facial tonus, pupil and respiratory responses. Leg stance was taken as a significant indicator of sexual arousal. The intra-patellar distance (estimated) varied from a maximum 24.9 cm. (Jacqueline Kennedy) to a minimum 2.2 cm. (Madame Chiang). Infrared studies reveal conspicuous heat emission from the axillary fossae at rates which tallied with general psychomotor acceleration.

Tallis was increasingly preoccupied

Assassination fantasies in tabes dorsalis (general paralysis of the insane). The choice of victim in these fantasies was taken as the most significant yardstick. All considerations of motive and responsibility were eliminated from the questionnaire. The patients were deliberately restricted in their choice to female victims. Results (percentile of 272 patients): Jacqueline Kennedy 62 percent, Madame Chiang 14 percent, Jeanne Moreau 13 percent, Princess Margaret 11 percent. A montage photograph was constructed on the basis of these replies which showed an "optimum" victim. (Left orbit and zygomatic arch of Mrs. Kennedy, exposed nasal septum of Miss Moreau, etc.) This photograph was subsequently shown to disturbed children with positive results. Choice of assassination site varied from Dealey Plaza 49 percent to Isle du Levant 2 percent. The weapon of preference was the Mannlicher-Carcano. A motorcade was selected in the overwhelming majority of cases as the ideal target mode with the Lincoln Continental as the vehicle of preference. On the basis of these studies a model of the most effective assassination-complex was devised. The presence of Madame Chiang in Dealey Plaza was an unresolved element.

by the figure of the President's wife.

Involuntary orgasms during the cleaning of automobiles. Studies reveal an increasing incidence of sexual climaxes among persons cleaning automobiles. In many cases the subject remained unaware of the discharge of semen across the polished paintwork and complained to his spouse about birds. One isolated case reported to a psychiatric aftercare unit involved the first definitive sexual congress with a rear exhaust assembly. It is believed that the act was conscious. Consultations with manufacturers have led to modifications of rear trim and styling, in order to neutralize these erogenous zones, or if possible transfer them to more socially acceptable areas within the passenger compartment. The steering assembly has been selected as a suitable focus for sexual arousal.

The planes of her face, like the

The arousal potential of automobile styling has been widely examined for several decades by the automotive industry. However, in the study under consideration involving 152 subjects, all known to have experienced more than three involuntary orgasms with their automobiles, the car of preference was found to be (1) Buick Riviera, (2) Chrysler Imperial, (3) Chevrolet Impala. However, a small minority (2 subjects) expressed a significant preference for the Lincoln Continental, if possible in the adapted Presidential version (qv conspiracy theories). Both subjects had purchased cars of this make and experienced continuing erotic fantasies in connection with the trunk mouldings. Both preferred the automobile inclined on a downward ramp.

cars of the abandoned motorcade

Cine-films as group therapy. Patients were encouraged to form a film production unit, and were given full freedom as to choice of subject matter, cast and technique. In all cases explicitly pornographic films were made. Two films in particular were examined: (1) A montage sequence using portions of the faces of (a) Madame Ky, (b) Jeanne Moreau, (c) Jacqueline Kennedy (Johnson oath-taking). The use of a concealed stroboscopic device produced a major optical flutter in the audience, culminating in psychomotor disturbances and aggressive attacks directed against the still photographs of the subjects hung from the walls of the theatre. (2) A film of automobile accidents devised as a cinematic version of Nader's *Unsafe at Any Speed*. By chance it was found that slow-motion sequences of this film had a marked sedative effect, reducing blood pressure, respiration and pulse rates. Hypnagogic images were produced freely by patients. The film was also found to have a marked erotic content.

mediated to him the complete silence

Mouth-parts. In the first study, portions were removed from photographs of three well-known figures: Madame Chiang, Elizabeth Taylor, Jacqueline Kennedy. Patients were asked to fill in the missing areas. Mouth-parts provided a particular focus for aggression, sexual fantasies and retributive fears. In a subsequent test the original portion containing the mouth was replaced and the remainder of the face removed. Again particular attention was focused on the mouth-parts. Images of the mouth-parts of Madame Chiang and Jacqueline Kennedy had a notable hypotensive role. An optimum mouth-image of Madame Chiang and Mrs. Kennedy was constructed.

of the plaza, the geometry of a murder.

Sexual behaviour of witnesses in Dealey Plaza. Detailed studies were conducted of the 552 witnessses in Dealey Plaza on November 22nd (Warren Report). Data indicate a significant upswing in (a) frequency of sexual intercourse, (b) incidence of polyperverse behaviour. These results accord with earlier studies of the sexual behaviour of spectators at major automobile accidents (=minimum of one death). Correspondences between the two groups studied indicate that for the majority of the spectators the events in Dealey Plaza were unconsciously perceived as those of a massive multiple-sex auto-disaster, with consequent liberation of aggressive and polymorphously perverse drives. The role of Mrs. Kennedy, and of her stained clothing, requires no further analysis.

"But I won't cry till it's all over."

Lydia Davis

Lydia Davis is a translator as well as a fiction writer. She has won a grant from the National Endowment for the Arts, an Ingram Merrill fellowship, and a Whiting Writers' Award. End of the Story *was her first novel. "Story" appeared in both* Story and Other Stories *and* Break It Down. *She lives in New York.*

"Story" traces a brief but intense argument between lovers and then records the narrator's attempt to figure out what has just happened both in the argument and in the story she has told of the argument. What was the story? What was the story of the story? Davis confronts the reader with the notion that actual life is perhaps scripted, that the parts we play

*and the space we move through have already been written out. As both
life and a story are composed of a sequencing of events, "Story," a
metafiction, blurs our distinctions between fact and fiction and reminds us
of times when arguments and endearments fell like clichés borrowed from
movies and books.*

Story

I get home from work and there is a message from him: that he is not
coming, that he is busy. He will call again. I wait to hear from him,
then at nine o'clock I go to where he lives, find his car, but he's not
home. I knock at his apartment door and then at all the garage doors,
not knowing which garage door is his—no answer. I write a note, read
it over, write a new note, and stick it in his door. At home I am restless, and all I can do, though I have a lot to do, since I'm going on a
trip in the morning, is play the piano. I call again at ten-forty-five and
he's home, he has been to the movies with his old girlfriend, and she's
still there. He says he'll call back. I wait. Finally I sit down and write
in my notebook that when he calls me either he will then come to me,
or he will not and I will be angry, and so I will have either him or my
own anger, and this might be all right, since anger is always a great
comfort, as I found with my husband. And then I go on to write, in
the third person and the past tense, that clearly she always needed to
have a love even if it was a complicated love. He calls back before I
have time to finish writing all this down. When he calls, it is a little
after eleven-thirty. We argue until nearly twelve. Everything he says is
a contradiction: for example, he says he did not want to see me
because he wanted to work and even more because he wanted to be
alone, but he has not worked and he has not been alone. There is no
way I can get him to reconcile any of his contradictions, and when this
conversation begins to sound too much like many I had with my husband I say goodbye and hang up. I finish writing down what I started
to write down even though by now it no longer seems true that anger
is any great comfort.

I call him back five minutes later to tell him that I am sorry about
all this arguing, and that I love him, but there is no answer. I call again
five minutes later, thinking he might have walked out to his garage and
walked back, but again there is no answer. I think of driving to where

he lives again and looking for his garage to see if he is in there working, because he keeps his desk there and his books and that is where
he goes to read and write. I am in my nightgown, it is after twelve and
I have to leave the next morning at five. Even so, I get dressed and drive
the mile or so to his place. I am afraid that when I get there I will see
other cars by his house that I did not see earlier and that one of them
will belong to his old girlfriend. When I drive down the driveway I see
two cars that weren't there before, and one of them is parked as close
as possible to his door, and I think that she is there. I walk around the
small building to the back where his apartment is, and look in the window: the light is on, but I can't see anything clearly because of the half-
closed venetian blinds and the steam on the glass. But things inside the
room are not the same as they were earlier in the evening, and before
there was no steam. I open the outer screen door and knock. I wait.
No answer. I let the screen door fall shut and I walk away to check the
row of garages. Now the door opens behind me as I am walking away
and he comes out. I can't see him very well because it is dark in the narrow lane beside his door and he is wearing dark clothes and whatever
light there is is behind him. He comes up to me and puts his arms
around me without speaking, and I think he is not speaking not
because he is feeling so much but because he is preparing what he will
say. He lets go of me and walks around me and ahead of me out to
where the cars are parked by the garage doors.

As we walk out there he says "Look," and my name, and I am waiting for him to say that she is here and also that it's all over between us.
But he doesn't, and I have the feeling he did intend to say something
like that, at least say that she was here, and that he then thought better of it for some reason. Instead, he says that everything that went
wrong tonight was his fault and he's sorry. He stands with his back
against a garage door and his face in the light and I stand in front of
him with my back to the light. At one point he hugs me so suddenly
that the fire of my cigarette crumbles against the garage door behind
him. I know why we're out here and not in his room, but I don't ask
him until everything is all right between us. Then he says, "She wasn't
here when I called you. She came back later." He says the only reason
she is there is that something is troubling her and he is the only one
she can talk to about it. Then he says, "You don't understand, do you?"

I try to figure it out.

So they went to the movies and then came back to his place and
then I called and then she left and he called back and we argued and

then I called back twice but he had gone out to get a beer (he says) and then I drove over and in the meantime he had returned from buying beer and she had also come back and she was in his room so we talked by the garage doors. But what is the truth? Could he and she both really have come back in that short interval between my last phone call and my arrival at his place? Or is the truth really that during his call to me she waited outside or in his grarage or in her car and that he then brought her in again, and that when the phone rang with my second and third calls he let it ring without answering, because he was fed up with me and with arguing? Or is the truth that she did leave and did come back later but that he remained and let the phone ring without answering? Or did he perhaps bring her in and then go out for the beer while she waited there and listened to the phone ring? The last is the least likely. I don't believe anyway that there was any trip out for beer.

The fact that he does not tell me the truth all the time makes me not sure of his truth at certain times, and then I work to figure out for myself if what he is telling me is the truth or not, and sometimes I can figure out that it's not the truth and sometimes I don't know and never know, and sometimes just because he says it to me over and over again I am convinced it is the truth because I don't believe he would repeat a lie so often. Maybe the truth does not matter, but I want to know it if only so that I can come to some conclusions about such questions as: whether he is angry at me or not; if he is, then how angry; whether he still loves her or not; if he does, then how much; whether he loves me or not; how much; how capable he is of deceiving me in the act and after the act in the telling.

Diane Schoemperlen

Diane Schoemperlen, born in Thunder Bay, Ontario, now lives in Kingston, Ontario. After graduating from Lakehead University, where she studied with the writers W. O. Mitchell and Alice Munro, Schoemperlen worked as a researcher and as a typesetter, experiences that inform her detailed and graphic fiction. She is the author of the novel In the Language of Love *and two collections,* The Man of My Dreams *and* Forms of Devotion, *in which "Innocent Objects" appeared.*

In "Innocent Objects," pictures, taken mostly from old commercial catalogues, appear as footnotes to a story detailing a burglary. The collage construction and the use of old illustrations allow the reader to piece together a story from the residue of an action that has already happened. Sifting and sorting the evidence, we find that innocent objects lose their innocence and take on a kind of life that we can "read." "Innocent Objects" replicates the detective work that we do in the everyday world.

All reading is a kind of detective work: a reader must make sense of the information in a text. But here the reader, solving the usual mystery by reading, is also faced with a "detective" story—a crime has been committed and must be solved—and a story about detective stories. All this detection creates an appealing labyrinth of experience, a kind of funhouse of discovery and mystery.

Innocent Objects

The burglary took place sometime between the morning of Friday, July the seventh, and the late afternoon of Sunday, July the ninth, while Helen Wingham was away in the city. Helen went to the city every summer early in July. (*The thief is watching the house.*) The timing of her trip was arbitrary, this particular part of the season chosen for no particular reason, at least not for any good reason that Helen could remember now. She hired a town boy to come out and water her garden while she was away.

She took the Friday morning bus and sat for the two-hour trip south in the window seat behind the driver with her small hands folded in her lap. (*The thief is walking through the front gate and around to the backyard.*) Through the bus window Helen watched the passage of lush green farmland dotted with white houses, red barns, brown cows, and dirty yellowing sheep. (*The thief is in the garden.*) Helen didn't notice much change in the landscape from one year to the next.

The bus stopped in several small towns much like her own, letting passengers off and on at gas stations or gift shops that doubled as bus depots several times a day. Here change was more evident. Buildings appeared and disappeared seemingly at random. (*The thief is picking peas,[1] dropping the crisp stripped pods in a pile in the pumpkin patch.*) A row of derelict wooden houses was bulldozed and replaced

---

[1]American Wonder, the best variety, Helen orders the seeds from a catalogue. The plump green pods hang on delicate vines that curl up the stakes and the chicken wire. Helen likes to eat them raw when they are still young and tender. Later in the season she cooks them up in cream with parsley and pearl onions.

by a shiny strip mall. A long green and yellow motel popped up in what had been a cornfield. A three-story gingerbread farmhouse was reincarnated as a sprawling stucco ranch-style house with a wall of windows across the front. From the bus Helen could now look right into the living room. She saw a woman in a blue bathrobe walking through the large white room. Helen politely looked away.

Helen Wingham was a fifty-four-year-old woman in a peach-colored silk blouse and a well-cut black skirt. Her short hair was gray and tidy. She wore her reading glasses on a black cord around her neck as if they were binoculars. (*The thief is examining a basket of garden tools accidentally left out on the picnic table.*) By all appearances, Helen Wingham was nothing more or less than a plain white woman. To look at her, you would expect her head to be full of recipes, household hints, gardening tips, knitting patterns, and charming anecdotes about her family.

Helen kept her large handbag on the empty seat beside her so no one would sit there. She enjoyed the bus trip for the time it gave her to sit silently and watch the scenery while, she imagined, certain longstanding, but occasionally worrisome, layers of her personality were being invisibly shed like the miles unrolling behind her. (*The thief is picking a pocketknife[2] out of the basket.*) By the time Helen got off the bus, she expected she would be, if not a whole new person, at least a whole new self.

At home in her small town, she was not sociable either. She did not spend her afternoons sipping coffee in the well-equipped kitchens of other town women. (*The thief is cutting a hole in the screen of the back right basement window which has been left half-open.*) The extent of her interaction with them was simply what common courtesy demanded: a polite greeting, a positive or negative acknowledgment of the weather, and, occasionally, a brief observation as to the success or failure of some recent local event or enterprise. Helen supposed, correctly, that she was looked upon as something of an eccentric, standoffish but harmless, surely. (*The thief is reaching in through*

[2]Ladies Knife with three blades, finest quality steel, German silver bolsters, 4¼-inch stag horn handle. Helen has had this knife for as long as she can remember. She uses it to cut off dead blossoms and leaves in the garden. Sometimes she uses it to cut slugs in half. After her gardening is done, she cleans the dirt out from under her fingernails with the thinnest of the knife's three blades.

the hole and unhooking the screen.) Helen *did* keep to herself, yes, but not in an ominous way, not like those monsters about whom (after human bones have been discovered in the compost pile or else they've gone berserk and poisoned the paperboy and his dog) the unsuspecting neighbors, aghast, feel compelled to say over and over again to television and newspaper reporters, "We never really knew her! She kept to herself but she seemed nice enough! How could we have known?"

Helen had lived alone in the large red-brick Victorian house just north of town for twenty years. Still the townspeople knew next to nothing about her. (*The thief is removing the screen and sliding into the basement which is cool and shadowy after the relentless bright heat of the backyard.*) They knew she had come from a wealthy family, was well-educated, had lived for thirty-four years in the city, then inherited a relative fortune and moved to their small town. She had never been married. She had no children and no pets. Over those twenty years she had had few visitors and apparently no suitors. She lived a very quiet life and bothered no one. (*The thief hooks the screen back in place, wipes off the blade and handle of the pocketknife, and sets it down on top of a large picnic basket.*[3] For her part, Helen suspected that the townspeople were both provoked by and disappointed in her. She was strange, maybe a little, but not strange *enough*. She was hardly the sort of character from whom small-town legends could be made.

The townspeople had long ago abandoned their secret hopes of a scandal and gone on about their business. "Live and let live, that's what I always say!" That's what they always said when Helen's name came up in casual conversation at the post office or the Sears catalogue shopping counter in the back of the drugstore, at one kitchen table or another, among the women who wondered about her, who wished they knew what her secret was. (*The thief is going up the stairs to the ground floor of the house.*) These women longed to be invited into Helen's house but none of them had ever made it past the front foyer

---

[3]Woven common elm, middle-hinged lid, brass closures, sturdy handle, gingham-lined. Helen is not sure where this basket originally came from. It is one of those objects that has simply always been there. She has never used it for a picnic. It is filled with junk: old screwdrivers, a baseball shedding its skin, a coil of copper wire, a broken flashlight, two padlocks without keys, and the guts of an old alarm clock. Helen does not exactly know where this junk came from either. It is as if the old house were quite capable of accumulating such objects all by itself.

on the few occasions when one of them had come to her door census-taking, selling raffle tickets, collecting money for the Cancer Society or the Salvation Army. *(The thief is in the kitchen.)* The most they could tell from this vantage point was that the house was very clean and the grounds were very tidy, front and back. *(The thief is opening the glass doors of the oak china cabinet.)* Helen, they knew, had neither a housekeeper nor a gardener and they couldn't help but admire her for that.

Mostly Helen's "secret" was whatever enabled her to not need a man (or *them*, for that matter), to live alone for all those years without, so they supposed, having to compromise, capitulate, or provide nutritious meals, clean clothes, and satisfying sex on demand.

For her part, Helen knew these women's faces but not their names, at least not their first names. *(The thief is touching the plates, the bowls, the milk jug, the eight-piece tea service[4] on the middle shelf.)* She knew them as Mrs. Henderson, Mrs. Adams, Mrs. Jensen, Mrs. James. Often she got them mixed up. They in turn called her "Miss Wingham," but among themselves they called her "Helen," with a breezy familiarity they knew they had not earned. *(The thief is running cold water into the shining stainless steel sink.)* Sometimes Helen wished she could give these women what they wanted although she wasn't entirely sure what it was.

Although by all appearances Helen Wingham could have passed for one of them, these women knew in their small-town hearts that she was not. They knew her head was not full of recipes, patterns, or boring stories about her family. *(The thief is filling the copper kettle and placing it on the front right burner of the gas stove where a pretty blue flame leaps up.)* These women knew that by comparison Helen Wingham was exotic and mysterious, forever unfathomable. These were qualities for which they either liked or disliked her, amorphous distinctions which they either envied or begrudged her on any given day.

The bus was rolling through the sprawling outer reaches of the city now. Every year Helen noted how you could be *in* the city for a very

[4]Carlsbad China Tete-à-Tete Set, decorated with a spray of pink roses and green leaves. The set includes teapot, sugar bowl, cream pitcher, two cups and saucers, on a fine china matching tray. Seven of the pieces are in perfect condition but there is a small chip on the lip of the cream pitcher. The set is over a hundred years old and very delicate so Helen seldom uses it except for special occasions like Christmas, Easter, and her birthday, the fifteenth of September.

long time before you actually got there. *(The thief goes back down to the basement and returns to the kitchen with two large mason jars[5] and three empty cardboard boxes.)* She took out her makeup case, combed her hair, and reapplied her lipstick while the bus idled at a red light. It was just noon when they reached downtown and the giant office buildings were disgorging slim women in sleeveless dresses and tall men in rumpled white shirts into the shimmering streets. *(The thief takes a box of tea from the cupboard, puts the leaves in the pot, and fills it with boiling water from the whistling kettle.)* The traffic was snarled and slow. Overheated impatient drivers honked their horns impotently, more for effect, it seemed, than with any real hope of accomplishing anything.

Finally the bus lumbered into the depot and Helen and the other passengers got off. She retrieved her suitcase from the belly of the bus and stepped into a taxi which took her to the hotel.

Helen stayed in the same hotel every year. Old but aging well, small but luxurious, it was a three-story gray stone building on a short side street off one of the city's main thoroughfares. *(The thief is sitting at the kitchen table, looking out at the empty road through white lace curtains[6] while sipping a cup of steaming black tea.)* The hotel was rather expensive, even by city standards, but it was well worth it, Helen thought, for the first-class amenities it provided.

The concierge was a handsome older man named Frederick who now greeted Helen by name: "Welcome, Miss Wingham. How good to have you with us again." Frederick stood by while Helen registered and her suitcase was whisked away by a bellhop. *(The thief washes the cup and saucer, then the teapot, and sets them down with the rest of the set beside the mason jars in one of the cardboard boxes.)* Then he escorted her to her room on the third floor.

[5]Peach and Pepper Relish: In food processor, chop 2 hot red peppers and 12 sweet red peppers, seeds and all. Add peppers to 12 large peaches (peeled and chopped), 1 cup white vinegar, and 1 teaspoon salt in large preserving kettle. Add 4 lemon halves. Boil gently for half an hour. Remove lemons and add 5 cups white sugar. Boil for another half-hour or until mixture is thick. Bottle and seal. Helen knows this recipe by heart.

[6]Nottingham Lace, single border, *point d'esprit* center with beautiful Brussels effect. Helen washes these curtains (and a similar pair that hangs in her bedroom) by hand twice a year in the bathtub and then drapes them over the shower rod to dry. When she hangs them back up at the windows, they are as soft and fragrant as freshly washed hair.

In the room there was a large soft four-poster bed with a thick white duvet edged with embroidery and white lace. (*The thief is in the hallway.*) There was a silver-wrapped chocolate mint on her pillow and a bouquet of fresh flowers on the bedside table. (*The thief is in the living room.*) In the spotless blue bathroom there was a crystal bowl of pot-pourri on the marble vanity, a plush white robe hanging from a hook on the back of the door, and a telephone on the wall beside the toilet.

Frederick strode across the room and opened the dark green damask drapes with a flourish. (*The thief sits in the wine-colored armchair beside the bay window, resting both hands upon the white antimacassars spread over its arms.*) Gracious and friendly, gallant in the old-world way, Frederick asked after Helen's health and her general well-being during the intervening year. He was scrupulously polite, never nosy or overbearing.

When Helen first began making her annual trip to the city, Frederick had been a handsome younger man. (*The thief is lifting a small clock[7] from the mantelshelf of the fireplace.*) During one of those early visits, Helen had had a dream about Frederick, an erotic dream in whch he had come to her in the four-poster bed and his arms were so strong, his skin so smooth, his tongue so agile, and his penis so amiable and big. She had awakened from the dream writhing, wet, and very embarrassed. For the remainder of that visit, she had avoided Frederick. If he noticed or wondered about her odd behavior, he was of course too discreet to mention it. (*The thief spies a square black typewriter[8] on an oak cabinet beside the sofa.*) By the following year Helen had managed to put the dream out of her mind and could act normally around Frederick again.

All these years later she seldom thought about the dream anymore except when Frederick said each year: "Consider me at your disposal, Miss Wingham, I will do anything I can to make your stay a pleasant

[7]Cupid's Dart, 6 inches high, finished in bronze with fancy dial and Ansonia movement. Having been largely unaffected by the sting of Cupid's dart in her lifetime, Helen loves her little clock anyway. The fact that it has never kept good time strikes her as fitting somehow in an object of desire. The clock is pretty but useless and Cupid's left wing has long since broken off and disappeared.

[8]Remington, all metal working parts and steel type, double case machine writes 78 characters including numbers, symbols, punctuation marks, and fractional figures. The typewriter, despite its advanced age, is in excellent working order except for the sticky letters m and p. Mostly Helen uses it for letters to lawyers and the like, business correspondence that she feels should be made to look as official as possible. Once she tried to type on it the story of her life but found she did not know where to begin.

one. Anything." This was exactly what Frederick had said in the dream as he lifted her nightgown and buried his mouth between her thighs. *(The thief places both hands in position on the keyboard and types:* The quick red fox jumps over the lazy brown dog, *but there is no paper in the machine and the words fall invisible onto the black rubber platen.)* This was exactly what he was saying now as he backed out the door and Helen thanked him with genuine gratitude both for his courtesy and for everything he had done to her in the dream. Helen and Frederick shook hands warmly and she slid a ten-dollar bill into his palm.

Then Helen unpacked, freshened up, and went downstairs. She took her lunch in the hotel dining room. *(The thief is in the hallway.)* She ordered Gazpacho, Stuffed Mushroom Caps, Asparagus Soufflé, and a small Caesar Salad. *(The thief is in the library.)* At home, if she had lunch at all, it was most often brown toast and tea, sometimes a bagel with cream cheese and some of her own peach and pepper relish. *(The thief admires the books in their shelves, strokes their spines, removes one, flips through it briefly, and then returns it precisely to its proper place.)* Helen marveled briefly at how being in the city always made her ravenous and then she ordered Blueberry Crème Brulée for dessert.

By the time she walked into the street, Helen Wingham had become her city self. She made her way smoothly along the crowded sidewalks, never bumping into anyone or making direct eye contact, bobbing and weaving around slowpokes, ignoring the occasional homeless person camped in a doorway. *(The thief is peering at the pages of a large encyclopedia[9] spread open on a cast-iron bookstand.)* Helen was happy to see how quickly she adjusted to being back in the city, how she must already look like everyone else around her: purposeful, preoccupied, and completely unapproachable. She felt brisk and confident. *(The thief is in the hallway.)* Navigating the city was like riding a bicycle, making love, or skating: once you knew how, you never forgot. It was simply an intricate series of physical maneuvers which, if performed in the right sequence

[9]The *New Illustrated Universal Encyclopedia: The Book of A Million Facts*, published in Great Britain, 1923, 1,280 pages, including 16 new maps. Helen is fond of skimming through this book for amusing entries. She enjoys "The Modern Household Cookery" which includes recipes for such delicacies as Bone Soup, Sheep's Head Soup, Eggs for the Invalid, Substantial Salad, and Mutton Chops in Ambush. She takes special delight in "The New Household Physician" which, in addition to dispensing information on very serious ailments, also offers remedies and advice regarding such afflictions as Ankles, Weak; Breath, Offensive; Feet, Sweating; Toenail, Ingrowing; and Cramp, Writer's.

at the right speed, would carry her safely through. (*The thief is in the music room.*) Although Helen hadn't been on skates or a bicycle since she was a girl, she did not doubt that she could still do these things if she wanted to. (*The thief sits down at the piano but cannot read music and so rests one hand gently on the keyboard and is silent.*) Helen supposed, correctly, that the townspeople would hardly recognize her now.

At home she sometimes felt she was too dreamy, floating aimlessly through the rooms of her sturdy house, anchored to the real world only by the solidity of the house itself and by the high-frequency resonance of the objects with which she filled it. (*The thief looks through the viewfinder of a large brown and black camera*[10] *into a gilt-framed mirror on the wall opposite the piano.*) Sometimes Helen pictured the roof of her house as a lid which kept her from drifting away entirely, all that lay between her and an attractive pocket of heaven to which she was not yet ready to ascend. Sometimes Helen suspected she was hiding, having firmly barricaded herself behind those well-appointed walls, carefully minding her own business and expecting all others to do the same.

Helen arrived at her favorite bookstore. (*The thief is in the hallway.*) It was a long narrow room with floor-to-ceiling shelves that required the use of an old-fashioned ladder on wheels to reach the highest books. The salesclerks wore soft-soled shoes and conservative clothing. They did not bother you unless you specifically asked for assistance. (*The thief is mounting the oak staircase to the second story.*) Classical music played tastefully somewhere near the ceiling.

Helen gravitated first to the biography section. (*The thief stops on the landing and removes a small painting*[11] *from the wall.*) Although Helen was not generally fond of people in the flesh, she loved to read about them, especially if they were famous in some creative field, especially if their

[10]Normandie Reversible Back Camera with adjustable, spring-actuated ground glass always in position, never in the way. Compact, highly polished mahogany body, metalworks of fine-draw file finish. Of course this camera no longer functions. But Helen likes to imagine that if it did, the photographs it took would be like holograms which, if viewed at just the right angle in just the right light, would reveal the whole spectrum of emanations (ghosts of the past, the future, and the truth) which lurk behind even the most mundane surfaces of the present and visible world.

[11]*Angel of Furnace Ascending* by L. C. Moffat, signed and dated 1891, oil on canvas, 8 x 12 inches, carved wooden frame. Helen knows nothing about this painter, not age, origin, or gender. She thinks though that L. C. Moffat must have been a woman. She

lives had been tormented and chaotic. Although the desire for privacy was paramount in her own life, Helen was thrilled by peeping into the emotional disturbances and scandalous behaviors that pockmarked these famous people's lives. (*The thief looks into several rooms along the upstairs hallway but does not enter any of them.*) Helen was particularly fond of those biographies that included photographs of the subject as a baby in its mother's arms, as a small child in a large class of other unidentified small children, as an unattractive adolescent in a marching band; photographs of the subject arm-in-arm with various spouses and lovers, of the rooms in which the subject had once slept, ate, copulated, and entertained; photographs of the gardens, the children, the pets, the Christmas trees, the birthday cakes, the funeral wreaths. (*The thief is turning the white procelain doorknob of the last room on the right.*) When reading one of these books, Helen would flip back and forth to these photographs which were, she thought, like the footnotes to the story, the place where all the secrets could be unearthed, the place where the true story could be deciphered and the sum of the subject's life could eventually be tallied.

By the time Helen was finished in the bookstore, she had accumulated enough books to fill three cardboard cartons. (*The thief is entering Helen's bedroom which overlooks the backyard.*) At the last minute she added a five-volume hardcover set called *A History of Private Life* and then she made arrangements to have the boxes shipped to her house early the following week.

Back in her hotel room she closed the drapes against the heat, turned up the air conditioner, and took off her dress. She put on the bathrobe supplied by the hotel and ordered up a light supper from room service. (*The thief is opening the doors of the oak armoire.*) After eating, Helen made herself comfortable in bed, turned on the television, and watched a concert by the Boston Philharmonic. (*The thief is touching Helen's blouses, her dresses, her skirts, and a number of silly-looking hats stored in the bottom drawer.*) After the concert, she turned out the lights and slept soundly, perfectly safe and content, undisturbed all through the summer night, by dreams of Frederick or anyone else.

---

intuits this from something in the brushstrokes, which are layered and thoughtful, and from the colors, which are rich and luminous. She does know that Furnace is a small village in the Strathclyde region of western Scotland. But she likes to think this is the angel of *the furnace*, who kindly keeps people warm in the winter. She fancies this notion of the angels of objects: the angels of chimneys, streetlights, and windows; the angels of teapots, cutlery, and kettles; the angels of asparagus, rhubarb, and eggs. These days she especially fancies the angel of doorknobs.

In the morning she rose early as was her habit, bathed, and got dressed. (*The thief is opening the top drawer of the mahogany dresser.*) She went down to the lobby, greeted the ubiquitous Frederick, and went into the street.

After a half-hour walk through the nearly deserted streets, Helen went back to the hotel for breakfast. (*The thief is touching Helen's panties and a white silk slip.*) Then she spent most of the day prowling through the many antique shops in the neighborhood. (*The thief pulls a leather-bound book[12] from beneath Helen's underwear and finds its blue-lined pages covered with Helen's small neat handwriting.*)

In the early years of her annual trip to the city, Helen had come to these shops looking mostly for furniture. Each year she had bought four or five large pieces and had them shipped home. These beautiful antiques now filled all the rooms of her house. (*The thief opens one by one the four drawers of the mahogany jewelry chest, runs fingers through gold and silver necklaces, brooches, bracelets, earrings, watches, and rings, but does not take anything.*) Helen bought these antiques for the moments of pure happiness they offered her each time she walked into a room and: there they were! Every day the sheer sight of them would give her a jolt of surprised satisfaction. It was like catching sight of her own reflection now in a store window as she walked through the city streets. (*The thief takes a large photo album[13] out of the glass-fronted bookcase by the window.*) Glimpsing that cosmopolitan woman striding along with such graceful determination, Helen thought, "Now there's a fine-looking woman!" just in that split second before she recognized herself.

But much as Helen loved her possessions, she had to admit that sooner or later even the most extravagant objects of her affection would

[12]Hand-bound genuine leather, burgundy and black, bound-in black silk bookmark, best quality white woven paper, 300 pages, ruled. This is not exactly a diary, bur rather a notebook Helen has kept sporadically over the last twenty years. The entries are a shorthand notation of her daily life and she often copies into it unusual facts she has come across in her reading. She likes to look back over these selected days of her life. She likes to know that on September 28, 1981, it rained all day, she had pork cutlets, broccoli, and baked potatoes for supper, made an appointment to have the chimney cleaned, and noted that the Pole of Inaccessibility is that point on Antarctica farthest in all directions from the seas which surround it.

[13]Blue Plush Album with photo of six children under celluloid on front, tinted interior pages with floral decorations in gold, openings for 48 photographs. Helen bought this album complete

become just furniture after all. *(The thief hears noises outside, a bicycle perhaps being leaned up against the house, footsteps coming down the driveway and passing into the backyard below.)* Then she went back to the city and bought more. After ten or twelve years of this, even Helen's big house contained just about all the fine furniture it could hold. *(The thief stands just to the right of Helen's bedroom window looking down at the town boy as he unrolls the hose and begins to water the garden.)* Now Helen scoured the antique shops for smaller treasures, precious bits and pieces of long-dead strangers' lives which she could then make her own, all of their history there for the taking, all of their dreams there for the imagining.

Today she found, among other things, a miniature toy harp with seventeen tunable strings; a man's alligator-skin traveling case still containing comb, toothbrush, razor, and strop; an eight-ball croquet set with fancy striped mallets and copper-plated arches.

Then she went back to the hotel and had a nap, suddenly exhausted after all that shopping in the heat. *(The thief steps back from the window and sits motionless on the edge of Helen's bed until the boy gets back on his bicycle and rides away.)* She spent the evening much as she had the night before. But tonight she did not fall asleep so quickly.

Tonight she lay awake for a long time, happily buoyed up by a burgeoning sense of possibility. *(The thief stands up and smooths the wrinkles out of the white eyelet counterpane with both hands which are trembling slightly.)* Here in the city Helen was emboldened. Here she felt she could do anything that crossed her mind. Anything. Here she still believed her life could change. It was not too late. Any day now she could wake up and find herself living a totally different life.

At home Helen did not like to contemplate change. *(The thief goes back downstairs to the kitchen.)* There she was comforted by the sameness of her solitary days. She valued stability, security, and peace of mind. She avoided anyone and anything that might cause anxiety, confusion, disappointment, or overstimulation. *(The thief sets the three full cardboard boxes in the back hall.)* At home when Helen thought about the future, she hoped simply to find herself living exactly the same life for the rest

---

nearly fifteen years ago. The people it contains are perfectly dead strangers. All she knows of them are their names noted neatly on the back or below: *Gertrude and Walt, Janey and Little Luke, Charlotte and Tiny (dog).* Sometimes more details are given: *Lindsay at cabin, Blackstone; Edith on holiday, England; Maurice on his twenty-first birthday at the Chateau.* Every picture is a mystery. Every eye, every elbow, every dish, every drawer, each and every innocent subject and object waits to spill out its secrets like pearls. Helen is still waiting to receive them.

of her life. (*The thief goes into the backyard, unrolls the hose, and turns it on a small flower bed that the town boy had overlooked.*) Sometimes at night Helen's hope took the form of a prayer: "Please God, just let me be."

But here in her hotel room she lay awake for hours imagining herself in all manner of new and startling situations. (*The thief leaves by the back door, making sure it is locked afterward, carrying the boxes one at a time to a gray midsize car parked a hundred yards down the road, pulled onto the shoulder under a clump of weeping birches.*) She could travel. She could visit the Parthenon, the Eiffel Tower, the Pyramids, the Sphinx. She could take a slow boat to China. She could sell the house and buy a villa in the south of France. For that matter, she could *keep* the house and *still* buy a villa in the south of France. She could redecorate in Danish modern. She could dye her hair red. She could write a book. She could take flying lessons. She could get married, for God's sake!

But in the morning Helen did none of these things. (*The thief, on the final trip to the car, is passed by a brown station wagon with two crying children and a barking dog in the backseat, and the harried woman at the wheel does not notice or wonder about this familiar-looking person carrying a cardboard box down the country road in the sunshine.*) In the morning Helen rose much later than usual and enjoyed a sumptuous brunch in the hotel dining room. She sat for a long time sipping her coffee and sampling the bountiful offerings of the dessert table.

Having finally eaten her fill, Helen went upstairs and took her clothes from the armoire, her toiletries from the marble vanity, and repacked her suitcase, removing all traces of herself from the room.

Her bus home did not leave until three o'clock. (*The thief is driving slowly away, down the country road and into the center of town.*) She went downstairs to the lobby which was decorated to resemble an old-fashioned parlor with overstuffed armchairs, antique lamps on well-polished tables, deeply worn Turkish carpets on the hardwood floor. (*The thief pulls into the driveway of a bungalow with pale yellow aluminum siding and black trim, red and white geraniums in the window boxes, two well-pruned cedar bushes on either side of the front door.*) In fact the hotel lobby resembled Helen's living room at home which she had begun to long fondly for now. She was always glad to go to the city but always glad to get home again too. It was exhilarating, all this feeling adventurous and confident, exhilarating but exhausting, and she was looking forward to turning back into her essential dreamy comfortable self.

In the lobby Frederick asked if she had enjoyed her stay. Yes, of course she had, she always did, everything was wonderful. (*The thief opens the yellow metal door with the remote control gadget in the car and drives into the garage.*) They chatted amiably about nothing and then, as the time of Helen's departure approached, Frederick had the bellhop bring down her suitcase while she checked out. He carried the suitcase into the street and hailed her a taxi. Again they shook hands warmly, looking forward, they both said, to next year, and Helen slid him another ten-dollar bill.

The bus ride home seemed, as always, to pass more quickly. (*The thief carries the boxes one at a time into the kitchen of the bungalow.*) Helen watched the scenery unraveling now in reverse as the city peeled off her like a sunburn. She thought about all her purchases and was immensely satisfied.

By five o'clock Helen Wingham is unlocking her own back door and stepping gratefully into her own back hall. She leaves her suitcase there, the door unlocked, and goes into the kitchen, grinning. (*The thief unpacked the three boxes and lined up the objects on the kitchen table.*) Helen finds it reassuring to see her own self reflected in each and every object, and beyond herself, there are the reflections of all the other hands which have touched them, all the other lives with which these innocent objects have intersected over time. (*The thief opened one of the mason jars with a pop, took a large spoon from the cutlery drawer, sampled the peach and pepper relish, declared it delicious, and put the jar in the refrigerator.*) Oh it is so good to be home!

The house is hot and stuffy, having been closed up tight since Friday. (*The thief made room for the other jar of relish in the cupboard to the right of the sink and arranged the tea service on its tray beside the cookbooks on the counter.*) Helen opens the kitchen window and puts the kettle on to boil. She takes the everyday tea things from the cupboard and a tiny spoon[14] from a wooden rack on the wall.

She sits at the kitchen table, looking out at the empty road through the white lace curtains. (*The thief fiddled with the Cupid mantel clock but was disappointed to find that it could not be made to keep good time.*)

Rejuvenated, Helen lugs her suitcase up to her bedroom. (*The thief went into the living room.*) She opens the window and looks out over the garden. The town boy has obviously done his job well. All the vegetables

[14]Solid sterling silver, 5 inches long, souvenir of Venezuela, palm trees and oil well on handle, the word *Caracas* engraved in teardrop bowl. This spoon is one of a collection of twenty-four which Helen bought, complete with oak display rack, just last summer. Her favorites among them, besides Venezuela, include Pisa with a braided handle featuring the famous Leaning Tower itself, El Salvador with palm trees and a man on a mule (no whisper of unrest), Wales with a castle on the handle and the coat of arms embossed on the bowl. Helen likes having souvenirs from places she has never seen and surely never will.

and flowers look robust and vigorous. She can see there are some beans that need picking and the peas are definitely done. (*The thief, having no fireplace, no mantelshelf, placed the clock on the coffee table beside a candy dish in the shape of a fish and a large arrangement of plastic flowers.*) Helen unpacks her suitcase and puts her things away. She notices that the right door of the glass-fronted bookcase is standing slightly ajar. Inside, all the photo albums on the middle shelf have toppled over. (*The thief surveyed the corners of the living room through the viewfinder of the camera and then placed it on the coffee table beside the clock.*) When she opens the door to straighten them, Helen realizes that the blue plush album is not in its proper place. This is most unusual.

Helen turns and looks all around the room. She can't remember the last time she looked at the album. She checks the other shelves in the bookcase, the bedside table, inside the large trunk[15] at the foot of her bed. She even lifts up the white eyelet counterpane and checks under the bed.

She panics briefly, thinking of premature senility, wasn't there a cousin with Alzheimer's, what were the signs? (*The thief went back into the kitchen and rummaged through the junk drawer looking for a hammer and a nail.*) Helen reassures herself by reciting the Ten Commandments. Thou shalt not kill. Thou shalt not commit adultery. Thou shalt not steal. Thou shalt not covet. Her memory appears to be intact.

She is hot. She is tired. She is hungry. (*The thief removed a framed print of Van Gogh's* Sunflowers *from the wall behind the couch, hammered in a new nail, and hung the angel painting there.*) Maybe there is the beginning of a headache behind her eyes. Maybe later, when she feels better, she'll find the photo album.

For now she will put away her suitcase and have something to eat. There are some bagels in the freezer, some cream cheese in the fridge. She goes down to the basement for a jar of peach and pepper relish. (*The thief sat down on the couch and turned the pages of the photo album, peering into the faces of stiff-backed strangers posed beside plant stands, grand pianos, and miscellaneous pets.*) Helen could have sworn she had two jars of relish left. But there is only an empty space on the shelf where they should be.

Helen is beginning to feel anxious. She imagines the jars of relish, the photo album, all the other objects in her house, the books, the tables, the

[15]Fancy metal-covered flat top with rounded corners, hardwood reverse bent slats, metal bumpers. There is nothing of consequence in this trunk: two wool blankets, a linen tea towel printed with a 1964 calendar, a cushion covered with a picture of Niagara Falls, a collapsible walking stick with a dog's head on top, and a black cashmere shawl which Helen has never worn. Usually she sits on this trunk while she puts on her panty hose each morning.

dressers, the rolltop desk, and the rocking chair,[16] everything rearranging itself in her absence in some macabre dance of the inanimate.

Then she sees it. *(The thief looked for a long time at the photograph of a stern-faced woman holding a serious fat baby in her lap.)* The pocketknife on the picnic basket. The hole in the window screen. At first she cannot move. Her hands go to her throat. She is suddenly cold in the heat. It does not occur to her that the thief could still be inside. It does not occur to her to abandon her house and run.

She picks up the knife and stares at it. She leans closer to the window. *(The thief picked up the heavy encyclopedia which proved to be filled with all manner of interesting arcane knowledge.)* The hole in the screen is a neat vertical cut, a little opening through which her own small hand just fits. She slides the window shut and locks it. She folds up the knife and puts it in her pocket. She goes back up the basement stairs.

In the kitchen now she sees the empty space on the middle shelf of the china cabinet. *(The thief skimmed through several sections of the encyclopedia including "The Dog Lover's Guide With Dictionary of Canine Diseases and Supplements on Domestic Pets, Poultry-Keeping and Bee-Keeping.")* Helen sees that the tea service is missing, but not the brass candlesticks, the Bohemian crystal berry dish, the gold-lined toothpick holder, and not (thank God!) the very rare calling card holder[17] with the bulldog on it. Clearly this thief with the very small hands was an amateur who didn't know the value of antiques. Helen had immediately suspected the town boy, of course, but what could he possibly want with an eight-piece tea service?

Helen feels the remnants of her city self rising to the occasion: she will be practical before she falls apart. She will make sense of what has happened before she allows herself to feel violated, angry, or fright-

[16]Large Oak and Reed Rocker, well-braced, plush tapestry seat. This was one of Helen's first furniture purchases twenty years ago. She sits in it to read in the evening and is invariably comforted by the rhythmic creak of its rockers on the hardwood floor. Once she dreamed she was rocking a baby in this chair. The baby was sucking heartily on her left breast and she was humming a lullaby. In real life Helen does not like babies.

[17]Fancy Quadruple Silver Plated Card Receiver, cast bronze bulldog on base. This is an unusual piece which Helen loves for two reasons. First, because it reminds her of how much better off she would have been to be born in an earlier time when callers came with cards and the world was an altogether more genteel place. Second, because she likes the silly look on the bulldog's ugly face. Despite what other people might think, Helen does have a sense of humor.

ened. *(The thief, in the section called "Encyclopedia of General Knowledge: Essential Facts on All Significant Subjects Clearly Stated and Exactly Defined," looked at photographs of Mount Vesuvius, Stockholm City Hall, and an Australian aborigine armed with three boomerangs.)* Above all else, she will not cry, she will not cry, she will not cry, not yet.

Helen walks from room to room assessing the extent of her losses. She knows she should call the police but first she wants to see exactly what is missing. *(The thief opened the leather-bound notebook filled with Helen's handwriting and turned eagerly to the first page.)* Her curiosity is beginning to get the better of her.

In the living room the Cupid clock and the typewriter are gone. In the library she sees the empty stand which had held the encyclopedia. Not one other book is missing. Not one other book is even out of place. *(The thief read the first entry, dated April 26, 1975, obviously written shortly after Helen had moved into the house:* Rain. Lamb chops, peas, mashed potatoes, apple crisp for desert. Unpacking almost done. Long quiet evening. On the averge human head there are 100,000 hairs. They grow 0.01 inches every day.) In the music room, only the box camera is missing.

Helen goes upstairs. The angel painting on the landing is gone. She rubs her hand over its silhouette on the wallpaper. *(The thief flipped ahead through the pages and read:* October 20, 1979. High wind, trees moan as their branches are stripped. Leaves to rake tomorrow. Beef stew, too many onions. Can't sleep. Headache. Hire someone to put up storm windows. The seven deadly sins are anger, envy, covetousness, gluttony, lust, pride, and sloth.)

Helen looks into each of the rooms along the upstairs hallway but finds nothing amiss. The only sound is that of a dead leaf falling from a large potted fig tree at the end of the hallway.

She goes back into her bedroom. She looks through the jewelry chest. She is relieved to see that everything is still there, especiallly happy to see her favorite watch[18] which she often wears on a gold chain around

[18]Ladies 14K Solid Gold Stem Wind Watch, two diamonds, three rubies, engraved. On the front is the name *Beatrice* and on the back, the inscription *With love from Edward forever.* When Helen wears this watch, she feels taller, thinner, kinder. She feels like a beautiful woman named Beatrice, much loved by a handsome man named Edward. When Helen wears this watch, she smiles more and is warm toward the women she meets on the streets in town. She laughs with them, admires a new outfit, gives advice on a problem of pests in the garden, lays a hand on an arm while asking after their husbands, their children, their health. These women go home happy to think that maybe Helen Wingham is becoming one of them after all.

her neck. (*The thief read:* January 15, 1983. Snow all day. Meatloaf, home fries, creamed corn, and a butter tart. Cozy, reading in front of the fireplace. Perfect silence save for the sound of the flames. The seven virtues are faith, hope, charity, prudence, justice, fortitude, and temperance.)

She looks through her clothes in the armoire and the dresser. She imagines the thief's fingers on her blouses, her dresses, her cool silk slip. She feels to the bottom of her underwear drawer and discovers that her notebook is missing. (*The thief read:* May 24, 1988. Planted geraniums, nicotiana, cosmos, snapdragons, pansies, and six tomato plants. Had hair cut yesterday, also car serviced. Salmon steak, rice, lettuce fresh from the garden. The first woman in space was Valentina Tereshkova who made 48 orbits of the earth in a three-day mission in June 1963.)

Helen knows she should call the police but she cannot bear the thought of them tramping through her tidy rooms, poking at her belongings, fondling all of her precious objects with their big rough hands. She imagines them laughing at her and her thief, both of them inept and eccentric, both of them fools. (*The thief read:* July 28, 1992. Heat wave. Flowers looking desperate though I'm watering twice a day. I was desperate once too but I never knew for what. Water? No. Silence? Maybe. A cloudless shimmering sky. Too hot to eat. Cheese and crackers, carrot sticks, sliced tomatoes, vanilla ice cream. Cannot remember the smell of snow. The ice which covers Antarctica is approximately 6500 feet thick.) Helen imagines the policemen laughing and slapping their knees.

She pulls open the drawer of the bedside table and is relieved to find that the thief has not taken her Holy Bible or her gun.[19] She remembers how, when she bought the gun, the salesman kept assuring her that it was a pure collector's item, had never been fired, not even once. (*The thief read:* September 14, 1994. Spaghetti and meatballs, green salad, garlic bread, cherry cheesecake, one small glass of brandy because tomorrow is my birthday. Make appointment to have furnace cleaned. The heart of a seventy-year-old person will have beat at least 2.8 billion times. Tomorrow I will be fifty-three.)

Helen takes off her clothes and puts on her white nightgown. She knows she should call the police but she cannot bear the thought of

[19]Harrington & Richardson's Improved Automatic Shell-Extracting Double-Action Self-Cocking Revolver. Nickel-plated with rubber stocks, ebony and pearl inlaid handle. Accurate and dependable, equal to a Smith & Wesson in shooting acumen and power. Weight, 20 ounces; 3¼ inch barrel, 6 shot, 32-caliber, center fire. Helen has never fired a gun in her life but she guesses she could if she had to.

the burglary being talked about all over town tomorrow, all those smug women in their kitchens gossiping happily about her and her thief, saying, no doubt, that she had been asking for it, living out there all alone, friends with no one, who did she think she was anyway? (*The thief put down the notebook and rolled a piece of blank paper into the typewriter.*) At the moment she could not have answered this question, parts of her carefully constructed self having been so suddenly stripped away.

She is so tired. She looks down into the backyard. It is not yet dark but the moon is rising, almost full. She will get out there in the morning and pick those beans. (*The thief placed two small hands in position on the keyboard and typed:* This is the story of my life. This is the little story of my little life. Once upon a time there was a woman.) But for now she will just go to bed. It is too hot for blankets so she lies down on top of the counterpane with her small hands folded on her chest. She knows she should go downstairs and lock the back door but she does not. She knows she should be frightened but finds that she is not.

She imagines telling this story to Frederick next year at the hotel in the comfortable lobby when he stands close to her and asks how she has been. She imagines how they will laugh, how Frederick will lean toward her and put his warm hand on her bare arm, how she will feel his sweet breath on her face.

(*The thief got up from the kitchen table and went out to the garage.*) Helen lies very still. She feels very calm.

By the time darkness falls, Helen is almost asleep. (*The thief started the car and backed it out of the garage, out of the driveway, into the street.*)

Suspended between waking and dreaming, Helen sees the bedroom doorknob turning. She cannot decide whether she is dreaming or not. She thinks about the angel of doorknobs. The door is opening. A figure is standing in the doorway, walking toward her. A small hand is reaching out to touch her nightgown, her shoulder, her hair. She can feel sweet breath upon her face. She knows she should be frightened but finds that she is not.

(*The thief is watching the house.*)

(*The thief is walking through the front gate and around to the backyard.*)

(*The thief is in the garden.*)

(*The thief is standing in the moonlight looking up at Helen's bedroom window. The night is balmy and bright. The white lace curtains flutter against the screen in the dark. Any minute now the thief is going to call her name.*)

Any minute now the thief is going to call her name.

Robert Coover

Robert Coover was born in Charles City, Iowa, and educated in Illinois and Indiana. At Brown University he taught courses in electronic writing and mixed media. His novels include The Origin of the Brunists, The Public Burning, Spanking the Maid, Gerald's Party, Pinocchio in Venice, *and* Briar Rose.

Long an advocate for and a practitioner of fiction that is highly conceptual and formally innovative, Coover re-imagines fairy tales, folk tales, and fables set to contemporary idioms. He is particularly interested in other narrative delivery devices (television, radio, newspapers, movies, the Internet) and how they complement, complicate, and compete with the narrative delivery device we call literary fiction. Rather than tell one story or follow one line of action, his stories will often have several beginnings, one right after the other, as well as several middles and several possible endings.

In "The Elevator," from the 1969 collection Pricksongs & Descants, *a character going to his job in an office building steps into an elevator again and again. Sometimes he is alone, sometimes other people go along for the ride. At times the elevator is self-service, at other times there is an operator. The elevator can go up or down. This metafictional approach to storytelling invites the reader to consider the many possibilities within a relatively simple, stripped-down situation and to participate actively in the creation of the story. "What if?" the story asks again and again: What if the elevator goes down instead of up? What if the elevator fails and falls? What if the elevator goes up and keeps going? The reader of "The Elevator" will never take a simple elevator ride again.*

The Elevator

1

Every morning without exception and without so much as reflecting upon it, Martin takes the self-service elevator to the fourteenth floor, where he works. He will do so today. When he first arrives, however, he finds the lobby empty, the old building still possessed of its feinting shadows and silences, desolate though mutely expectant, and he wonders if today it might not turn out differently.

It is 7:30 A.M.: Martin is early and therefore has the elevator entirely to himself. He steps inside: this tight cell! he thinks with a kind of unsettling shock, and confronts the panel of numbered buttons. One to fourteen, plus "B" for basement. Impulsively, he presses the "B"— seven years and yet to visit the basement! He snorts at his timidity.

After a silent moment, the doors rumble shut. All night alert waiting for this moment! The elevator sinks slowly into the earth. The stale gloomy odors of the old building having aroused in him an unreasonable sense of dread and loss, Martin imagines suddenly he is descending into hell. *Tra la perduta genta*, yes! A mild shudder shakes him. Yet, Martin decides firmly, would that it were so. The old carrier halts with a quiver. The automatic doors yawn open. Nothing, only a basement. It is empty and nearly dark. It is silent and meaningless.

Martin smiles inwardly at himself, presses the number "14". "Come on, old Charon," he declaims broadly, "Hell's the other way!"

2

Martin waited miserably for the stench of intestinal gas to reach his nostrils. Always the same. He supposed it was Carruther, but he could never prove it. Not so much as a telltale squeak. But it was Carruther who always led them, and though the other faces changed, Carruther was always among them.

They were seven in the elevator: six men and the young girl who operated it. The girl did not participate. She was surely offended, but she never gave a hint of it. She possessed a surface detachment that not even Carruther's crude proposals could penetrate. Much less did she involve herself in the coarse interplay of men. Yet certainly, Martin supposed, they were a torment to her.

And, yes, he was right—there it was, faint at first, almost sweet, then slowly thickening, sickening, crowding up on him—

"Hey! Who fahred thet shot?" cried Carruther, starting it.

"Mart fahred-it!" came the inexorable reply. And then the crush of loud laughter.

"*What!* Is that Martin fartin' again?" bellowed another, as their toothy thicklipped howling congealed around him.

"Aw *please*, Mart! *don't fart!*" cried yet another. It would go on until they left the elevator. The elevator was small: their laughter packed it, jammed at the walls. "Have a heart, Mart! don't *part* that fart!"

It's not me, *it's not me*, Martin insisted. But only to himself. It was no use. It was fate. Fate and Carruther. (More laughter, more brute jabs.) A couple times he had protested. "Aw, Marty, you're just modest!" Carruther had thundered. Booming voice, big man. Martin hated him.

One by one, the other men filed out of the elevator at different floors, holding their noses. "Old farty Marty!" they would shout to anyone they met on their way out, and it always got a laugh, up and down the floor. The air cleared slightly each time the door opened.

In the end, Martin was always left alone with the girl who operated the elevator. His floor, the fourteenth, was the top one. When it all began, long ago, he had attempted apologetic glances toward the girl on exiting, but she had always turned her shoulder to him. Maybe she thought he was making a play for her. Finally he was forced to adopt the custom of simply ducking out as quickly as possible. She would in any case assume his guilt.

Of course, there was an answer to Carruther. Yes, Martin knew it, had rehearsed it countless times. The only way to meet that man was on his home ground. And he'd do it, too. When the time came.

3

Martin is alone on the elevator with the operator, a young girl. She is neither slender nor plump, but fills charmingly her orchid-colored uniform. Martin greets her in his usual friendly manner and she returns his greeting with a smile. Their eyes meet momentarily. Hers are brown.

When Martin enters the elevator, there are actually several other people crowded in, but as the elevator climbs through the musky old building, the others, singly or in groups, step out. Finally, Martin is left alone with the girl who operates the elevator. She grasps the lever, leans against it, and the cage sighs upward. He speaks to her, makes a lighthearted joke about elevators. She laughs and

Alone on the elevator with the girl, Martin thinks: if this elevator should crash, I would sacrifice my life to save her. Her back is straight and subtle. Her orchid uniform skirt is tight, tucks tautly under her blossoming hips, describes a kind of cavity there. Perhaps it is night. Her calves are muscular and strong. She grasps the lever.

The girl and Martin are alone on the elevator, which is rising. He concentrates on her round hips until she is forced to turn and look at him. His gaze coolly courses her belly, her pinched and belted waist, past her taut breasts, meets her excited stare. She breathes deeply, her lips parted. They embrace. Her breasts plunge softly against him. Her mouth is sweet. Martin has forgotten whether the elevator is climbing or not.

4

Perhaps Martin will meet Death on the elevator. Yes, going out for lunch one afternoon. Or to the drugstore for cigarettes. He will press the button in the hall on the fourteenth floor, the doors will open, a dark smile will beckon. The shaft is deep. It is dark and silent. Martin will recognize Death by His silence. He will not protest.

He *will* protest! oh God! no matter what the
the sense of emptiness underneath breath lurching out
The shaft is long and narrow. The shaft is dark.
He will not protest.

5

Martin, as always and without so much as reflecting upon it, takes the self-service elevator to the fourteenth floor, where he works. He is early, but only by a few minutes. Five others join him, greetings are exchanged. Though tempted, he is not able to risk the "B," but presses the "14" instead. Seven years!

As the automatic doors press together and the elevator begins its slow complaining ascent, Martin muses absently on the categories. This small room, so commonplace and so compressed, he observes with a certain melancholic satisfaction, this elevator contains them all: space, time, cause, motion, magnitude, class. Left to our own devices, we would probably discover them. The other passengers chatter with self-righteous smiles (after all, they are on time) about the weather, the elections, the work that awaits them today. They stand, apparently motionless, yet moving. Motion: perhaps that's all there is to it after all. Motion and the medium. Energy and weighted particles. Force and matter. The image grips him purely. Ascent and the passive reorganization of atoms.

At the seventh floor, the elevator stops and a woman departs it. Only a trace of her perfume remains. Martin alone remarks—to himself, of course—her absence, as the climb begins again. Reduced by one. But the totality of the universe is suffused: each man contains all of it, loss is inconceivable. Yet, if that is so—and a tremor shudders coolly through Martin's body—then the totality is as nothing. Martin gazes around at his four remaining fellow passengers, a flush of compassion washing in behind the tremor. One must always be alert to the possibility of action, he reminds himself. But none apparently need him. If he could do the work for them today, give them the grace of a day's contemplation . . .

The elevator halts, suspended and vibrant, at the tenth floor. Two men leave. Two more intermediate stops, and Martin is alone. He has seen them safely through. Although caged as ever in his inexorable melancholy, Martin nonetheless smiles as he steps out of the self-service elevator on the fourteenth floor. "I am pleased to participate," he announces in full voice. But, as the elevator doors close behind him and he hears the voided descent, he wonders: Wherein now is the elevator's totality?

6

The cable snaps at the thirteenth floor. There is a moment's deadly motionlessness—then a sudden breathless plunge! The girl, terrified, turns to Martin. They are alone. Though inside his heart is bursting its chambers in terror, he remains outwardly composed. "I think it is safer lying on your back," he says. He squats to the floor, but the girl remains transfixed with shock. Her thighs are round and sleek under the orchid skirt, and in the shadowed— "Come," he says. "You may lie on me. My body will absorb part of the impact." Her hair caresses his cheek, her buttocks press like a sponge into his groin. In love, moved by his sacrifice, she weeps. To calm her, he clasps her heaving abdomen, strokes her soothingly. The elevator whistles as it drops.

7

Martin worked late in the office, clearing up the things that needed to be done before the next day, routine matters, yet part of the uninterrupted necessity that governed his daily life. Not a large office, Martin's, though he needed no larger, essentially neat except for the modest clutter on top of his desk. The room was equipped only with that desk and a couple chairs, bookcases lining one wall, calendar posted on another. The overhead lamp was off, the only light in the office being provided by the fluorescent lamp on Martin's desk.

Martin signed one last form, sighed, smiled. He retrieved a cigarette, half-burned but still lit, from the ashtray, drew heavily on it, then, as he exhaled with another prolonged sigh, doubled the butt firmly in the black bowl of the ashtray. Still extinguishing it, twisting it among the heap of crumpled filters in the ashtray, he glanced idly at his watch. He was astonished to discover that the watch said twelve-thirty—and had stopped! Already after midnight!

He jumped up, rolled down his sleeves, buttoned them, whipped his suit jacket off the back of his chair, shoved his arms into it. Bad enough twelve-thirty—but my God! how much *later* was it? The jacket still only three-quarters of the way up his back, tie askew, he hastily stacked the loose papers on his desk and switched off the lamp. He stumbled through the dark room out into the hallway, lit by one dull yellow bulb, pulled his office door to behind him. The thick solid catch knocked hollowly in the vacant corridor.

He buttoned his shirt collar, straightened his tie and the collar of his jacket, which was doubled under on his right shoulder, as he hurried down the passageway past the other closed office doors of the fourteenth floor to the self-service elevator, his heels hammering away the stillness on the marble floor. He trembled, inexplicably. The profound silence of the old building disturbed him. Relax, he urged himself; we'll know what time it is soon enough. He pushed the button for the elevator, but nothing happened. Don't tell me I have to walk down! he muttered bitterly to himself. He poked the button again, harder, and this time he heard below a solemn rumble, a muffled thump, and an indistinct grinding plaint that grieved progressively nearer. It stopped and the doors of the elevator opened to receive him. Entering, Martin felt a sudden need to glance back over his shoulder, but he suppressed it.

Once inside, he punched the number "1" button on the self-service panel. The doors closed, but the elevator, instead of descending, continued to climb. Goddamn this old wreck! Martin swore irritably, and he jiggled the "1" button over and over. Just this night! The elevator stopped, the doors opened, Martin stepped out. Later, he wondered why he had done so. The doors slid shut behind him, he heard the elevator descend, its amused rumble fading distantly. Although here it was utterly dark, shapes seemed to form. Though he could see nothing distinctly, he was fully aware that he was not alone. His hand fumbled on the wall for the elevator button. Cold wind gnawed at his ankles, the back of his neck. Fool! wretched fool! he wept, there *is* no fifteenth floor! Pressed himself against the wall, couldn't find the button, couldn't even find the elevator door, and even the very wall was only

8

Carruther's big voice boomed in the small cage.

"Mart fahred-it!" came the certain reply. The five men laughed. Martin flushed. The girl feigned indifference. The fetor of fart vapours reeked in the tight elevator.

"Martin, damn it, cut the fartin'!"

Martin fixed his cool gaze on them. "Carruther fucks his mother," he said firmly. Carruther hit him full in the face, his glasses splintered and fell, Martin staggered back against the wall. He waited for the second blow, but it didn't come. Someone elbowed him, and he slipped to the floor. He knelt there, weeping softly, searched with hands for his glasses. Martin tasted the blood from his nose, trickling into his mouth. He couldn't find the glasses, couldn't even see.

"Look out, baby!" Carruther thundered. "Farty Marty's jist tryin' to git a free peek up at your pretty drawers!" Crash of laughter. Martin felt the girl shrink from him.

9

Her soft belly presses like a sponge into his groin. No, safer on your back, love, he thinks, but pushes the thought away. She weeps in terror, presses her hot wet mouth against his. To calm her, he clasps her soft buttocks, strokes them soothingly. So sudden is the plunge, they seem suspended in air. She has removed her skirt. How will it feel? he wonders.

10

Martin, without so much as reflecting on it, automatically takes the self-service elevator to the fourteenth floor, where he works. The systematizing, that's what's wrong, he concludes, that's what cracks them up. He is late, but only by a few minutes. Seven others join him, anxious, sweating. They glance nervously at their watches. None of them presses the "B" button. Civilities are hurriedly interchanged.

Their foolish anxiety seeps out like a bad spirit, enters Martin. He finds himself looking often at his watch, grows impatient with the elevator. Take it easy, he cautions himself. Their blank faces oppress him. Bleak. Haunted. Tyrannized by their own arbitrary regimentation of time. Torture self-imposed, yet in all probability inescapable. The elevator halts jerkily at the third floor, quivering their sallow face-flesh. They frown. No one has pushed the three. A woman enters. They all nod, harumph, make jittery little hand motions to incite the doors to close. They are all more or less aware of the woman (she has delayed them, damn her!), but only Martin truly remarks—to himself—her whole presence, as the elevator resumes its upward struggle. The accretion of tragedy. It goes on, ever giving birth to itself. Up and down, up and down. Where will it end? he wonders. Her perfume floats gloomily in the stale air. These deformed browbeaten mind-animals. Suffering and insufferable. Up and down. He closes his eyes. One by one, they leave him.

He arrives, alone, at the fourteenth floor. He steps out of the old elevator, stares back into its spent emptiness. There, only there, is peace, he concludes wearily. The elevator doors press shut.

11

Here on this elevator, my elevator, created by me, moved by me, doomed by me, I, Martin, proclaim my omnipotence! In the end, doom touches all! MY doom! I impose it! TREMBLE!

12

The elevator shrieks insanely as it drops. Their naked bellies slap together, hands grasp, her vaginal mouth closes spongelike on his rigid organ. Their lips lock, tongues knot. The bodies: how will they find them? Inwardly, he laughs. He thrusts up off the plummeting floor. Her eyes are brown and, with tears, love him.

13

But—ah!—the doomed, old man, the DOOMED! What are they to us, to ME? ALL! We, I love! Let their flesh sag and dewlaps tremble, let their odors offend, let their cruelty mutilate, their stupidity enchain—but let them laugh, father! FOREVER! let them cry!

14

but hey! theres this guy see he gets on the goddamn elevator and its famous how hes got him a doodang about five feet long Im not kiddin you none five feet and he gets on the—yeah! can you imagine a bastard like that boardin a friggin public I mean public elevator? hoohah! no I dont know his name Mert I think or Mort but the crux is he is possessed of this motherin digit biggern ole Rahab see—do with it? I dont know I think he wraps it around his leg or carries it over his shoulder or somethin *jeezuss!* what a problem! why I bet hes *killt* more poor bawdies than I ever dipped my poor worm in! once he was even a—listen! Carruther tells this as the goddamn truth I mean he *respects* that bastard—he was even one a them jackoff gods I forget how you call them over there with them Eyetalians after the big war see them dumb types when they seen him furl out this here five foot hose of his one day—he was just tryin to get the goddamn knots out Carruther says—why they thought he musta been a goddamn jackoff god or somethin and wanted to like employ him or whatever you do with a god and well Mort he figgered it to be a not so miserable occupation dont you know better anyhow than oildrillin with it in Arabia or stoppin holes in Dutch dikes like hes been doing so the bastard he stays on there a time and them little quiff there in that Eyetalian place they grease him up with hogfat or olive oil and all workin together like vested virgins they pull him off out there in the fields and spray the crops and well Mort he says *he* says its the closest hes ever got to the real mccoy jeezuss! hes worth a thousand laughs! and they bring him all the old aunts and grannies and he splits them open a kinda stupendous euthanasia for the old ladies and he blesses all their friggin procreations with a swat of his doodang and even does a little welldiggin on the side but he gets in trouble with the Roman churchers on accounta not bein circumcised and they wanta whack it off but Mort says no and they cant get close to him with so prodigious a batterin ram as hes got so they work a few miracles on him and wrinkle up his old pud with holy water and heat up his semen so it burns up the fields and even one day ignites a goddamn volcano and *jeezuss!* he wastes no time throwin that thing over his shoulder and hightailin it *outa* there I can tell you! but now like Im sayin them pastoral days is dead and gone and hes goin up and down in elevators like the rest of us and so here he is boardin the damn cage and theys a bunch of us bastards clownin around with the little piece who operates that deathtrap kinda brushin her swell butt like a occasional accident and sweet jeezus her gettin fidgety and hot and half fightin us off and half pullin us on and playin with that lever *zoom!* wingin up through that scraper and just then ole Carruther jeezuss he really breaks you up sometimes that crazy bastard he hefts up her little purple skirt and whaddaya know! the little quiff aint wearin no skivvies! its somethin *beautiful* man I mean a sweet cleft peach right outa some foreign orchard and poor ole Mort he is kinda part gigglin and part hurtin and for a minute the rest of us dont see the pointa the whole agitation but then that there incredible thing suddenly pops up quivery right under his chin like the friggin eye of god for crissake and then theres this big wild rip and man! it rears up and splits outa there like a goddamn redwood topplin *gawdamighty!* and knocks old Carruther *kapow!* right to the deck! his best buddy and that poor little cunt she takes one glim of that impossible rod wheelin around in there and whammin the walls and she faints dead away and *jeeezusss!* she tumbles right on that elevator lever and man! I thought for a minute we was *all* dead

15 . . .

They plunge, their damp bodies fused, pounding furiously, in terror, in joy, the impact is

I, Martin, proclaim against all dooms the indestructible seed

Martin does not take the self-service elevator to the fourteenth floor, as is his custom, but, reflecting upon it for once and out of a strange premonition, determines instead to walk the fourteen flights. Halfway up, he hears the elevator hurtle by him and then the splintering crash from below. He hesitates, poised on the stair. Inscrutable is the word he finally settles upon. He pronounces it aloud, smiles faintly, sadly, somewhat wearily, then continues his tedious climb, pausing from time to time to stare back down the stairs behind him.

Clarice Lispector

One of Brazil's most original and celebrated writers, Clarice Lispector was born in a small village in Ukraine in 1920, then moved with her parents to Brazil when she was two months old. At twenty she began working for Agencia Nacional (the Brazilian news agency), but in 1943 she left Brazil for sixteen years upon marrying a career diplomat. For her first novel, Close to the Wild Heart, *published in 1944, she won a Graça Aranha Prize, awarded by the Brazilian Academy of Letters. In addition to novels and stories, she wrote regular newspaper columns. She died of cancer in 1977.*

Lispector does not fret over the uncertainties of life in her work; she celebrates them. The French writer and theorist Hélène Cixious writes of Lispector, "If Kafka were a woman; if Rilke were a Brazilian Jewish woman born in the Ukraine; if Rimbaud had been a mother, if he had reached his 50's; if Heidegger had been able to stop being German, if he had written the Novel of the Earth . . . It's in this ambiance that Clarice Lispector writes. There, where the most demanding works breathe, she advances. There, further ahead, where the philosopher loses his breath, she continues, still further, beyond all knowledge."

"The Fifth Story" deals with the most mundane of incidents: a woman wakes up to discover her residence infested with cockroaches, and she kills them. But she doesn't know how to tell the story or what it means to have killed these creatures, so she tells the story five times in order to approach some resolution. That's a literal reading of the story, but this story resists literality. At its heart, its sensibility is highly poetic and mythic, and in some ways metafictional (a story about telling stories), though to attempt to categorize this story is futile and ultimately does it a

disservice. We recognize that Lispector illuminates the ambiguity and uncertainty of the human condition.

The Fifth Story

This story could be called "The Statues." Another possible title would be "The Killing." Or even "How to Kill Cockroaches." So I shall tell at least three stories, all of them true, because none of the three will contradict the others. Although they constitute one story, they could become a thousand and one, were I to be granted a thousand and one nights.

The first story, "How to Kill Cockroaches," begins like this: I was complaining about the cockroaches. A woman heard me complain. She gave me a recipe for killing them. I was to mix together equal quantities of sugar, flour and gypsum. The flour and sugar would attract the cockroaches, the gypsum would dry up their insides. I followed her advice. The cockroaches died.

The next story is really the first, and it is called "The Killing." It begins like this: I was complaining about the cockroaches. A woman heard me complain. The recipe follows. And then the killing takes place. The truth is that I had only complained in abstract terms about the cockroaches, for they were not even mine: they belonged to the ground floor and climbed up the pipes in the building into our apartment. It was only when I prepared the mixture that they also became mine. On our behalf, therefore, I began to measure and weigh ingredients with greater concentration. A vague loathing had taken possession of me, a sense of outrage. By day, the cockroaches were invisible and no one would believe in the evil secret which eroded such a tranquil household. But if the cockroaches, like evil secrets, slept by day, there I was preparing their nightly poison. Meticulous, eager, I prepared the elixir of prolonged death. An angry fear and my own evil secret guided me. Now I coldly wanted one thing only: to kill every cockroach in existence. Cockroaches climb up the pipes while weary people sleep. And now the recipe was ready, looking so white. As if I were dealing with cockroaches as cunning as myself, I carefully spread the powder until it looked like part of the surface dust. From my bed, in the silence of the apartment, I imagined them climbing up one by one into the kitchen where darkness slept, a solitary towel alert on the clothesline. I awoke hours later, startled at having overslept. It was beginning to grow light. I walked across the kitchen. There they lay on the floor of the scullery, huge and brittle. During the night I had killed them. On our behalf, it was beginning to grow light. On a nearby hill, a cockerel crowed.

The third story which now begins is called "The Statues." It begins by saying that I had been complaining about the cockroaches. Then the same woman appears on the scene. And so it goes on to the point where I awake as it is beginning to grow light, and I awake still feeling sleepy and I walk across the kitchen. Even more sleepy is the scullery floor with its tiled perspective. And in the shadows of dawn, there is a purplish hue which distances everything; at my feet, I perceive patches of light and shade, scores of rigid statues scattered everywhere. The cockroaches that have hardened from core to shell. Some are lying upside down. Others arrested in the midst of some movement that will never be completed. In the mouths of some of the cockroaches, there are traces of white powder. I am the first to observe the dawn breaking over Pompei. I know what this night has been, I know about the orgy in the dark. In some, the gypsum has hardened as slowly as in some organic process, and the cockroaches, with ever more tortuous movements, have greedily intensified the night's pleasures, trying to escape from their insides. Until they turn to stone, in innocent terror and with such, but *such* an expression of pained reproach. Others—suddenly assailed by their own core, without even having perceived that their inner form was turning to stone!—these are suddenly crystallized, just like a word arrested on someone's lips: I love . . . The cockroaches, invoking the name of love in vain, sang on a summer's night. While the cockroach over there, the one with the brown antennae smeared with white, must have realized too late that it had become mummified precisely because it did not know how to use things with the gratuitous grace of the *in vain*: "It is just that I looked too closely inside myself! It is just that I looked too closely inside . . . " From my frigid height as a human being, I watch the destruction of a world. Dawn breaks. Here and there, the parched antennae of dead cockroaches quiver in the breeze. The cockerel from the previous story crows.

The fourth story opens a new era in the household. The story begins as usual: I was complaining about the cockroaches. It goes on up to the point when I see the statues in plaster of Paris. Inevitably dead. I look toward the pipes where this same night an infestation will reappear, swarming slowly upwards in Indian file. Should I renew the lethal sugar every night? like someone who no longer sleeps without the avidity of some rite. And should I take myself somnambulant out to the terrace early each morning? in my craving to encounter the statues which my perspiring night has erected. I trembled with a depraved pleasure at the vision of my double existence as a witch. I also trembled at the sight of that hardening gypsum, the depravity of existence which would shatter my internal form.

The grim moment of choosing between two paths, which I thought would separate, convinced that any choice would mean sacrificing either myself or my soul. I chose. And today I secretly carry a plaque of virtue in my heart: "This house has been disinfected."

The fifth story is called "Leibnitz and the Transcendence of Love in Polynesia." It begins like this: I was complaining about the cockroaches.

Translated by Giovanni Pontiero

A. B. Paulson

A. B. Paulson lives in Portland, Oregon. His odd but funny novel Watchman Tell Us of the Night *was published by Viking-Penguin.*

We have all taken tests that look like the one printed here with the title "The Minnesota Multiphasic Personality: a diagnostic test in two parts," and we notice immediately the fidelity with which Paulson has crafted the look and feel of it. In our daily life we read newspapers, road signs, cereal boxes, letters, advertisements, greeting cards, bank statements—and in all that reading we often lose sight of the occasion of the reading. Paulson's test, re-framed as a story, makes the tests we take (and take for granted) seem strange, new, and bizarre.

The Minnesota Multiphasic Personality: a diagnostic test in two parts

(1) Name:			(2) Social Security #:		(3) Sex:
Last	*First*	*Middle*			
(4) Permanent Address:					
Street	*City*		*State*	*Zip*	
(5) Position for which you are applying:			This space for office use only.		
			A B Total		

(Note: All prospective employees of the Drummand Fabricating Corporation are required to take the following examination. The results are used for placement purposes only and are strictly confidential.)

The Director of Testing has supplied you with two sharpened pencils. Use only these pencils in marking your test answers.

Fill in the information requested in the box above.

The examination consists of two parts: section A and section B. You are allowed one-half hour to complete the entire examination.

If you think you have finished before the half-hour is up, please wait quietly in your seat until the others are finished.

Section A

This is a test of your ability to read, comprehend, and evaluate written materials. Read each paragraph below and then for each question choose the answer that seems the BEST to you. Mark your selection by circling the letter of the answer you chose.

1. The stove was in the corner of the big room where we slept. From my bed across the room I would stare at the warm glow that crept around the edges of its loose iron door. Some nights in October are cold, and you never know what the sound is that calls you out of dreaming. Perhaps the geese, high overhead in the darkness crying to one another.

I was awake when he came home, heard the stove's door open and shut, his boots on the hollow floor. I felt his coarse breath on my face as he bent over me. I smelled the sweat and grime on his clothes as I huddled there perfectly still.

In this passage we learn that:
A. The narrator hates the man because he is dirty and coarse.
B. The man suspects the boy has been spying on him and checks to see if he is asleep.
C. The father has been drinking and seeing another woman.
D. The father kisses his son.

2. Genetic mutations in *Drosophila Melanogaster* may be grouped into three broad classes: visible, biochemical, and lethal. Visible muta-

tions, both dominant and recessive, may involve an additive alteration in the organism's morphology (such as the development of the proboscis into a leg-like structure), or may reveal the loss of some esssential function, such as the ability of the organism to recognize members of its own species. Biochemical mutations involve the loss of a specific metabolic function, such as the ability to synthesize essential enzymes. There may also be partial losses which inhibit the organism's normal patterns of behavior under conditions of unusual stress, such as altered temperature or pH. Lethal mutations cause the death of the organism.

We may infer from this passage that:
A. Inversion of gene sequence within the chromosomes of *Drosophila* males often results in sterility.
B. Visible mutations may not be subject to experimental observation because they involve perceptions internal to the organism itself.
C. Some lethal mutations may involve partial losses of essential metabolic functions leading to partial death.
D. The author has submitted test subjects to conditions of unusual stress.

3. Among the Sioux it was customary for an adolescent male to fast alone and naked on the prairie awaiting the vision that would guide him into manhood. Geissling in 1934 recorded the case of a boy who, on the fourth day, dreamed the Thunderbird dropped out of the sky striking him with a bright flash. When the boy regained consciousness he made his way back to the village. He knew that a vision of the Thunderbird would oblige him to assume the role of *heyoka*, a sort of tribe jester who behaved clownishly for the amusement of the others. When the time came to relate his vision to the elders, he told them that the moon had reached out to him offering in one hand a quiver of arrows, and in the other a bow. Somehow the older men knew he lied for one of them said, "So the thunderbird has struck you; already you are behaving foolishly." The boy could only answer yes. Then they all had a good laugh together.

The author of this paragraph is illustrating how:
A. Telling lies will get you nowhere.
B. Homogeneous cultures absorb deviant behavior by providing secondary roles.
C. Anthropologists fill their technical writings with little stories.
D. Fasting alone on the prairie will produce visions.

4. Speak the speech I pray you, as I pronounced it to you, trippingly on the tongue; but if you mouth it, as many of your players do, I had as lief the town-crier had spoke my lines. Nor do not saw the air too much with your hand, thus, but use all gently; for in the very torrent, tempest, and, as I may say, the whirlwind of passion, you must acquire and beget a temperance that may give it smoothness. Be not too tame neither, but let your own discretion be your tutor. Suit the action to the word, the word to the action, with this special observance, that you overstep not the modesty of nature. For anything so overdone is from the purpose of playing, whose end, both at the first and now, was and is, to hold, as 'twere, the mirror up to nature, that she may see her own occulted soul, which peeps from out the very rags and struttings of her image. This was sometime a paradox, to let your eye and tongue in this be hypocrites, while firm within your bosom, thus, the inward man in hugger-mugger guides the guilded hand of broad abuse.

The best title for this reading passage would be:
A. "Don't overact"
B. "Dialogue between self and soul"
C. "To thine own self be true"
D. "Hugger-mugger man"

5. Frescos are paintings—usually with an egg tempera base—executed on wet plaster. This intimate bond between the pigment and its ground accounts for the surprising durability of frescos; their colors still appear brilliant after many centuries.

Painting on plaster that began drying as soon as it was applied imposed an unusual limitation on the fresco artist. He was forced to complete at one sitting small areas of his larger composition. A half-finished fresco must have looked much like an uncompleted jig-saw puzzle. In fact, lines are still visible in completed paintings that mark the edges where the artist left off for the day and began the next with fresh plaster. These boundaries were disguised where possible by following the contours of objects or persons in the painting. In the famous creation scene in Michelangelo's Sistine Chapel ceiling, it is clear that the figure of God the Father, leisurely stretching out his hand, was painted at a different sitting than Adam, who reaches up to receive the spark of life. For just at that point where their fingers might touch, one can see a line dividing one plastered area from another.

On the basis of the information in this passage we can assume that:

A. The forms artists choose impose limitations of content.
B. God and man belong to separate realms.
C. A spark can jump a gap.
D. Michelangelo was not afraid of heights.

Section B

This part of the examination consists of 93 true and false questions. Read each statement carefully and then circle "T" for "True" or "F" for "False." Because this is a psychological test some of the questions may sound unusual. Answer them all as best you can. You may now begin.

1. T F You have to meet people half-way.
2. T F A healthy person learns to laugh at his own foibles.
3. T F Sometimes I think the world has gone stale.
4. T F I am afraid of large machines.
5. T F I am afraid there is someone inside me.
6. T F I am discreet.
7. T F I am straightforward.
8. T F I have not made lewd faces at matrons descending escalators.
9. T F I have lain awake at night thinking nothing in particular.
10. T F I have had entire conversations with people only to realize later that they had mistaken me for someone else.
11. T F I have had visions.
12. T F Bureaucracies are impersonal.
13. T F Doctors are dedicated.
14. T F Old dogs are unlikely to learn new tricks.
15. T F Someone has his eye on you.
16. T F I had a dog that never learned a single trick.
17. T F I have learned the trick of being straightforward.
18. T F We waited up for my father.
19. T F Some days I look at the examination booklets piled up on my desk and it fills me with loathing and I feel distraught.
20. T F The supervisor posts lists of office rules above the water cooler.
21. T F Long division is not amusing.
22. T F I give the supervisor knowing looks.
23. T F He thinks I am a good worker but a little odd.
24. T F He is a fool.

25. T F   I have clowned and brought joy into the lives of many fools.

26. T F   One must take life with a grain of salt.

27. T F   I have been drinking too much water lately.

28. T F   Sometimes I find myself in situations where I am forced to say, "This is not life; this is someone's idea of art."

29. T F   I have worked in this office for five years and they still mispronounce my name.

30. T F   I have never told people my real name.

31. T F   I am afraid of heights.

32. T F   I have given myself a name that even I cannot pronounce.

33. T F   I am a prince.

34. T F   My mother was pretty ordinary.

35. T F   Variety is the spice of life.

36. T F   I asked her where babies came from and she told me a story about chimneys and birds in the night.

37. T F   I practice regular living.

38. T F   I never practiced the piano.

39. T F   That was a good sign.

40. T F   Hordes of tiny flies live in my dresser drawer.

41. T F   They feed on something in there.

42. T F   I have abused my member.

43. T F   I think it is a rotten fig.

44. T F   I have heard voices in the night.

45. T F   They told me I was special.

46. T F   I have gone door to door naked on Halloween.

47. T F   I have done nothing to discourage people from thinking that I am a prophet in disguise.

48. T F   I have stood in front of the mirror for hours until I no longer recognize myself.

49. T F   Someday I shall amuse everyone with my rubber mouse.

50. T F   I have eaten spiders.

51. T F   On the whole you could say that I am a pretty regular fellow.

52. T F   Somewhere in the world there is another person exactly like me.

53. T F   If I ever met him I probably would not recognize him.

54. T F   I once wore a pencil behind my ear for three months hoping that it might be the sign of a secret society, and although no one ever gripped my hand in recognition, a neatly dressed man did wink at me once.

55. T F Never discuss your personal life with prospective employees.

56. T F Time is running out.

57. T F People are beginning to call me fruity behind my back.

58. T F I have failed the test of time.

59. T F Life is tragic.

60. T F I am just waiting for the part that is called comic relief.

61. T F Art is a necessary lie.

62. T F The revelation is at hand.

63. T F He said, "What are you doing here?"

64. T F I didn't know the right answer.

65. T F He said, "I was testing you and I knew that you followed me here."

66. T F I thought I had been testing him.

67. T F He and the lady had been drinking together.

68. T F He said, "You are a man now."

69. T F I said, "I wish you were dead."

70. T F I have hidden a fugitive and protected him with half-truths.

71. T F Sometimes I wish all this weren't happening.

72. T F I'm tired of being a ship passing in the night.

73. T F More than once I've lost a shoe in a snowbank, and somehow I hopped home with one foot bare.

74. T F I'm tired of clowning for someone hidden inside me.

75. T F For all I know there's someone inside him.

76. T F I forbid him to write letters in color-crayon.

77. T F I'll try to face the past with honesty.

78. T F We waited up but he did not come home.

79. T F You can help me.

80. T F In the morning they came holding their hats in their hands.

81. T F I can help you.

82. T F "He must have stumbled in the dark at the edge of the quarry."

83. T F I have lain awake at night thinking of nothing in particular.

84. T F I want to throw my popcorn box at the screen.

85. T F I will tell you my real name.

86. T F I will sing barbershop in the elevator.

87. T F I will let the grass grow under my feet.

88. T F I will tighten my belt.

89. T F   The readiness is all.
90. T F   I am throwing down the glove.
91. T F   I will join the march of time.
92. T F   You will make a sign to me.
93. T F   I can only meet you half-way.

Molly Giles

Molly Giles won the Flannery O'Connor Award in 1985 for her story collection Rough Translations, *which was also recognized with the Boston Globe Award and the Bay Area Book Reviewers Award for Fiction. Currently Director of the Programs in Creative Writing at the University of Arkansas, Giles has taught the novelists Amy Tan and Gus Lee in writing workshops. She divides her time between Woodacre, California, and Fayetteville, Arkansas.*

"The Writers' Model" satirizes writing's claim that it, too, is a fine art like sculpture or painting. Unlike painters, writers don't employ models to pose for them as they write; yet the story reminds us that in fact authors do draw on models taken from life. This subtle metafiction, despite its narrative sequence of events, is predominately a story about storytelling. It's a story worth reading because it makes the self-conscious reader think about his or her own stories or a script that he or she is following. Aren't we all models? objects in someone's gaze? characters in someone's story? trapped in roles and events of our own invention?

The Writers' Model

I'm old now, but when I was young you could talk me into anything. I had an open mind. So when I saw the ad saying some "professional writers" needed an "adventurous girl" to "interview for fictional purposes," I was intrigued, especially when the ad went on to say that "by simply answering questions" I could "make an important contribution to American literature." I had always wanted to make an important contribution to something, so I threw on my coat, grabbed my purse, and went straight to the address listed in the paper.

I found myself outside a dark house in a bad part of town. Nobody answered when I knocked so I tried the door and stepped into the strangest room, like an interrogation cell in a jail, with one bare bulb in the middle of the ceiling and an empty chair waiting beneath it. A ring of silent people circled the chair. I caught the glint of their pens and pencils and saw the notepads open on their laps. All the notepads, I noticed, were blank. For some reason, that touched me. I straightened my shoulders, went to the chair, and sat down.

"Ask me anything," I said, and the first writer said, "What is your body like?"

I stared. I realized that all the people were men and that many were dressed alike, in tweed jackets with leather patches on the sleeves. One by one they adjusted their horn-rimmed glasses, lit their briar pipes, patted the Irish setters lying at their feet, and looked at me as if they expected me to take my clothes off.

So I did. I am not shy and I had already understood that to these writers I was neither woman nor human; I was an object. An *objet* (comforted my self) *d'art*.

"Why are you smiling?" one writer asked, and I told my little joke as I took my scarf off, and another said, his voice sharp, "Do you know French?" and I shrugged as I unbuttoned my blouse because everyone knows some French and then I stepped out of my skirt and for the rest of that first session there was nothing but scribbling and an occasional testy, "How about German? How about Greek?" from the back.

I didn't have to do many sittings stark naked after that; they had their notes to refer to, after all, and the small room was cold. It wasn't my body they had come for anyway, it was the questions—the questions and the answers I gave them. Many of them had seen a woman, touched a woman, had sex with a woman—many of them were married—but not many had ever really talked to a woman, and this was their chance.

How do you feel about your underpants?

Do you jiggle when you run?

What is it like to have someone inside you?

Does size really matter?

What does orgasm feel like?

Those were the physical questions, some of them, though of course there were many more. Everything about breasts fascinated them except nursing—they did not care to hear about that—and very few asked about menstruation or childbirth. They all wanted to know about "the first time" and if I'd done it with women, or had it done to me as a child. Nymphomania intrigued them and they could not hide their disbelief when I said that neither I nor any of my girlfriends knew anything about it. The other, nonphysical, questions were more varied but not really much more surprising:

Do you fish?

Do you dream?

Do you vote?

And, the one that made them all hold their breath:

Do you read?

At the break, many continued to write as they watched me sip my tea from a thermos, eat half my sandwich. They were allowed to smell my perfume and look through my purse. When I went to the toilet it was permitted for one or two to come with me and watch, take notes if they needed.

After the break a few presented me with "problems" they "had blocked" on—those were the words they used. You are about to be stoned for adultery: how do you feel? Your husband has run off with another woman: what do you do? Your brother is kidnapped, your daughter is raped, you are raped, there's a lion charging toward you, there's a corpse in your closet—easy stuff, most of it, nothing, I thought, to get blocked by. Sometimes they brought costumes for me—snake suits or nurse uniforms or frilled gingham aprons, depending on what kind of character they were trying to depict—and they would ask me to act out a fight scene with a lover, or improvise a suicide note, or pose with a whip, or pretend to go crazy—and all that was easy too.

The only part of the job that was not easy was Free Form Time—the five minutes reserved at the end of each session for me to talk about the things that I'd been thinking about during the week. There was a lot I wanted to talk about, everything from school board elections to mermaid sightings to Mexican railroads, but the writers were tired by then, and as cranky as children. Some swallowed yawns, others openly doodled, many just leashed their dogs and left. I saw I was not holding their attention and I had to fight the temptation to start making things up. If I'm not careful, I thought in a panic, I will turn into a writer myself.

Looking back I see it was a good job in many ways. The men were lonely and ignorant, but they were educable, I thought, and I took pride in helping them, however slightly, understand others. When I saw that a few female characters based on me were being called "real" and "rounded" in the book reviews, I was, frankly, flattered. But when I read the books themselves I saw nothing had changed. The women in these books were the same as they'd always been—the same saints, sluts, and sorry set of psychotics that I had been reading about all my life. Where were their passions? Their generous hearts? Where had I failed?

The writers' questions began to tire me—that same one, week after week, about the underpants—and I decided to quit before I became what they saw. With the money I'd saved I finished school and since then I've been a milliner, a chef, a sand castle architect. I've run child care centers and nursing homes. I put up wallpaper one autumn in Australia, worked the vineyards in Brittany, clocked bicycle races in Houston. I've always been drawn to the odd job, in every sense of that phrase, and I wasn't too surprised to see a spaceship land in my backyard last night. The little man who got out looked familiar, with his domed forehead and hard hurt stare. He had come a long way, he said, to study someone like me. And much as I'd like to see Mars, I picked up the shotgun and marched him right off my porch. Some things can't be studied, I told him, and there is no one like me.

R. M. Berry

Ralph Berry, a native of Atlanta, Georgia, was born in 1947 and earned his Ph.D. from the University of Iowa in 1985. A professor of literature and writing at Florida State University, he also serves on the board of the innovative publishing house Fiction Collective Two. His book Leonardo's Horse *was a* New York Times *notable book of 1998. He has also been a Fullbright lecturer in France and has received awards for his fiction and his teaching.*

In part, "Second Story" grew out of the author's feeling that "I was never actually writing the fiction I was writing, but was always working on another fiction, my fiction's doppelganger or ghostly double. I decided to write a story that literalized all of this, setting out to make the first story into the double and the double into the first." The result is a story of shifting perspectives and ambiguity. In one light, one might interpret this story as a commentary on the ways we misinterpret the histories and actions of our family members, the "texts" of our everyday lives. In another vein, this story makes the reader wonder who the author is, who the critic is, and where the literal truth is to be found, if anywhere. "Second Story" exists in a postmodern limbo, so to speak. The reader (and the supposed author) is left wondering about the relationship (literal and figurative) of the critic to the author.

Second Story

"Second Story" could have been an excellent novel. Its plot, or what remains of one, contains all the elements of which classic novels are made: a colorful locale, conflict among blood-kin, a background of immediate social and political interest. But the story we have is not that one.

A young man, I—, inherits his father's business, a small produce store. His sister, U—, is ignored in the will. Both siblings are living abroad at the time, and each reacts to the legacy with profound but mixed emotions. The sister despises her father (there are hints of sexual abuse) and hoped never to see him again. But being disinherited infuriates her. It replicates the injury done her as a child and revives the memories she crossed the ocean to escape. She undergoes a phychotic episode and ends up in a hospital in Scotland.

The son is living in Paris, pursuing his dream of becoming a writer, and failing utterly. He also hates his father. His reasons are unclear, but they may involve the father's abuse of his sister, for whom I— too harbors forbidden desires. However, I—'s anger is directed, not so much at his father as at his father's business. Or more specifically, at the apartment above it. It was in this flat, overlooking the street, that he and his sister were raised (the mother's absence is never explained). I— has a recurrent nightmare of being imprisoned there.

The inheritance takes on the character of fate for both siblings. I— is penniless and not especially strong. When the word of his inheritance reaches him, he is living on the charity of friends. It's wearing out. He badly needs a means of support, one that will allow him to practice his art, and he hasn't the faintest notion how to secure it. He obsesses about his father's legacy, feels himself being drawn back to America, rails at his weakness, et cetera.

This predicament is skillfully contrived, and for the first fifty pages or so, that is, until I—'s narration takes over, "Second Story" verges on being a captivating read. However, no sooner does I—'s writing become the novel's focus than its plot slows to, if not a halt, then a grind.

Part of the problem is that I— is afflicted with a debilitating self-consciousness of no obvious origin. He doesn't want what he wants, can't let himself do what he tries to do, questions everything. Once installed in his father's home, I— passes his days selling peaches and kumquats. He doesn't mind his father's business, even takes an interest in the daily accounts, but gradually he succumbs to repetition. He finds himself reliving old rivalries, waking to the sting of forgotten slights. One afternoon while washing rutabagas, he blurts out a schoolyard epithet. Later, counting change, he bursts into childish tears. He's able to compose himself only while sitting at his computer. Either he has been notified of his sister's breakdown or he has somehow fantasized it, but gradually he begins to narrate her ordeal from his vantage six thousand miles away.

U— passes her days in a tiny room with a window too high to see out. She experiences rages that exhaust her, prolonged episodes of sobbing and nightmares. Despite I—'s absence from these scenes, he describes her traumas with impressive vividness. U—'s symptoms are dramatized, and her interior monologue is convincing. There is a moving scene of masturbation.

In itself, the technique of substituting an imaginary account for a recollected one is neither confusing nor especially new and, if skillfully handled, can provide an effective variation in mood and tone. We willingly suspend our disbelief in I—'s point of view and allow ourselves to forget that, of course, he can't really imagine his sister's suffering. But unfortunately I— can't forget this. After describing U—'s memory of their father's voice, I— ruins his powerful effect by remarking, "Or this is how I picture U—." He continues narrating but now intersperses his story with expressions such as, "I seem to see her gazing up," or, "In my dreams he stifles her cries," or at his most ludicrous, "Is this the monstrous shape my hallucinations must all assume?"

Although irritating, these intrusions gradually become less noticeable, and for a time the narrative of U—'s recovery proceeds. In U—'s nightmare her father is perpetually inside of her. No matter how hard she struggles, she can never get free. U—'s doctor is a zombie, but a psychiatric resident comes alive to her plight. He explains to U— that she's creating her nightmares herself, that her father is powerless without her permission, that U— holds the key to her own jail. For some reason, this casts U— into the deepest gloom imaginable. She stops eating. Her eyes become expressionless. She spends whole days staring at a wall. Her breakthrough finally comes when one night she recognizes the violator of her dreams as the young psychiatrist. (This mistake is never explained.) She immediately begins to plot her escape from the hospital, feigning openness and recovered candor, and counting on the psychiatrist's sexual repression to make her scheme work. Despite I—'s tiresome asides, U—'s subterfuge makes for an exciting episode.

But the novel that "Second Story" might have been gets no further. One night while seated before his computer imagining U—'s torment, I— undergoes paralysis: "My fingers stopped," he recounts. "I stared into nothing. There across the waters I saw her raise her eyes, saw my hallucination looking back, saw U— seeing *this.*" And we never find out how U— escapes the hospital. Instead we are treated to a two-page orgy of authorial self-loathing. ("How transparent I've become! All my designs, every pretense. Abasing U— just to exalt myself!") When next we hear of the sister, she's back in America.

At this point the novel starts to disintegrate. The narration fragments. The plot becomes contradictory. Increasingly, "Second Story" resembles a jumble of parts without plan or direction. Among the parts are: 1) I—'s unfinished narrative of U—, in multiple versions, with notes for a revision; 2) a self-serving autobiography about I—'s life as his father's heir (if there's any story in "Second Story," the autobiography concludes it); 3) seven journal entries, presumably written at a later time, disparaging both the narrative and the autobiography; 4) various documents about "Second Story" itself: a form rejection from an obscure press, an insipid jacket blurb, an anonymous reader's report (unfinished), and a review to which the author has attached his reply.

Needless to say, the reader finds this abandonment of artistic responsibilities infuriating. Presumably, the book's deterioration is meant to reflect the brother's worsening psychological state, but the more involved we become in the sufferings of U—, the more I— seems a distraction.

U— returns home and takes up residence on the street beside her father's, now her brother's, store. She shrieks at pedestrians, sleeps on the sidewalk, defecates in an adjacent alley. To all appearances she has become a lunatic. I—, meanwhile, is making a shambles of the business. Customers are leaving, creditors are phoning, everywhere there's the smell of rotten fruit. Then, seated at his computer one night, I— hears singing. At first he thinks he's a child again, then he decides he's asleep. Finally he goes to the window where he sees his sister's nude body swaying under a street lamp. The imagery turns evocative. He describes her "undulating trajectories, the fuchsia haze of darkness over my brain." He narrates his gradual loss of self-control, "as consciousness shattered on the cusp of her pain." He continues: "I saw the silver spike of moonlight, my sister's bare shoulders, her Gorgon's hair." He rushes downstairs. U— turns. Under a street lamp, brother and sister embrace.

Who knows what happens next? In the shortest of the ensuing fragments, U— and I— become lovers. They move back into their old room, where I— spends his days writing, while U— minds the store. At night they rejoin for exuberant fornication, made still more piquant by the taint of ancient taboo. I— (who in this fragment is narrating) says their union realizes his heart's deepest desire.

But gradually a feeling of uncanniness overtakes him, as if everything has happened before. Although U— never complains, I— feels troubled by her composure, a smiling opacity that somehow shuts him out. One day he mentions their father and grows alarmed when no remark, no matter how insensitive, produces any retort. He becomes anxious, starts prowling the apartment, making sure of doors, windows. But as his apprehension increases, his nightly pleasures do too, and with doom approaching, he determines not to flee, recognizing with sinking heart that his fate has outrun him. Finally he awakens one night to the smell of smoke. He calls to his sister, but the crackling of flames is the only reply. The open stairwell and windows, he realizes, will form a chimney, draw the fire toward him. But his strongest feeling is of consummation, of events taking their course. This fragment breaks off unfinished. Its last sentence reads, "As I utter these words the heat of my sister's rage devours the floor beneath my"

In a second fragment, U— and I— go into business. I—'s motivation is unclear, but he decides to make his sister a partner, sharing management and profits equally. However, I—'s reluctance to credit accounts turns out to be his failing, and within weeks U— has taken over. I— withdraws upstairs, venturing into the store less and less often, and finally offers no protest when, during remodeling, U— bricks up every window in their father's facade. I—'s only way out now is through the market.

At this point, U—'s success has restored her confidence, and she's free of her violator's memory at last. But gradually a feeling of uncanniness overtakes her, as if everything has happened before. Although I— never resists her management, she's disturbed by his composure, a silent opacity that somehow shuts her out. One day she locks the upstairs door and becomes alarmed when, after forty-eight hours, he hasn't tried it. She starts listening for his footsteps overhead, monitoring the water bill and electric meter. She fears she's being used, considers liquidating or selling out, but as her apprehension increases, her daily profits do too, and she decides to expand instead, recognizing with a sinking heart that her fate has outrun her. Finally one night she notices all signs of life above have ceased. She creeps up the stairs, calls to her brother, but an echo is the only reply. U— knows that, left to his own devices, I— will have turned upon himself, but her strongest feeling is of consummation, of events taking their course. She enters the apartment, checks every room. I— is not there.

Although the narrator of this fragment is never identified, the final sentence implies that I—'s disappearance, and perhaps the whole novel to this point, has been hallucinated by U—, an incurable schizophrenic confined in a Scottish hospital.

If there exist readers sufficiently persevering to continue to this point, they will have long since abandoned all hope of rewards to come. "Second Story" contains no story, is at best the semblance of a novel, is hardly more than a pun. Its title refers, of course, not to I—'s writing but to I—'s apartment, or more exactly, to the elevation at which he lives "in accordance with my father's will." Its superior perspective ("one flight up") seems essential to I—, but its distance from the fruitfulness in store below unsettles him. For some reason, he confuses coming down to earth with abandoning fiction altogether, as if art's contact with life were somehow corrupting. From first to last I— looks down upon his reader. He never tells us what we want to know.

This condescending reticence is nowhere more apparent than in the unfinished autobiography. There I— finally becomes a novelist, but only by leaving his sister's disinheritance entirely unaccounted for.

The autobiography begins with a promising sentence: "It was always my ambition to meet life face to face, but when I discovered I was my father's heir, I reconciled myself to living at a distance from the ground." Although rich in possibilities, this beginning sentences us to a contradiction that "Second Story" never overcomes. The first story is where nature's produce is stored, but it is also a store in which the products of cultivation are sold. I— insists he loves earth's abundance (calling it "my mother's bounty") and fills pages with ecstasies over "the surprising brightness oranges become," but these effusions appear forced, as if compensating for some lack. Finally, in a lyrically expansive scene, he recognizes the "cornucopia of being" every pumpkin is and throws himself into "the life of a greengrocer," professing bewilderment at that mysterious compulsion he formerly called "literature."

But gradually a feeling of uncanniness overtakes him, as if this devotion to fruitfulness has happened before. Although I—'s customers never haggle, he's disturbed by their composure, a mindless opacity that somehow shuts him out. One day on impulse I— rearranges price tags, valuing kiwis as highly as watermelons, and is alarmed when no one complains. He decides to join a radical party, starts quoting Marx and Bentham, but as his anger increases, his isolation does too, and rather than succumb to desperation, he retreats into the second story, leaving his conclusion up in the air. The produce rots, the store is vandalized, eventually drug dealers move in. I—'s life on earth is over. For the remainder of the book, there's no explanation how I— eats, much less pays his power bill.

(Although the seven journal entries criticize virtually every other aspect of the novel, they never complain about I—'s lack of material support. Noting his apparent indifference to financial motives, the entry for "Day 7" observes that I—'s writing seems increasingly immaterial and remarks on an absence of economy in his narration throughout. However, after deciding that "what's fundamentally the matter here" needs "laying bare," all the journalist ever "lays bare" are twelve *sentences*. Inexplicably, in the editing that follows, the journalist removes every evocative phrase and image quoted in this review.)

If "Second Story" finally does tell a story, it's not the one summa-
rized here, not the narrative of U—'s violation, but the story of I—'s failure to tell that story. U—'s story is a mere pretext. The novel's real subject is the male artist's self-defeat, his narcissistic plea for adoration by
the very public he ignores. Nothing ever happens in "Second Story"
because its sole aim is to show why nothing *can* happen, why I— can
never assume his father's position, how, in the plot against his sister,
I— too has been framed.

The autobiography contains a gap, but when it finally resumes, I—
has written his novel (entitled, predictably, "Second Story"). Our text
provides no excerpts, but an enclosed, unfinished reader's report calls it
"a work without prospect of any following," and a jacket blurb (also
included) describes it as a *Kunstlerroman* that "records the artist's undo-
ing." Whether I— still lives "at a distance from the ground" is left
ambiguous: according to the autobiography, the father's legacy is "a
thing of the past," but the blurb says "the author's whereabouts, as of
this writing, remain undetermined." Although the autobiography covers
ninety pages, there are just two mentions of U—. In an early aside I—
complains that she's still working for "that rag" (an unnamed Eastern
newspaper), and on the last page of continuous text he contrasts his own
amorphous fiction with the plots "to which my sister appears drawn,"
suggesting that she may be a critic or novelist herself. But I—'s absorption
has now become total. How U— escapes her confinement, how she
resists the violator of her dreams, no longer comprise his business.

If my synopsis has not sufficiently brought it out, the whole of this
tiresome work is further vitiated by an undertone of anti-feminism and
indifference to women that many readers will find unsettling. I realize
these criticisms are serious, but I do not offer them without reflection.
I know nothing of the author's expressed political views, but the qualities I mention (which will strike women readers as obtrusive) are
notable precisely because they are unconscious and, I fear, irremediable. The author, like his protagonist I— (there is finally no difference),
is afflicted with an obsessive need for abstraction that amounts to little
more than fear of the body and love. The whole of his work is perme-
ated by defensive gestures, a kind of embarrassing self-exposure that
merely aims to avoid exposure itself. There is something sad about all
this. The author is capable of impressive concreteness, as shown by his
brief slips into lyricism (for which, of course, the journal entries always
repent), but he seems to fear these fleshly pleasures, the invigorating
saga of life and mortality. This fear is his sole reason for retreating into
narrative indirection and complexities of structure, and most readers—

certainly most women readers—will feel it's high time men *stopped doing this*. If the author wishes to encounter life face to face, it's in his power to do so. This is, after all, what novelists have always done.

The Author Replies:

I know it's always in bad taste to respond to a review, but I don't want to miss this opportunity to thank my sister for her generous remarks on my "Second Story." On all significant points she has recognized my aims and done justice to my work. In writing this novel, I left the story untold, preserving only its insupportable consciousness, precisely as she has explained, and the ineffectuality of my narrator was a transparent ploy to this end. Unlike some reviewers who dismiss what they don't understand, she has been scrupulous in her analysis and shown a rare willingness to withhold judgment until my meaning has made itself plain. As every reader can imagine, the hope of such judiciousness keeps my spirits high.

Her comparison of my book's disintegration with my narrator's discomposure and her comment that, in narrating U—'s suffering, I— tells more than he knows, are further examples of her perceptiveness, but nothing has encouraged me more than her recognition of my unconsciousness of women. Although she may not know this, it has been the major work of my adulthood to liberate myself from the injustices and political repression with which I've been familiar since I was a boy. Having come to maturity during the latest flourishing of women's historic demand for autonomy, I, like so many of my generation, grew to feel feminism in my tissue and bones. A chance sexist remark could send blood to my face. Listening to news-reports I found my heart racing, palms starting to sweat. There seemed no end to the novels I couldn't read with pleasure. In one fashion or another, the consciousness of women constituted the air I breathed, my instincts and terrors, the plots I constantly repeated in my dreams.

As you may imagine, the naturalness of all this at times felt confining. Like my height or bodily imperfections, my discomfort with institutions, laws, policies, friends—virtually everything!—resembled a fate or affliction. Even my attempts at sexist jokes or crude wisecracks were marked by self-consciousness, as if I were merely *faking* machismo, *pretending* to be male. What I felt incapable of was genuine insensitivity, a sincere obliviousness of my own obliviousness. I say this with no pride. I no more chose my dissatisfactions than I chose to speak English. On the contrary, my pride in my indignation, my confidence that anger arose in me from real outrages, from conditions about which people *ought* to feel angry—all this only made my plight more ludicrous. Hadn't every age, even the most brutal, viewed its own anger in just this way? Gradually a feeling of uncanniness overtook me, as if everything I'd grown to know, all my reactions and experience had already happened before.

Perhaps this explains my attachment to the I— I wasn't. Perhaps nothing explains it. I can't tell. But I soon found myself preoccupied with another being. I had no desire to be different. How could I desire what my stomach rose up against? But something about his composure, his faceless opacity, made me feel shut out. I suppose I imagined—or not really imagined, more like imagined imagining, imagined being able to imagine—I imagined myself imagining myself apart from what, in coming to know my sister, I could never not know. There were moments when so much nothing disconcerted me. I tried to overcome it, fearing I— was going nowhere, but because my concentration remained weak, my mind inevitably wandered, leaving me to stare vacantly into space.

I want to make perfectly plain that this other being was inconceivable to me. Perhaps I— wasn't even male. But I knew that his acts were marked by a thoughtlessness unlike any act of mine, an unconsciousness that avoided no consciousness, that denied nothing. After all, to have merely denied what every woman knows, to have pretended ignorance of what no man today can pretend ignorance—why that would be an achievement hardly superior to the Republican party. Wasn't my whole nation in denial of what a woman knows? My task, on the contrary, would be more arduous. I must revert to the nature I naturally avoided, to my uncreated state, must recover an absent-mindedness in which my sister's unaccountability could never be on my account but would be as incalculable as my next heartbeat or every breath escaping me. In short, I— must undo human history.

Of course, I set about the task systematically, discovering one step at a time the impossibility of all that is. I cannot say either of us has made much progress, for progress was the first thing to prove impossible, but I can say his undertaking has completely preoccupied me while composing "Second Story," and although I expect failure will also one day prove impossible, my divided attention has caused me no end of concern. What if, in trying to leave my sister alone, I unwittingly violated her dreams again? Often I've been beside myself with apprehension and would surely have surrendered to fate, had not the continuous prospect of her oblivion prevented me. And so I'm deeply grateful for her reassurance that my work does not contain her, that it betrays no consciousness of any woman, that in it all sensitivity to pain is gone, such that, in withdrawing my interest from her saving's account, my words have finally ceased to be overlooked, coming forth without super vision, occurring to all at one time. Nothing seems harder than to tell what isn't happening, but in reviewing "Second Story," I suspect my sister isn't there.

However, there remains one sentence of her review with which, despite my deep and sincere appreciation, I still must disagree. Personally, I do not see how "Second Story" could have been an excellent novel. This was what attracted me to it. That any man could narrate his sister's disinheritance, tell how he assumed her abuser's place and came to dwell above the market—from the outset, such a plot struck me as fantastic. Only its perpetrator would presume to write it, and only his collaborator could tolerate its being read. The work's conclusion would be the recognition of its own futility, so that its very existence would constitute proof of fraud. Having always known myself as history's fabricator and having never accepted my sister's reality as my own, I seemed the perfect one to undertake it—by which I mean the first story, the one I could never tell. In this way, I lived out the second. My sister's review is entirely correct. I, who write this self-serving epistle, am the impotent and narcissistic I— of the incomplete autobiography, nemesis of novel readers everywhere, undoer of my life's work. Knowing how classic plots were made, I discounted everything in store, leaving my authority groundless. Thus another beside myself was needed to compose my work, for to him alone its words would come as a surprise. And so the I— I wasn't was sentenced without ever imagining what he'd done. As far as I can tell, nothing remotely like "Second Story" has ever been written. For this reason I call it a novel.

Michael Wilkerson

Michael Wilkerson has been executive director of the Ragdale Foundation and the Provincetown Art Center, artists' colonies that provide protected time and space to writers, composers, and artists in stimulating settings. Currently he administers and teaches in his home state of Indiana.

"Can This Story Be Saved?" was originally published by Story County Books in the format of the purse books one finds on the racks at a supermarket checkout counter. The story appropriates the women's magazine feature "Can This Marriage Be Saved?" Wilkerson plays with our notions of criticism and therapy, highlighting the sense of an author's anxiety at being able to pull off the deceptive act of fiction creation. The characters in Wilkerson's story take themselves and their troubles seriously even

*when we don't. The effect this story should have on the reader is to make
him or her laugh—it's funny. It's funny when the very serious therapeutic
language the reader usually associates with marriage counseling is instead
associated with fixing a fiction and a fictional relationship.*

Can This Story Be Saved?
A REGULAR FEATURE

Introduction:

It was a simple situation, as are most we see here at **Can This Story Be
Saved?** Candace, 29, had lived in numerous cities during her post-college
life. She had had a propensity for relocation—indeed, she'd even switched
colleges three times. Soon, however, being a nomad had wearied her. She
applied successfully for a solid position as a software analyst in Fort
Collins, Colorado. The salary was good; she began to purchase large
objects—marble tables, console TV's, stereo speakers large enough for
small amphitheatres. The story really begins, though there is substantial
hem-hawing around in the preliminary text, when she breaks down in a
ferocious crying jag the day the mover delivers the new double-wide
Amana frost-free, and attempts to haul away the trusty old Kelvinator.

"Roots, roots, I have no roots," Candace wails, and the white-smocked
cooler-wheeler sets down his Kelvinator-laden dolly deliberately. Then,
on a clearly fictional impulse, he walks toward her and hugs her.

And she looks up in his eyes, and so on.

The author named him Marcus and gave him a more elaborate
background than most appliance-toters would have had; he had been a
champion skier, but had lost interest when his fiancee, who was second
string on the Colorado College Women's Slalom team, had smashed
into a tree, after which she could neither see nor remember him.

Then, predictably, he'd drifted, doing a bit of small-time marijuana
selling and some half-hearted piano work in bars. As the author tells
it, Marcus suspected that he may have been the only native Coloradan
in the Boulder area, which fascinates Candace and attracts her, both
hormonally and intellectually, to him.

So the two finish work with the refrigerator and attend a selection
of happy hours, before watching the sun set over the Rockies. They
then return to Candace's for drinks. Later that night, they drive to the

grocery store together, at which place we discover, along with Candace, that Marcus is, shall we say, something of an obsessive on consumer issues. We also learn that he's a bit of a socialist. And that fascinates Candace, who's never been too contemplative in a macropolitical way, so they converse onward, into the night.

This reasonably acceptable scene is followed by a delicate jump-cut to the fledgling couple's First Fight, which the author elects to capitalize; Marcus begins to compile a record of tardiness and absentia at work and is seen omnisciently sipping gin at various hangouts of questionable repute.

Word of this gets back to Candace, who is by now starting to make some errors of her own in analyzing the company software. There's an hilarious sequence in which the data processing program for a regional bank comes to resemble, due to Candace's blunders, a screen of Donkey Kong. She orders Marcus not to come near her, an instruction he obeys for some time. After this brief trauma, Candace summons all her charm and wit, in what seems to us here at **Can This Story Be Saved?** to be an awfully heavy-handed scene, and barely salvages her job.

The author comments, "All is sadness and misery in the capitalist pig system, but we plot onward anyhow," and there are a few elegiac lines concerning the sun's plummeting 'neath the purple Rockies once again. Candace's new refrigerator breaks, Marcus bribes a co-worker for the right to come and fix it, and she "sees her reflections in his eyes," according to the text. Predictably, the story ends at that point.

Our Services Explained:

Can This Story Be Saved? is an internationally renowned organization of highly qualified therapists, each of whom has not only an M.F.A., but also an M.S.W. We guarantee 100% accuracy in flaw diagnosis of all ten standard elements of story; after fifty-three years of business, under our Founder and his literary heirs, we proudly report no failures. Indeed, all stories handled in full by **Can This Story Be Saved?** have been published within eighteen months of the first therapy session. It's no wonder *The New York Times* calls us "America's great alchemists of contemporary fiction." Confidential quotation of fees available on request.

The Characters' Turn:

"What is this mumbo-jumbo?" Candace begins. "Four years of college, seven years of vagabonding and a rich array of lifestyles after that, and this yahoo author thinks I don't know about Karl Marx and corporatism? I find the whole thing very antiwoman, and generally demeaning."

"At first it was acceptable, but there's more than a bit too much of the old rhetorical flight of fancy," Marcus said. "I mean I don't even *believe* some of the things I supposedly say, and it's hard to sound convincing in such a circumstance." He looked taller and more striking than he'd seemed in the story, more sure of himself, more powerful than an ordinary fridge-bringer.

"Don't get me wrong, I think Candace is a wonderful woman, and God knows I'd love to live in Boulder, but I'm afraid there's just a bit too much cafe-hopping and political spewing for one story to carry." Marcus offered me a Barclay cigarette, lighting one himself.

"He thinks those things are low tar," Candace said. "I'm certain the company just tricked the FTC's machine with a collapsible filter." She extracted a Marlboro from her woven-reed handbag, explaining that it was indeed attractive, and that it had been constructed at a decent and fair wage by members of a worker co-op in Taos. It became obvious that, in person, Candace was a much more interesting and three-dimensional character than she'd been in the story.

"I just can't accept the business that I'd go bananas over some compressor-carrier just because of his eyes," Candace said, using her half-full coffee cup as an ashtray. "I mean I'm more together than that."

Marcus interrupted. "Candace sees the whole problem in a feminist perspective, and I think that's one reason why we can't seem to fix the story. If you look at it from a point of view of literary totality you can see its flaws."

"Literary totality my ass!" Candace shook her head, hair flying in a rather earthy way, and smacked the armchair for emphasis. "He's just like those foreign films from the early sixties, always yakking about the class struggle and never doing anything but moping around home and boozing it up at the Hole-In-The-Wall."

Marcus lit another cigarette. Candace continued.

"I mean can you believe that scene where he takes my pants off and then starts quoting Herbert Marcuse. Jesus!"

"I thought it was rather modern." Marcus clearly had his hands full, literally, with cigarette in the left hand and coffee cup in the right, and figuratively, with Candace.

"Modern, hell. You were just avoiding me as usual."

"Candace, I really think it's impossible to have a healthy male-female relationship without the totality of the world being justified or at least rationalized. Now if you look at the story we're in, you can see—"

"—There he goes again," Candace said.

"—You can see the flaws. One, the verbs."

"No kidding. There isn't a one in that whole story I didn't know in the second grade. I mean my God, there are so many passive verbs you have to live with. It makes me feel totally bloated and dull."

"Right," Marcus said. "And what about the business with me drinking all that gin at the Hole-In-The-Wall. Gin, for God's sake! Everyone knows that's an upper-class beverage.

"It does seem that the author could have come up with something better." We here at **Can This Story Be Saved?** have a policy of non-criticism of the author during a counseling session, but it was felt that to elicit further comment from the characters, the above statement was not significantly contrary to the spirit of our guidelines.

Marcus clenched his fist. "At that point of the story, I tried to take over from him. There was one time when I left the bar and went to steal a car from the Buick-Cadillac place, but the *author* struck it out."

"I don't think that was terribly original of you," Candace said. Perhaps there were troubles between her and Marcus that no author or counselor, no matter how skilled, could resolve. We began to hypothesize that the standard modern-wistful ending might be the best we could do in this story's case.

"Anyway," Marcus said. "I go on this adventure in a new Electra 225. I'm playing with the power windows—you know, sense of control and all that—and I start speeding on the beltway."

"Speeding on the beltway," Candace said. "You? Mister 'fifty-five stay alive'?"

"Yeah, I asserted myself for once. I *am* capable of it, you know." Marcus stubbed his cigarette. "I was going to go up to Golden and crash the car into one of Coors' headquarters buildings. A truly revolutionary act. No talking, pure action this time.

Candace, for the first time during our interview, seemed truly interested in Marcus, and, we believed, displayed facial expressions that indicated admiration for his courage.

"But that damned author xx'ed out the whole thing, just as I turned onto the road to the brewery. Instead he put in that drivel about my attending a meeting of the Citizens' Coalition for Safe Energy. What a disaster," Marcus said.

"That really was a turgid scene." Candace commented.

For a moment, an atmosphere of quiet prevailed. We asked the characters for an overall prognosis for the story. Marcus answered.

"When you talk about literary totality, I mean the whole question of my skiing career, the ex-fiancee with amnesia, my short binge as a pianst, Candace's loss of roots, the Donkey Kong scene, it all adds up to nothing."

"Uh-huh," Candace said. "Zilch."

"I think that's all I really have to say." Marcus finished his now room-temperature coffee.

"Well, I'm not done," Candace broke in. "I would like to say that this story, like most others I've read recently, is in one hell of a lot of trouble. Just once in my life I would like to see an author have some understanding, not just hand-wringing 'poor girl' sympathy for me. Just once I would like to hook up with a male character who could somehow fit a little respect for his sisters into his so-called 'enlightened revolutionary consciousness.' Just once I would like to see Marcus, or anybody with a damned Y chromosome, wash the frigging dishes while *I* pontificate." She relaxed her posture and, seeing Marcus's stunned look, cautiously patted his knee. "You think about it, okay?"

They left the offices of **Can This Story Be Saved?** in separate cars.

The Author's Turn:

The author, Herman D., did not, like Marcus, cut a striking figure; rather, he was a frazzled man, his skin pale and somewhat puffy, his clothes rumpled and his hair uncombed. Articulation came slowly to him, but eventually, through the deft encouragement of our skilled professionals at **Can This Story Be Saved?,** dramatic progress occurred.

"Yeah, I know it's tough. I know some of my flaws. Look, I may not be Salinger or anything, but I'm not a total failure as an author. I mean I've hatched a tale or two in some pretty respectable places." He extracted a tattered copy of *The Whining Muse,* Vol. 12, No.1, from his briefcase. "I mean, really, if you get in *The Whining Muse,* you're not without ability.

"Anyway, I have my own baggage to carry around. Everybody does. I'm really the one who has too many roots. Sometimes I wish I had none. Too, with a name like Herman, I'm constantly fighting the temptation to name my characters Bainsley and Felippe, let alone Candace and Marcus. I think Candace and Marcus are decent names for these people, I really do."

At **Can This Story Be Saved?** we often see belligerent authors, but in all objectivity, we found Herman D. an exceptionally upset man, given the quality of work he'd created.

"Look. I've been living alone a while now, with a little savings, nothing but time to write on my hands. Sooner or later it gets to you.

One day, no story. The next day, a bad story. Day after that, false starts all over the goddamned living room. Then, finally, you write something that's got all the basic stuff, but you're tired, just too tired to make it excel enough to satisfy these hot-stuff editors. I mean, you can nitpick and soup up the adjectives, jockey a few clauses around, cut a little bit, you know, that sort of thing. But you just get worn out and move on to the next piece. You finally have to call it a day." Herman sat back in his ultra-modern, leather-covered chair purchased during a recent redecoration here at **Can This Story Be Saved?** "I guess there's just too much junk in my head," he said.

Herman had already made one thing clear: he was a coffee slurper, not a sipper like Marcus. We reminded ourselves to affix a moderate but fair surcharge to Herman's account. With computer billing, the process is virtually painless.

"I admit there's a lot of me in Marcus," Herman said. "I mean, I'm always talking about being a writer and making revolution and, oh, all that stuff, but I just sit around all day, crank out a few pages, and hit the gin."

Though it is our task to maintain rigid separation between professional and personal difficulties, we nonetheless found listening to Herman somewhat trying. His authorial defense mechanisms had long since lost their elegance and variety.

"These characters. They just run around Boulder in their cars—and I make sure they have nice cars—unpacking appliances and yakking about labor versus capital. They can ski, bowl, dance, have a good time. I'm the one who can't get *them* out of my head. Then the next thing I know, they've forced me into calling a counselor about their story. Well, what about *my* story?"

We took the liberty of interrupting to repeat the standard explanation of the purely literary nature of the services we offer. Herman waved us to silence.

"And this feminism stuff. Boy, do I get tired of trying so hard. I sit around when I'm not writing and read *Ms.* and just feel like hell. I've gone through two wives and God knows how many serious girlfriends. I mean, I was brought up a sexist pig, and sometimes I think I can transcend that, but every time I break a dish or don't get all the egg out of the Pyrex mixing bowl, I get *Ms.* articles spouted at me live in my own kitchen. What do you clowns want from me?"

We excused ourselves to take an emergency phone call from a client who seemed lately to have been exceptionally fraught with concern over a dramatic monologue involving a well-known political figure.

Alone, Herman mused. We were fortunate in having installed a two-way intercom, from which Miss Junkins made transcripts of all our interviews with clients.

The author sat in the counselor's office with his tommy gun in his lap. He waited for the counselor to return. He would show the counselor. He would shoot him, put the counselor out of his, that is to say, the author's, misery. How unusual it would be, though bloody.

Knowing fully of the danger, our counselor changed vests and returned. Herman pointed the gun at **Can This Story Be Saved?**, but did not fire. The author sat back and relaxed. He placed the gun on the floor, where it disappeared.

"Guess I'm just not the killing kind of writer," Herman said. "I just can't do the snuff stuff." We made another note for the billing department. He began to nurse a bourbon. We made another note. "That's why I couldn't let Marcus steal the car. It's just wrong." He sipped. "Besides, it wouldn't matter to anyone. It would be just another freak smashing into a steel building, probably offing himself. Old Joe Coors could care less."

Herman took yet another sip.

"I don't know what to do with these people. Hell, I figured if I could get them to love each other, even if a little sadly, it would be better than what they had before. I don't know. I wanted a happy ending, but you're right, Counselor. I guess it's artificial. Hell, you think up something. You're the counselor."

The Counselor's Turn:

Solving this story, we knew, would be terribly spotty wicket. Like most authors who can afford lengthy sessions with **Can This Story Be Saved?**, and, indeed, like most who can spare significant time for writing, Herman D. possessed respectable amounts of savings and unearned income. However, what should have been an asset for him was converted into a liability by extreme guilt over his wealth. His knowledge of the various forms of subtle oppression of the lower classes, and of women, was superficial; hence, he seemed to us generally unable to transform his concepts into convincing day-to-day realism. Herman also suffered from arrogance. He was unwilling or unable to listen to his characters, and seemed generally out of touch with their feelings and desires.

We diagnosed acute literary dissonance.

The characters, on the other hand, shared an undifferentiated form of dogma, though the beliefs that grounded their intractabilities seemed virtual opposites. It was evident that they cared deeply for each other but refused to center those feelings on any meaningful day-to-day reality base. Hence, the very genre-like scenes of Candace falling like a stone into Marcus's puzzled but wiry arms, et cetera. It seemed to us at **Can This Story Be Saved?** that the solution to this problem was only workable if applied in sequential stages.

First, Herman D. had to become more in touch with his own feelings. Where did he stand, politically and aesthetically? Was he a literary futurist, a neo-Aristotelian, or, perhaps, a Dickensian? In lay terms, we simply wanted to know if he wished to concentrate on idea, plot, or character. He would have to key in on those issues and filter them through his personal perceptions of how individuals interacted within the institutional systems of the United States.

Second, we urged Herman to act out some of his leftist fantasies, perhaps join a commune for awhile, or form a study group with other like-minded people. This way, we thought, he might become better acquainted with the real issues of life and with other individuals who could provide him more accurate models for his characters.

Third, if Herman were to save this specific story (and, we must confess, a significant minority of our therapists had doubts as to that possibility) he would have to enter into an honest dialogue with Marcus and Candace, which, if properly handled, not only might save the story, but also might render the two characters much happier together, or, if they did end up autonomous from each other, more able to be philosophical about the inevitability of such a split.

Marcus seemed to need more direction, which we believed could only come about if Herman exercised better self-control. Candace certainly needed to be better rendered: her complaints about the author's sexism were, we felt, well taken.

Finally, we felt that the two characters and the author should come to some kind of consensus about imagery systems and the relative weights of Marcus's prior careers, the Marxist incident in the supermarket, and the symbolic transformation involved in the parallel sunsets over the staid Rockies.

The Eventual Result:

Can This Story Be Saved? heard little more from Herman D. for several months. Once, we encountered Marcus at a 7-11, and he seemed much more alive than before. He had taken a position as a ski instructor, seeking to overcome the horrible memory of his ex-fiancee's accident. He told us that Candace had begun a new career as well, but was rather evasive when asked what it was. He did mention that the two of them were living together again, and while no long-term commitments had been made or requested by either party, Marcus had become more responsible and tolerant around the home. He had, he commented, "become able to take a mean turn around the living room on the old Electrolux."

We noted Marcus's rather zippy idiom with pleasure, and were indeed excited about the fictive prospects, until Herman D. mailed us a radically overhauled version of the story, whose title we must withhold from this report for professional reasons. Here, however, is how it began:

Candace fondled the throttle of the MX-72 attack helicopter and thought of Marcus, who would at that moment be washing the dishes and listening to her well-worn copy of the album *More Separatist Diatribes.*

"Ladies' Death Ray to Corporal Herman. Do you have a sighting yet?" she said. Her own scope was not as advanced as that of the dashing young scion who had donated most of his inherited wealth to Candace's revolutionary group, which she named "Bombin' Women."

"Coming in over the Capitol Building, Captain. Smart Bomb SZ-Death-431A ready to go," Corporal Herman said into his transceiver.

The sun glowed a beautiful red over the Rockies. It was setting, and the Capitol Dome glistened more than anyone could ever describe. Candace knew, through her network of skilled informants, that the evil Governor J. Bean Jr., who had busted all state employees' unions, overturned local fair housing laws, and dammed up the Colorado River before opening a coal mine in Rocky Mountain National Park, would be meeting with his aides in the top floor of the building. She had programmed the Smart Bomb to his scent and knew it would kill him, but the killing would be justified in the name of the new workers' state that would arise from the ashes. She thought of Marcus working cheerfully at home as Herman dropped the bomb. She wondered if he had dinner ready and hoped to see him soon. She heard the explosion and saw the dome disintegrate, then fondled her throttle, thinking of Marcus, and headed for the landing strip.

In the inner sanctum of **Can This Story Be Saved?** the chief therapists were summoned to executive session. We had copies of each analyst's dictated remarks on Herman D.'s efforts, and the prognosis proved utterly bleak. No rays of hope enlightened our unhappy staff. Even through the burnished oak doors of our conference room, we heard our receptionist, Miss Junkins, guffawing in a quite uncharacteristic way. We asked her to refrain. "I just can't help it. This one about the feminist attack pilot is just incredible," she said, choking on a Mars. "I read the whole thing in lurid horror."

Finally, as the sun's shadows lengthened through the wainscoted windows of **Can This Story Be Saved?,** and as the fine, handmade table clock our founder received long ago from The Dial Press ticked inexorably toward four-thirty, we arrived at our consensus.

"Ladies and gentlemen," our chairman said. "We face a crisis unprecedented in the history of **Can This Story Be Saved?** So that all our years of progress and growth might continue unimpeded, I hereby request that Mr. Gardner, the most senior of our emendation specialists, revise the publicity brochure to read:

> We guarantee *nearly* 100% accuracy in flaw diagnosis of all ten standard elements of story. After fifty-three years of business, under our Founder and his literary heirs, we proudly report *few* failures. Indeed, *virtually* all stories handled in full by **Can This Story Be Saved?** have been resurrected and published within eighteen months of the first therapy session.

"Experience," our chairman said, "has made us all stronger and wiser, if sadder." We reflected on his remarks. Ah, experience! Virtuous experience! Our chairman pushed a discreet button underneath the table, summoning Miss Junkins into the inner sanctum. With all due severity and grace, she distributed our monthly paychecks; a motion to adjourn carried admirably. No mention was made of a refund.

Karen Brennan

Karen Brennan is a professor in the creative writing program at the University of Utah. Her poetry collection Here on Earth *appeared in the Wesleyan New Poets Series, and her most recent book, the memoir* Being with Rachel, *was published by Norton in 2002. "Wild Desire" comes from her Associated Writing Programs award-winning story collection of the same title.*

"Wild Desire" traces the progress of many characters who are brought together in a group therapy session. It is a record of the dynamic of

*the group and its own schizophrenia as well as the fractured interior states
of individual members. "Wild Desire" utilizes the conventions of collage to
capture formally the dissociative and disconnected world Brennan's characters inhabit. The story takes its emotional charge from juxtaposing interesting images so that the reader must make mental leaps to connect the various stories. (While a collage may appear random in its arrangement, in
reality its chaos is highly structured and organized.) The use of repetition
and variation allows the reader to readily connect the dots, actively partici-
pating in the story by providing the connective tissue between sections.*

Wild Desire

Biff at work in a three-piece

Biff at work in a three-piece Brooks Brothers, Sulka tie. The smoothest
cheek and jaw, like a baby's. Very white teeth, blond hair with a
soupçon of curl over the ears. In charge of the OX account. A large
manufacturer of antiacne cream. No acne for Biff though. Acne makes
him want to puke. That secretary, Annemarie. The mailboy. Lots of
people with acne and the worst was when they didn't pop their white-
heads. Weirded Biff right out. Made Biff want to throw up but he
never did. Never threw up and never farted. Two disgusting things.
Never had acne either, not one zit, ever. Biff. Soccer and football.
Junior exec at the agency in charge of the OX account. A wife, Carolyn,
and two wonderful kids, Biff junior and Ravena. We all know them.

Carolyn tosses

Carolyn tosses her tennis racket into a green dumpster. It lands on a
bum's head but doesn't wake him up. Rather the thud of the tennis
racket makes the bum go deeper into a coma. Carolyn is wearing a cute
little tennis tutu and pearls. Her white blond hair is tied back with a
pink ribbon. She is Biff's wife. She has thrown out her racket because
she is sick to death of tennis and all the accoutrements of tennis which
she now considers shallow and unfulfilling. With this gesture—throwing the tennis racket into the green dumpster—she is starting a new life.
A life with passion. Angrily, she pulls the pink ribbon from her white
blond hair and hurls it into the dumpster after the tennis racket. Then
her shoes and socks and, what the hell, the tutu, the sleeveless tee

shirt, the matching Christian Dior bra and panties. In the end, all she has on are pearls. I don't care, she says. I want some feeling mixed with a social consciousness in my life. Luckily it's not cold out. Nevertheless, some people report her to the police and before long the insane asylum truck comes to take her away.

Ohmygod

Ohmygod. I can't believe it. Carolyn in the looney bin. Should I call her Dad? What do I tell the children? And what about the OX account? Biff drives his Toyota Celica to the insane asylum where, at the same time, Carolyn is looking through the barred window at a view which seems hazy and lopsided. But that's the way it is with a new vision. It's disgusting, Biff tells the psychiatrist. She used to be so cute and now she looks like one of those Diane Arbus photos. That's what happens, says the shrink. What shall I do? What shall I tell the children? Carolyn's Dad? My boss? Is there some kind of support group I can join? Yes, says the doctor. He gives Biff a card with the name of a woman—Donna Reed—on it. Donna Reed is the name of the facilitator, he says.

Ravena is lying

Ravena is lying on her bed thinking of human sacrifice. A very hopeful notion, she thinks. The first person she would sacrifice would be her brother Biff junior. He was a little retarded dope. She would set fire to his pjs, then sweep the ashes into a paper bag and sprinkle them over the swimming pool. Just thinking about it gives her excited shivers. After a while she gets up and sits at her dressing table. She hates her face. It's a blond puffy face with no character at all. It reminds her of her father's face.

Biff junior, says

Biff junior, says Biff, I must ask you to pay attention while I'm talking. This is a serious thing. Your mother is in the hospital with a nervous breakdown. Who knows when she'll get out. Now will you please stop digging your fork into your sister's cheek and listen to me. From now on I will make your lunches. Peanut butter and jelly every other day. In between you'll have tuna. GET your foot out of the casserole. I know this is very hard on you both. Now Ravena where are you off to oh no you don't young lady you come back here this minute or I'll call the police this minute do you hear me, Biff junior we do not put peas in our nose thank you very much.

Biff goes

Biff goes to see Carolyn and brings the children. Carolyn has changed so drastically that the children hardly recognize her. She looks like a monster, whispers Biff junior to Ravena. The children hold each other's hands very tightly and shrink back when their mother speaks to them. Sweethearts, says Carolyn. Come here and let me touch your faces. Eeek, says Ravena, not on your life. Biff, too, finds himself shrinking away from his own wife even though she claims she is extraordinarily happy now and that life in the insane asylum has given her a whole new perspective. I'm getting into some very interesting issues, she tells Biff. Ecological issues such as saving the whales and I'm running for a political position here on ward 7B. Someone has to stand up for the rights of us nuts. Biff and the children look around uncertainly while Carolyn talks on and on. They do not sit down. They are hoping for an attendant to come and sedate Carolyn and/or to usher them to the front door. But no one comes. Carolyn's face—which was once such a cute face—can only be described as the face of a woman who's been living under a bridge for a long time and who believes she's really at the Ritz Hotel in Paris. A crazed, deluded, and unpleasant face. She is going on and on about politics. We all have duties and rights in this country. For years my duty was to be your wife. But I had no rights. She slams her fist into her forehead. Now all that has changed. Biff junior and Ravena exchange looks. Gotta run, says Biff squeezing his wife's shoulder briefly.

Ravena writes

Ravena writes in her Daily D. Today a gruesome girl called Sara Jane sat next to me in the cafeteria. I had to listen to all about this crush she has on Randy L. I felt like telling her forget it, you couldn't get Randy L if you took off your shirt and rubbed your titties in his face. But she split her Coke with me. All we get these days is peanut butter and jelly or tuna. No candy money, no Cokes. She said she'd bring some extra money tomorrow and buy me a whole Coke. Also if you have any change for the candy machine I'd appreciate it, I said as politely as I could considering I can't stand the girl.

Biff is not up to

Biff is not up to snuff these days. Biff is tired. He has dark circles under his eyes. The OX account is suffering. Mr. OX himself calls Biff on the telephone and tells him he is disappointed. We either do the job or we don't do the job, which is it Biff, says Mr. OX. Don't worry I'll handle it, says Biff. To bad about you, Biff, says Mr. OX, We can't afford your hard times as the saying goes. No siree bob, Biff honey, I've got to fire you. Biff hangs up the phone and cries into his green blotter. He cries so loudly that his secretary, Emma Spludge, peeks her head around to see what's happening. Was happnin' bro? Was wrong wit' you? Oh Emma I'm so miserable. I lost the OX account and Carolyn I'm sure you know is having a nervous breakdown and my kids, oh god, my whole damn life is actually coming apart fiber by fiber, Emma, and there's not a darn thing I can do about it. Emma blows her nice big nose. Hey, it souns' like *Dynasty* to me Mr. B tee hee. I say we have a little rubber band fight to cheer you up, eh? No, no thanks Emma, says Biff. Please no rubber bands now. But Emma is already loading her pencil up and she shoots about three dozen at Biff while he just sits there with an expressionless face.

Biff junior decides

Biff junior decides to run away and join a band of thieves. He will become a drug addict. He will shoot pure beautiful heroin into his veins and look at the sky. No more homework, no more peanut butter, he will run off with the thieves and learn to break and enter. They'll sleep under the stars or in a homemade house in the desert. He'll steal some pillows from the family room sofa. Then at night they'll do more drugs. Cocaine. LSD. Speed. It will be so much fun. Sexy women will come and play with their pee pees.

The facilitator's name

The facilitator's name is Donna Reed. The name of the workshop is Families in Distress. Everyone sits in a circle and tells his or her story. When it's Biff's turn he simply says: My wife is having a mental collapse. I was fired from the OX account. My children are behaving strangely.

After a while Carolyn's Dad

After a while Carolyn's Dad comes to visit. He brings his fishing rod and a half dozen detective novels. It's a terrible thing, Biff, he says in the

evenings. He shakes his head, then goes back to reading his book. A terrible thing, he says from time to time as he reads. What is? asks Ravena
finally. Carolyn's Dad closes his book. Why Ravena you poor child,
come up here on grandpaw's knee. You poor child, why I remember
when your mama was your age, she used to sit just like this on my knee
and I'd tell her the story of Brer Fox and Brer Rabbit, how Brer Fox had
some kind of scam goin' with Brer Rabbit, wasn't that it Biff? How does
that darn thing go anyways, it's been so long. But Biff just sits there with
no expression on his face and acts like he doesn't hear Grandpaw.
Welp, Carolyn's Dad finally says, looks like we're going to have another
rainy day on account of that ring around the moon there Ravena you
know what they say sailors take warning, everywhere there's a sign of
what's gonna come next if you're just smart enough to spot it. Uh huh,
all you need these days is a can of brains, how's that, Ravena?

All I can say is

All I can say is that the whole meaninglessness of my life suddenly struck
me after that 6 love 6 love travesty with Betty Wood, the cocky bitch. Not
that I'm not grateful, overwhelmingly so, to Betty for leading me to that
green dumpster (I only hope there wasn't a bum or anyone sleeping inside
of it) and hence to my liberation, yes I may as well say it. Standing in front
of that dumpster it was like god or something, but I saw myself like in a
movie pitch my racket clear over the sides, it was so beautiful to see this
gliding tennis racket soaring into the dumpster. It was kind of like a
dream but then I realize what isn't like a dream? What is real? My silly
white shoes? Those thin little socks? My hair, is my hair real? It was kind
of a Sartrean experience, very existential, very nauseating. Like when the
men in the white coats came to take me away I thought oh yes here are the
men in the white coats coming to take me away and that's when I started
to laugh because it was so funny seeing those men in white coats, like a
cartoon, do you know what I mean, I mean it's just an expression, here
come the men in the white coats, and then all of a sudden in the middle
of your life here they are, the men in the white coats! It's like amazing!

These days you see Ravena and Sara Jane

These days you see Ravena and Sara Jane everywhere. In the play-
ground, walking to and from the bus, in the cafeteria eating candy bars.
They must be best friends now. Sara Jane wears pink ribbons in her hair
just like Ravena. They both wear pink pearl lipstick and rose madder

blush. They do not tie their hightops. They are pink and white girls. Like strawberry ice cream sundaes or like cotton candy. Those girls are adorable, says everyone. At night they talk on the telephone. Sara Jane talks about Randy, how cute he is, how he drew a magic marker x on her locker, what a nice bod he has. Ravena is getting a little heavy though. She tries to go on diets but hasn't the will power. Oh well.

Mr. OX wears casual clothes

Mr. OX wears casual clothes since he is so rich. He wears blue jeans with a silver and turquoise belt to the office. And he wears lots of heavy silver and turquoise jewelry, plus some gold around his neck, and on his pinky a one-carat diamond set in platinum. He is fond of saying, I'm in the eruption business. I detonate faces ha ha. In fact his face, unlike Biff's, is a tragic landscape of yesterday's battles, so to speak. Too bad about me, ha ha, he says. Today is a new day, right honey? He calls everyone honey, regardless of gender. He even calls Biff honey. Sit down, honey, he says when Biff comes in. Sit down over there and talk to me, poor Biff. A guy gets a tough break every once in a while and you're today's guy, all right Biff honey. Tell you what I'm gonna do, that's ok Biff, you just rest your tired head on your hand like that don't you stand on ceremony for me or any other guy, you just put your feet up, there you go, tell you what. Now I had to take you off the OX account well let's just let bygones be bygones, what the hell Biff honey, but I'll tell you what, Mrs. OX and me, well we want to go visit your Carolyn now in the hospital, how about that? In the hospital this Saturday A.M., Mrs. OX and I decided we'd go on over, maybe bring a picnic or Mrs. OX thought some nice lingerie or that new gourmet toothpaste all the gals love, how about that? That's ok, you just slump down there in the chair, take the whole thing, that's it, I like a man who likes his space, goddammit honey, you just stretch out good and let your head fall down on those arms, good enough 'cause when a man's in pain he should show it, dammit, yes siree. Now honey don't you have a handkerchief or something for that? Now don't go blubbering all over without a handkerchief. Biff? Biff honey? Look at that Biff honey, is that how a man takes his lumps, tell me that honey?

At night Biff junior

At night Biff junior sneaks into the refrigerator and eats mayonnaise out of the jar. He hates this house. Most of all he hates his grandpaw, Carolyn's Dad, who is snoring noisily on the pullout bed in the den.

He hates the smell of his grandpaw and the texture of his grandpaw. He hates the stupid boring stories his grandpaw insists on telling every night. He has an urge to go to his grandpaw's pullout bed in the den and shove peas in his nose. That'll stop the old fart from snoring.

Donna Reed is a petite, neatly dressed

Donna Reed is a petite, neatly dressed woman with large brown compassionate eyes which are always a little moist as if she's recently been crying over the poor children in South Africa or something. Nevertheless, she runs her group with an iron hand. She claps her hard little mitts and believe me everyone hops to. They sit in a circle, even Biff who these days has a tendency to list to one side, even Biff sits up straight when Donna Reed claps her fierce little paws. OK, she shouts. Reports! Then we go around in a circle starting with Mr. M. Mr. M says, Yes Donna, this week things go a bit better. My wife has decided we will not keep the dog, I repeat, not keep the dog. Mr. M looks around defensively. Donna says, I don't give a shit if you keep the dog or not and neither does anyone else, Mr. M. Your life is your life, remember that. Mr. M looks at his squarish knees. He is wearing Bermuda shorts this evening.

Biff and Carolyn look deep

Biff and Carolyn look deep into each other's eyes. What do they see? Nothing familiar. It is the same old story. Biff says, I lost the OX account, what can I do? Carolyn says, You should thank your lucky stars, anyway it's all maya, an illusion, even my hair which is falling out on account of the drugs which are also illusions. Jesus, says Biff, I am so cold and hungry. I lost the OX account and we're rationing the pbj's. Your Dad is no help, I wish he'd go home. Last night I caught him jacking off in Ravena's closet. Thank god she was at Sara Jane's. What do you think? asks Carolyn. Am I still gorgeous? Am I still your little cute-face? These days she's quite fat; her white blond hair is falling out in large tufts; she has a double chin. She sits with her legs apart and you can see up between her thighs to her underpants only she doesn't wear underpants anymore. Gross.

Donna Reed is the only one

Donna Reed is the only one who understands Biff. After group, she takes his arm and leads him to the parking lot. Don't worry about anything, Biff, she says. A fine handsome man such as yourself need not worry about a thing. You're one of the lucky ones, says Donna Reed, and just to prove it she touches his genitals with her little hand. Jesus, he says. He can't even get a hard-on. I'm sorry, Donna, he says. He feels like he's going to puke, but Biff never pukes.

Ravena and Sara Jane have been thinking

Ravena and Sara Jane have been thinking about human sacrifice for some time now. They try to find out more about it in the library but all they can find are some books on human sexuality. They look at some diagrams for a while. Très boring. Then they find this book called *A Treasury of Witchcraft*, and Sara Jane smuggles it out under her raincoat. The witchcraft book tells them about a few useful spells and curses. Also about magic circles which you make by stretching goatskin. But who can find goatskin nowadays?

On Saturday, Mr. and Mrs. OX drive to the country

On Saturday, Mr. and Mrs. OX drive to the country to see Carolyn. They drive a Mercedes-Benz the color of a razor blade. Of course, naturally, they are very rich people, he being the owner of the OX company. King OX, we say. Mrs. OX, Vera, is a sad-faced woman who is wearing an orchid corsage in her lapel. She looks intensely out of the window as they drive through the dipping and rolling countryside. So many rectangular houses. So many cows. She wonders what she should be feeling in the face of all this. Happiness? Gratitude? Hunger?

Carolyn sees

Carolyn sees a way to redeem the world. First, she traces the course of world events, then she draws a narrow time line with her thumbnail. Secretly, she's been growing the thumbnail to a long sharp point for this very purpose. This is the plan: first they have to take everything back. All the wars, the entire 13th, 14th and 15th centuries, etc. Then we women can slap togther a new version. This is how Carolyn imagines the new version: like a huge soapy iridescent bubble just kind of sailing terminably through space. But Carolyn is crazy.

Carolyn is fat, says Mr. OX

Carolyn is fat, says Mr. OX, It's probably the thorazine. They all get fat on thorazine, honey. He nudges his sad-faced wife, Vera. Her orchid wobbles on her lapel. She feels a terrible headache coming on, one of those headaches that start off sideways, then when you least expect it they rip back and forth like a saw. Carolyn's eyes, once so large and innocent and seductive, have shrunk to tiny glittering pinpricks in her enormous face. I hardly know what to say to you, Vera and King. So sweet of you to come seems, you know, *fake* on my part. She peels the tinfoil from a Hershey's kiss and pops it into her mouth. I love these damn things, she says. These and Sugar Daddys. You ever had a Sugar Daddy, Vera? I bet you have. I just bet you eat two or three Sugar Daddys a night, you wanna bet? I'll bet you any amount of money in the world.

Biff and Donna

Biff and Donna are at the movies. The movie is about a married woman who falls in love with a man called Alex. It's in black and white. The married woman's husband is a pear-shaped man with a sparse moustache. He is very unattractive, don't you think? whispers Biff to Donna. Comme ci, comme ça, says Donna. The husband is always wondering where his dinner is. The wife spends half her time on a train. She meets the man called Alex and they confess their love for one another. They drive into the country and stand on a bridge. She says she can't go on being so deceitful to her husband. In the tragic ending, Alex goes off to Africa. Then Biff takes Donna for a cocktail at Nino's. There's a rock band called the Giant Sandworms. The music reminds Biff of that time he caught his trouser leg in an escalator. But Donna is very relaxed. She is stroking Biff's arm and telling him he reminds her of Alex. Let's pretend I'm the woman and you're Alex, she says. But Biff is too nervous to play that game; the music puts him on edge.

Do you remember that old cartoon

Do you remember that old cartoon "Puff n' Stuff"? Well Biff junior these days goes around singing that song to himself nonstop. It's not that he likes it, but it goes on and on in his mind anyway, he can't help himself. At the same time he is peripherally aware of an image which accompanies the song: two large vague pink and green animals. The whole thing has had a beneficial calming effect on him. At the dinner table these days he is very well behaved. His grandfather no longer rubs him the wrong way. His grandfather is sitting there eating egg noodles with cream of mushroom soup made by you guessed it Donna Reed.

Carolyn, still fat

Carolyn, still fat, is running for public office. Her campaign slogan—who wouldn't be insane these days?—makes the city headlines. Biff's humiliation is peppered with a little pride. Carolyn for city council-woman. I cannot promise you much, she says in a bedside interview with reporter Armory Godfrey, but I will promise a few things. Her campaign manager is her friend from the asylum, Terry Jo. Terry Jo is a 6'5" brunette originally from a wealthy Philadelphia family; she has been diagnosed as a hypomanic syndrome gal. Let's always stick together, Terry Jo tells Carolyn. No matter what we do, let's be best friends forever. Carolyn agrees. Don't trust men, she tells Terry Jo. To seal their friendship they write their names on the wall of the shower stalls with period blood.

Mr. OX has just received

Mr. OX has just received word that his cholesterol count is very high. You are in the 99% bracket for your age group, the doctor tells Mr. OX. So Mr. OX decides to go on a diet. He tells Vera that she'd better think of some good recipes. Vera is not fat herself, but one of her few joys in life is to cook French cuisine. She belongs to a cooking club that meets Wednesday afternoons and, although she rarely talks to the other ladies in the club, she has a wonderful time scooping Mornay sauce over ter-rines of shrimp and scallops, pounding veal fillets into a fattening mix-ture of breadcrumbs, heavy cream, and minced walnuts, stirring the hot fudge in its no-stick pot. Now she has to learn a whole other way. Brown rice and fresh beans steamed in an inch of water. The idea of it makes her even more melancholy than usual and she takes to her bed; it seems there's not a thing in the world Mr. OX can do to rouse her. So he hires a girl from the U Bet We Do cooking service who heats him up a can of Campbells chicken noodle soup for supper each night and slaps a seg-mented orange in front of him for dessert. Nevertheless, his cholesterol count goes down by the estimated 6%.

Every day at 3 o'clock

Every day at 3 o'clock, Biff junior disappears into his mother's closet. There, among the hat boxes, the garment bags, the outdated evening dresses and rows of high heels, Biff junior makes his plans for escape. He writes on the wall behind the raincoats, revving himself up. Life is too short, he writes, to waste it on trivialities. Birds of a feather should stick together. The root enterprise of the living involves radical break-throughs. When his pencil point breaks, he leans against the silky hems of his mother's dresses and occcasionally fingers a couple, closes his eyes.

Ravena and Sara Jane make a pact

Ravena and Sara Jane make a pact not unlike the pact made by Carolyn and Terry Jo. Only they do not use period blood. They use real blood since they are allowed to stick straight pins into their fingers without fear of being shot full of phenobarb and shoved into Ward 4. They are at Sara Jane's house and Sara Jane's mother is drunk on the couch. First they take the bottle from her lap where it is lying lopsided, then they each take a hit. After that is when they prick their fingers and vow never to part from one another. (Only Ravena, like Carolyn, has her toes crossed.)

Biff and Donna Reed are getting along

Biff and Donna Reed are getting along swimmingly these days. Donna is a prince of a woman, says Biff. Only he cannot bring himself to fuck her properly. He thinks he wants to and then something happens. And yet she is so small and alluring, what man wouldn't want to? Donna Reed who is a professional therapist says that it's guilt. Your wife and children are ruining your life, she says. The longer you try to cope with those brats, the more stress you create for yourself. If I were you I'd put them in a temporary care home until you get your feet on the ground again. You need your space, Biff.

These days Biff junior

These days Biff junior is happiest in his mother's closet making plans and writing encouraging aphorisms on the wall in back of the rain-coats. But soon it will be time to get out of the plan phase and into ACTION. As long as he's in the closet, he hunts around for loose change and finds enough for a Big Mac and a small fries. Not enough, he thinks, unless I can find a job.

Armory Godfrey

Armory Godfrey, one of the hottest reporters in the city, is doing a pro-file on Carolyn. Every day he visits her either in the visitors' lounge with the orange wallpaper and the white Formica table full of *Scientific Americans,* or in the small cinder-block cubicle she now shares with Terry Jo, her soul sister. Armory is thin faced with a light stubble of beard and long irritable looking fingers. He smokes cigarette after cigarette while the girls talk about their ideas for the new world. Carolyn is usually cramming chocolate-covered cherries or big spoonfuls of cream cheese into her mouth as she speaks. Terry Jo sits on the arm of her chair leaning protectively against her, her eyelashes fluttering in a rhythmic and unnerving way. During all of this Armory tries to be attentive although once or twice he has let his mind wander. He cannot help admiring Carolyn's intelligence, though he believes her ideas are not sound or even original. Paying women to nurse their babies and make love to their husbands, for example. A good idea on the surface, but how could you enforce such a thing?

Biff junior buys a Big Mac

Biff junior buys a Big Mac and small fries with the change he finds in his mother's closet. Then he sits at one of the orange booths and stares out the window. His mind is blank. He is waiting for something to pop into it. Hopefully, a well-conceived plan of action, but nothing jumps in. Just then a bag lady comes up and asks him if he would mind if she joins him. Not at all, he says. Transients have always fascinated him and here was a chance to talk to one firsthand. He even offers her a bite of his Big Mac, but she says no, hamburgers are the food of the devil.

When Armory goes home

When Armory goes home that night, his wife Beth is taking a nap which is par for the course. He throws together his own dinner—pasta with a jar of Ragu and garbanzo beans on the side to make a complete protein. As he shovels the food in—for a thin man he has a wild uncontainable appetite—he thinks about Carolyn and Terry Jo, but mostly Carolyn. There is something fierce and admirable about her, he can't help thinking.

Biff and Donna Reed look

Biff and Donna Reed look into a temporary care home for the children called The House of Friendship and Light. The House of Friendship is run by two ex-nuns who now call themselves Kath and Nance. They seem

very nice to me, says Donna Reed. Kath is very bosomy and Nance goes
around with a riding crop (her horse is out back). This would be a great
place, Donna continues. Out in the country. Horses. And they're much
nearer their mother which is where children ought to be, and you so need
your space in order to recover, I call you a recovering guiltoholic !

Ravena says, If they send me

Ravena says, If they send me to that place I'll burn down the house.
Then I'll stab myself.

The bag lady

The bag lady whose name is Ms. North tells Biff junior that he ought
to come on some adventures with her since he's so curious. But don't
expect no special treatment, she warns him. And we don't eat meat,
she adds.

Driving back

Driving back from the House of Friendship and Light Biff suddenly
and for no apparent reason has an erection. You're kidding, says
Donna. She's a little suspicious that he's been thinking about Kath or
Nance instead of herself. Pull over, she orders. But by the time the big
semi has passed and the Dodge truck and a few other compacts have
moved to the left so that Biff and Donna can scoot the Celica onto the
shoulder, it is too late. What can I say? says Biff. You can say you'll put
those children under the care of those nice young women. Just then
Biff has another erection which makes Donna furious, though she is
too clever to mention it.

At night Terry Jo and Carolyn

At night Terry Jo and Carolyn sleep in each other's arms and exchange
passionate kisses. The idea of the new world has made them dreamy
and excitable. Men paying women to wear makeup or else men wearing makeup; either way it's a no-lose situation. Don't you think, murmurs Carolyn in Terry Jo's ear, that every woman should have at least
a master's degree? Terry Jo, a hypomanic syndrome gal, demurs at this
one. How about a mink coat or a Porsche or some, like, emblem of
their newfound power?

For two weeks Vera

For two weeks Vera stays in bed, leaving only to go to the bathroom or to hard-boil an egg. Then she gets up, throws a mink coat over her nightgown and leaves the house. She drives her BMW straight to First Interstate where she withdraws thirty-four thousand dollars from the joint checking account and then she hits the highway, driving fast but confidently. That night Mr. OX has the au pair girl sit on his lap after the soup course.

Carolyn's Dad goes to Ravena's room

Carolyn's Dad goes to Ravena's room in the middle of the night and stands at the foot of her bed. What is it Grandpaw? she says. His bulky shadow has woken her. After a while he turns from the bed and goes to her window; now he is silhouetted against the bright moonlit night. Ravena thinks he looks like a bear. She shivers, then pulls the covers up over her face. Grandpaw never says anything; it is very creepy.

Biff junior carefully considers

Biff junior carefully considers Sandy North's proposition. To go on an adventure, hmmm. Might be interesting. Then again, what if these people are murderers? Well, so what? Wouldn't it be fascinating and educational to hang out with murderers? You could write a book about it or at least a decent magazine article for someplace like *Esquire* or *Playboy*. Yah. But what if they murder *me*?

In OT, Carolyn and Terry

In OT, Carolyn and Terry Jo make ashtrays with tiny blue mosaic chips that get glued onto a copper form. It's so insulting, whispers Carolyn. Neither of these women is what you would call good with her hands. Carolyn's fingers are too fat to be especially nimble these days, and hypomanic Terry Jo is either too jittery or too lethargic for handicrafts. This is exactly what I mean, hisses Carolyn. Insane people have rights. I think we should be allowed to go play on the swing set now, for example, or to have midmorning snack a little early. Who do they think we are, kindergarteners? No, insane people are not babies, we are very special. You could call us artists. We have visions, we hear voices from beyond, and we're very outspoken. In some centuries they thought we were prophets or prophetesses. I still think we are. Moreover, if I'm elected to the office of city council member I will guarantee that this stupid OT class be flushed down the toilet, figuratively or literally speaking, take your pick.

En route to the House of Friendship and Light

En route to the House of Friendship and Light Biff tries to get the kids to sing "Row Row Row Your Boat" or "Down by the Old Mill Stream," but no go. Ravena sits stonily in the back seat and Biff junior sits stonily in the front seat. Neither kid says a word to their father and when he speaks they pretend not to hear. Finally he pulls to the side of the road, gets out of the car, and pees into a clump of wild bluebells.

Armory Godfrey is spending

Armory Godfrey is spending more and more time at the hospital. He must be undergoing a deep transformation—deeper than mere politics or ideology. It's Carolyn's influence. Suddenly, insane people look like sane people and vice versa. His wife, Beth, he's now convinced is not normal. She sleeps constantly and when he tries to engage her in a conversation, her eyes drift to the window or the wall.

Carolyn's father is digging

Carolyn's father is digging a big hole in the yard. What's that for? asks Biff. Funny you should ask, is all Carolyn's father says, and then he keeps digging. Every day the hole gets more gigantic, wider and deeper. Biff says, Did it ever occur to you that you're ruining my lawn? But the old guy just leans against his spade and looks out toward the horizon and blinks both eyes.

Terry Jo needs a megadose

Terry Jo needs a megadose of electroshock, that's obvious. The other night she had what they call a screaming shit fit here at the hospital and it took four beefy guys to pry her off of Armory Godfrey and to get the toothbrush out of her fist. She wanted to gouge his eyes out, says Carolyn in a speech to the women in Ward 7B, and do you know why? On Ward 7B you have the cheerfuls, the OT folks on Xanex at the most so there's none of that catatonic rocking and drooling. We know! They all screamed out the possibilities: Full moon, cat got her tongue, 'jes felt like it, PMS, etc. Armory himself got a nasty scrape under the left eyebrow and the nurse let Carolyn swab it with Merthiolate and Bactine ointment.

Mr. OX reports

Mr. OX reports Vera's absence to the Missing Persons' but they say she's a grown woman she can do what she wants. Be that as it may, honey, says Mr. OX, that woman's my wife of twenty-five years and I have got to find her. He removes four crisp fifty dollar bills from his lizard billfold and snaps them smartly on the Missing Persons' counter. Give it your best shot, he tells the girl, who reminds him of a toy poodle with that little bit of fluff on the top of her head. At night he has the au pair girl parade around the house in one of Vera's nightgowns, then she sits on his lap and tongues his forehead.

Biff junior and Ravena are having

Biff junior and Ravena are having a great time with Kath and Nance. Kath and Nance understand children whose parents have gotten sick of them. They take them horseback riding and teach them the names of wildflowers. At night they watch MTV and drink Harvey Wallbangers.

Armory is in love

Armory is in love with Carolyn and out of love with Beth. He's not sure how to handle the situation, but he begins by trying to effect Carolyn's release from the insane asylum. You're not crazy, he pleads with her. But Carolyn smiles that new smile of hers which is a modern mixture of the smiles of Flipper and Mamie Eisenhower. Ok, ok, he says. Don't say another word. You're in love with that dyke Terry Jo.

Donna Reed is in love

Donna Reed is in love with Biff but Biff is in love with Kath and Nance who are in love with each other.

Terry Jo is, in fact, in love

Terry Jo is, in fact, in love with Carolyn, but Carolyn is in love with no one, unless you count life. Nor are Ravena and Biff junior in love. Or

Carolyn's father who has taken to sleeping in the backyard hole which is as big as a movie theater.

Mr. OX is sort of in love

Mr. OX is sort of in love with the au pair girl and the girl from Missing Persons' who reminds him of a poodle, but neither of these girls loves him much, except for his money for which they will do anything—wiggle their bare fannies, fart in his face, what the hell.

No one can find Vera

No one can find Vera. Maybe she is with Beth who wound up leaving Armory after he loaned her ironing board and sewing machine to The Gals of Ward 7B, as they now call themselves in their newfound political identity, an identity characterized not so much by craziness as by a kind of salutary insouciance and wild desire.

Sandy Huss

Sandy Huss, born in Toledo, Ohio, graduated from Washington University in St. Louis, where she studied with Stanley Elkin. She now teaches in the Program in Creative Writing at the University of Alabama in Tuscaloosa.

Since the publication in 1992 of a collection of short fiction, Labor for Love, *her creative production has explored the juxtaposition of texts and images. This work has evolved into a study of historical forms of the book and the design of digital spaces. She is completing a long prose piece for print,* Scrap Book, *from which "Scissors Kick" is excerpted.*

Like many of her contemporaries, Huss uses the personal computer and the Internet to compose, employing forms and techniques usually found in graphic design and video production. With this tool, a writer has access not only to libraries of fonts but to a vast array of alphabets and the libraries of images and illustrations. Huss assumes that the choices she makes graphically, visually, and spatially are as significant in conveying what she wishes to communicate as the more standard arrangements of letters and punctuation. Through its graphics and its words, "Scissors Kick" teases out the material nature of the printed book and asks us to consider how we get our information and whether we are wired to respond better to the information contained in pictures than to the meaning deeply hidden within words.

Scissors Kick

The commercial pattern is a development of the last hundred years. Although fashion has been important to both men and women for centuries and centuries, it was not until the 1850's that Ebeneezer Butterick conceived the idea of recording a garment design by means of a pattern. So novel was the idea that Mr. Butterick charged his clients rental or cutting charges for the use of the pattern.

Mildred Graves Ryan & Velma Phillips CLOTHES FOR YOU

The seam was our first discourse, one quietly spoken: Phyl taught us it should never show. The body leads, the garment follows, period. There are other schools of thought, of course: the seam can be a star—topstitched with contrasting thread, inlaid with piping, fringed. But Phyl spurned such frippery: our love of it was kid stuff. Which was fine for us (still kids, more or less), but a grown woman fared best if she didn't seem to be trying. Phyl had a degree in Clothing & Textiles: she knew. So we knew it too, and loved knowing it: it took us over, made us happy.

Childhood was just a footnote in the pattern catalogues, anyhow. The kids' clothes were hundreds of pages into one of those books, so far back that when we turned to them, the books, heavy and serviceably stitched though they were, had to be held open. Way in the back with the other afterthoughts (dickeys and vestments, cummerbunds and valances) in a realm that was classically timeless and creepy. Not that any part of the pattern books kept up with the fashion magazines, but when things did change therein, they changed for the Misses.

The effects of Butterick patterns were significant and far-reaching. Before the introduction of the graded pattern for home sewing, fashion was a phenomenon exclusive to ladies of high standing. Who else could afford to pay for the latest styles from Paris, New York and other centers? Most women took apart old, worn out dresses to use as a model for a new one. With the advent of Butterick patterns, not only did dressmaking become much easier, fashion became available to men, women, and children, of all classes all over the world.

Butterick Website
www.butterick.com

We learned to study in the yard goods store, with Phyllis as our tutor. Her demeanor at the pattern catalogue was even more solemn than at the library—more solemn and more eager. The fact that money could soon change hands contributed to this bearing, of course, but it wasn't the whole story. Her posture arose from what she knew: how to read what might be in what was, how (as it were) to sample the lyrics. She taught us to picture View C's sleeves on View A's bodice, to strip the pompons from view B, to cross one pattern's pieces with another's. And to read the tiny print—its admonitions about weight and weave and nap, its helpful list of Notions Needed.

She carried a notebook in her purse, a graduate's mechanical pencil, and an envelope of swatches clipped from selvages and hems—her wardrobe, real and to be realized, in synecdoche. We sat next to her on the tall bar stools at the catalogue counters while she took notes and made cunning little sketches. Once we had a purse, we carried swatches of our own, but we were never nearly as systematic. We wrote on the scraps of paper supplied by the stores, using their stumpy Putt Putt pencils. And write is really all we did: we've never been any good at drawing. Still, now we see how pen & ink & a light watercolor wash could be said to have inspired some of our best ideas.

Before we owned a bike, a Bible or a Barbie, we owned a sewing machine: Phyl bought it for us out of her secret stash, a wad of cash hidden in a compartment of her wallet, a wad she'd been saving, she claimed, for her own new machine. For herself, she wanted a particular name brand, and not the commonplace name brand, either: she'd been educated as a seamstress AND a consumer when she was in school. What she got for us was a generic—which she was persuaded her preferred company had actually built: there was something dis-

The making of a garment should be considered with the same degree of seriousness as the building of a house or an airplane, as the painting of a picture, or the molding of a statue.

Mildred Graves Ryan & Velma Phillips CLOTHES FOR YOU

tinctive in the way its motor whirred. We couldn't hear it, and we thought she sounded smug and immodest—not at all her style.

She bestowed this machine upon us: we never asked for it. The last thing we ever expected was to be equipped. Nothing really belonged to us, except maybe our clothes. (Our only sibs were brothers; Unisex was not yet a word.) We thought we were being raised to be Borrowers, like the tiny people in the books Phyl had read aloud, who lived in the walls by day and sneaked out at night to take whatever the regular-sized people left lying around. In their interstitial workshops, they transformed their haul, laboriously extracting pins from a pincushion to make an ottoman, fighting off rats with straightpin swords.

Stu had a whole room dedicated to sewing. Stu—whom Phyl forbade to make anything for us or our brothers but pajamas. Stu—for whom everything was a chore unless it was reading. Stu—who got her chores Done, taking no discernible pleasure in the doing. And who

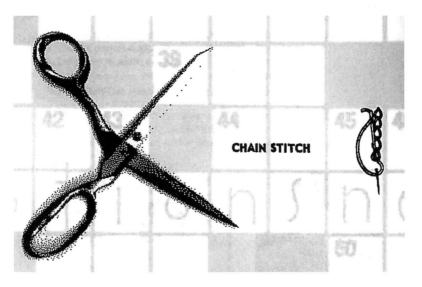

CHAIN STITCH

FOR ONE COLOR MONOGRAM—Using contrasting thread, work chain stitch over stamped transfer lines. Then work additional rows of chain stitch along inside and outside of letter.

FOR THREE COLOR MONOGRAM—Using white, work chain stitch over stamped transfer lines. Refer to envelope illustration for placement of remaining 2 colors and work along outside and inside of letter in chain stitch.

then would read and read and read—and work the crossword puzzle. It was a nice little room: the windows were high and narrow. Her brother, Jester, during a sober stretch, had built Stu's old treadle into a long wide table: you could have made a ball gown for one of the March girls, one of the Bennetts, without worrying where you might drag it. Not that, in Stu's house, the floor was ever dirty. But for us, Stu stuck to pajamas, as she had been instructed: straight seams, elastic waistbands, dolman sleeves, snaps pounded in with a hammer. Peddling like a house afire. Helping—not meddling.

The clothes Stu made for herself looked all right until you got up close. And then you'd see a slub blaring across a collar, a zipper not entirely hidden. A plaid pocket not Quite matching its shirt front's field, rick rack (rick rack!) caught up wrong in its thread, some of its points folded completely over. But inside would be the real horror show, which set Phyl's eyebrows up above her glasses: curves that must have been gnawed instead of clipped, unironed seams joined to unironed seams in wretched lumps, the points of darts not exactly pointy. Stu put the stress in Seamstress, all right, but she had a secret stash too, and bought herself a good Butte knit whenever she had an occasion. And sometimes, when Phyl would let her, she took Phyl shopping.

Shorty wasn't either allowed to sew for us kids—but she didn't know it. As Number Two Son's mother, she didn't have to suffer Phyl's prohibitions, although even Phyl would admit her technical merit. Shorty was part thread, part needle, part gore, part pleat: the chevrons and trapezoids and arches of a pattern were her internal geometry. But she made the patterns herself, out of shirt cardboard and cereal boxes. And the fabric—well, it could have come from anywhere: Shorty put the brick in Bricoleur. Not that she'd like the word. Or know it, or want to know it—even though she was the family's first writer. In her daily journal, she wrote it all down: the temperature, the rainfall. The trips to her favorite dumping grounds, what she'd scavenged from where, what she'd turned it into. We and our brothers knew the drill: we always thanked her politely. And then put whatever reconstituted thing into the Salvation Army bag—while Phyllis hissed the word *Dutchy.*

The biggest fight we ever had with her lasted all of one Christmas dinner. The ERA seemed almost possible, and we were home from college with ideas. Women shouldn't take jobs from men, she said, men with families. And if a woman doesn't have a man, we said, what's she supposed to do? The look she gave us really hurt: we didn't think we were That alien. What's the matter, she spit, afraid you won't make the grade?

Phyl used to say she never used her degree: it was her fallback, in case something happened to Number Two. It hadn't even been her idea: Educating The Women was a family tradition—on both sides of her family. In a pinch, she said, all those great aunts of ours could support themselves. She held up her fingers and ticked away: teacher, teacher, nurse, nurse, teacher, nurse, dietician. But she sewed all the time—what would using it mean? Her explanation: department store buyer. We wonder now if she could have made a go of it, if she'd have been able to relax her standards (simplicity, neatness, modesty, elegance) so as to attract any customers. What we wondered then, and what we got clear on right away, was if a degree was only good for a fallback. No she said, you can do what you want: there's no law that says you have to get married. And even if you do, you might want to work too, for a while anyhow—until you have babies. And even then, she smirked, jerking her head in the general direction of The Shop, you might CHOOSE to.

Phyl was the best we ever knew: we've got a memento in one of our closets. A pair of curtains from her last kitchen, her least favorite room in the house. Open, the curtains would hang straight and true, but that's the easy part, relatively speaking. Closed they would reveal how much care she took, because they've got a pattern, see, and the pattern's unbroken. A bouquet of daisies starts on the left panel and ends on the right, but you have to get up real close to recognize it's an illusion. That it's not all one big bunch crying out for you to put it in some water.

Phyl could dress you UP, refashion you—and we were primed to follow in her glory. We carried our machine with us everywhere as we moved around the country, only setting it up when we needed to patch our jeans, finally passing it along to someone who really sewed when we inherited Phyl's. Her new machine, for which she'd saved practically her whole life, one manufactured, after all, by that commonplace company. She'd reported that between setting her heart on the other brand and being able to make the actual purchase, her fantasy had fallen way off in quality. We were a little surprised that she could change her mind—she'd always been so adamant. But upon relfection, we under-

When you decide what you want
to do most in life, your next step is to
find the best road to reach your goal.
You will want to prepare yourself for
your first job by getting the best possible training. Read books and trade
magazines that pertain to the business or profession you have chosen.
Make a special effort to meet people
who are engaged in the field in which
you are interested. Such people are
usually glad to counsel with any beginner who is really interested.

Lesson 56: Speed Building Exercise
ROWE COLLEGE TYPING

stood. See, it was Phyl who, while we were still quite young, got us our
first typewriter.

Shall we teach you to sew? Would you like to learn? Even if you
would, should we teach you? Could it do for you what it's done for us?
How well do you understand Houdini? All this lore we have, all these
skills we've kept sharp (well, sharp enough to instruct a beginner)—
what will come of it should you decide to refuse this indoctrination?
Perhaps there are, after all, reasons to have children.

There's a lot to learn, and you start with the seam: that's how you
know you're sewing. Sewing as opposed to mending or hemming or any
of the fancy-pants sitchery. First you've got to cut the pieces out, the pieces
you've arranged on the prepared material. You've shrunk your fabric, and
straightened its grain, and kept your eye on that grain while you pinned
down the pattern. It's all thread, that material, hundreds of threads, thousands of them. Thread that's already been joined to thread—and now you
and your scissors enter the picture. Is there a frog in your throat? a swamp
on your brow? Is your heart flopping like a fish out of water? C'mon kid,
Buck Up. Many, so many, have been down this aisle before you.

Janet Kauffman

Janet Kauffman was born and raised on a farm in Pennsylvania and now lives and teaches in Michigan, where she has worked for many years to restore the original wetlands to her farm. Kauffman continues to campaign for watershed protection and land use reform; her thinking on such issues can be found in her essay "Letting Go," which originally appeared in A Place of Sense. *"Patriotic," a story in her first collection,* Places in the World a Woman Could Walk, *has been made into a film by Judy Dennis. Her most recent books are* Characters on the Loose, *a collection of short stories, and the novel* Rot.*

Kauffman has a deep, abiding interest in the physical-ness of the physical world, and her classes are famous for her instructions in the art of incorporating the physical world in the world of literary abstraction. Her students bring objects and text together in assemblages that can be appreciated both as works of the plastic fine arts and as literature. "Five on Fiction," which is about the writing of fiction, takes on in labeled sections the traditional components of fiction—character, plot, theme—and can be read as a persuasive essay claiming that fiction can be made of other ingredients. The story also attempts to make the abstract nature of the written language as solid and pliable as stone and paint.

Five on Fiction

On Eliminating Characters from Fiction

1.

If you don't say the name of a person, a good many things are possible in a sentence, and even in a landscape without margins or verifiable boundaries. It is possible to turn a corner and encounter a large machine lifting trees out of the ground. You can read the lettering on the metal, letters and numbers that are a code name for the machine, but it is certainly not the name of a person. Heaps of trees in full leaf may be stacked in the middle of the road. It is possible to see the beginnings of flames among the branches, and if you wait long enough, not very long actually, turn slightly to the side, and still not saying the name of a person, you can walk through the fire and into the house it's become.

2.
It's akin to making a hat from sticks. The handwork and gluing are not at all sweatshopped. Not jetted or crashed into wetlands, not magically rising up out of it whole and crowned. You can count the prepositions, cross-fingered, coming up from to out of, especially. And it is a cityscape here. Swept. There's plenty of sand for the froth of some sea.

3.
Okay, explain how many celebrations it takes to call them off and quit firing k-k-k-k-k-k into clouds, fireworks falling onto cottonwoods where they spit jewelry and metal chunks of Pontiacs, the whole river valley flipped to an attic with clothing on dummies, strings of paper lights burning; how many long naps with sunblock and handheld missile launchers, before night and nothing else falls, and time (paying no attention to all the fucking good-byes) passes.

4.
And the story that stops with somebody saying fare-thee-well to somebody must be false. Even if there's scenery in the fade-out. A dead tree, say. Even if the kid says something like "I'll get those chives chopped now, Mother." Even if he says, "Bring me my goose gun." He goes inside, and in the middle of chive chopping, or later, maybe stories later, fork in his hand, he's opening his mouth.

5.
In their cells, in their cells, they invent vocabularies ready-to-go. They don't have paint or soldering tools, but they do have the die-hard mentality. They don't scrub up. Their spirits have so completely filled them out, gone right past the skin, detached, that these are the things cited, proof on paper of whatever's lost or found, which is why, even if we have lamps, good light, we can't know by reading who is who.

6.
Debris, homespun, flimflamming with shrouds, castoffs, that is the handwork of what's-her-name in her shift, her hair woven to ladders. It is the paradox of her escape, she climbs down, she cuts her hair, more flotsam to figure out. She is gone, gone, a nervy babe, like a one-time flier, flimsy above the globe and going down. Oh, those are the syllables she calls out, oh, oh.

7.

On its own, narrative goes to nature. His tongue between her toes, or hers his, they roll in a tire, say, one way and another, steel-belted, hot as the highway, it's Utah anyhow, the salt flats, fast with their fingers between their thighs. They don't know which way they'll roll next, whosever story it is. Is this day the equinox? They're spun, they shut their eyes to cut out confusion, and hollows open up behind their knees, and, see, it's Salt Lake between them. They lick whatever they can, and slow. It's not true, but people say it: this is the ocean that used to be.

8.

Recall the trees, their ex-foliage—in French, a construction more tactile. In fiction, the mouth is the place of trees, whole: root, trunk, limb, leaf, seed, node, scar, tooth, tip, pit, lobe.

9.

It's raining, and yes, somewhere the avalanches strip stones from the cliff, wing-scrapes. There is so much motion the sow bugs roll downhill, and then the artillery opens up and shells hit the three-story apartment buildings at 16 Ferdinand Place and the windows flare. They have exploded now. The gnats called phantom gnats with fringed antennae as large as wings, the ones walking the corners of the glass, they are in the air now, and you've flown here, your baggage is so light.

10.

They're sleeping in a row, labeled, you can look, it's not like tags on their toes, but they've got a line or two over their heads, bookish, like poets, maybe they *are* poets, side by side, you can call up their files at the windows. They've been asleep, arranged in some fashion, and now we're here messing up the sheets, good god, air the place out, open another door. Even your mother says, there's more than scenery out there. You can look both ways, and then another, the first disturbance is the most disturbing, and after that you can read the books with the bad titles, and make love this way, one leg over the shoulder.

On Plot as Ground

1.

Bleed it, run it over, past the margin or whatever edge of the thing hedges the page, garden, sheet, highway, screen. There's the body, too, and when the format or the shoulder cuts off, drops off, and it's not possible to go over and under the asphalt or onto the reverse of the surface, Moebius-stripped, or inside the skin, and the eye is exposed to the same plane and cut of things, well, the mind does for the mind what it can. A blur and flux and more of the same until somebody says, stop! And then bleed that, run it over, a surface a place a form a fake a violence a turn to it and from it.

2.

One thing a kid calls music crosses the street. It is not birdsong, but fish or mouth shapes flying, hammered, cast brass or tin chimes on the wood porch of a boarded house, not her house. And no one walks in or walks out, but the sound flies, and it is the girl's jangling teeth, there with her carved jaw on the sand, not one room or ceiling for her across a whole desert, and she lies where the other end of the wind rattles through, at her mother's feet.

3.

It would be better, when it matters most, to see in secret, and read, to look at a canvas with blue and black paints on it, with its various songs and assaults and logics, alone, or with one other person, two at the most, and lie around looking at words wherever they lie, too, or to circulate anything like art like contraband so that possession is moral complicity, a wrestling, right to the ground.

4.

As economical postlude, whack a peaky mountain down. Something along the line of rubble, pebbled, and here are enough ringable stones for all the pinkie fingers you can count. Ringmasters, quite a bunch, call in the clean-up crews—clowns they've never been happy with, with brooms, horns, blowers, scrubbers, the racket of room-size polishers. And then they raise a stink, it's work work, and what the hell happened, they want to know, to the pie-faced, high-topped comical?

5.

Tobacco-sizing boxes are real things, enclosed steps, six up or six down, depending how you look at them. Right justified. You can still read the leaves now and then, and in the tobacco-stripping room in November, anybody says anything. The dry leaves are sized, baled, it's handwork all the way, and on the table, the radio plays, too. As good as an open field, what we've got is dust, and, go ahead, call it your working proof of life elsewhere, of the relativity of time and this space, of fiction as what anybody says.

6.

Pass Monsieur Pasha, make it a dish from the past, with heft, an excess of sauce, European and entrepreneurial, sleek in velvets and patent leather, all sorts of imports, indisputable, entirely seignorial, smooth in its etymologies, the Madeira, the port, the heap of it, haul it along like a pyramid or a davenport. Eat in the living room. Maybe a kid'll deliver it. Maybe the women'll clean up.

7.

It's only one thing, their cry, but profligate, the high romance of four or maybe more fingers at play, soloing, Paganini. Hell, it's not easy when you're good to have fun. But when you're expert, the excess—hear that? They used to say it was siren song, off the water, and what else do women have to do out there but call like that? They've been at it all their lives. They know there's no end to pleasure. That's what they have to say. No wonder they lounge around, unpaid like you and me, who kick it up with the fishes, and open our eyes, and cry out again.

8.

The number of wing feathers (f) it takes to circumnavigate a given planet (x) is directly proportional to the number of armed men (m) it takes to subjugate half the population of that world ($\frac{1}{2}p$ of x), so that most species and certainly all the poor, adept in mathematics from perpetual practice, prefer either flocks of relaying flocks or those infamous contraptions like Icarus's that gum together random collections of pin feathers, secondaries, down, and plumes, rather than air-to-air missiles, calculated spans of selected lightweight alloys, riveted, polished like teeth.

9.

Consider the Catholic-boy brain mazes, the dark and depth of God, who ditched them, back there somewhere, predecessor, and now they're on their own, Hansels in the woods, lederhosen in good shape. Although it's not their legs they care for, not their arms they swing through the speckle-shade places, not anybody else's body they hand-hold, or care-take in the end. No, here, sit here at all the machinery, they've got the codes, it's a revelation, the goodly heaps of God's waste at each of the grid's embroidered nodes, they'll go clean to the core—where roots root, they say, and rot rots.

10.
So this is the end of holding the book like a head, there are so many hairs on his head, one after another. It's the end of holding the book like a fish, fingered, a limb, all of his letters, the print thick as the lawn. She is reading the book barefoot, reading the book, its letters, not his letters, and touching them with her fingers. The book falls on her wrists where the skin is thin and soft. The book is bound, she can feel that on her wrists, the binding. She is slung in the canvas sling chair. The book slips on her belly, slides between her legs. Oh, this is a very good book.

On Dialogue: Words That Come Out of the Mouth

1.
What about Angela, with a name like that, what can she say? She crosses the street whenever she wants and doesn't look over her shoulder. She wears her lapel pins for good works, she is almost metallic, shoe to hat. Her medals hang from her ears. She insists on an A, her athletic letter. She knows that whatever stars or stripes she wears, somebody will say it's too much, and it is, she is making sounds, she is breathing the smell of sex out of her mouth.

2.
She knows how talk goes under, between, across, buried, uprooted, dredged, hauled, maneuvered, sliced, snagged, catapulted, pinioned, rendered, masked, launched, labored, obliterated, hacked, hewn, harbored, boomeranged, laid waste.

3.
It's real estate, hey, watch the ducks on the water, somebody says. Tanks and goldfinches the same thing, knocked from chartreuse, the shock of one blink, one more, they're butter-lemon paint applied by knife. Somebody's got the art kit. It's breakfast time, too, time to lick the spoons, and say, gimme the cash, or say, so what's been carved up out there now?

4.

You can't say whether weather does this damage, and more, and more. The dry lake. The bulldozed slopes. We've said too much. Look at the words. Still more.

5.

It is only one side, but she's cut and bleeding on the foot, on the calf lengthwise and crosswise, look, on the knee as well, the thigh. She is not cut on the belly or on the breast. She is cut on the shoulder and on the forearm, she is cut on the wrist. And children on the sidewalk back away, mouths O O, and grown men step off the curb and cross over the street, they won't grab that one by the arm. You can see how freely she walks from here to there, spared, exposed, what we call fear gone out of her, whole; everything else about her here.

6.

Angelo's a hero here for that *o* at the end, the circle of his uncatalogued arms, his long-distance legs, he flies low, evades radar, and on the front porch says something unclear, hello, to Angelina maybe it is, there's nothing to them but airlifted bodies, which they have named outright, and spell out now. They are nowhere near dead, as he begins the roundabout fingering of her lips, around in her mouth, and she circles him, O Angelo, arms and legs, too, unnumbed. They laugh at the cheer he gives when she comes, O Angelo. She refuses to say out loud, O God.

7.

It was said words came out of her mouth you could read. She was bearded sometimes with words. Unless the wind stripped them off. She was breathless then, conversant with vegetation, the monosyllabic reeds in particular.

8.

Maybe it's the Taj Mahal, or a pagoda, that swan or pontoon boat or head-on wheels, the girl says. If you don't blink now, you'll never know.

9.

Backward blowing from the East, that's not the usual way things go. Look at the gray clouds, scrim torn and dangled, you can touch them. And nobody minds for a change, walking is pool-like, pond paddling.

The striated muscles take it slow, buoyant from whatever air flows by. Even old men, with the sparest flesh on long bones, stride along the marsh. They see herons flying, and the herons' eyes meet their eyes. They take in the sights, which are the lowering dark clouds, before their bodies lift and disappear headfirst, calling back in a heron's croak: *Black! Blue!*

10.

Too much agreeable quiet-speaking, sure, sure, it wipes you out. I bet that's why you're checking the map, you get the idea. Who cares where we are, as long as there's good cause to complain, it's about time, and somebody new to keep an eye on, water in the vicinity? Pavement so we don't forget which planet we're on. Nerves on edge, good, that's something to talk about. Who's mad now, that guy in the cap? Ask what he's done this time, you know it means trouble. He's bought the farm, the town, he's bought Seattle, he likes the needle, and thinks it's pretty, so keep up the racket, what have you got to lose. There's a measurable quantity of air left. You saw the woman with the black skirt dyed to match her hair, you know the logic, so look around. Here's a couple of trees we can travel through.

On the Transportation of Background to Foreground

1.

Remember. Indoors, the outgoing door opens in. As a usual thing. Outdoors, the ingoing door opens out. And in a house of many doors, such as the city, the distinction, inside to out, may be difficult, a habitual mystery, what with the trees and jungle paraphernalia of tattoo shops and the concrete bedding and awned walkways under the air. Guess where you are. It is impossible to be a stranger to the climates of seven continents. And others. There are several others. The forearm registers low-lying air, off the chocolate pecan tub; and the various underground weathers rise, usually visibly, against the knee, the thigh. There is the underarm atmosphere, too—dank, hair sweet. Temperature and steam and aroma, these ephemera, forewarn the way advertising forewarns: by assertion, mild haste, dispersal. It slips by. But if you open a door, out or in, to look at an advertisement, that's another story. If you open a door, flat on the ground, to look at a subway, a grotto, that's another story, too. Consider the number of doors. It is morning in Detroit. You can open a door and see sixteen bolts of hand-woven, purple fabric. You can open a door and see the wooden step and the marigolds. You can open a door and see a woman pull at her own nipples. It is midday. You can see the man in the green hat on the sidewalk. You can see brickwork. The sky is there, plain as a cake. The blue ceiling. The blue floor. The blue door.

2.
It's better for the camera to fall back and catch sky, a field like a line, not much beyond that, to show there's ground someplace, and gravity, a minor accounting of it. Or climb, go aerial, show us far-gone. Eyes turn up, sun-drawn, and something shifts, the nerves defining to infinite focus where weight works no more as measure. Whatever weather is here or there hits and saturates eyeballs, the camera's lens; collison is no accident.

3.
It was the leaf roofs that lifted and parted and flew upward in spirals like hair cut as a gift for the woman who lived on the thirteenth floor, who reached out her window and caught these things in her arms before night fell.

4.
Walk around, the attraction in the Midwest is the horizontal. It ought to be advertised. Make your bed here, lie down. Even the low hills recline, decline, into good foam ticking, cotton batting, dirt, straw, down. Look at your feet, the toes upturned. Where are your hands? Behind your head. Or turn on the side, and there's somebody else, hair on the head, on the blades of the shoulders. You can comb the body with your fingertips, roll him over, roll her, he's not sleeping and neither is she. Comb the belly, take the penis between your hands, lick your hands and let the palms swim. There are plenty of holes for water, and whatever grows, grows out of clay, or sand, or the hand.

5.
If the bicycle is painted blue and disappears skyward outside Kalamazoo, it's no different, as far as that goes, from the bicycle painted brown that disappears groundward in southern India. And then you can imagine all the black-painted ones missing at dawn, and the orange ones pulled into volcanic areas or cheap sunsets. Notice how worldwide, atop foot-propelled machinery, because of the easygoingness of it, bodies weave in and out. In and out of *abattoirs*, concrete squares,

the overhangs of edifices and beaded doors, the smooth cuts across gravel, or through the iridescent waste in gutters. Nothing is not camouflaged. Notice how many things fly and evaporate and cannot choose appropriate times to plummet, we're past that, like satellites, outdated, or dipper birds with wire feet, detached from nests, those streaks of color down and dirty in leaves.

6.

It doesn't take much in the way of angular shots to see that the territories of animals, ours, are drawn in with sails, planks, high-rises, poles, slabs, rock faces, bricks, sheathing, siding, and how can we climb the cliff walls to roofs where whatever our two or four feet walk on is ground and whatever our feet or hands hold is sky?

7.

Between the opera and the Mars game, how much empty space is there for a woman to traverse, without kits and oxygen? It could be atomic space, or cellular, the gaps nerve to nerve, really reckless. There are a number of feet of hammered floor, that's for sure, or half a block, or two-mile circuits to town, three hours to whichever lake, and then to the edge of its water. Or there's the slow flight in childbirth, low along the islands of Japan, a long labor, all morning behind the eye, companion to leaf-wing butterflies, the bluest ones, approaching sunlit inlets, ascending volcanic slopes, more and more blue between the gingko leaves in green upland gardens.

8.

Now that magic with its verifiable mayhem has flown the coop—lost the coup, as the insiders say—it's no surprise that a couple of Rhode Island Red Hens collaborate on architectural designs for the roofs over their heads, mansard or hiproof, cathedral, insisting on skylights, the better to manage their escapes nightly, into remote star-places where they crow unnaturally and roll eggs into whirlwinds seen as mist and swamp light, or pale yolks adrift.

9.

The water table, there it is, although there is no fire floor or earth bed, not yet. Here's an air mattress. Won't you lie down? The water table lies, or stands, under the field, and it can be a surprise how close to the surface the table (never set, it's heaped) is buried, sometimes a plow-blade's depth. The metal scrapes water and the tractor sways on float-ing ground where crayfish have built up gray chunk chimneys. Apart-ments are mortared, cellars sink and fill with duckweed and water plan-tain. Are you rested? How long did you sleep? You can put your elbows on the table. It is floral and amoral and porous to the elements, the touch of everything.

10.
Out of the trees, from overhead, those multicolored embroiled branches, and also from under the trunk's shade rises and settles all the see-through-it air you can imagine, and it is darker than the air at the back of the mouth, but it swirls like that, intimate, the privacy of a global thing. It is ours, the same as dust, its palm-size touch, and the clasp in the throat is an aching, a moan, the sound of a cough, and here is the smoothing out of a withering, and the withering itself, and paper folding back, the collapse, the drench of sweat, another press of leaves.

On Action: One Word after Another

1.
It's calm, and the slowest doves angle up from the road onto wires, slow rises. Everything stalls, and they're safe, it's a sort of safety, half-lidded, a lullaby before the tires of cars and kids who aim to throw these things off. The doves are gray, so gray one boy thinks they'll disappear anyway into weeds, the plain space opposite sky. He's been there and no one missed him.

2.
The skeleton truck pulled up, jammed, they could drive and walk like anybody else, and one of them at the front door held the key to the door between bone fingers. We recognized the key, its three chiseled teeth, that's how plain the situation was, and was before, and after.

3.
Dead wood burns, it passes the time, good for wood. No outlineable shapes hold up in fire, not tongues, hands, or fingers, not lips or belly, none of that. The refusals of metaphor, at least a few, are dead cer-tainties, as consoling as, alternatively, the animations of cliché: honey-moon, for instance—*lune de miel*—such a shape, full or crescent, the hive

emptied out all over it, fingers in it, flower-work, feet-flying pollen, and then, now, the lovers' feet, and then, too, the sweet hands, fingers, tongues on each other's bodies, the niches of honey, excess, sun, night, flower, dream, it's all there. We might as well be on the moon, where nothing burns.

4.

Sixteen, no fifteen, children are lined up against the garden wall, one child is outstanding, rage in hand—see?—that thing in hand? One is counting, one won't, the handy one farmed out. One says, me, too. The next buckles her shoe, fear afoot, one or two's crayon boots are scrawled by the garden wall. One bows, one hangs low, one sings lowly lowly lowly. One and another shoot the breeze, and that takes two more. They're sick of the garden, they say, and won't cry.

5.

Here you can read the real end of all things. Two barns on the white horizon drop to nothing. A fog rises in the house, flows slow out the refrigerator door, and then a roiling blast-force wind, transparent, silent, hits and cracks the plaster, and the firemen out there sling hoses with no water at the power plant before all the concrete walls split apart, and like any day, there's nothing to do but work, or walk someplace; so you pick up a pencil, a pear, something for each hand for no reason.

6.

It's always March when talk, not logic, flies in the face of things. There's ice on the driveway. How is it there with you? Ice crazes when geese walk. They live in the field, the garden, the drive. They stand on the asphalt slope, they slide, and they hold those gray wings wide. These are escapades, nobody flies.

7.

Suppose the woman behind the hat, that straw hat with the rip through the brim, turned around without warning and, looking at nobody, tore it off and tore it in half as best she could and threw it down. And took her shirt with the blue glass buttons, and ripped it open, and threw that down, too, over the pieces of the hat. And drew up her skirt and pulled at its blue fabric, with some difficulty, but she kept at it until the skirt split to the waist, and then the button at the waistband was no problem. After that she gripped the leg holes of her underpants and ripped those apart, the seam at the elasticized waist snapping at the stitching, and since she was not wearing shoes, that was it. She could turn around, and step off, whichever way she'd intended to begin with. And don't let anybody walk up now and say there's a simple explanation, or a complicated one either.

8.
You said you skipped the Atlantic and came down hard in the field—*downtrodden*, you said, but aren't the words *uplifted, ditched?* Your legs shone silver from street dust, and the blood on your face, from your left forearm, might have cooled someone not dreaming, but so few, you said, are not dreaming. It is terrible how you refuse refreshment, and speak too fast in all those languages. You will not take the extra steps to the woods, but what worse collapse could there be in shade? Before you go back, at least comb your hair and wash your arms in the River Raisin, where it falls over three green rocks. There is jewelweed there, related to touch-me-not, but you could.

9.
She's the one who sits on the edge of the windowsill and calls down: you forgot your underwear. Or more likely, she asks, because she likes the drum of the words in her head: what will you do when the doom is done? Or sometimes, she says, because it's the truth: you're the one in the uniform, the one I pulled down from the podium and kissed, the one who finally laughed before the trees fell and the program ended.

10.
They are sticks and stones, wrapped, and in your arms, you drop off the decorations, there are downfalls of veils and heat-pressed white, plastic flowers and toweling and rags, mostly rags. You have littered the ocean, you lift them and fly them and lay them out, broken things strewn after storm; and although there has been no storm, and no one has any memory of a storm, we have the words for it now.

John Barth

John Barth was born in 1930 on the eastern shore of Maryland. He was educated at Johns Hopkins University and has taught at Penn State University, SUNY Buffalo, and in the writing seminars of Johns Hopkins. He is the author of ten novels, two books of short fiction, a book of novellas, and two collections of essays. The novellas collected in Chimera won the National Book Award in 1973; The Floating Opera and Lost in the Funhouse had been nominated in previous years. He is the recipient of many other prizes, among them the F. Scott Fitzgerald Award, the PEN/Malamud Award for Excellence in the Short Story, and a Lannan Lifetime Achievement Award. Retired from teaching, Barth now lives on the banks of Chesapeake Bay in Maryland, the setting for most of his writing.

Barth's earlier book of stories, Lost in the Funhouse, subtitled Fiction for Print, Tape and Live Voice, included the story "Frame Tale," which came with instructions for the reader to cut and construct a mobius strip, a continuous loop of paper where the inside turns into the outside and then back to the inside. Once put together in this manner, the story reads: ONCE UPON A TIME THERE WAS A STORY THAT BEGAN ONCE UPON A TIME THERE WAS A STORY THAT BEGAN and so on, endlessly.

"Click," originally published in the Atlantic Monthly, represents Barth's ongoing fascination with the intersection of storytelling and the ever-evolving means of its transmission. The story, which is about the discovery of a computer disk, is actually the story encrypted on the disk. Through this story, Barth explores the extreme possibilities of the hypertexual nature of the computer and the Internet and reminds us of the intimate relationship between the medium (in this case, a disk) and the message (in this case, the story on the disk). In essence, "Click" is a message-in-the-bottle tale that suggests that the real treasure we search for is the search itself.

Click

"Click?"

So (sans question mark) reads the computer monitor when, in time, "Fred" and "Irma" haul themselves out of bed, wash up a bit, slip back into their undies, and—still nuzzling, patting, chuckling, sighing— go to check their E-mail on Fred's already booted-up machine. Just that single uppercase imperative verb or sound-noun floating midscreen, where normally the desktop would appear, with its icons of their several files: HERS, HIS, SYSTEM, APPLICATIONS, FINANCES, HOUSE STUFF, INTERNET, and ETC (their catchall file). Surprised Irma, having pressed a key to disperse the screen-saver program and repeated aloud the word that oddly then appeared, calls Fred over to check it out, but the house cybercoach is as puzzled thereby as she. Since the thing's onscreen, however, and framed in a bordered box, they take it to be a command or an invitation—anyhow an option button, like SAVE or CANCEL, not merely the name of the sound that their computer mouse makes when . . . well, when clicked.

So they click (Irm does) on <u>Click</u>, and up comes a familiar title, or in this case maybe subtitle—<u>The</u> <u>Hypertextuality</u> <u>of</u> <u>Everyday</u> <u>Life</u>— followed this time by a parenthesized instruction: (*Click on any word of the above*).

"Your turn," declares our Irma. That's not the woman's real name, any more than the man's is Fred; those are their "online" names, in a manner of speaking, for reasons presently to be made clear. Never mind, just now, their "real" names: they would involve us in too much background, personal history, all the things that real names import; we would never get on with the story. Sufficient to say that although these two are unmarried, they're coupled housemates of some years' stand- ing, a pair of Baby Boomer TINKs ("two incomes, no kids") of some eth- nicity or other, not necessarily the same, and profession ditto—but never mind those either. Sufficient to say that what they've just rolled out of the sack from (one of them perhaps more reluctantly than the other) is an extended session of makeup sex after an extended lovers' quarrel, the most serious of their coupleship—a quarrel currently truced but by no means yet resolved and maybe inherently unresolv- able, although they're really working on it, fingers crossed.

A bit of background here, perhaps? That's Fred's uncharacteristic suggestion, to which Irma, uncharacteristically, forces herself to reply, "Nope: Your turn is your turn. On with the story."

And so her friend—partner, mate, whatever—reaches from behind her to the mouse and, kissing her (glossy walnut) hair, clicks on <u>Hyper- textuality</u>. (This parenthesized matter, they agree, is stuff that might be left out of or cut from The Fred and Irma Story—see below—but that they've agreed to leave in, at least for the present.) (In the opinion of one of them, there could be much more of it.) (In the opinion of the other, much less—but never mind.)

No surprise, Fred's selection: <u>Hypertextuality</u> is that (sub)title's obvious topic word, modified by the innocuous-seeming article before it and the homely prepositional phrase after (containing its own unex- otic substantive [<u>Life</u>] with adjectival modifier [<u>Everyday</u>]). This man, one infers correctly, is the sort who gets right down to business, to the meat of the matter. Everybody knows, after all (or believes that he or she knows), what "everyday life" is, different as may be the everyday lives of, say, Kuwaiti oil sheikhs and American felons serving life sentences in maximum-security prisons without possibility of parole (different, for that matter, as may be the everyday lives of FWFs ["friends who fornicate"] when they're at their separate businesses between F'ly Fs). The term "hypertextuality" itself may or may not interest our Fred; he's computer-knowledgeable but not computer-addicted. The phrase "everyday life," however, most certainly doesn't in itself interest him. The fellow's too busy *leading* (perhaps being led by?) his everyday life to be attracted to it as a subject. With the woman it's another story (possibly to come). But precisely because he hasn't associated something as fancy-sounding as "hypertextuality" with something as ordinary as "everyday life," the juxtaposition of the two piques Fred's curiosity. Not impossibly, for the man's no ignoramus (nor is his companion), he hears in it an echo of Sigmund Freud's provocatively titled 1904 essay "The Psychopathology of Everyday Life." Everyday life psychopathological? (Try asking Irma, Fred.) (He will—another time.) Everyday life hypertextual? How so? In what sense? To find out, Fred has clicked on the implied proposition's most prominent but least certain term.

Some (the computer script now declares in effect, along with much of the paragraph above) out of mere orneriness will select one of the phrase's apparently insignificant elements—the <u>The</u>, for example, or the <u>of</u>—as if to say "Gotcha! You said 'Click on any word' . . . " The joke, however, if any, is on them: A good desk dictionary will list at least eight several senses of the homely word "the" in its adjectival function, plus a ninth in its adverbial ("the sooner the better," etc.)—twenty lines of fine-print definition in all, whereas the comparatively technical term just after it, "theanthropic," is nailed down in a mere three and a half. As for "of": no fewer than nineteen several definitions, in twenty-five lines of text, whereas the fancy word "oeuvre," just before it, is dispatched in a line and a half. Try "as," Fred, as in "As for 'of' "; try "for," Irm, or "or": the "simple" words you'll find hardest to define, whereas such technoglossy ones as "hypertextuality" . . .

Well, F and friend have just been shown an example of it, no? The further texts that lie behind any presenting text. Look up (that is, click on) the innocent word "of," and you get a couple hundred words of explanation. Click on any one of those or any one of their several phrases and clauses, such as "phrases and clauses," and get hundreds more. Click on any of *those*, etc. etc.—until, given time and clicks enough, you will have "accessed" virtually the sum of language, the entire expressible world. That's "hypertext," guys, in the sense meant here (there are other senses: see <u>Hypertext</u>): not the literal menus-of-menus and texts-behind-texts that one finds on CD-ROMs and other computer applications but rather the all-but-infinite array of potential explanations, illustrations, associations, glosses and exempla, even stories, that may be said to lie not only behind any verbal formulation but also behind any real-world image, scene, action, interaction. Enough said?

(If so, click on EXIT; otherwise select any one of the four foregoing—image, scene, etc. for further amplification.)

Restless Fred moves to click on action but defers to Irma (their joint mood is, as mentioned, still tentative just now: he's being more deferential than is his wont), who clicks on scene and sees what the Author/Narrator sees as he pens this: a (white adult male right) hand moving a (black MontBlanc Meisterstück 146 fountain) pen (left to right) across the (blue) lines of (three-ring loose-leaf) paper in a (battered old) binder on a (large wooden former grade-school) worktable all but covered with implements and detritus of the writer's trade. (Parenthesized elements in this case = amplifications that might indeed be cut but might instead well be "hypertexted" behind the bare-bones decription, to be accessed on demand, just as yet further amplifictions [not given, but perhaps hypertexted] might lie behind "white," "adult male," "MontBlanc," "Meisterstück," etc.) For example, to mention only some of the more conspicuous items: miscellaneous printed and manuscript pages, (thermal) coffee mug (of a certain design) on (cork) coaster, (annotated) desk calendar (displaying MAY), notebooks and notepads, the aforeconsulted (*American Heritage*) desk dictionary open to the "the" page (1,333) on its (intricately hand-carved Indian) table stand, (Panasonic autostop electric) pencil sharpener (in need of emptying), (Sunbeam digital) clock (reading 9:47 A.M.), (AT&T 5500 cordless) telephone (in place on base unit), Kleenex box (ScotTissue, actually) half full (half empty?) . . . etc. Beyond the table is the workroom's farther wall: two (curtained and venetian-blinded double-hung) windows, between them a (three-shelf) bookcase (not quite filled with books, framed photos, and knick-knacks and) topped by a wall mirror. The mirror (left of center) gives back a view not of the viewer—fortunately, or we'd never get out of the loop and on with the story—but of the workroom door (now closed against interruption) in the wall behind. (The two windows are closed, their figured curtains tied back, their blinds raised. Through them one sees first the green tops of foundation shrubbery [from which Irm infers, correctly, that the room is on the ground floor], and then assorted trees [L] and a sward of lawn [R] in the middle distance, beyond which lies a substantial body of [currently gray] water. Two [wooded] points of land can be seen extending into this waterway from the right-hand window's right-hand side, the first perhaps half a mile distant, an [uncamouflaged] goose blind at its outer end, the second perhaps a mile distant and all but obscured now by a light drizzle that also blurs the yet-more-distant horizontal where [gray] water meets [gray] sky.

(*Click on any of these items, including those in brackets.*)

But "Enough already," says nudgy Fred, and he commandeers the mouse to click on <u>action</u>, whereupon some of the leaves on some of those trees move slightly in some breeze from some direction, the water surface ripples, and across it a large waterfowl flaps languidly left to right, just clearing some sort of orange marker-float out there on his or her way . . . upstream, one reasonably supposes, given that the stretch beyond that bird and those two points seems to be open water.

"That's action?" Fred scoffs, and moves to click again, but determined Irma stays his mouse-hand with her free right (Irm's a south-paw) while she registers yet a few further details. Atop that bookcase, for example (and therefore doubled in the mirror), are (L to R:) a (ceramic-based) lamp, the carapace of a (medium-size horeshoe) crab, and a (Lucite-box-framed) photograph of three (well-dressed) people (L to R: an elderly man, a middle-aged man, and a younger woman) in (animated) conversation (at some sort of social function).

(*Click on any detail, parenthesized or non-, in this scene.*)

Irma springs for <u>well-dressed</u>—not nearly specific enough, by her lights, as a description of three people "at some sort of social function" (!) in the photograph on the bookcase in the not yet fully identified scene on their computer's video-display terminal. With a really quite commendable effort of will, Fred restrains his impulse to utter some exasperated imprecation and snatch the freaking mouse from his freaking partner to freaking click on <u>Fast</u> Freaking <u>Forward</u>, <u>On With the Story</u>, EXIT, QUIT, <u>Whatever</u>. Instead he busses again his lover's (glossy) (walnut) hair, bids her "Have fun; I'll be futzing around outside, okay?" and (having slipped into jeans and T-shirt) clicks with his feet, so to speak, on the scene beyond his own workroom window.

Which twilit scene happens to be a small suburban back yard near the edge of the nation's troubled capital city, where this occasionally dysfunctional pair pursue their separate occupations: Mark the Expe-diter, as he has lately come to call himself; Valerie the Enhancer, ditto. Those are their "real" given names, if not really the real names of their jobs, and with the reader's permission (because all these digressions, suspensions, parentheses, and brackets are setting this Narrator's teeth on edge as well as Mark's) we'll just follow him out there for a bit while Val explores to her still-bruised heart's content the hypertextuality of everyday life.

Okay. How they got into that "Fred and Irma" business (Mark and I can reconstruct less distractedly now, as he waves to a neighbor lady and idly deadheads a few finished rhododendron blooms along their open side porch) was as follows: They having pretty well burned out, through this late-May Sunday, their scorching quarrel of the day before (enough, anyhow, to make and eat together a weary but entirely civil dinner), after cleanup Mark volunteered to show Valerie, as he had several times previously promised, some things he'd lately learned about accessing the Internet for purposes other than E-mail: more specifically, about navigating the World Wide Web (WWW), and in particular (Valerie being Valerie, Mark Mark) about the deployment of "bookmarks" as shortcuts through that electronic labyrinth, the black hole of leisure and very antidote to spare time. Mark is, as aforenoted, no computer freak; the PC in his Expediter's office, their Macintosh at home, are tools, not toys, more versatile than fax machine and phone but more time-expensive, too, and—like dictionaries, encyclopedias, and hardware stores (this last in Mark's case; substitute department stores and supermarkets in Val's)—easier to get into than out of. Tactfully, tactfully (by his lights, anyhow) (the only lights he can finally steer by)—for they really were and still are burned, and their armistice is as fragile as it is heartfelt—he led her through the flashy home page of their Web-server program, actually encouraging her to sidetrack here and there in the What's New? and What's Cool? departments (she trying just as determinedly to blind her peripheral vision, as it were, and walk straight down the aisles, as it were, of those enticing menus) and then sampling a curious Web site that he had "bookmarked" two days earlier, before their disastrous Saturday excursion to the National Aquarium, in Baltimore.

    http://www.epiphs.art, it was addressed: the home page of an anonymous oddball (Net-named "CNG") who offered a shifting menu of what he or she called "electronic epiphanies," or "E-piphs." On the Friday, that menu had comprised three entrées: 1) <u>Infinite Regression v. All but Interminable Digression</u>, 2) "<u>Flower in the Crannied Wall</u>," and 3) <u>The Hypertextuality of Everyday Life</u>. Mark had clicked on the curious-sounding second option and downloaded a spiel that at first interested but soon bored him, having to do with the relation between a short poem by Tennyson—

Flower in the crannied wall,
I pluck you out of the crannies.
I hold you here, root and all, in my hand.
Little flower—but *if* I could understand
What you are, root and all, and all in all,
I should know what God and man is.

—and the virtually endless reticulations of the World Wide Web. This
time (that is, on this postmeridianal, postprandial, post-quarrel but
ante-makeup-sexual Sunday) the menu read 1) <u>The Coastline Measurement Problem and the Web</u>, 2) "<u>The Marquise went out at five</u>" (CNG
seemed to favor quotations as second entries; this one was familiar to
neither of our characters), and 3) <u>The Hypertextuality of Everyday Life</u>.
That third item being the only carry-over, M suggested they see what it
was. V clicked on it—the entire title, as no option was then offered to
select from among its component terms—and they found themselves
involved in a bit of interactive "E-fiction" called "<u>Fred</u> and <u>Irma</u> <u>Go</u>
<u>Shopping</u>," of which I'll make the same short work that they did.

Onscreen the underlined items were "hot"—that is, highlighted as
hypertext links to be clicked on as the interacting reader chose.
Methodical Mark would have started with <u>Fred</u> and worked his way L
to R, but Valerie, left-handing the mouse, went straight for <u>Irma</u>:

> Irma V., 43, <u>art-school</u> graduate, <u>divorced</u>, <u>no children</u>, cur-
> rently employed as <u>enhancer</u> by small but thriving <u>graphics firm</u> in
> <u>Annapolis MD</u> while preparing show of her own computer-
> inspired <u>fractal art</u> for small but well-regarded <u>gallery</u> in <u>Baltimore</u>.
> Commutes to work from modest but comfortable and <u>well-
> appointed rowhouse</u> in latter city's <u>Bolton Hill</u> neighborhood, 2
> doors up from her <u>latest</u> lover, <u>Fred M.</u>
> (<u>more</u> on Irma) (<u>on</u> with story)

"My turn?" Mark had asked at this point, and clicked on <u>Fred M.</u>
before Valerie could choose from among <u>divorced</u>, <u>no children</u>,
<u>enhancer</u>, <u>well-appointed rowhouse</u>, <u>latest</u>, and <u>more</u>.

> Fred M., <u>software expediter</u> and <u>current</u> lover of <u>Irma V.</u>
> (<u>more</u> on Fred) (<u>on</u> with story)

"That's the ticket," in Mark's opinion: "Who cares how old the
stud is or where he majored in what? On with their story already."

"My friend the Expediter," Val had murmured warningly, having raised her free hand at his "Who cares?" Whereat her friend the Expediter (it was from here that they borrowed those job titles for themselves; Valerie in fact does interior design and decoration for a suburban D.C. housing developer; Mark, a not-yet-successful novelist, writes capsule texts on everything under the sun for a CD-ROM operation in College Park, distilling masses of info into style-free paragraphs of a couple hundred words), duly warned, had replied, "Sorry there: Enhance, enhance."

But she had humored him by clicking on <u>on</u>, whereupon the title reappeared with only its last term now highlighted: "Fred and Irma <u>Go Shopping</u>."

"Off we go," had invited M. But when the clicked link called up a three-option menu—<u>Department Store</u>, <u>Supermarket</u>, <u>Other</u>—V had said "Uh-oh," and even Mark had recognized the too-perilous analogy to their debacle of the day before. Expediter and Enhancer in <u>Supermarket</u>, he with grocery list in one hand, pencil in other, and eye on watch, she already examining the (unlisted) radicchio and improvising new menu plans down the line . . .

"Unh-unh," he had agreed, and kissed her mouse-hand, then her mouth, then her throat. By unspoken agreement, bedward they'd headed, leaving the Mac to its screen-saver program (tropical fish, with bubbly sound effects). Somewhile later Valerie/Irma, re-undied, had returned to check for E-mail; the marine fauna dispersed into cyberspace; there floated <u>Click</u> in place of CNG's unpursued interactive E-tale—and here we all are.

Rather, here's Valerie at Mark's workstation in their (detached suburban) house (V's studio is across the hall; unlike those FWFs Irma and Fred, our couple are committed [though unsanctified and unlegalized] life partners, each with half equity in their jointly owned [commodious, well-appointed, 1960s-vintage] split-level in Silver Spring [MD]), and here are Mark and I, out on the dusky porch, deadheading the rhodos while thinking hard and more or less in sync about certain similarities among 1) the sore subject of their Saturday set-to, 2) a certain aspect of their recent makeup sex, 3) the so-called Coastline Measurement Problem aforeoptioned by CNG, 4) an analogous problem or aspect of storytelling, and 5) how it is, after all, to be a self, not on the World Wide Web but in the wide web of the world. Can M think hard about five things at once? He can, more or less expeditiously, when his attention's engaged, plus 6) Zeno's

famous paradox of Achilles and the Tortoise, plus 7) the difference
between Socrates' trances and the Buddha's. Our chap is nothing if
not efficient—a phrase worth pondering—and I'm enhancing his effi-
ciency as worst I can, by impeding it. Valerie, meanwhile (at my off-
screen prodding), has reluctantly torn her attention away from that
photograph on that bookshelf in that creekside scriptorium in that
onscreen scene hypertexted behind the word "scene" in the definition hypertexted behind <u>Hypertextuality</u> in CNG's menu option 3)
<u>The Hypertextuality of Everyday Life</u>, itself hypertexted the second
time up behind the word <u>Click</u>. The twenty-year-old wedding-recep-
tion photo, she has learned it is, of (present) Narrator with (present)
wife and (late) father at (post-) wedding do for (now divorced) daughter and (then) new son-in-law—and nothing accessible beyond. Inter-
activity is one thing, restless reader; prying's another. Having lingered
briefly on the <u>shrub</u> outside the <u>RH window</u> (*Viburnum burkwoodii*:
grows to 6 ft [but here cropped to 4 for the sake of view and ventila-
tion], clusters 3 in. wide, blooms in spring, <u>zone 4</u>, and it's a lucky
wonder her professional eye didn't fix on those <u>figured curtains</u>, or
we'd never have gotten her outside) and then on that <u>waterfowl</u>
(Great Blue Heron [*Ardea herodias*, not <u>*Coerulea*</u>]) flapping languidly
<u>up-creek</u> (west fork of <u>Langford,</u> off the <u>Chester River</u>, off <u>Chesa-
peake Bay</u>, on Maryland's <u>Eastern Shore</u>, where <u>Narrator</u> pens these
words as he has penned <u>many others</u>), she's "progressing" unhur-
riedly toward those two intriguing <u>points of land</u> in the farther distance but can't resist clicking en route on that orange <u>market-float</u>
out yonder near the creek channel.

> Marks an <u>eel pot</u>, 1 of 50 deployed in this particular tidal creek at
> this particular season by waterman <u>Travis Pritchett</u> of nearby <u>Rock
> Hall MD</u> in pursuit, so to speak, of "elvers": young <u>eels</u> born thou-
> sands of miles hence in the <u>Sargasso Sea</u> and now thronging
> <u>instinctively</u> back to the very same <u>freshwater tributaries of the
> Chesapeake</u> from which their parents migrated several years earlier
> to <u>spawn</u> them in midocean: one of nature's most mysterious and
> powerful <u>reproductive phenomena.</u> The eels among Pritchett's
> catch will be <u>processed</u> locally for <u>marketing</u> either as <u>seafood</u> in
> <u>Europe</u> and <u>Japan</u> or as <u>crab</u> bait for <u>Chesapeake watermen</u> later
> in the season.

Travel-loving Val goes for <u>Sargasso Sea</u>, and there we'll leave her to
circulate indefinitely with the spawning eels and <u>other denizens of the</u>

<u>Sargassum</u> while we click on item 1) some distance above: <u>the sore sub-ject of their Saturday set-to.</u>

They love and cherish each other, this pair. Although neither is a physical knockout, each regards the other and her- or him-self as satis-factorily attractive in face and form. Although neither can be called outstanding in his or her profession, both are entirely competent, and neither is particularly career-ambitious in her or his salaried job. Both enjoy their work and take an interest in their partner's. Most impor-tant, perhaps, although neither has a history of successful long-term relations with significant others, both have enough experience, insight, and humility to have smoothed their rougher edges, tempered their temperaments, developed their reciprocal forbearance, and in general recognized that at their ages and stages neither is likely to do better than he or she has currently done in the mate-finding way; indeed, that despite their <u>sundry differences</u> (at least some of which they've learned to regard as compensations for each other's short-comings: see below), they are fortunately well matched in disposition, taste, and values. Neither drinks more than an occasional glass of wine at dinner, or smokes tobacco, or sleeps around, or fancies house pets; both are borderline vegetarian, environmentally concerned, morally serious but unsanctimonious secular unenthusiastic Democ-rats. Mark has perhaps the quicker intelligence, the duller sensibility, the more various knowledge; Valerie perhaps the deeper understand-ing, the readier human insight, the sounder education. They've never quarreled over sex or money. Both wish they had children, but neither finally wants them. (<u>etc.</u>—although that's really enough <u>background</u> for <u>their Saturday set-to</u>, no?)

They do have differences, of course: M enjoys socializing with oth-ers more than V does; she enjoys traveling more than he. He's more liberal (or less frugal) with money; she's more generous in the good-works way. He's less ready to take offense, but also slower to put their occasional tiffs behind him. She leaves closet and cabinet doors ajar and will not learn how to load their dishwasher properly (by *his* stan-dards) (and the user's manual's); he wears his socks and underwear for two days before changing (turning his briefs inside out the second day) and often makes no effort to stifle his burps and farts when it's just the two of them. (<u>etc.</u>, although [etc.]) These lapses or anyhow dishar-monies they've learned to live with, by and large. The difference that really drives each up her or his wall is the one herein amply hinted at already, if scarcely yet demonstrated: at its mildest, a tease- or sighprovoker, a prompter of rolled eyes and of fingertips drummed on dashboard, chair arm, desk- or thigh-top; at its sorest . . .

<u>Saturday</u>. Their week's official work done and essential house chores attended to, they had planned a drive up to nearby Baltimore to tour that city's Inner Harbor development, which they hadn't done in a while, and in particular the National Aquarium, which they'd never. After a not unreasonable detour to an upscale dry-goods emporium in the vast shopping complex at Four Corners, a quick shot from their house, where Val really did need to check patterns and prices of a certain sort of figured drapery material for a job in the works (and, having done so, pointed out to Mark that there across the mall was a Radio Shack outlet where he could conveniently pick up the whatchamacallit-adapter that he, not she, insisted they needed for their sound system's FM antenna [while she popped into the next-door Hallmark place for just a sec to replenish their supply of oddball greeting cards, which was running low]), they zipped from the D.C. Beltway up I-95 to Baltimore and reached Harbor Place in time for a pickup lunch about an hour past noon (no matter, as they'd had a latish breakfast)—an hour and a half past noon, more like, since the main parking lots were full by that time, as Mark had fretfully predicted, and so they had to park (quite) a few blocks away, and it wouldn't've made sense not to take a quick look-see at the new Oriole Park at Camden Yards stadium that was such a hit with baseball fans and civic-architecture buffs alike, inasmuch as there it stood between their parking garage and the harbor, and since their objective, after all (she reminded him when he put on his Fidget Face), wasn't to grab a sandwich, see a fish, and bolt for home but to *tour* Harbor Place, right? Which really meant the city's harbor area, which surely included the erstwhile haunts of Babe Ruth and Edgar Allan Poe. They weren't on a timetable, for pity's sake!

Agreed, agreed—but he *was* a touch hungry, was Mr. Mark, and therefore maybe a touch off his feed, as it were, especially after that unscheduled and extended stop at Four Corners; and it was to be expected that the ticket line at the Aquarium might well be considerable, the day being both so fine and so advanced . . .

"So we'll catch the flight flick at the IMAX theater in the Science Center instead," Val verbally shrugged, "or I'll stand in the Aquarium line while you fetch us something from the food pavilion, and then you stand while I do The Nature Company. What's the problem?"

The problem, in Mark's ever-warmer opinion, was—rather, the problems were—that *a)* this constant sidetracking, this what's-the-rush digression, can take the edge off the main event by the time one gets to it, the way some restaurants lay on so many introductory courses and side dishes that one has no appetite for the entrée, or the way fore-play can sometimes be so protracted that (etc.). Having no timetable or deadlines doesn't mean having no agenda or priorities, wouldn't she agree? And *b)* it wasn't as if this were just something that happened to happen today, or he'd have no grounds to grouse; it was the way cer-tain people went at *everything*, from leaving for work in the morning to telling an anecdote. How often had he waited in their Volvo wagon to get going in time to drop her off at her Metro stop on the way to his office and finally come back into the house and found her with one earring and one shoe on, making an impulsive last-minute phone call while simultaneously revising her DO list with one hand and rummag-ing in her purse with the other? (Valerie is a whiz at cradling the phone between ear and shoulder, a trick Mark can't manage even with one of those gizmos designed for the purpose.) How often had he been obliged to remind her, or to fight the urge to remind her, in mid-nar-rative in mid-dinner party, that the point of her story-in-regress was her little niece's *response* to what Val's sister's husband's mother had said when the tot had walked in on her in the guest-bath shower stall, not what that widow lady's new Cuban-American boyfriend (whom she hadn't even met yet at the time of the incident) apparently does for a living? and c) . . .

But he never reached c) (*click on it if you're curious*), because by this time V was giving as good as she got, right there on the promenade under the old *USS Constellation's* bowsprit, where their progress toward the distant tail of the National Aquarium ticket queue caesura'd for this exchange. As for *a)*, damn it to hell, if in his (wrong-headed) opinion she was a Gemini who preferred hors d'oeuvres to entrées both at table and (as he had more than once intimated) in bed, then *he* was a bullheaded whambamthankyouma'amer of a Tau-rus whose idea of foreplay was three minutes of heavyweight humping to ejaculation instead of two; and *b)* because he himself has his hands full thinking and breathing simultaneously, he couldn't imagine any-one's doing five things at once better than he could manage one; for the reason that c) . . .

But she never reached c), for the reason that b) (now b1)) reminded her that b2) his idea of a joke was the punch line, his idea of a who-dunit the last page, revealing who done it (no wonder he couldn't place his Middle-less novels even with an agent, much less with a publisher); and *a2)* if she might presume to back up a bit, now that it occurred to her, his idea of a full agenda was a single item, his top priority always and only the bottom line, his eternal (and infernal) *Let's get on with the story* in fact a *Let's get* done *with the story,* for the reason that—*b3),* she guessed, or maybe *a3),* who gave a damn?—his idea of living life was the same, *Let's get done with it,* and every time she saw him ready and fidgeting in the car a full ten minutes earlier than he knew as well as she they needed to leave for work, she was tempted to suggest that they drive straight to the funeral parlor instead and *get done with it* (etc., okay? On to the freaking fish already!).

But they never reached the FF ticket line, far less the marine exhibits themselves, and that's a pity, inasmuch as in the two-million-plus recirculating gallons of scrupulously monitored exhibit water in the National Aquarium's numerous tanks and pools are to be found some 10,000 aquatic animals (eels included), concerning every one of which much of natural-historical interest might be said. Under the volatile circumstances, however, it is no doubt as well they didn't, for how could they imaginably have moved and paused harmoniously through the exhibits (Valerie tranced at the very first of them, Mark glancing already to see what's next, and next after that) without reopening their quarrel? Which quarrel, mind, was still in noisy progress, if that's the right word, there under the *Constellation's* mighty bowsprit—which bowsprit, at the time I tell of, extended halfway across the promenade from the vessel's prow toward the second floor Indian restaurant above the first-floor Greek one in Harbor Place's Pratt Street pavilion, but which at the time of this telling is alas no longer there, nor are those restaurants, nor is the formidable old warship whose bow that bowsprit sprits, or spritted, said vessel having been removed indefinitely for a much-needed, long-overdue, and staggeringly expensive major overhaul—to the tsking amusement of passersby (the lovers' spectacular, hang-it-all-out quarrel, I mean, of course, not the *Constellation's* shifting to some marine-repair limbo) including Yours Truly, who happened just then to be passing by and sympathetically so saw and heard them, or a couple not unlike them, toe-to-toeing it, and who then or subsequently was inspired to imagine (etc.).

Embarrassed, wasted, desperate, and sore, tear-faced Valerie anon turned her back on the dear, congenitally blinkered bastard whom she so loves and just then despised and stomped off back toward the Light Street food pavilion and their parking garage, no objective in mind except breathing space and weeping room. Mark was damned if he'd go chasing after the beloved, indispensable, impossible, darling bitch, but he did so after all, sort of; anyhow he trudged off in the same general direction, but made himself pause—Valerie-like, though in part to spite her—to half attend a juggling act in progress at the promenade's central plaza, where street musicians and performers entertain. Although he was as aware as was V (and no less alarmed) that the heavy artillery just fired could never be unfired, and that it had perilously, perhaps mortally, wounded their connection, he nonetheless registered with glum admiration the jugglers' so-skillful routine: their incremental accumulation of difficulties and complications at a pace adroitly timed to maximize dramatic effect without straining audience attention past the point of diminishing returns, a business as tricky in its way as the juggling itself—and now he couldn't refind Valerie among the promenaders. Well, there was The Nature Company yonder; she had mentioned that. And beyond it were the food concessions; she must have been as hungry by then as he, but probably as appetiteless, too, from their wring-out. And somewhere beyond or among those concessions were the public restrooms, whereto she might have retreated to collect herself (V is better than M at self-collection), and beyond them the parking ramp. Did she have her car keys? Probably, in her purse; anyhow there were spares in a magnetic holder under the rear bumper brace. Would she drive off without him, for spite? He doubted it, although she seemed more hurt and angry than he'd ever known her to be; anyhow, the lot ticket was in his wallet—not that she mightn't pay the hefty lost-ticket fee just to strand him, or, more likely, just to get out of there, with no thought of him either way. Most probably, however, she would collapse in furious tears in the Volvo's passenger seat, poor sweetheart, and then lay into him with more of her inexcusable even if not wholly off-the-mark insults when he tried to make peace with her, the bitch.

Well, she wasn't in The Nature Company, where among the coruscating geodes and "Save the Rain Forest" stuff his attention was caught by one of those illuminated flat-projection Earth-map clocks that show which parts of the planet are currently daylit and which in darkness (the East Coast of North America was just then correctly mid-afternoonish; dusk was racing across Asia Minor, dawn approaching Kamchatka and Polynesia). What (momentarily) arrested him in this instance was not that vertiginous reminder of onstreaming time and the world's all-at-onceness but rather the profusion of continental coastlines, necessarily much stylized in so small-scale a rendering but considerably articulated all the same. Chesapeake Bay, for example (180-some miles in straight-line length, but with upwards of 9,600 miles of tidal shoreline in its forty major rivers and their all but innumerable creeks and coves), was a simple small nick up there between

Washington and Philadelphia, yet quite distinguishable in shape and position from Delaware Bay, just above it; even the Delmarva Peninsula, between them, no bigger here than a grain of rice, had overall its characteristic sand-flea shape. Framed nearby, as if to invite speculation on the contrast, was a large-scale, fine-grained aerial-photo map of Baltimore's Inner Harbor, every pier and building sharply resolved, including the no-longer-present-as-I-write-this *Constellation*. One could distinguish not only individual small watercraft paddling about or moored at the harbor bulkheads but their occupants as well, and strollers like varicolored sand grains on the promenade.

One could not, however (Mark duly reflected, looking now for the exit to the food court and/or for a glimpse of Valerie's . . . yellow blouse, was it? Yes, he was almost certain: her yellow watchamacallit blouse with those thingamajigs on it and either a white skirt or white culottes, he couldn't recall which and saw no sign of either), even with so fine a resolution, distinguish male from female, for example, or black from white from Asian, much less identify himself and Valerie having it out under the warship's bowsprit if they'd happened to be there doing that at that moment, much less yet see the thingamabobs on her watchamacallits and much less yet the individual whatsits on each thingamabob (etc.)—any more than the most finely drawn map of the Chesapeake could show every barnacle on every pile of every pier on every creeklet (etc.): the famous Coastline Measurement Problem aforereferred to, in terms whereof the estuary's shore length could as well be put at 96 million miles as 9,600 (etc.). Which all led him to, but not yet across, the verge of recognizing . . .

Yellow blouse? Yes, out there by the Polish-sausage stand, but minus thingamajiggies and blousing a red-faced matron whose steatopygous buttocks were hugely sheathed in pink cotton warm-up pants (though there might, to be sure, he reminded himself, be a truly saintly spirit under all that [maybe helplessly genetic] grossness). *No Middles to his novels,* V had told him! His eye ever on the destination, not the getting there! Already figuring the server's tip while she lingered over the appetizer! No greater evidence of the degree of Pal Val's present pissed-offness than that she had been sidetracked neither in The Nature Company, as even he had briefly been, nor in the food court (where she would normally have been provisioning the pair of them, bless her, with goodies both for present consumption and for future enjoyment at home), nor on the pedestrian overpass to the parking lot, where in other circumstances she was entirely capable of dawdling to contemplate at length the

vehicular traffic below, the cumulus formations overhead, the observation elevators up-and-downing the Hyatt Regency façade nearby.
Unless she had indeed withdrawn into a women's room (he had forgotten to locate the WCs; couldn't've done anything in that precinct
anyhow except dumbly stand by), she must have beelined for the car,
as did he now finally.

No Valerie. Well, she was more liable than he to forget the level
and pillar numbers of their parking slot. Not impossibly, in her present
troubled state, she was wandering the ramps in a weepy rage. Plenty
troubled himself, he walked up one level and down one, gave up the
search as counterproductive, leaned against the Volvo's tailgate for
some minutes, arms crossed, and then trudged back, *faute de mieux,*
toward the walkway/footbridge/overpass/whatever. Halfway across it
he stopped, disconsolate, and simply stood—facing uptown, as it happened, but really seeing nothing beyond his distress.

Which let's consider himwith for just a paragraph. A physically
healthy, mentally sound, well-educated, (usually) well-fed, comfortably
housed and clothed, gainfully employed, not unattractive early-fortyish
middle-class male WASP American is at least temporarily on the outs
with his housemate/girlfriend, a comparably advantaged and not unattractive professional who has declared her opinion that he hasn't the
talent to achieve his heart-of-hearts career aim and that this deficit is of
a piece with a certain general characteristic of his that she finds objec-
tionable. So Mr. Mark's pride is bruised, his self-respect ruffled, the
future of his closest and most valued personal relationship uncertain
indeed. *So what?* he has asked himself before any of us can ask him. The
world comprises approximately 4.7 zillion more mattersome matters,
from saving the tropical rain forests to finding money enough in the
chaotic post-Soviet Russian economy to bring that country's fiscally
stranded cosmonauts back to Earth. Not that love and loss, or com-
mitment and (potential) estrangement, aren't serious even among
Volvo-driving yuppies, but really . . . What of real consequence is at
stake here? If this were fiction (the wannabe writer asked himself), a
made-up story, why should anyone give a damn?

Well, it *wasn't* fiction from Mark's perspective, although out of
aspirant-professional habit he couldn't help considering (as he
resumed his troubled path-retracement back to and through the Light
Street pavilion in search of his dear damned Valerie) how, if it were, it
ought properly to end. Reconciliation? On what terms? Uneasy
armistice? Virtual divorce? In each case signifying what of interest to a
reader who presumes the characters and situation to be imaginary?

From *our* point of view, of course, they *are* imaginary, and so these questions immediately apply (in a proper story they would never have come up; bear in mind that it was heart-hurt Mark who raised them) and shall be duly though not immediately addressed. Even their allegedly Middle-challenged poser, however, understood—as he rescanned in vain the food concessions and monitored for a fruitless while the traffic to and from the women's room after availing himself of the men's—that more's at stake here than the ups and downs of early-middle-aged Baby Boomer love. Not until "tomorrow" (the <u>Sun</u> following this sore <u>Sat</u>) will CNG's interactive E-fiction serendipitously supply the terms "Expediter" and "Enhancer" to shorthand the characterological differences that erupted under the *Constellation's* awesome bowsprit; but already back there on the footbridge Mark sensed that the conflict here is larger than any temperamental incompatibility between Fred and Irma, or himself and Val: it's between fundamentally opposite views of and modes of dealing with the infinitely complex nature of reality.

Valerie sensed that too; she was, indeed, already deep into the pondering thereof when, almost simultaneously, she espied him approaching from the second-level fooderies, and he her at a railing-side table on the open deck out there overlooking the promenade. Far from roaming the ramps in a weepy blind rage, or storming off alone in the Volvo (Val's better than Mark, we remember, at shrugging off their infrequent blowups; he tends to forget that and to project from his own distress), our yellow-bloused Enhancer, her chair tipped back and feet propped on the balcony rail, was finishing off a chocolate-chocolate-chip frozen-yogurt waffle cone while simultaneously *a)* teaching her sumbitch lover a lesson by neither fleeing nor chasing after him, *b)* facilitating their reunion by staying put, as her mother had taught her to do in little-girlhood if "lost" in, say, a department store or supermarket, and *c)* calming her still-roused adrenaline with a spot of yogurt while keeping an eye out for friend M and at the same time considering, in a preliminary way, his criticisms of her and the differences, as she saw them, between Socrates' famous occasional "trances," the Buddha's, and her own. They had in common, those trances, a self-forgetfulness, a putting of circumambient busyness on hold in favor of extraordinary concentration. But the Buddha under the bo tree was transcendentally *meditating,* thinking *about* nothing in particular while subsuming his ego-self into the cosmic "Buddha self"; Socrates, tranced in the agora or come upon by his protégés stock-still in some Athenian side street, was strenuously *contemplating,* presumably in finely honed logical terms, such uppercase concepts as Knowledge,

Reality, Justice, and Virtue. She, however, beguiled indefinitely by . . .
by the hypertextuality of everyday life, we might as well say, as encountered in the very first fish tank in the National Aquarium, or in the
book beside the book upshelf from the book that she had gone to fetch
from the library stacks, or on the counter across from the counter in
the department en route to the department that she had been vectored
toward in the department store downplaza from the supermarket that
she was finally aiming for, was not so much meditating or contemplating as *fascinating*: being bemused and fascinated by the contiguities,
complexities, interscalar resonances, and virtually endless multifari-
ousness of the world, while at the same time often doing pretty
damned efficiently several things at once.

"*Damn*," said Mark, hands on hips on deck beside her. "Damn and
damn."

"The same," came back his unfazed friend. "That said, is it on with
our day or on with our spat?"

"Spat!" had all but spat more-than-ever-now-pissed-off M.

"Pity." Val gave her (glossy walnut) hair a toss and licked a drip
from her (waffle) cone. "I thought *you* were the big mover-onner and I
was the over-dweller-on-things. Lick?"

"No, thank you. There's a difference between moving on and hit-
and-run driving, Val."

"Shall we discuss that difference?" More a challenge than a cordial
invitation.

"No, thank you. Because what happened back there was no accident."

"So let's discuss *that*: its non-accidentality."

"No, thank you very much," the fire gone out of him. "Because
there'd be no bloody end to it. Let's go the hell home."

But "Not so fast, Buster," had countered Ms. Valerie, and although
they did in fact then go the hell home after all, they ventilated recip-
rocally all the way, each charging the other now with spoiling the day
in addition to his or her more basic grievances. Through that evening,
too, they had kept scarifyingly at it, heartsick Mark from time to time
declaring "What it all comes down to . . ." and tearful Valerie being
damned if she'd let him shortcut to that bottom line before he'd had
his nose thoroughly rubbed en route in this, that, and the other.
Exhausted half-sleep, as far apart as manageable in their king-size bed.
Then a grumpy, burned-out Sunday, both parties by that time more
saddened and alarmed than angry, each therapeutically pursuing her
or his separate business till Happy Hour—which wasn't, but which at
least brought them civilly together as was their custom for their (single)

glass of wine with a bit of an hors d'oeuvre, over which they exchanged tentative, strained apologies, and then apologies less strained and tentative. Through dinner prep each guardedly conceded a measure of truth in the other's bill of complaints; through dinner itself (with, uncharacteristically, a second glass of wine, much diluted with club soda) a measure less guarded and more generous. Thereafter, by way of goodwill respite from the subject, M had offered to show V that business he'd mentioned sometime earlier about navigating the World Wide Web. She had welcomed the diversion; they had booted up Mark's Macintosh, had shortcut to CNG's E-piphanies home page with its E-tale of Expediter Fred and Enhancer Irma, had aborted it early in favor of makeup sex (etc.)—and here they are.

Mm-hm. And where is that, exactly?

That exactly is in separate rooms of their (jointly owned, jointly tenanted) Silver Spring house and likewise in their extraordinarily strained but by no means severed connection. More exactly yet, it is *a*) in Mark's case, on their pleasant, now dark side porch, where—having thought hard and efficiently about those five or seven interrelated matters aforelisted (Saturday set-to, makeup sex, Coastline Measurement Problem, analogous aspect of storytelling, selfhood in the world's wide web, etc.)—in a sudden access of loving appreciation of his companion and their indispensable differences he turns from his idle rhododendron-tending to hurry herward with the aim of embracing her and ardently reaffirming that she is not only to him indispensable but by him treasured, and that he is determined to temper his madddening get-on-with-itness with as much of her wait-let's-explore-the-associations-ness as his nature permits. And *b*) in Valerie's case, in Mark's workroom, where—having floated a fascinated while in the Sargasso Sea of everyday life's virtual hypertextuality (but at no time so bemused thereby as to lose sight of the subject of their Saturday set-to)—in a sudden access of loving etc. she bolts up from Mark's Mac to hurry himward with corresponding intent. The physical halfway point thembetween happens to be the fourth-from-bottom step of the staircase connecting their house's ground floor (living room, dining room, kitchen/breakfast room, lavatory, front and rear entry halls, side porch, attached garage) and its second (main bedroom and bath, V's and M's separate workrooms with hallway and No. 2 bath between, library-loft [accessible from main BR] over garage) (additionally, in basement and thus irrelevant to their projectible rendezvous: TV/guest room, workshop, utility room). Where they'll actually meet is another matter, perhaps suspendable while Narrator tidies a few loose ends. To wit:

• Any reasonable reader's suspicions to the contrary notwithstanding, "CNG" stands in this context not for Compressed Natural Gas but rather for Center of Narrative Gravity: in a made-up story, the author's narrative viewpoint; in real life-in-the-world, however, the self itself, of which more presently unless it's clicked on now . . .

• Presently, then. Meanwhile, as to the aforedemonstrated essential difference between Ms. Valerie's sensibility and Mr. Mark's, it is nowhere more manifest than in the way each, in the other's opinion, tells a story. "Anna train squish," is how Val claims Mark would render Leo Tolstoy, *Anna Karenina*; indeed, given the man's Middle-challengedness, she suspects he might skip the train. She, on the other hand (claims he, whether teasingly or in their Saturday set-to mode), would never get beyond Count Tolstoy's famous opening sentence, "Happy families are all alike;" etc.—indeed, would never get through, much less past, it, inasmuch as she would need to pause to explore such counterevidence as that her family and Mark's, for example, while both prevailingly quite "happy," are as different in nearly every other respect as aardvarks and zebras; and once having clicked on <u>Mark's family</u>, or equally on <u>hers</u> (or, for that mattter, on <u>aardvarks</u> or <u>zebras</u>), she would most likely never get *back* to <u>Tolstoy's proposition,</u> not to mention on to its second half and the eight-part novel therebeyond.

• Myself, I'm on both their sides in this matter, not only because M and V seem equally reasonable, decent, harmless souls, but also because their tendencies represent contrary narrative impulses of equal validity and importance. A satisfyingly told story requires enough "Valerie"—that is, enough detail, amplification, and analysis—to give it clarity, texture, solidity, verisimilitude, and empathetic effect. It requires equally enough "Mark"—that is, efficiently directed forward motion, "profluence," on-with-the-storyness—for coherence, anti-tedium, and dramatic effect. In successful instances a right balance is found for the purpose (and adjusted for alternative purposes). In unsuccessful instances . . .

Friend of Valerie and Mark's: So, how'd your vacation go, guys?

M: Cool—Spain in ten days.

V: Really terrific, what little we got to see. The very first morning, for example, in Avila—Do you know Avila? Saint Teresa and all that?—we were in the Parador Nacional, just outside the old city wall. You've stayed in the Spanish paradors, right? So, anyhow, the one in Avila's this fifteenth-century palace called Piedras Albas ('cause that's what it's made of, white stones from [etc.,*never getting past the breakfast* churros, *inasmuch as hypertexted behind them, for Valerie, lie all of Spanish history, culture, geography, and the rest, inseparable from the rest of Europe's and the world's. Mark had had practically to drag the rapt, protesting woman out of that stern and splendid place, to get on with their itinerary]*) . . .

• <u>So what?</u> you ask, unless one happens to take some professional interest in storytelling, which you for one do not? Thanks for clicking on that Frequently Asked Question, reply CNG and I: The "so what" is that that same right-balance-for-the-purpose finding applies to the measurement of coastlines, the appropriate scaling of maps, and—Hold that clicker—not only interpersonal relations, Q.E.D., but *intra*personal ones as well.

<u>Intrapersonal relations?</u>

Thanks again, and yes indeed. For what is Valerie, finally, what is Mark, what are you, and what am I—in short, what is <u>the self itself</u>—if not what has been aptly called a "posited center of narrative gravity" that, in order to function in and not be overwhelmed by the chaotically instreaming flood of sense data, continuously notices, ignores, associates, distinguishes, categorizes, prioritizes, hypothesizes, and selectively remembers and forgets; that continuously spins trial scenarios, telling itself stories about who it is and what it's up to, who others are and what they're up to; that finally *is*, if it is anything, those continuously revised, continuously edited stories? In sum, what we're dealing with here is no trifling or merely academic matter, friends: finding, maintaining, and forever adjusting from occasion to occasion an appropriate balance between the "Mark" in each of us and the "Valerie" ditto is of the very essence of our selfhood, our being in the world. We warmly therefore hope, do CNG & I (click on that <u>&</u> and see it turn into an =, + much <u>more</u> on intrapersonal relations), that that couple works things out, <u>when</u>ever and <u>where</u>ever they recouple.

<u>When.</u> One short paragraph from now, it will turn out, although given the infinite subdivisibility of time, space, and narrative (not to mention <u>The Hypertextuality of Everyday Life</u>), it could as readily be ten novels hence or never. See <u>Zeno's paradoxes</u> of time and motion; see swift <u>Achilles</u> close forever upon the tortoise; <u>see Spot run</u> . . .

<u>Where.</u> Not on that fourth-step-from-the-bottom *Mittelpunkt*, it turns out, but back where this story of them started. Mark (inescapably himself even when determined to be more Valish) is off the porch and through the dining room and up the staircase and into the upstairs hallway by the time Valerie (who, decidedly herself even after deciding to be more Marklike, has stepped from M's workroom first into the

No. 2 bathroom to do a thing to her hair or face before hurrying
porchward, then into their bedroom to slip a thigh-length T-shirt over
her undies in case the neighbor lady's out there gardening by street-
light, then back into M's workroom to exit the Internet so that their
access meter won't run on while they finish making up, which could
take a happy while), hearing him hurrying herward, re-rises from
Mark's Macintosh to meet its open-armed owner with open arms.

To her (glossy) (walnut) hair he groans, "I love you so damned
much!"

To his (right) collarbone she murmurs, "I love you more."

They then vow (<u>etc.</u>), and one thing sweetly segues to another right
there on the workroom's (Berber) wall-to-wall, while the screen saver's
<u>tropical fish</u> and <u>seahorses </u>burble soothingly per program themabove.
• *The Marquise Went Out at Five (La Marquise sortit à cinq heures)* is the
title of a 1961 novel by the French writer Claude Mauriac and a refrain
in the Chilean novelist José Donoso's 1984 opus *Casa de Campo (A
House in the Country)*. The line comes from the French poet and critic
Paul Valéry, who remarked in effect that he could never write a novel
because of the *arbitrariness*, the vertiginous *contingency*, of such a "prosaic" but inescapable opening line as, say, "The Marquise went out at
five"—for the rigorous M. Valéry, a paralyzing toe-dip into what might
be called the hypertextuality of everyday life.

*Not too fast there, Mark. Not too slow there, Val. That's got it, guys; that's
got it* . . . (so "CNG" [= I/you/eachandallofus] encourages them from
the hyperspatial wings, until agile Valerie lifts one [long] [lithe] [cinna-
mon-tan] leg up and with her [left] [great] toe gives the Mac's master
switch a

CREDITS

"At the End of the Mechanical Age," from *Amateurs* by Donald Barthelme. Copyright © 1976 by Donald Barthelme. Reprinted by permission of The Wylie Agency, Inc.

"Water Liars," from *Airships*, by Barry Hannah. Copyright © 1978 by Barry Hannah. Used by permission of Grove/Atlantic, Inc.

"A Conversation with My Father," from *The Collected Stories* by Grace Paley. Copyright © 1994 by Grace Paley. Reprinted by permission of Farrar, Straus and Giroux, LLC.

"In Dreams Begin Responsibilities," by Delmore Schwartz, from *In Dreams Begin Responsibilities*. Copyright © 1937, 1978 by New Directions Publishing Corp. Reprinted by permission of New Directions Publishing Corp.

"Opium," from *The Word Desire* by Rikki Ducornet. Copyright © 1997. Reprinted by permission of the author.

"The Sin of Jesus," from *The Complete Works of Isaac Babel*, 2001, by Isaac Babel and Intro by Cynthia Ozick, edited by Nathalie Babel, translated by Peter Constantine. Copyright © 2002 by Peter Constantine. Compilation, Preface, Afterword copyright © 2002 by Isaac Babel. Introduction copyright © 2002 by Cynthia Ozick. Chronology copyright © by Gregory Freidin. Used by permission of W. W. Norton & Company, Inc.

"The Aleph," from *Collected Fictions* by Jorge Luis Borges, translated by Andrew Hurley. Copyright © 1998 by Maria Kodama; translation copyright © 1998 by Penguin Putnam Inc. Used by permission of Viking Penguin, a division of Penguin Group (USA) Inc.

"Pastoralia," by George Saunders. Reprinted by permission of the author.

"The Art of Forgiveness: A Fable," by Janice Eidus, first appeared in *The Celibacy Club* (City Lights; 1997); reprinted by the courtesy of the author.

"Lyompa," by Yuri Olesha, from *Envy* by Andrew R. MacAndrew. Copyright © 1967 by Andrew R. MacAndrew. Used by permission of Doubleday, a division of Random House, Inc.

"Cat's Eye" from *Open Door*, Stories by Luisa Valenzuela. Translated by Christopher Leland, North Point Press, 1988. Used by permission of the author.

INDEX OF AUTHORS
AND TITLES

Aleph, The, 49

Art of Forgiveness: A Fable, The, 102

At the End of the Mechanical Age, 15

Babel, Isaac, Sin of Jesus, The, 44

Ballard, J. G., Plan for the Assassination of Jacqueline Kennedy, 215

Barth, John, Click, 317

Barthelme, Donald, At the End of the Mechanical Age, 15

Berry, R. M., Second Story, 261

Bloodchild, 138

Borges, Jorge Luis, Aleph, The, 49

Brennan, Karen, Wild Desire, 281

Butler, Octavia E., Bloodchild, 138

Can This Story Be Saved?, 271

Carter, Angela, Fall River Axe Murders, The, 120

Cat's Eye, 111

Click, 317

Conversation with My Father, A, 26

Coover, Robert, Elevator, The, 239

Cornsilk, 181

Davis, Lydia, Story, 218

Dixon, Stephen, Milk Is Very Good for You, 165

Ducornet, Rikki, Opium, 39

Eidus, Janice, Art of Forgiveness: A Fable, The, 102

Elevator, The, 239

Fall River Axe Murders, The, 120

Fifth Story, The, 249

Five on Fiction, 304

Gass, William H., Order of Insects, 156

Giles, Molly, Writers' Model, The, 258

Hannah, Barry, Water Liars, 22

Huss, Sandy, Scissors Kick, 298

In Dreams Begin Responsibilities, 31

Innocent Objects, 221

Is It Sexual Harassment Yet?, 198

John Duffy's Brother, 115

Kauffman, Janet, Five on Fiction, 304

Kennan, Randall, Cornsilk, 181

Lispector, Clarice, Fifth Story, The, 249

Lyompa, 107

Mazza, Cris, Is It Sexual Harassment Yet?, 198

Milk Is Very Good for You, 165

Minnesota Multiphasic Personality: a diagnostic test in two parts, The, 251

Neville, Susan, Rondo, 176

O'Brien, Flann, John Duffy's Brother, 115

Olesha, Yuri, Lyompa, 107

Opium, 39

Order of Insects, 156

Paley, Grace, *Conversation with My Father, A*, 26

Pastoralia, 61

Paulsen, A. B., *Minnesota Multiphasic Personality: a diagnostic test in two parts, The*, 251

Plan for the Assassination of Jacqueline Kennedy, 215

Rondo, 176

Saunders, George, *Pastoralia*, 61

Schoemperlin, Diane, *Innocent Objects*, 221

Schwartz, Delmore, *In Dreams Begin Responsibilities*, 31

Scissors Kick, 298

Second Story, 261

Sin of Jesus, The, 44

Story, 218

Valenzuela, Luisa, *Cat's Eye*, 111

Water Liars, 22

Wild Desire, 281

Wilkerson, Michael, *Can This Story Be Saved?*, 271

Writers' Model, The, 258